AF600104

HAUNTED NARRATIVES

Life Writing in an Age of Trauma

Haunted Narratives

Life Writing in an Age of Trauma

EDITED BY
GABRIELE RIPPL, PHILIPP SCHWEIGHAUSER,
TIINA KIRSS, MARGIT SUTROP, AND
THERESE STEFFEN

UNIVERSITY OF TORONTO PRESS
Toronto Buffalo London

Toronto Buffalo London
www.utppublishing.com

ISBN 978-1-4426-4601-8

Library and Archives Canada Cataloguing in Publication

Haunted narratives : life writing in an age of trauma / edited by Gabriele Rippl ... [et al.].

Includes bibliographical references and index.
ISBN 978-1-4426-4601-8

1. Autobiography. 2. Biography as a literary form. 3. Literature – 20th century – History and criticism. 4. Autobiography in literature. 5. Biography in literature. 6. Psychic trauma in literature. 7. Memory in literature. I. Rippl, Gabriele

PN56.A89H39 2013 809′.93592 C2012-908214-7

University of Toronto Press acknowledges the financial assistance to its publishing program of the Canada Council for the Arts and the Ontario Arts Council.

Canada Council for the Arts Conseil des Arts du Canada

University of Toronto Press acknowledges the financial support of the Government of Canada through the Canada Book Fund for its publishing activities.

Contents

Part Four: Fictions of Loss and Trauma

HAUNTED NARRATIVES

Life Writing in an Age of Trauma

Introduction: Life Writing in an Age of Trauma

GABRIELE RIPPL, PHILIPP SCHWEIGHAUSER, AND THERESE STEFFEN

Writing Lives of Pain

At the beginning of Raj Kamal Jha's novel *Fireproof*, the narrator gives emphatic advice: "Don't listen to the dead, please do not listen to the dead – whatever they tell you, whatever fancy name or un-name they wish to go by, howsoever lyrical they may wax, because once you lend them your ears, they will nibble at your guilt, feed on your pity, swallow you whole, from head to toe, make no mistake" (11).

Obviously, listening to the dead is a dangerous thing to do. Once they have a grip on the living, they will trigger strong emotions such as guilt and pity before finally devouring the living completely. Yet while there is no doubt that listening to the dead – like listening to sirens – harbours many risks, it is equally obvious that *not* listening to the dead, *not* trying to come to terms with them can also lead to calamities. As the psychoanalytic work on transgenerational haunting done by Nicolas Abraham and Maria Torok has shown, undisclosed traumas of the past may come to haunt later generations in significant ways. The phantoms of dead ancestors tend to be particularly disturbing psychological presences in cases where the pain and violence of the past remain concealed: "The phantom which returns to haunt bears witness to the existence of the dead buried within the other" (175). All of the texts discussed in *Haunted Narratives: Life Writing in an Age of Trauma* face such phantoms; most of them also engage with traumatic events and situations of the past that haunt whole communities.

We chose "Haunted Narratives" as the title of our volume to stress both the lingering, haunting presence of the past in the present and the psychological, ethical, and representational difficulties involved in narrative negotiations of traumatic memories. In "haunting," then, a variety of theoretical concerns intersect: Abraham and Torok's work on transgenerational haunting, Jacques Derrida's reflections on spectrality, trauma theory, memory studies, and more general reflections concerning the representability of experiences and events that test the limits of representation. Our focus is on life writing in the broadest sense of the term: auto/biographies that deal with traumatic experiences, autobiographically inspired fictions of loss and trauma, and limit-cases that transcend clear-cut distinctions between the factual and the fictional. Though our double focus on life writing and trauma memory may be taken to suggest this, we do not consider "haunting" a purely individual psychological category. As Tiina Kirss writes in our volume's first essay, "Both trauma theories and psychoanalytic approaches focus on the individual psyche and intimate social relations, perhaps to the neglect of ways in which the consequences of an uncannily present violent past are transmitted through social networks and through contiguity among those who inhabit the same place." In line with this observation, the present book brings together studies of life writings from a variety of cultural contexts to gain new insights into how individuals and communities across time and space deal with traumatic experiences and haunting memories. Resulting from a transnational research project of the Universities of Berne (Switzerland) and Tartu (Estonia) that first met in 2006 and has since brought together literary and cultural scholars on a regular basis, we focus on anglophone and Estonian life writings that revolve around individual and collective acts of remembering painful pasts.

If one looks at recent developments in book markets around the globe, one is bound to recognize that life writing has become an especially powerful aesthetic and economic force.[1] This has also had major repercussions on literary and cultural studies. In Sidonie Smith's words from her presidential address at the 2011 MLA annual convention:

> My co-author Julia Watson has observed that our contemporary memoir boom has become a financial boon to the publishing business. Memoirs appear on the book shelves of stores that are still brick and mortar, and they pop up regularly on sites such as amazon.com ... Many of us in the field of autobiography studies began our scholarly labors some forty years ago now on the periphery ... In the last two decades, life writing studies has moved from the periphery to an academic center. In dissertations and

> in critical studies, the field has gotten some satisfaction. Indeed, autobiography studies, with its capacious reach, is now a site of prodigious theoretical activity ... Narrating lives becomes an occasion for assembling and claiming identities, securing and releasing social relations and negotiating affective attachments. These acts connect people to an intimate past, animating a historical imaginary identified with family and nation.

Memoirs are only one form of life writing among many, and Smith's comments emphasize their function as representations of not only individual lives but also the cultural situations and historical moments from which they originate. In this sense, too, autobiographical lives are always "relational lives" (Eakin, "Relational Selves"), that is, lives that are related to other subjects as well as to real and imagined communities as small as the family or as large as the nation.

Already in the 1970s, critics such as James Olney emphasized the dominance of autobiography and also paid some attention to the fictional aspects of life writing (Olney's *Metaphors of Self: The Meaning of Autobiography* from 1972 is an early example), but the phenomenon has greatly diversified and expanded since then. Today, there are new, prolific possibilities of writing one's life and "getting a life" (Smith and Watson, *Getting a Life*) due to the availability of electronic mass media such as TV, video, and Web-based means of expression. The "I" is ubiquitous in the virtual world; it is well documented and documentable thanks to Facebook, online diaries, blogs, and other communication platforms. To account for this multiplicity of forms, one needs the kind of broad notion of life writing that informs the contributions in our volume. Already in more narrow understandings of the term, "life writing" refers to a wide variety of non-fictional autobiographical and biographical texts, including memoirs, diaries, journals, testimonies, letters, autobiographies, personal essays, and sometimes also biographies. Yet since the 1980s, scholars such as Paul John Eakin (1985), Marlene Kadar (1992), Sidonie Smith and Julia Watson (1992, 1998, 2001; Smith 2011), and Leigh Gilmore (2001) have further broadened the notion of "life writing" by more radical challenges to the fiction/non-fiction dichotomy that still underlies more narrow definitions of the term and by problematizing some of the claims to objectivity and truthfulness that build on that dichotomy. In many cases, such attempts at redefinition go hand in hand with a more general preference for the term "life writing" over "autobiography" that is energized by a well-founded suspicion that the latter tends to privilege certain ways of writing about the self – those that conform to the Western Enlightenment narrative of the autonomous, self-determined (and at least implicitly male) individual, and which usually favour "narrative regularity" (Kadar 4) – over those by women, people of colour, post-colonial subjects, and other historically marginalized groups, whose stories of violence and oppression are often rendered in non-linear and fragmented narrative forms. Smith and Watson's 1992 essay collection *De/Colonizing the Subject: The Politics of Gender in Women's Autobiography* has been particularly instrumental in opening up the discussion to life stories told by subjects other than Western males: "What has been designated as Western autobiography is only one form of 'life writing.' There are other modes of life-story telling, both oral and written, to be recognized, other genealogies of life-story telling to be chronicled, other explorations of traditions, current and past, to be factored into the making and unmaking of autobiographical subjects in a global environment" (xviii).

Following these two critics' lead, "life writing" has become the preferred term, both in discussions of colonial, post-colonial, and neocolonial sites and in more general reflections on the multiple aesthetic forms the genre encompasses and the social functions it performs. Smith and Watson helpfully define the term as "writing of diverse kinds that takes a life as its subject. Such writing can be biographical, novelistic, historical, or an explicit self-reference to the writer" (Smith and Watson, *Reading Autobiography* 3). This broad definition of "life writing" does not erase all distinctions between autobiography, historiography, and fiction. In fact, referring to Philippe Lejeune's 1975 definition of autobiography as a special pact between a real author and readers, Smith and Watson maintain that "autobiographical narrators establish for their readers a different set of expectations, a different pact, than the expectations established in the verisimilitude or suspension of disbelief of the novel or the verifiable evidence of biography and history writing" (12). Most recently, Max Saunders has pointed out that, from the late nineteenth century onward, the "categories of autobiography, biography, fiction, and criticism beg[a]n to interact, combining and disrupting each other in new ways" (1). When postmodern writers began to play games with the concept of autobiography, the boundaries between autobiography, biography, and fiction became even more porous. Their blurring of generic distinctions has created new types of texts for which Saunders coins neologisms such as "auto/biography" and "auto/biografiction" – terms that are based on earlier coinages such as "autofiction" (Doubrovsky 1977) and "biofiction" (Middeke 1999). Saunders's terms indicate "both that auto/biography can be read as fiction, and that fiction can be read as autobiographical" (Saunders 7).

Against the backdrop of these broad definitions, we use "life writing" as an umbrella term which allows us to read biographies and autobiographies side by side with autobiographically inspired fictions as well as what Leigh Gilmore calls "limit-cases" of life writing, that is, texts such as semi-autobiographical novels, meta-biographies, and fictionalized memoirs that self-consciously sit on the fence between fiction and non-fiction to "confront how the limits of autobiography, multiple and sprawling as they are, might conspire to prevent some self-representational stories from beginning to be told at all if they were subjected to a literal truth test or evaluated by certain objective measures" (14). The "self-representational stories" Gilmore here refers to are the kinds of trauma narratives our contributors also focus on: life writings about extremely painful experiences that are particularly difficult to verbalize. For Gilmore, trauma tests the limits of self-representation in ways that force us to rethink more narrow conceptualizations of autobiographical writing that subscribe to legalistic definitions of truth, sharply distinguish between the private and the public as well as the individual and the collective, and presuppose a sovereign self as the teller of the tale. Broad definitions of life writing such as Smith and Watson's and Gilmore's are entirely appropriate for discussing the texts our authors focus on, not only because these texts consistently challenge the fact/fiction dichotomy, but also because the harrowing experiences they recount are for the greatest part embedded in larger structures of violence and domination such as (post-)colonial oppression, Stalinist terror, and the Holocaust.

And indeed, while three of our contributors focus on life writing in a more narrow sense (Julia Straub on a memoir; Nora Escherle on a biography; Leena Kurvet-Käosaar on deportation narratives), a second group of contributors discusses limit-cases that sit on the fence between life writing and fiction (Stefanie Preuss on Scottish documentary and biographical plays; Eneken Laanes and Aija Sakova on autobiographical novels; Eva Rein on two historiographic metafictions), and a third group deals with autobiographically inspired fictions (Christa Schönfelder on a fictional autobiography; Maarja Hollo on works of fiction that incorporate events of their author's life; Annie Cottier on a novel whose footnotes include fictional autobiographical narratives). We have divided the core of the present volume into three sections (2–4) that reflect these divergent yet overlapping interests and foci:

"2. Auto/biographies as Trauma Narratives," "3. Limit-cases: Exploring the Limits of Telling Pain," and "4. Fictions of Loss and Trauma." To represent the interactive nature of our research group and to ensure a true exchange of ideas across national borders, we have also solicited shorter essays that critically respond to the main contributions.

Focusing on texts that highlight the precariousness of our tripartite division in especially poignant ways – Toni Morrison's *Beloved,* Ene Mihkelson's *Plague Grave,* and Elie Wiesel's *Night* – the two essays in part 1 frame the debates and discussions that take place in our volume from a more theoretically inclined perspective: In chapter 1, Tiina Kirss engages with the minor scholarly industry of *hantologie* as it emerged in response to Jacques Derrida's *Spectres of Marx: The State of the Debt, the Work of Mourning, and the New International* as well as Nicolas Abraham and Maria Torok's psychoanalytic work to suggest two alternative theoretical models of haunting that emerge from fictional texts themselves: Toni Morrison's "rememory," which is crucial to her 1987 novel *Beloved* (1987), and Ene Mihkelson's historical analogy of the long-term latent toxicity of the plague grave, which she develops in her 2007 novel *Plague Grave.* In chapter 2, Philipp Schweighauser draws on the work of Walter Benjamin and Theodor W. Adorno to explore the relations between two notions that seem opposed to one another at first sight: trauma and utopia. Writing against the background of the First World War, the Second World War, and the Holocaust, both Frankfurt School theorists insist on the difficulty of thinking utopia in times of trauma. For both, utopia must not be depicted from within a radically debased world, but they also join Elie Wiesel, who in his radically dark Holocaust memoir *Night* asserts that the utopian imagination is needed in a world that has seen the Shoah because utopias promise to liberate the individual and open the present up to that which may transcend it. Together, Kirss's and Schweighauser's essays prepare the ground for our volume's negotiation of both the difficulty of coming to terms with painful pasts and the necessity to do so from a vantage point that allows for the imagination of a better future.

Trauma and the Need for Narratives

All our contributors have taken to heart a lesson literary studies has been teaching us at least since the beginning of the twentieth century, and which media theorists such as Friedrich A. Kittler – who has elaborated on Marshall McLuhan's dictum from 1964 that "the medium is the message" (24) – have adopted to study a variety of cultural artefacts: that both the individual and the social functions media serve crucially depend on their form and materiality.[2] This is especially true for the texts discussed in this volume: life writings that revolve around individual and collective processes of identity formation under conditions of trauma. As we know from memory studies and trauma theory, traumatic experiences are especially hard to verbalize and therefore push self-representation towards its limits:

> Trauma, from the Greek meaning "wound," refers to the self-altering, even self-shattering experience of violence, injury, and harm. Crucial to the experience of trauma are the multiple difficulties that arise in trying to articulate it. Indeed, the relation between trauma and representation, and especially language, is at the center of claims about trauma as a category ... Trauma mocks language and confronts it with its insufficiency. Yet at the same time language about trauma is theorized as an impossibility, language is pressed forward as that which can heal the survivor of trauma. (Gilmore 6)

Post-traumatic stress disorder (PTSD) was officially recognized as a medical condition by the medical and psychiatric professions only three decades ago, when it was introduced into the third, 1980 edition of the *Diagnostic and Statistical Manual of Mental Disorders* (American Psychiatric Association, *DSM-III*). In the *DSM-III*, "trauma" refers to the traumatic event itself rather than the medical condition, but most contemporary trauma theorists in literary and cultural studies use the notion of "trauma" more loosely to encompass both the event and its aftermath. For them, trauma as condition relates to trauma as event primarily in the sense that the event cannot be integrated into one's memory and for that reason threatens or shatters the construction of a vigorous and self-sufficient self-image. To this, literary and cultural theorists add that trauma defies verbalization and narration. In this, clinical and cultural approaches to trauma converge: both recognize that trauma often registers as gaps in the narrative structures of autobiographical memory.

Accordingly, in current trauma scholarship such as Elizabeth A. Kaplan's *Trauma Culture: The Politics of Terror and Loss in Media and Literature* (2005), the crucial question of how the unspeakable can be talked or written about is tackled not only from the perspectives of literary studies and post-structuralist reflections on the unreliability of language but also from psychoanalytical angles that take account of the linguistic turn. Trauma specialists note that patients' re-confrontation with the traumatic experience and attempts to verbalize and narrativize the trauma may support the process of recovery. In many cases, such attempts at expressing trauma take oral forms, for instance in talking cures. But *writing* about one's traumatic experiences may also facilitate the transformation of speechless threats into embedded and narrative memory. Suzette A. Henke speaks of "scriptotherapy" in this context, which she defines as "the process of writing out and writing through traumatic experience in the mode of therapeutic re-enactment" (xii). As Cathy Caruth has noted, though, putting the unspeakable into words may create problems of its own. Caruth, who draws on Bessel Van der Kolk's and Otto Van der Hart's neurological research, acknowledges that only a conscious effort via linguistic endeavours helps to release the threatening power of trauma and to integrate it into memory; at the same time, she points out that the process of putting memories of trauma into language, the effort to shape and contain the unspeakable by way of words, may in fact result in even greater imprecision and loss: "Trauma thus requires integration, both for the sake of testimony and for the sake of cure. But on the other hand, the transformation of the trauma into a narrative memory that allows the story to be verbalized and communicated, to be integrated into one's own, and others' knowledge of the past, may lose both the precision and the force that characterizes traumatic recall" (153).

As Julia Straub's essay on Wollheim's *Germs* (chapter 3) reminds us forcefully, not all life writing about painful experiences is a therapeutic exercise: Wollheim's memoir probes painful and humiliating experiences of his childhood from within a Freudian analytic framework, but ultimately questions the usefulness of life writing as a therapeutic tool. Yet whether we follow Henke in thinking of certain types of life writing as scriptotherapy or not, it is clear that in oral as well as written attempts at verbalization, trauma and memory are closely connected with storytelling.

An Age of Trauma: Remembering the Twentieth Century

This holds true not only for accounts of individual suffering and pain but also for attempts to work through and grapple with what is variously called collective or cultural trauma – a term usefully defined by Neil J. Smelser as "a memory accepted and publicly given credence by a relevant membership group and evoking an event or situation which is (a) laden with negative affect, (b) represented as indelible, and (c) regarded as threatening a society's existence or violating one or more of its fundamental cultural presuppositions" (44). In view of the twentieth-century history of political violence, we need a notion of collective trauma to account for the haunting presence of the 187 million human lives claimed by wars, genocides, and atrocities committed by totalitarian regimes.[3] While the last century was the one during which the project of the Enlightenment was supposed to reach its peak in Europe and the Western world in general, in retrospect it seems clear that the civilizing efforts of the Enlightenment, the striving for individuality, emancipation, and freedom, were thwarted in many respects. Remembering the sight of "trainloads of Jewish children standing at Austerlitz station," François Mauriac puts it thus in his foreword to the English translation of Elie Wiesel's Holocaust memoir *Night*:

> The way these lambs had been torn from their mothers in itself exceeded anything we had so far thought possible. I believe that on that day I touched for the first time upon the mystery of iniquity whose revelation was to mark the end of one era and the beginning of another. The dream which Western man conceived in the eighteenth century, whose dawn he thought he saw in 1789, and which, until August 2, 1914, had grown stronger with the progress of enlightenment and the discoveries of science – this dream vanished finally for me before those trainloads of little children. And yet I was still thousands of miles away from thinking that they were to be fuel for the gas chamber and the crematory. (vii–viii)

In *Liquid Modernity* (2000), Zygmunt Bauman analyses the outcome of the struggle for freedom and emancipation and, like Giorgio Agamben in *Homo Sacer: Sovereign Power and Bare Life* (1998), highlights the problems and paradoxes of modernity. Throughout the last century, power politics violated social and political core values to an almost unimaginable extent. Due to Verdun, Auschwitz, Vietnam, Cambodia, the Gulag Archipelago, the Partition on the Indian Subcontinent, and Rwanda, the twentieth century will undoubtedly be remembered as the century of ethnic conflicts and genocides. Political oppression, persecution, ethnic cleansing, wars, and ultimately experiences of exile, transculturation, and cultural hybridity created fault lines in the lives of many people and peoples that deeply affected the construction of individual and collective identities. While any cognitive or affective return to these experiences may open up new wounds, remembering the dark and even traumatic sides of twentieth-century history is indispensable for both individuals and collectives in order to come to terms with the past and its lingering, haunting presence. Many of the texts discussed by our contributors participate in that process of remembering. As life writings, these texts tell stories of personal and familial pain that are embedded in larger structures of oppression: the Holocaust in Vikram Seth's biography *Two Lives* (chapters 5 and 6), Indian communal violence in Jha's *Fireproof* (chapters 21 and 22), the long-term effects of British colonialism in the Scottish plays discussed by Stefanie Preuss (chapters 9 and 10), and Soviet totalitarianism in the testimonies, life stories, and fictions our Estonian contributors focus on (chapters 7, 11, 13, 15, and 19). All of these texts both stage individual acts of remembering and, in the process of doing so, participate in the construction of collective forms of memory. In taking account of this collective dimension of trauma, our contributors follow the lead of sociologists such as Smelser and Kai T. Erikson, who propose a broad understanding of PTSD that includes collective traumas as well. In Erikson's words, "Sometimes the tissues of community can be damaged in much the same way as the tissues of mind and body … But even when that does not happen, traumatic wounds inflicted on individuals can combine to create a mood, an ethos – a group culture, almost – that is different from (and more than) the sum of the private wounds that make it up. Trauma, that is, has a social dimension" (185).

And yet, our contributors are very much aware that insights gained from the study and psychoanalytic treatment of traumatized individuals cannot easily be transferred to the analysis of collective states of trauma. Trauma, like "collective memory," is a "tantalizingly elusive concept" which has propelled methodological concerns about the fact that "the connections between collective and individual memory are poorly theorized, that collectives may respond very differently than individuals to traumas and other life experiences, and that the important relationship between memory and identity has been largely neglected" (Lebow 9–10). It is not without a sense of unease that our contributors move from the level of individual experience to that of collective experience and vice versa, a fact that becomes particularly clear in Christa Schönfelder's essay (chapter 17), which relies heavily on a clinical-psychological understanding of trauma to challenge a number of the broad claims made by scholars working within the "cultural trauma" paradigm. The contact zones between the private and the public remain contested grounds, both in our contributors' essays and in the cultures they write from.

Yet while our contributors' different cultural situatedness – half of them are Estonian, the other half Swiss – shapes the work they do, their concerns are neither primarily "Eastern" nor primarily "Western"; they are cross-cultural. This is perhaps most immediately apparent in Escherle's discussion of Vikram Seth's double biography *Two Lives* (chapter 5). She traces how the pasts of the biographer's two subjects come to haunt them in ways that transcend national, cultural, and linguistic boundaries: Seth's great-aunt Henny Seth (a German Jew whose family was killed in Nazi Germany) and his great-uncle Shanti Behari Seth (an Indian man who came to Germany to study dentistry at the age of twenty-three) met and became a couple in Berlin in 1931, were separated during the Second World War, and finally reunited when they met again in England after the war. While Henny had to cope with the loss of her family in the Holocaust, Shanti suffered from wounds inflicted during his service in the British Army Dental Corps. The language they spoke at home when no one else was present was neither English nor Hindi but German, Henny's mother tongue, which is the language the two had spoken while in Berlin. Escherle's essay focuses on both Vikram Seth's and his great-aunt's complex relationships to the German language, which in the writer's case changes from love to hate and back to love again, and in Henny's case involved a strict separation between spoken German, which was the "medium of partnership, friendship, and love that allowed her to relate to positive experiences of the past as well as to her life in the present" and written German, which served her "to confront painful memories, to analyze and judge the negative experiences of the past." Escherle's essay paradigmatically shows how migration and political violence have brought forth subject positions that transcend the boundaries of national cultures. The cross-cultural dimension of many a twentieth-century biography also comes very clearly to the fore in the comparative essays by Aija Sakova and Eva Rein (chapters 13 and 15). Sakova's essay on Estonian writer Ene Mihkelson's *Ahasveeruse uni* and German writer Christa Wolf's *Kindheitsmuster* engages with the two key historical reference points our contributors return to again and again: Soviet totalitarianism and the Third Reich. In doing so, she explores how both writers' re-experiencing of traumatic events in fictional form is a working through that comes at great personal pain but opens up their understanding of what happened and ultimately enables a thorough revisioning of the past. Rein's discussion of *Ahasveeruse uni* and Japanese-Canadian writer Joy Kogawa's *Obasan* not only stresses how experiences of political oppression and exile position individuals between cultures (between Estonia and Soviet Russia in Mihkelson's case; between Japan and Canada in Kogawa's case); its comparative approach also emphasizes that such experiences are shared across cultures.

Yet lest we get carried away with highlighting the post-national, boundary-crossing nature of our volume, Margit Sutrop's afterword to this volume is there to remind us that the two culturally and historically specific traumatogenic configurations discussed in Sakova's essay remain constant reference points. While Soviet totalitarianism is the central focus of for all our Estonian contributors' discussions of collective traumas, our Swiss contributors touch on a variety of traumatogenic historical configurations but in many cases do so with the Holocaust at least in the back of their minds – Straub's and Escherle's contributions (chapters 3 and 5) are good examples here. In her afterword, Sutrop comments on those different foci as she revisits the political as well as ethical implications of life writing. In doing so, she focuses on our contributors' different choices of key historical reference points. What does it mean for the Estonian contributors to return again and again to the legacy of Soviet totalitarianism, while for the Swiss contributors, "any discussion of trauma and the past automatically [takes] place against the background of the Holocaust"? As she asks that question in our volume's final text, Sutrop again takes us to the heart of our project as she explores the related questions of how individual acts of life writing insert themselves into cultural memory and how they can help us develop a responsible relationship to both the dead and the not-yet-born.

In staging a dialogue across nations that acknowledges the cultural specificity of not only the texts we discuss but also the different places from where we write about them, we aim to make a significant contribution to the study of life writing in an age of trauma that also allows for a reconsideration of current theorizations of a genre that continues to proliferate and renew itself as we write these words. If the present volume helps readers become acquainted with trauma narratives that are not so well known in the English-speaking world, this is a very welcome side effect.

The editors would like to thank the Gebert Rüf Foundation for generously financing the conferences of the Berne-Tartu research group and for supporting this publication. Without Gebert Rüf, this project would have never materialized. At the University of Toronto Press, we are indebted to the splendid work of Barbara Porter, Shoshana Wasser, John St James, and especially Richard Ratzlaff, the acquisitions editor whose belief in this project made a real difference. Many thanks are also due to Triin Paaver, Christa Schönfelder, and Stephanie Hoppeler for taking care of the logistical needs at the two conferences and Marianne Hofstetter, Daniel Allemann, Naomi Shepherd, Charif Shanahan, Daniela Casanova, Triin Pisuke, Aire Vaher, and Laura Lilles for their diligent proofreading of the manuscript. Derek Gottlieb deserves thanks for preparing the index with great care. Our special thanks go to Julia Straub for contributing to this research project in more ways than we can count.

NOTES

1 As Laurenz Bolliger, the editorial director of foreign-language literatures at DuMont publishing house, asserts in an email communication, life writings such as Shalom Auslander's *A Foreskin's Lament*, Rafael Yglesias's *A Happy Marriage*, and Helen Garner's *The Spare Room* are regularly categorized, marketed, and sold under the general heading of "Belletristik" (*belles lettres*). While Auslander's narrative about his own childhood is further categorized as a "memoir," the latter two, which revolve around the cancer illness and dying of a real-life loved one (Yglesias's wife and a good friend of Garner's, respectively), are labelled "novels." Note that to conceptualize autobiography as a literary genre is by no means a recent gesture. The first sentence of Georges Gusdorf's classic 1956 essay on autobiography is "Autobiography is a solidly established literary genre" (28). Other early conceptualizations of autobiography as literature include Shapiro (1968), Mandel (1968), and Olney (1972).

2 For a classic exploration of the question of literariness, see Victor Shklovsky's 1917 essay "Art as Technique." For splendid introductions to Kittler's work, see Geoffrey Winthrop-Young and Michael Wutz's "Translators' Introduction" to Kittler's *Gramophone, Film, Typewriter* and David E. Wellbery's foreword to Kittler's *Discourse Networks 1800/1900*.

3 In his enlightening article "Why Is the Twentieth Century the Century of Genocide?" Mark Levene even speaks of a statistical platitude: "a platitude, a statistical one at that: 187 million is the figure, the now more or less accepted wisdom for the number of human beings killed as a result of political violence … in this, our bloody century" (305). Levene draws on Eric

Hobsbawm's seminal book *Age of Extremes: The Short Twentieth Century, 1914–1991.*

WORKS CITED

Abraham, Nicolas, and Maria Torok. *The Shell and the Kernel: Renewals of Psychoanalysis.* Vol. 1. Chicago: University of Chicago Press, 1994.

Agamben, Giorgio. *Homo Sacer: Sovereign Power and Bare Life.* Stanford: Stanford University Press, 1998.

American Psychiatric Association, ed. *Diagnostic and Statistical Manual of Mental Disorders. DSM-III.* 3rd ed. Washington, DC: American Psychiatric Association, Washington, 1980.

American Psychiatric Association, ed. *Diagnostic and Statistical Manual of Mental Disorders. DSM-IV-TR.* Text Revision. 4th ed. Washington, DC: American Psychiatric Association, 2000.

Bauman, Zygmunt. *Liquid Modernity.* Cambridge: Polity Press, 2000.

Bolliger, Laurenz. "Re: addendum." Email to Philipp Schweighauser. 10 June 2010.

Caruth, Cathy, ed. *Trauma: Explorations in Memory.* Baltimore: Johns Hopkins University Press, 1995.

Derrida, Jacques. *Spectres of Marx: The State of the Debt, the Work of Mourning, and the New International.* Trans. Peggy Kamuf. New York: Routledge, 1994.

Doubrovsky, Serge. *Fils.* Paris: Éditions Galilée, 1977.

Eakin, Paul John. *Fictions of Autobiography: Studies in the Art of Self-Invention.* Princeton: Princeton University Press, 1985.

Eakin, Paul John. "Relational Selves, Relational Lives: The Story of a Story." In *True Relations: Essays on Autobiography and the Postmodern*, ed. G. Thomas Couser and Joseph Fichtelberg, 63–81. Westport, CT: Greenwood Press, 1998.

Erikson, Kai. "Notes on Trauma and Community." In *Trauma: Explorations in Memory*, ed. Cathy Caruth, 183–99. Baltimore: Johns Hopkins University Press, 1995.

Gilmore, Leigh. *The Limits of Autobiography: Trauma and Testimony.* Ithaca, NY: Cornell University Press, 2001.

Gusdorf, Georges. "Conditions and Limits of Autobiography." In *Autobiography: Essays Theoretical and Critical*, ed. James Olney, 28–48. Princeton: Princeton University Press, 1980.

Henke, Suzette A. *Shattered Subjects: Trauma and Testimony in Women's Life Writing*. Houndmills: Macmillan, 1998.

Hobsbawm, Eric. *Age of Extremes: The Short Twentieth Century, 1914–1991*. London: Michael Joseph, 1994.

Jha, Raj Kamal. *Fireproof*. London: Picador, 2006.

Kadar, Marlene. "Coming to Terms: Life Writing – From Genre to Critical Practice." In *Essays on Life Writing: From Genre to Critical Practice*, ed. M. Kadar, 3–16. Toronto: University of Toronto Press, 1992.

Kaplan, Elizabeth A. *Trauma Culture: The Politics of Terror and Loss in Media and Literature*. New Brunswick, NJ: Rutgers University Press, 2005.

Kittler, Friedrich A. *Discourse Networks 1800/1900*. Trans. Michael Metteer, with Chris Cullens. Stanford: Stanford University Press, 1990.

Kittler, Friedrich A. *Gramophone, Film, Typewriter*. Trans. Winthrop-Young and Michael Wutz. Stanford: Stanford University Press, 1999.

Lebow, Richard Ned. "The Memory of Politics in Postwar Europe." In *The Politics of Memory in Postwar Europe*, ed. Richard Ned Lebow, Wulf Kansteiner, and Claudio Fogu, 1–39. Durham: Duke University Press, 2006.

Lejeune, Philippe. *Le pacte autobiographique*. Paris: Éditions du Seuil, 1975.

Levene, Mark. "Why Is the Twentieth Century the Century of Genocide?" *Journal of World History* 11, no. 2 (2000): 305–36. http://dx.doi.org/10.1353/jwh.2000.0044.

Mandel, Barrett John. "The Autobiographer's Art." *Journal of Aesthetics and Art Criticism* 27, no. 2 (1968): 215–26. http://dx.doi.org/10.2307/428849.

Mauriac, François. Foreword to *Night* by Elie Wiesel, trans. Stella Rodway, vii–xi. New York: Bantam Books, 1986.

McLuhan, Marshall. *Understanding Media: The Extensions of Man*. New York: McGraw Hill, 1964.

Middeke, Martin. "Introduction." In *Biofictions: The Rewriting of Romantic Lives in Contemporary Fiction and Drama*, ed. Werner Huber and Martin Middeke, 1–25. Rochester, NY: Camden House, 1999.

Olney, James. *Metaphors of Self: The Meaning of Autobiography*. Princeton: Princeton University Press, 1972.

Saunders, Max. *Self Impression: Life-Writing, Autobiografiction, and the Forms of Modern Literature*. Oxford: Oxford University Press, 2010.

Shapiro Stephen, A. "The Dark Continent of Literature: Autobiography." *Comparative Literature Studies* 5, no. 3 (1968): 421–54.

Shklovsky, Victor. "Art as Technique." Trans. Lee T. Lemon and Marion J. Reis. In *Contemporary Literary Criticism: Literary and Cultural Studies*, ed. Robert Con Davis and Ronald Schleifer, 261–72. New York: Longman, 1994.

Smelser, Neil J. "Psychological Trauma and Cultural Trauma." In *Cultural Trauma and Collective Identity*, ed. Jeffrey J. Alexander et al., 31–59. Berkeley: University of California Press, 2004.

Smith, Sidonie. "2011 Presidential Address." 2011 MLA Annual Convention, Modern Language Association, 6 May 2011. http://www.mla.org/pres_address_2011.

Smith, Sidonie, and Julia Watson, eds. *De/Colonizing the Subject: The Politics of Gender in Women's Autobiography*. Minneapolis: University of Minnesota Press, 1992.

Smith, Sidonie, and Julia Watson, eds. *Getting a Life: Everyday Uses of Autobiography*. Minneapolis: University of Minnesota Press, 1996.

Smith, Sidonie, and Julia Watson. Introduction to *Women, Autobiography, Theory: A Reader*, ed. Smith and Watson, 3–52. Madison: University of Wisconsin Press, 1998.

Smith, Sidonie, and Julia Watson, eds. *Reading Autobiography: A Guide for Interpreting Life Narratives*. Minneapolis: University of Minnesota Press, 2001.

Van der Kolk, Bessel, and Otto Van der Hart. "The Intrusive Past: The Flexibility of Memory and the Engraving of Trauma." *American Imago* 48 (1991): 425–54.

Wellbery, David E. Foreword to *Discourse Networks 1800/1900* by Friedrich A. Kittler, trans. Michael Metteer, with Chris Cullens, vii–xxxiii. Stanford: Stanford University Press, 1990.

Winthrop-Young, Geoffrey, and Michael Wutz. "Translators' Introduction: Friedrich Kittler and German Media Discourse Analysis." In *Gramophone, Film, Typewriter*, by Friedrich A. Kittler, trans. Winthrop-Young and Wutz, xi–xxxviii. Stanford: Stanford University Press, 1999.

PART ONE

Life Writing and Trauma: Theorizing the Vicissitudes of Representing Violence

1 Seeing Ghosts: Theorizing Haunting in Literary Texts

TIINA KIRSS

What haunts is not subject to conscious memory: unbidden, it comes back for visits, and recurs through uncanny phenomena, personified or atmospheric. The ontological status of the visitor is unclear: it both invites and defies naming. Where is the "place" where the ghostly lies harboured, and from whence does it return? What is the ghost's time, what are the rhythms and circumstances of its return and departure? What kind of hospitality, protection, or transaction does the ghost ask for – or accept? Does the ghost speak a "language," and, if so, how does it "signify"?

Ghosts are more than literary personifications or theoretical metaphorics. Historical events of mass human destruction – the middle passage, Stalin's Great Terror in the Ukraine in the 1930s, civilian massacres during the Vietnam war, the disappearings in Argentina beginning in the mid-1970s, and postcolonial conditions – urge the raising of questions about haunting that relate to remembering and the past. Among these is a range of complex phenomena through which suppressed, erased, unvoiced, and misappropriated aspects of the past reappear, or are explicitly and deliberately reconfigured. For the personal testimonials of victims and witnesses of violence to be believed requires the appropriate political and social circumstances for them to be heard. In the context and the aftermath of twentieth-century historical cataclysms, scholarly reflection and therapeutic practices responding to eloquent symptoms of traumatic events in individual and social lives have led to a range of "trauma theories." According to the psychoanalytic model developed by Nicolas Abraham and Maria Torok, the unmastered and unprocessed past is trapped and sequestered, encrypted in the deep unconscious of the individual, and this secret material is unconsciously passed on to others, particularly intergenerationally in families. Both trauma theories and psychoanalytic approaches focus on the individual psyche and intimate social relations between families and kin. Trauma theories do not always negotiate effectively the social, public, and political consequences of an uncannily present violent past in places, social networks, and commemorative practices. The model of the traumatized psyche cannot be extended or allegorized to a collective subject of trauma. "Hauntological" models and theories based on extensive critical reflections on Maurice Halbwachs's "collective memory" emphasize processes of social remembering, rituals, and institutions of commemoration. The realm of "ghosts," ghostliness, and spectrality refers to the intermittent symptomatology of the larger story refused by public actuality. Encryptment (individual and social) is not correlative in simple terms to the "belatedness" of public articulation, commemoration, and history-writing.[1] Revisionary history writing and the institutionalization of commemoration evade and foreclose the ghostly, since these efforts often serve nationalist or identitarian projects.

Spectrality may be seen as a threshold phenomenon rendered potentially and intermittently visible between what Jan and Aleida Assmann have called "communicative memory" and "cultural memory," before official versions of history solidify, often minimizing and erasing the traces of violence, and at a point of generational transition when a cohort of witnesses is passing on, whether or not they have been offered the opportunity to record what they remember. Changes in the political order – such as the collapse of the Soviet Union and the political independence of countries in eastern Europe – that allow these buried issues to be legitimately reopened to public discussion do not, however, constitute automatic invitations to an exorcism. As has been seen after 1989 in east European countries, particularly the former GDR, the sudden opening of archives of state surveillance provides an excruciating twist that continues the trauma, causing a sudden flood of withheld information that is both unassimilable and irreconcilable. Previous, partial versions of reality may have been easier to bear than the knowledge that there exists a transcript of ongoing reports by an intimate informer. Ghosts do not disappear when brought to light: the power dynamics of lustration in many eastern European societies have shown that the semi-darkness of transition may make them yet more visible tenants of the common house that cannot bear too much "reality."

Theories of haunting might be considered a supplement (in the Derridean sense) to the new interdiscipline of "memory studies," not only because they explore the textures of ordinary language around uncanny phenomena, but also because they address the dimension of the social imaginary, including the generation of what James V. Wertsch has called the "textual resources" of social memory. Arguably, writing about haunting in the context of processes of social remembering brings into view intermediate levels between "individual" and "collective" memory, between the covertly individual and the overtly public. Paradoxically, the poetics of haunting provides a richly metaphoric repertoire of conceptual tools which, if used with caution and sensitivity, can enable more precision about those interstices and intervals where remembering happens.

However, as can be seen in Derrida's reading of *Hamlet* in *Spectres of Marx*, the theoretical force of haunting pushes radically beyond *Vergangenheitsbewältigung*. As Gayatri Chakravorty Spivak points out in her critical reading of *Spectres of Marx*, "because it coordinates the future in the past, the ghost is not only a revenant (a returner, the French for 'ghost'), but also an arrivant, one who arrives" (Spivak 71). In similar terms, Avery Gordon argues that "ghostly matters" is far from being a euphemism for superstition or folk belief deemed obsolete in a modern age. They designate real social phenomena: the ghost, very much alive, is a symptom of what is missing and brings a "charged strangeness" into a situation. "It gives notice not only to itself but also to what it represents" (63).

Anthropologist Heonik Kwon points to ghosts as "constitutive of social life"; in his fieldwork in Vietnamese villages, the "vitality" of ghosts attests to "a set of inventive wartime and postwar kinship practices" in response to the violence of the war, which due to combat and civilian massacres resulted in the burial of large numbers of "strangers" on village land (7). The "ghost stories" – narratives of encounters with apparitions that Kwon has collected in Vietnamese villages – are a cultural form; both narrative and ritual respond to the social experience of continuing to live with the presence of this violent past:

> The vitality of ghosts in Vietnam is not only a literary affair; nor is it oblivious to pressing issues in society. The phenomenon is founded upon the intense popularity of ghost-related stories across Vietnamese communities and the growing ritual intimacy with memories of tragic war death in their everyday life. Ghosts are a preeminent popular cultural form in Vietnam and also a powerful, effective means of historical reflection and self-expression. As such, they constitute a legitimate field of sociological inquiry against the discipline's received wisdom. (2)

As both Kwon and Gordon are careful to point out, hauntings are not to be dismissively categorized as "folk beliefs," nor should their connection to religion be sanitized by secular explanations. Nevertheless, spectrality in social experience can be "de-transcendentalized" (according to Spivak's way of speaking), its magic dimensions seen in terms such as Kwon's "vitality" or Gordon's "animation." Paradoxically, one can also crave to be haunted: "You crave to let history haunt you as a ghost or ghosts, with the ungraspable incorporation of a ghostly body, and the uncontrollable, sporadic, and unanticipatable periodicity of haunting ... It is not, then, a past that was necessarily once present that is sought. The main effort is to compute with the software of other pasts rather than reference one's own hallucinatory heritage for the sake of the politics of identitarian competition" (Spivak 70).

As I seek to show in this essay, theories about haunting, spectrality, and ghosts have become a richly provocative source of theoretical metaphors and models in literary and cultural studies over the last ten to fifteen years, drawing upon variegated layers of (not new) thinking and practice embedded in many of the world's cultures as well as on compelling readings of canonical literary texts: Derrida's – and through Derrida, Marx's readings of Shakespeare's *Hamlet*. Extensive and varied epistemological work is expected from "hauntology," as it veers between seductively compelling tropology and conceptual regularity. Gordon has turned to spectrality as a means of insisting that the sociological imagination recognizes the recurrence of the repressed at various levels of political reality. She pragmatically privileges literary texts that figure and seek to come to terms with haunting, texts such as Toni Morrison's *Beloved* and the novels of Argentine writer Luisa Valenzuela, which, in Spivak's terms, issue "prayers to be haunted."

As Colin Davis suggests, hauntology not only has a heterogeneous plurality, but a bifurcated theoretical and textual genealogy: on the one hand, there is Derrida's *Spectres of Marx* (1993) and the vigorous polemic that attended it; on the other, we have Abraham and Torok's psychoanalysis of encryptment. It is intriguing to note, with Davis, that partly by way of a footnote trick, the Derridean inflection given to the psychoanalytic approach elides from view the distinction between Derrida's "specters" and Abraham and Torok's "phantoms." Derrida's own curiously folded evasion of the psychoanalytic conversation – in his introductory essay "Fors" to Abraham and Torok's revisionist exploration of the Wolfman, *Le verbier de l'homme aux loups* – belies a conversation waiting to happen. Derrida does not engage the topic of phantoms in

Abraham and Torok's work, nor does he indicate points of connection with his own writing on phantoms.

A particularly productive (and often also generative) use of the theoretical tropology of ghosts has been in the context of literary and cultural texts concerned with the analysis and figuration of the postcolonial. Michael O'Riley uses the post-1997 novels of Assia Djebar to argue, somewhat tendentiously, that "postcolonial haunting ... is very much about the way that the story of transition to independence in former colonies at the end of long periods of colonial rule has gone, for the most part, very much awry. The spectre of colonialism that appears in the form of social division, civil warfare, and authoritarian regime in many post colonies is but a remainder and a reminder that colonialism has only been reincarnated differently" (2). Such an evocation of "haunting" in O'Riley's opening chapter, as a synonym for "remainders and reminders" of colonial power relations, is an allegorical device, much like what Kwon sees as the idiom of the "collective phantom" of the Vietnam war in American public media, and falls somewhat short of engaging the dynamic of the future anterior urged by the readings of Derrida and Spivak. Another theoretical implementation of spectrality in the context of postcoloniality can be seen in Pheng Cheah's analysis of Javanese writer Pramoedya Ananta Toer's four-volume historical novel *Buru Quartet*. He posits a "spectral public sphere" in the novel, which attempts to "reincarnate the spirit of national awakening" that has gone awry in neocolonial circumstances: "This constitutive haunting of the living nation by the death-dealing state – from which Pramoedya tries to guard it – puts into question the organismic-vitalist philosopheme of culture as the power of human self-actualization" (264). Flickering behind both of these studies of "postcolonial haunting" by the colonial past is a genealogy (ontology) of "ghosts" as represented figures, structures, practices, and circumstances that play out the recursion of the "past gone awry." The theoretical paradox of postcolonial temporality has implications for narrative and other discursivities, and Cheah's reading of *Buru Quartet* richly evokes the double valence of the ghost as arrivant/revenant. If time is "out of joint," and if postcolonial hopes have turned into neocolonial realities, the ethical imperative of postcolonial "hauntology" entails a utopic aspect, a "future anterior" rather than a "future present" (Spivak 70). As in Cheah's examples from *Buru Quartet*, literary texts use various structural devices not only to represent the complex melancholy of the postcolonial condition, but to potentially stage these utopic possibilities, keeping the "ghost" alive. In postcolonial theory that uses the trope of haunting, we can legitimately speak of glossing a tropology of spectrality already latent in writings of postcolonial struggle, such as the works of Fanon and Ngugi: a postcolonial social reality remains elusively apparitional as revolution stops in its tracks and emancipatory impulses are neutralized and co-opted by "native" power structures that replay their colonial antecedents. In the context of postcolonialities, then, theoretical considerations of haunting have referred not to the remains of actual or terrible pasts, but to the failure or short-circuiting of a future that has failed to materialize. Without proclaiming a facile symmetry between postcolonial and post-communist, post-Soviet social reality can be said to bear similar spectralities.

Because of the potency and polyvalency of the trope of haunting, "hauntologies" risk generating a poetic, rather than a rigorously conceptual vocabulary. The "work" of the literary text must thus be situated among other kinds of cultural texts in which and through which the "ghost dance," the "ethical relation with history" that Spivak calls for, can be observed. Life writing, as defined in the introduction to this volume, along with its fluid and open boundary with literary texts and fiction, is another site where coming to terms with trauma, exploring the traces and elisions of the past, deploys the vocabulary of interacting with "ghosts." What do we mean when we refer to a narrative as "haunted" or as a "ghost story?" How do literary texts and life writing participate in cultural and historical phenomena of seeing and naming ghosts? Some of the texts our contributors discuss concern themselves with the elusive and halting ways that people and communities remember or refuse to remember, not only thematizing these processes, but allowing them in various innovative ways to engender literary form.[2] Psychoanalytic hauntology of the Abraham and Torokian lineage provides fruitful possibilities for literary analysis of texts where haunting undergoes figuration or narration as secrets, as shown by Esther Rashkin's work on family secrets and haunted children. However, Rashkin's as well as Nicholas Rand's studies of secrets raise insistent limiting questions: Is the text the patient under analysis, or is it, covertly, its author who reclines on the couch? Is a literary text tantamount to a case history, an allegory of symptomatology which requires the transpiercing and discarding of aesthetic effect and form? However carefully deployed, psychoanalytic terminology (no more or less perhaps than any other psychoanalytic hermeneutics) may subtly instrumentalize the literary text, either towards a diagnosis of perpetrators or towards a therapeutics of the victims.

When we refer to "ghost stories" and "haunted narratives," it is tempting to imply that it is the duty of the interpreter to "cure" the text of its haunting in something like a demining operation: once brought to light, the text's bitter or toxic secret will cease to be transmitted to the next reader or to an unsuspecting community of interpreters. The positive purchase of this possibility is that when decoded, the "secret" will be an open one and will be transmitted consciously. More dangerous, and more limiting, however, is the implicit assumption that the secret haunting of the text is the author's "dirty" or "guilty" secret for which he or she must be held accountable. Beyond these interpretive traps, "haunted" texts may be sites where narrative is resisted, where the assumption of the adequacy or healing potential of narration is questioned. "Haunted" texts do not pretend that people and cultures can be "delivered" of ghosts "merely" by telling stories about them. As Gordon has suggestively pointed out, the "ghostly haunt" in a text gives "notification" of the unfinishable yet demanding quality of the past, and issues an imperative for close, persistent ethical attention (179). At best, the interpretive teasing forth of ghostly disturbances in literary texts may talk back to theory. If it seems appropriate to propose the question of haunting preliminarily with respect to literary texts, and through according a (temporary) privilege to narrative, we should do this in what follows in view of both Gordon's and Kwon's warnings: it is the "social vitality" of ghosts and spectrality that is thereby brought into view. I shall broach "haunted narratives" through a contrapuntal reading of two literary texts, Toni Morrison's novel *Beloved*, and Ene Mihkelson's novel *Katku-haud* (Plague Grave, 2007).

Revenants and Spectres: *Beloved*

In Toni Morrison's *Beloved*, which fictionalizes the 1856 case of Margaret Garner, the title character is figured as a ghost, the *revenant* of the "crawling already" child that Sethe killed when threatened with recapture by her slave-owner, and buried under a partially marked headstone. Reading *Beloved*, Homi K. Bhabha sees the appearance of the ghostly character Beloved as an "invasion of the projective past" in a situation of time-lag or belatedness that allows for a novelistic representation of the narrative of slavery. At closer glance, Bhabha can be seen to draw (generatively) on Walter Benjamin's much quoted "Stillstand," and the dialectical image, a subtext that underlies and energizes several other articulations of postcolonial temporality in which the magical or "religious" aspect of spectral phenomena is not dismissed outright, but acknowledged in a secular, material frame. For Hershini Bhana Young, the trope of haunting in Morrison's novel thereby enables a reading of the "affective nature of racial injury" (54).

At the opening of Morrison's novel, Paul D, who only just reappeared in Sethe's life after an absence of many years, stills the ghost and stops the moving furniture in "spiteful 124." Paul D knows that what he encounters in the house referred to as "124" is a haunting, the activity of a ghost, and he meets it with physical, not ritual, force:

> The quaking slowed to an occasional lurch, but Paul D did not stop whipping the table around until everything was rock quiet. Sweating and breathing hard, he leaned against the wall in the space the sideboard left. Sethe was still crouched next to the stove, clutching her salvaged shoes to her chest. The three of them, Sethe, Denver, and Paul D, breathed to the same beat, like one tired person. Another breathing was just as tired. (22)

There is, however, no "successful" exorcism. Ghosts are neither to be evicted, domesticated, contained, nor dismissed. Sethe's baby, who haunts her house, is an open, even familiar secret to those who live there. Paul D's manoeuvre is a temporary measure, perhaps even, unbeknownst to him, a conjuring. The crisis occasioned by Paul D's return presages the emergence of Beloved in a symbolic scene evocative of birth, and her residence in 124 is a study in haunting, a surrogate existence that threatens to engulf the destinies and stories of all the other characters in the household.

What is the ontological status of ghosts in the novel's life-world? For the African-American characters in Morrison's novel, the sociality of revenants is acknowledged, allowed for, and (at least partially) interpretable, regardless of individual squeamishness or scepticism. That is, for the characters in the novel, "believing" in ghosts is not a question, but a matter of a short stretch of the imagination, of (un)common sense about the uncanny. The question of the origin and identity of the character Beloved is, however, a larger issue, persisting past the outpost of apparitional occurrences. Placing Beloved in the category of "phantom" or "ghost" is necessary but not sufficient – be it in relation to the drama in the 124, or to understand Sethe's personal drama of mourning and

Denver's story of longing, jealousy, and affiliation. The character Beloved addresses the reader at least as a revenant, but quickly becomes a more complex signifier. At the end of the novel's second section, the departure of Paul D and the withdrawal of the women of Sethe's household into enclosure opens onto a glossolalia of ancestral voices, and the "baby ghost" begins to resonate with a collective dimension of trauma, multiply evocative of the middle passage and its victims. According to Gordon, though Beloved is for Sethe a screen for the memory of her dead child, the "more" of Beloved's story is beyond the horizon of Sethe's remembering in 1873: "the more of Beloved's story as a slave-to-be who never arrived, a history of barely legible traces imagined or conjured up out of *Documents Illustrative of the Slave Trade*" (175). As a collective "screen," Beloved as ghost becomes more, not less anonymous, and the past speaks through her as medium.

While critics have argued at length about whether Beloved has a "supernatural existence" or whether she can be explained in the novel in more ordinary ways, as a trick of mind and memory, the interpretation of Beloved as a revenant signifies in the novel's symbolic economy. Shlomith Rimmon-Kenan astutely differentiates between the narrative significance of Beloved's insubstantiality for the reader on the one hand and for the ghost's intratextual interlocutors – Sethe and Denver in particular – on the other:

> That the dead baby who first returned as a ghost has now come back in the flesh is unquestionably accepted – though often resented – by the various characters in the novel, as is the supernatural character of this occurrence ... The invasion, I am afraid, cannot be so unquestioningly accepted by the reader, not because of a modern skepticism about supernatural events but because of conflicting evidence within the novel itself. (118)

This is a vital distinction, as Rimmon-Kenan goes on to show when she explores the internal contradictions between various levels in the text. Beyond the transferential dynamics enacted in the mother-daughter-sister triad of Denver, Beloved, and Sethe, and distinct from the collective historical transference of the "unspeakable things unspoken" of part II of the novel is the question of Beloved's place and status in the narrative. Analytical attention to this "middle" level short-circuits or at least tempers the reader's mythological projections onto the text and on Beloved as its ghostly messenger. Such careful narratological attention serves the sobriety of the moral imagination over against the pathos of projection or identification.

Morrison's novel also enriches the metaphorics of memory in a gesture which has engendered a small critical literature of its own.[3] The defamiliarizing linguistic shock delivered by the noun "rememory" substantivizes the more familiar process of remembering, which seems to suggest a more intrusive, opaque reality for the recurrent past, which the perceiver encounters in a bodily way. However "rememory" is spun in Morrison criticism, it belongs neither to dialect nor idiolect; it is a buried word reclaimed and foregrounded from the *OED*. It is helpful to resituate the concept in its textual environment and to read it there, as Rimmon-Kenan replaces the ghost in its narratological dynamics. The scene where "rememory" is first mentioned in the novel is focalized through Sethe's daughter Denver, who is watching her mother praying: "Maybe the white dress holding its arm around her mother's waist was in pain. If so, it could mean the baby ghost had plans. When she opened the door, Sethe was just leaving the keeping room" (42). The conversation between mother and daughter that follows allows Sethe to elaborate on the "talking" she was doing in the keeping room. Rememory is connected with the palpable persistence of the past in places:

> I was talking about time. It's so hard for me to believe in it. Some things go. Pass on. Some things just stay. I used to think it was my rememory. You know. Some things you forget. Other things you never do. But it's not. Places, places are still there. If a house burns down, it's gone, but the place – the picture of it – stays, and not just in my rememory, but out there, in the world. What I remember is a picture floating around out there outside of my head. I mean, even if I don't think of it, even if I die, the picture of what I did, or knew, or saw, is still out there. Right in the place where it happened.
>
> Can other people see it, asked Denver.
>
> Oh, yes, Oh, yes, yes, yes. Someday you be walking down the road and you hear something or see something going on. So clear. And you think it's you thinking it up. A thought picture. But no. It's when you bump into a rememory that belongs to somebody else. Where I was before I came here, that place is real. It's never going away. Even if the whole farm – every tree and grass blade of it – dies. The picture is still there and what's more, if you go there – you who never was there – if you go there and stand in the place where it was, it will happen again; it will be there for you, waiting for you. So, Denver, you can't never go there. Never. (42–3)

To overhear the conversation between Denver and Sethe, and to lend at least tentative credence to Sethe's statements here is to test a hypothesis, namely, that "rememory" is not a thought-picture confined to one person's perception, but a thing, a thing "out there" and intersubjectively available, at least potentially owned in common. Others make tactile contact with "rememory," on a threshold or at a juncture of visibility or perceptibility, and without a story "in between." It is not far-fetched for the reader to accept this possibility. Eerie and spooky as it may be, rememory is a cognitive entity, an ineluctably embodied one; it represents a connected and connecting encounter with the traces of events that have transpired. Due to the intensity of these events – which are far from extraordinary in the violent social world in which slavery is a brute fact – perceiving them would seem to require no more than "ordinary" sight and hearing and common sense: one simply bumps into them in the road. This explanation is plausible to Denver, since it coheres with her own line of sight, with what she has "seen" in and around her mother, encircled by the arm of a phantom white dress. From the reader, the occurrence of rememory in the fictional world requires no epistemological leaps, but an extension of the seeing and hearing range of the moral imagination to include the uncanny side of the horrors of history.

Far from any intention to generalize "rememory" beyond the boundaries of Morrison's novel, or to build theories from it, it is important to note that the reader of Morrison's novels will recognize its genealogy and circulation among other novels. How is haunting related to rememory, and how do both, and their relation, raise questions for theorizing literary haunting? For Sethe, being able to articulate rememory is not sufficient to cope with Beloved's residence in her house. Beloved's departure is made possible by coming to terms with the personal past she carries through Sethe's projection, her "bearing" – to light and to understanding – Beloved's story. Before this is possible, Sethe gives in to Beloved, and is almost engulfed by her. The hold of the ghost is broken, the disproportionate grasp of her power is contained by the ritual of the thirty singing women led by Ella who "descend" on 124 for an exorcism of the "devil-child" – a scene that for Sethe recalls and reanimates Baby Suggs's sessions in the Clearing: "For Sethe it was as though the Clearing had come to her with all its heat and simmering leaves, where the voices of women searched for the right combination, the key, the code, the sound that broke the back of words" (308).

Haunting and rememory demand similar moral and psychological reckonings. For the contemporary reader, this involves "the ethical task at hand to make a community of the past through narration, figuration, and naming, even if the community of Morrison's characters cannot house Beloved's presence because she is too close to home" (Handley 688). Gordon's gloss on the above-quoted passage of Sethe's narrative naming of rememory articulates the more intimate connections between haunting and rememory most suggestively:

> What can we make out of this rememory that forgets some things and never ever others, a memory already indicated as uncanny by its fundamental repetitiousness and by its gesture to the haunted house? We could make out of this deeply social memory the kind of historical materialism an awareness of haunting would produce. For Morrison's social memory is not just history, but haunting, not just context, but animated worldliness, not just the hard ground of infrastructural matters, but the shadowy grip of ghostly matters. (165–6)

The articulation of haunting with rememory insists on a history with a will to materiality that eludes or resists narrative. If narrative is not a vehicle – or at least not a privileged vehicle – for this "historical materialism," its subtending textuality is understood to accommodate phenomena deemed uncanny in a range of alternative ways.

An "allergic," modest, or wary attitude towards narrative is revealed in the last two pages of the novel in a passage which has been interpreted pessimistically as a regrettable forgetting of Beloved: "It was not a story to pass on. They forgot her like a bad dream. After they made up their tales, shaped and decorated them, those that saw her that day on the porch quickly and deliberately forgot her" (274). The formula about passing on the story is repeated at three junctures in this final passage, and the third time with a change in the first word: "This is not a story to pass on." It seems important to heed this shift in register, and to interpret the sentence that critics have most focused on in the final paragraph in its light: "The rest is weather." By seemingly drawing a line under the tale of Beloved, the narrator creates a deliberate rupture and opts, like the others, for forgetting over remembering. What does it mean to say that "the rest is weather"? To point to weather in the context of Morrison's narrator's life world is not at all to trivialize, nor is it to understate. Under what circumstances and to what end might it not only be that "remembering is unwise" but that forgetting is wiser; that forgetting is not a lapse, a process left ravelling, but a step beyond the foreclosure of a future fraught and blocked by repeated remembering? Far from being "worked (over and) through," the space of this third declaration seems to resituate narrative within a hospitable, perhaps even a hopeful space of a process left incomplete. Giving those who have suffered the space not to re-call and re-member may seem to dishonour the testimonial imperative that seeks ever new groups of "compassionate listeners" earnest not to allow historical injustice to repeat itself. Beloved, materialized ghost that she was, wrought her harm and set her lessons. Perhaps the narrator forecloses further narrative of and about her, eschews her remembering because she has done enough, filled the shoes of her epitaph with the fullness of a name, and she calls for no more intimacy: "The rest is weather. Not the breath of the disremembered and unaccounted for, but wind in the eaves, or spring ice thawing too quickly. Just weather. Certainly no clamor for a kiss. Beloved" (274–5).

Kathleen Marks reads the stopping point of remembering at the end of the novel primarily in terms of its benefit for a community with a tangled and terrible history:

> The figure Beloved is the difference between what ought to be saved from the past and what needs to be discarded, the limit between what can and cannot be known … As a catalyst to memory, however, Beloved sets the boundaries of the new order, boundaries that the community works together to define – boundaries that exclude Beloved herself and that yet retain what it means to be loved. (101)

I would add that this refusal is a forbidding limit, apotropaic in its very function – not an ending that rounds things off, but an acknowledgment that memory work can only go so far before it goes too far, becoming inexorable or tyrannical. The reticence of refusing further narrative – not passing on the story – should be respected. *Beloved* is not only a book about historical "haunting," a "haunted" narrative in which "haunting" is a structure of poetic form, but a haunt-ing narrative, one that performs and sustains, and provokes a "ghost dance," issues a summons to the scene of "ghostly matters." A most provocative conclusion to be drawn from the novel's narrative structure is that granting and submitting to the persistence of haunting is a compelling, perhaps ethically more consequential, alternative to the self-agency of conducting (or enforcing) "memory work."

Plagues and Their Graves

A contrapuntal reading of *Beloved* and Estonian writer Ene Mihkelson's 2007 novel *Katku-haud* (Plague Grave) provides further insights into the presence of haunting in fictional texts and its relation to models of memory. *Plague Grave*, a novel of intimate inquisition about post-war terror in Estonia, probes the limits of how the past can return and explores the receding horizon of its reconstructability. It also hollows out the romanticized national myth of heroic resistance of the Forest Brethren, who fought a desperate guerrilla war from the end of the Second World War until the early 1950s, when the NKVD had flushed all but the last diehards from the woods in southern and northeastern Estonia. One of the ironies of Ene Mihkelson's novels is their refusal to "be autobiographical," though critics and the author herself have publicly dialogued about the issue of the relation of her novels to life writing (see Aija Sakova's and Eva Rein's essays in this volume [chapters 13 and 15]). It would be a consummate category mistake to situate Mihkelson's novels as "life writing" in any narrow sense, both in view of the banalizing "memoir boom" in Estonia and, more significantly, in view of the "memory culture" she seeks to singe and crack since it serves the nationalist project of writing the history of a suffering nation and its freedom fighters.

Plague Grave figures haunting through revisiting a relation, a series of conversations between the narrator and her mother's sister Agaate (Kaata), who was the narrator's temporary guardian and legal foster mother in the early 1950s, when both of her parents were Forest Brethren. The narrator's father, who bears the name Valter in *Plague Grave* (and the name Meinhard in Mihkelson's previous novel, *Ahasveeruse uni* [The Sleep of Ahasuerus]), was killed in a raid on the Forest Brethren's bunker. The opening, and one of the premises of the novel's inquisition/confession, is a contradictory interval between two dates of Valter's death – was it in 1953 or 1955? This uncertainty belies the scuffed chronology of the narrator's childhood, and a cluster of symptoms that point to other, more dangerous versions of the narrative of that time in her life.

In *Plague Grave*, Kaata is a querulous, smelly, frail, old woman, living in a house referred to as a "haunted castle" (*tondiloss*), a colloquial term in post-Soviet Estonia for both abandoned dwellings and half-completed building projects. Indeed, the word *tondiloss* is nothing extraordinary – even casual, in keeping with the ruses of the uncanny.

Kaata's house at the edge of the city had been built neatly and well – but it has since fallen into disrepair. By post-Soviet standards, it is good real estate – but it is a big storage shed for accumulated clutter, too big for one person, and in need of renovations. Kaata is the ghost in her own house, not unlike other elderly people who, in the eyes of their younger, busier relatives, have become physically disgusting and cantankerous, hardly worth the time of frequent visits and loving care, let alone the planning and cost of renovations to her house. After all, it is more convenient to wait until she dies. The deeper background "haunting" of Kaata's dwelling, beyond the ordinariness of the post-Soviet *tondiloss* – and by close implication and metonymy, her psychic haunt – has to do with her need to confess the unspoken, concealed underside of her foster-motherhood, as becomes apparent when the narrator, who has already been taking a walking tour of the places where she lived as a child, decides that Kaata is a key witness, the one to visit next.

As becomes clear early in the novel, Kaata, a pretty village girl who flirted and danced well, was recruited as an informer in the early post-war years. She collaborated with the NKVD/KGB over a long period of time, was assigned to frighten people with threats, to gather information in the village, and deliver reports. The dirtiest part of the secret for the narrator is that Kaata informed on the band of Forest Brethren to which her own sister and brother-in-law belonged, and kept her vigilant eye on their little daughter: quite directly and ultimately, then, Kaata was responsible for Valter's death. The conversations between the narrator and Kaata constitute an interrogation, with the narrator designating herself as a "bold huntsman," baiting her gaunt, helpless, and incontinent aunt with gifts of food and adult diapers, chopping wood, and providing company. She is hunting down the veiled and unspoken chapters of her fear-saturated childhood, and in the intimate politics of innuendoes and barbs, having her revenge upon two failed mothers – her biological mother, who abandoned her, and her duplicitous foster mother, who betrayed her.

The interrogation is intercalated with the narrator's visits to the historical archives, where she reads court records from central Estonian villages from the middle of the nineteenth century. Post-Soviet genealogical research focused on finding "noble ancestors" is a veneer, not only on the undeniable fact of miscegenation and cultural hybridity, but on much uglier stories. With little effort, "digging" in the archives reveals the subtext of ressentiment, and the magical effects of believing in the "noble ancestor"; this is shown in the cameo biography of the narrator's relative Anna von Stauden. Browsing in the county court records also "translates" off-the-cuff remarks passed on in family history. Ethnic slurs quoted by the narrator's grandfather become linked with their antecedents, such as a gruesome report of the trial of participants of village folk in a pogrom-like episode in Põltsamaa in 1882. Despite the random gaps (and gaping holes) created during the reorganization of archives in the first Soviet years, there is enough to sketch out boldly the broader implications of colonial social relations. The "middle layer" of colonial society in the Estonian and Livonian provinces, composed of "house servants" and other skilled labourers and craftspeople who worked on the baronial estates, "collaborated" with the landlords, and rose to a higher status than the peasants. Ironically, as is true of colonial power relations at various locations and historical situations, this "intermediate layer" later became a seedbed for the nationalist educated elite that sought to define the ethnic autochthonicity of the Estonian people in the national awakening of the third quarter of the nineteenth century. The question of "miscegenation" and the attribution of "noble birth" is, of course, one of the intimate transcripts of this relation.

In *Plague Grave*, the colonial past browsed forth from the archives "haunts" the recent past in brutally palpable ways: as the narrator ponders it, continuities are not matters of blood, but of mentality; coping and survival strategies die hard. "Native informers" had had centuries of practice informing on each other. Villagers such as Kaata were only too ready to practise similar informancy and betrayal with respect to their immediate neighbours in the time of the burning of villages in 1940 and 1941, and in the post-war forests filled with Forest Brethren and other civilian fugitives. The narrator finds no need to see Soviet times as a state of exception: to blame or exonerate Kaata's behaviour on Soviet terror, and the attendant fear and panic (the murky post-war circumstances Kaata refers to as *mäsu* – a jumbled mess), would be much too facile (and fatally wrong) an explanation.

The interrogation (hearing Kaata's confession) is carried out relentlessly, in a reversal of the caregiving functions the narrator received as a child. After each conversation with Kaata, the narrator writes down the keywords of what she said. She also takes photographs. In between visits to Kaata, the narrator has to process inner data – the dreams and physical symptoms that are the consequences of tracking the elusive truth. She learns to scrutinize Kaata's shadowily familiar body language for discrepancies. If as a child the narrator had realized that Kaata was a gifted "performer," convincingly feigning illness and weakness as circumstances required, she refines her decoding of Kaata's performances by closely reading her body: the "bird struggling for air under her throat" is a sign that Kaata is telling the truth. A photographic image of Kaata's eyes supplements these tactile impressions: "Seeing after the fact (rereading and checking the facts) takes place when I look at the photos I took that evening. Kaata's eyes are burning with the fire of inner torment. Eyes like that are inconsolable." Congruent with the Freudian unconscious, Kaata has a fetish about washing her hands often, and with ceremony. The narrator digs into the ground beneath the hand-washing fetish, and finds habitus: the meticulous cleanliness for which Sanna and Kaata's family was acclaimed among their fellow villagers was the heritage passed on by generations of foremothers, female house servants on the baronial estate.

At this point, with the freeze-frame of Kaata's inconsolable eyes, at the exact midpoint of the novel, and by moving the image of the "haunted house" around on the mental screen, the narrator creates a presumptive "theoretical" end to the story, a moratorial interruption in the investigation, and a second narrative threshold for the reader to cross. She scrolls Kaata's tale forward into the future anterior, beyond her death and "burial by fire": "Yes, I could put a period here, and stay here, with Kaata's glowing eyes, in that house that stands in wait for renovations, with its rooms turned into storerooms, in that cold haunted house with its overgrown garden" (138). After Kaata's death, the narrator limits herself only to giving Kaata's son Tõnu practical advice – not to sell a well-made house. Almost in the same breath, the narrator restrains her impulse to tell Tõnu anything else about his mother – the story of Kaata's haunted psyche, the substance of her confession, is a story not to be passed on.

In the same chapter, having revealed that Kaata was (to be) "buried by fire," in keeping with the villages that burned in 1941, the narrator shifts the subtext of the novel (and the interrogation) towards a different register of metaphors connected with exhumation and reburial. What is buried in the earth is available to excavation, to those who can bear it: "to begin excavations in order to find out who has been carefully buried under the slabs of stone. If there even is anybody or anything, except for the knowledge that there is not a single place on this land of repeated exhumations and reburials, that remains entirely untouchable and neutral with respect to the present time" (140). This meditation makes way for the metaphor of the novel's title: the graves on the land of recurrent reburial are "plague graves," infected for indeterminate future time, perhaps in perpetuity.

Mihkelson's novel evokes the trope of the tainted grave with reference to Estonian plague folklore, creating a network of allusions rippling from mass epidemics in the sixteenth and eighteenth centuries to the tainted and infected graves of Forest Brethren in the woods near the village.[4] This folkloric material is within range of articulability for the narrator, who seems to be conversant with it, but it offers neither interpretive or ritual succour for the dangers of the past: while various personifications of the plague (a sinister visitor in innocuous guise) are evoked, there is silence concerning the magical spells and ceremonies for protection against the plague, and ritual means of cure. This is a salient and significant exclusion. Folkloric "possibilities" are evoked only to be refuted, any utopic potential on the narrative level is firmly foreclosed: the infection, and the suspicion of infection remain – in the ground. Though the narrative is thus "disciplined" away from tendencies to romanticize folk tradition, the selective use of these "folkloric textual resources," by means of their very exclusions, alert the reader to follow metaphorical networks more closely. What lie in the ground are infected bones, skeletons, that give rise to ghosts. As readers we may surmise, Mihkelson's novel has more to do with skeletons in the closets of public and private memory than with ghosts who may be appeased, fed, satisfied by ritual means, and thus induced to silence. Skeletons must be exhumed, uncovered, and, if dismembered, put back together again if they are to rest in peace. Is this distinction between skeletons and ghosts more than a metaphoric shift – and does it share some of Kwon's stated intention to make distinctions when reading the ghost stories of the Vietnamese villages between ancestors (the dead that are our own) and ghosts (that belong to strangers not of our kin)? Interestingly, the narrator of *Plague Grave* calls repeated attention to Kaata's skeletal thinness, complete with the tic of a self-mocking, grimacing grin as she approaches particularly pernicious memory matter. Kaata is repeatedly referred to as a skeleton barely clothed with skin, ironically dissonant with the uncannily robust appetite that manifests upon offers of food. Throughout the novel, the narrator meditates in short poetic passages on the meaning of skeletons.

Mihkelson's novel documents a process of psychic exhumation with respect to her very real dead kin, and her functional covering version of her own childhood past, relentlessly crumbling and falling to pieces as she engages in the interrogational "dance" with Kaata. On one level, she is the perpetrator, brutally jarring and jogging the memory of an older relative who tenaciously resists remembering, and who is baited to deliver up her repressed tale of guilt. It is important to remember, however, that the initial gesture to confess belongs to Kaata herself. The tag line "I have committed great evil against you" (*Ma olen Sulle väga palju kurja teinud*) arouses the narrator's "hunter's instinct" only after the bait has been offered twice, but the obverse of the situation is that she has less to gain than she has to lose. She is the victim of her own hunt, its doubled quarry. The language of her symptoms, her dreams, and her conscious self-reflections show that she finds it hard to relinquish the "acceptable" version of her childhood – the one with only some of the gaps filled in, the one where at least theoretically there was a whiff of a good-enough mother. While a thirst for the truth and its concomitant rage to revenge goad her on, her symptoms and dreams provide a physical restraint to the relentlessness of the "hunt," thus perhaps tempering it and keeping it within humane bounds. The space for narrating "truth" is scripted, almost with minuscule precision, by the gap between Kaata's "performance" and her narrative. The interrogation maintains that space by calibrating the questions with the syncopated rhythm of Kaata's body language, reclaiming the narrator's own kinaesthetic memory from childhood, when she read the sign language of her caretaker's body anxiously, noting, but not comprehending, the contradictions. Indeed, early in the novel, silences become marked by "empty" question marks on the page – question marks that are placeholders for the untold story and its proleptic, perhaps inexhaustible, excess.

Only implicitly and grudgingly, despite rather than because of the narrator's inquisitorial activities, the novel points to the kind of mercy that might be shown towards skeletons, and living skeletons on the verge of the grave, even if the process remains permanently incomplete. Readers, reaching the limits of their own tolerance as witnesses to the inquisition, may rage at the abjection enacted by the narrator in the course of her excavation, and perhaps even wonder where the ethical limits of such inquiry may be, even if Kaata's suffering is intricately mirrored in the after-symptoms of the narrator herself. As is true in two of her previous novels, *Nime vaev* and *Ahasveeruse uni*, Mihkelson's reconstructions follow the trail of the narrator's headaches, heart palpitations, the graph of elevated and fluctuating blood pressure.

The traces arising from the barely remembered past of the narrator must partake of a painful process of reconstructing the elusive remainder – be it of the paternal family story in *Ahasveeruse uni*, or the mother-daughter-aunt drama of *Plague Grave*. Indeed, this missing part is encrypted, like the secrets analysed by Rashkin and Rand. Readers of Mihkelson's novels justifiably find it difficult to avoid amalgamating the narrators in these two novels, as well as those of her previous novels *Matsi põhi* and *Nime vaev*: these novels all share the same crypt. Though Ene Mihkelson herself has resolutely resisted any psychoanalytic interpretation of her works, the documentation of the memory seismograph in all four of her interlocked novels about Estonia's haunted half-century invites an Abraham-Torokian reading. The distinctive signature of the voice in all four of Mihkelson's novels overrides even major differences in literary form that mime and model memory work, such as the complex rhetoric of third-, first-, and second-person narration in *Ahasveeruse uni*.

On the level of public reception, Mihkelson's novels have become signifiers for the necessity of *Erinnerungsarbeit*, "memory work" – and their "difficult form," the very reflexivity of their aesthetics, their compelling and dangerous hollowing out of seemingly innocent everyday locutions, (supposedly) constitute the means of its apotropaicity. Such is the story line of respectful literary-critical orthodoxy, which surrounds Ene Mihkelson's fiction in abundance. Unfortunately and ironically, however, Estonian readers seem to have delegated the dirty work of memory to writers such as Mihkelson – her sibylline, rough-textured voice is a good surrogate – and this is "literature," after all – not testimony, to which one might be held publicly accountable. Kaata was no KGB boss – not a mass killer, only an "ordinary criminal." It is enough to read about her, if one can overcome squeamishness.

To fall into this trap is to miss the point: the imperative of memory work rises out of the narrator's exhumation of her own truth, including the exposure of herself as interrogator, as the hungry child seeking revenge for a double abandonment. In a telling double entendre (and returning to the metaphor of the haunted house), the place of the ghostly past is quite literally *hinge taga* (behind the soul, in the soul's back parts). But in another, more material meaning of that phrase, what is in the back room of the soul is what the careful and provident (peasant) housewife has put up for storage for a time of need – a personal and collective resource hard to contain or stabilize to a paradigm of private ownership. In the novel the impact of collective or communal providership is sharpened by the presence of another well-built house in the opening framing chapters: the storehouse (*ait*) of the Vakeristi estate, built by the narrator's uncle, and equipped with a massive iron key wrought by the local blacksmith, which has a sly tendency to get lost, thus leaving its trace in the archival transcripts of the local court. Who is the owner of this (these) haunted house(s)?

How are the summonses issued by literary "haunted narratives" such as Morrison's *Beloved* and Mihkelson's *Plague Grave* related to the genre of life writing? Literary scholars and historians (Ansgar Nünning, Aleida Assmann, and Astrid Erll among them) have noted that autobiographical texts are "memory places" (*lieux de mémoire*), belonging within the purview of cultural memory – while the boundary between life writing and "autobiographical" fiction remains open, mobile, and ambiguous. What relevance does haunting (and hauntology) have for this open border? The terms and the spaces that *Plague Grave* establishes for "memory work" are precisely a function of the fact that it is *not* an autobiography, not a testimonial text that can be read over and against the "real" biography of the author and checked for "the facts." It must emphatically be said that this is not an evasion, nor is it primarily a "distancing manoeuvre" or "displacement" in a psychological sense. Perhaps it would be more precise to say that by choosing the ruse of fictionality, Mihkelson has made of the autobiographical material of her own family story what Spivak has called a "regulative psychobiography" – for, in, and about post-Soviet Estonia. Not only because of its intense and unrelenting imbrications of narration with the somatization of psychic symptoms and dreams, *Plague Grave* is a "symptomatic" text – but not an exceptional one. It is not "about" exceptions: these hauntings are quite "ordinary." *Plague Grave* and *Beloved* harness any mimetic resemblances to the larger, more haunting "facts": they are texts with the poetic power to induce and to continue haunting.

Does reading *Plague Grave* as a "haunted narrative" entrust too much power to the literary text? Despite hopes that the literary text will provoke and stun the reader into "digging," into "doing" memory work (expressions such as "competent reader" should be shunned here!) – do Estonian readers want to be disturbed by their unburied dead, or would they rather be entertained by their parodic representations (as can be seen in some of Andrus Kivirähk's recent writing)? As if the implicit summons to the reader in Kaata and the narrator's painful dialogue – this implicit summons to self-interrogation – were not enough, apotropaic conjuring happens from the first beat of the novel, in its outer frame, bounded by the neon-yellow plastic of a police ribbon, squarely in the path of the present, always already apparitional. The disturbing future-before-the-past temporality of the novel's first scene preceded the political reality of the Bronze Soldier, which took place in the streets of Tallinn in April 2007 while the novel was already at the printer's, a mere few days before the publisher's book launch. This fortuitous event, this uncanny "coincidence" is partly the after-effect of careful reading on the part of the writer – reading in the "future anterior," not too deeply "between" the lines. After all, it would not have taken much guessing to figure out that the public expression of passions surrounding the moving of the Bronze Soldier (and the bones of the dead buried beneath the monument) from Tõnismäe to the military cemetery at the edge of town were only a matter of time – and that the Estonian government would predictably fumble with the timing and decorum of that ceremony. Such predictions required no prophetic prescience, or even acute intuition – only common sense. The Bronze Soldier was an alarm signal for "their" nasty stories, barely tolerated, still waiting to be told. "Haunted narratives" and the hauntological theories built from reading them in the singular power of literary imagination, have double force. On the one hand, instead of exorcistic spells, containing and managing the ghosts in putatively aesthetic "safe spaces," they issue a "prayer for haunting" and an invitation to a "ghost dance," holding open narrative space in "intermediate time" between time present and time future for that telling. On the other hand, such texts interrupt kinds of aesthetic pleasure that repeat with a peculiarly obscene indulgence, scandalous perhaps even to mention – the stories that keep the trauma going by reopening the wound. That pleasure, as the narrators of both *Beloved* and *Plague Grave* know well – offers no safety. Thus, "haunted narratives" do not proclaim the end of storytelling but ask about its limits: when does narration need to stop and be allowed its silence proper? Are there stories (not) to be passed on?

NOTES

1 Eda Kalmre's study of rumours of cannibalism in post – Second World War Tartu is an interesting example of the genesis of ghost stories on the popular level.
2 Among the texts analysed in this volume, European examples include Christa Wolf, Ingeborg Bachmann, and Estonian writers Ene Mihkelson and Bernard Kangro. See chapters 13, 15, and 19.
3 See Rushdy.

4 Plague folklore in Estonia has been thoroughly researched in an international frame by Reet Hiiemäe.

WORKS CITED

Abraham, Nicolas, and Maria Torok. *The Shell and the Kernel: Renewals of Psychoanalysis*. Vol. 1. Chicago: University of Chicago Press, 1994.
Assmann, Aleida. *Der lange Schatten der Erinnerung: Geschichtskultur und Erinnerungspolitik*. München: Beck, 2006.
Assmann, Jan. *Religion and Cultural Memory: Ten Studies*. Stanford: Stanford University Press, 2006.
Benjamin, Walter. "Theses on the Philosophy of History [On the Concept of History]." Trans. Harry Zohn. In *Illuminations*, ed. Hannah Arendt, 253–64. New York: Schocken, 1986.
Bhabha, Homi K. "Conclusion: 'Race,' Time and the Revision of Modernity." In *The Location of Culture*, 236–56. New York: Routledge, 1994.
Cheah, Pheng. *Spectral Nationality*. New York: Columbia University Press, 2003.
Davis, Colin. "Hauntology, Spectres and Phantoms." *French Studies* 59, no. 3 (2005): 373–9. http://dx.doi.org/10.1093/fs/kni143.
Derrida, Jacques. *Specters of Marx: The State of the Debt, the Work of Mourning, and the New International*. Trans. Peggy Kamuf. New York: Routledge, 1994.
Gordon, Avery. *Ghostly Matters: Haunting and the Sociological Imagination*. Minneapolis: University of Minnesota Press, 1997.
Halbwachs, Maurice. *The Collective Memory*. Trans. Francis J. Ditter and Vida Y. Ditter. New York: Harper & Row, 1980.
Handley, William R. "The House a Ghost Built: 'Nommo,' Allegory, and the Ethics of Reading in Toni Morrison's *Beloved*." *Contemporary Literature* 36, no. 4 (1995): 676–701. http://dx.doi.org/10.2307/1208946.
Hiiemäe, Reet. *Eesti katkupärimus. Eesti muistendid. Mütoloogilised haigused I. Monumenta Estoniae Antiquae II*. Tartu: Estonian Folklore Archives Publications, 1997.
Kalmre, Eda. *Hirm ja Võõraviha sõjajärgses Tartus: Pärimuslooline uurimus kannibalistlikest kuulujuttudest*. Tartu: EKM Teaduskirjastus, 2007.
Kwon, Heonik. *Ghosts of War in Vietnam*. Cambridge: Cambridge University Press, 2008.
Marks, Kathleen. *Toni Morrison's Beloved and the Apotropaic Imagination*. Columbia: University of Missouri Press, 2002.
Mihkelson, Ene. *Ahasveeruse uni* [The Sleep of Ahasuerus]. Tallinn: Tuum, 2001.

Mihkelson, Ene. *Katkuhaud* [Plague Grave]. Tallinn: Varrak, 2007.

Morrison, Toni. *Beloved*. New York: Knopf, 1991.

O'Riley, Michael. *Postcolonial Haunting and Victimization: Assia Djebar's New Novels*. New York: Peter Lang, 2007.

Rand, Nicholas. *Le cryptage et la vie des oeuvres: Étude du secret dans les textes de Flaubert, Stendhal, Benjamin, Stefan George, Edgar Poe, Francis Ponge, Heidegger et Freud*. Paris: Aubier, 1989.

Rashkin, Esther. "The Haunted Child: Social Catastrophe, Phantom Transmissions, and the Aftermath of Collective Trauma." *Psychoanalytic Review* 86, no. 3 (June 1999): 433–53. Medline:10550869.

Rimmon-Kenan, Shlomith. "Narration, Doubt, Retrieval: Toni Morrison's *Beloved*." *Narrative* 4, no. 2 (1996): 109–23.

Rushdy, Ashraf H.A. "'Rememory': Primal Scenes and Constructions in Toni Morrison's Novels." *Contemporary Literature* 31, no. 3 (1990): 300–23. http://dx.doi.org/10.2307/1208536.

Spivak, Gayatri Chakravorty. "Ghostwriting." *Diacritics* 25, no. 2 (1995): 64–84. http://dx.doi.org/10.2307/465145.

van Alphen, Ernst. "Symptoms of Discursivity: Experience, Memory, and Trauma." In *Acts of Memory: Cultural Recall in the Present*, ed. Mieke Bal, Jonathan Crewe, and Leo Spitzer, 24–38. Hanover, NH: University Press of New England, 1999.

Wertsch, James V. *Voices of Collective Remembering*. Cambridge: Cambridge University Press, 2002. http://dx.doi.org/10.1017/CBO9780511613715.

2 Trauma and Utopia: Benjamin, Adorno, and Elie Wiesel's *Night*

PHILIPP SCHWEIGHAUSER

On 26 October 2005, the American writer James Frey appeared on *Oprah's Book Club* to promote *A Million Little Pieces* (2003), his graphic autobiographical narrative of drug addiction, alcohol abuse, crime, and eventual recovery in a twelve-step program.[1] Oprah Winfrey had already selected his book as one of her show's picks and, largely as a result of that endorsement, Frey's book rose to the top of the non-fiction titles on the *New York Times* best-seller list, where it stayed for fifteen weeks. When, on 8 January 2006, the investigative website The Smoking Gun reported that part of Frey's tale was fabricated ("The Man"), Winfrey at first defended the author on *Larry King Live*, saying that "although some of the facts have been questioned, the underlying message of redemption in James Frey's memoir still resonates with me, and I know it resonates with millions of other people who have read this book and who will continue to read this book" (quoted in Wyatt, "Writer Says" A20). Two weeks later, on 26 January, Winfrey invited Frey as well as his publisher Nan A. Talese back to her show to tell him, "I feel duped … But more importantly, I feel that you betrayed millions of readers" (quoted in Wyatt, "Author" A1). Apparently, Winfrey had changed her mind.[2]

Winfrey's next selection for her book club was another piece of life writing that records personal suffering, though on an entirely different scale: the new, 2006 English translation of Elie Wiesel's Holocaust memoir *La Nuit* (1958). After the Frey debacle, this seemed a smart decision. I am not being cynical: as the memoir of one of the most prominent Holocaust survivors and a winner of the Nobel Peace Prize, *Night* seemed a paradigmatic example of life writing that adheres to precisely those standards of truth telling that Frey's semi-fictional memoir violated. This also corresponds to Wiesel's own assessment of *Night*, which he calls his "testimony" and "deposition" (71 and passim) in his 1994 memoir *All Rivers Run to the Sea*. When interviewed by the *New York Times* shortly after the publication of the new English translation and in the context of its selection by *Oprah's Book Club*, Wiesel elaborated on his earlier assessment. While he acknowledged that some commentators had referred to the book as a novel, "mainly because of its literary style," he maintained that it was "not a novel at all ... I know the difference ... I make a distinction between what I lived through and what I imagined others to have lived through ... All the people I describe were with me there. I object angrily if someone mentions it as a novel" (quoted in Wyatt, "Oprah's Book Club" B8). Yet that did not prevent commentators from asking similar questions about *Night* than they did about *A Million Little Pieces*.

Debates concerning the veracity of Wiesel's account most often revolve around significant differences between a first, longer Yiddish version of the text that was published under the title *Un di velt hot geshvign* (And the World Remained Silent) in Argentina in 1956 and the second, French version published by Les Éditions de Minuit as *La Nuit* in 1958. Both English translations, the first by Stella Rodway, the second by Wiesel's wife Marion Wiesel, are based on the French version and were published by Hill & Wang in 1960 and 2006, respectively. In 1996, Naomi Seidman, a professor of Jewish culture at Berkeley, had published a comparative analysis of the Yiddish and French texts in *Jewish Social Studies*. Seidman claimed that while the Yiddish version offers a historical account of events written from the perspective of an angry survivor, *La Nuit* is an autobiographical novel with strong religious overtones in which, "in the aftermath of God's abdication, the site and occasion of this abdication – 'the Holocaust' – takes on theological significance, and the witness becomes both priest and prophet of this new religion" (2). Seidman's essay has generated a lively and often fierce debate that was re-energized by Winfrey's selection of Wiesel's book. What is at stake in that debate is not merely the genre of *Night* but the veracity of Wiesel's account and his moral authority as a witness. Thus, when we read Gary Weissman's list of the wide variety of generic labels that have been adduced to classify *Night* ("novel/autobiography," "autobiographical novel," "non-fictional novel," "semi-fictional memoir," "fictional-autobiographical novel," "fictionalized autobiographical memoir," "memoir-novel" [Weissman 65]), we need to remain aware that each choice of a label has significant ethical and political ramifications. Considering that "life writing" is not an established term in the publishing world, publishers' and booksellers' choices of the labels they used to market *Night* further complicated the issue. In the case of the 2006 English translation of *Night*, Amazon.com allegedly first categorized it as "fiction and literature," but then switched to "biography and memoir" (Italie). What the debates surrounding the generic status of *Night* make clear is that Wiesel's text is a liminal case of autobiography. Unlike several other texts discussed in this volume, though, it is not a "limit-case" as defined by Leigh Gilmore. *Night* does not "confront how the limits of autobiography, multiple and sprawling as they are, might conspire to prevent some self-representational stories from beginning to be told at all if they were subjected to a literal truth test or evaluated by certain objective measures" (14). *Night* is not a text that self-reflexively probes the limits of autobiography; the debates surrounding its truthfulness and authenticity are neither elicited by the text itself nor desired by its author; they were brought to bear on it by third parties. These caveats need to be kept in mind when I refer to *Night* as Wiesel's "Holocaust memoir" in what follows.

What I find particularly intriguing about the debates that sprung up around Frey's and Wiesel's books, though, is less what they tell us about the kinds of expectations readers and critics alike bring to bear on memoirs than the religious register critics tap into as they discuss life writing that revolves around painful experiences. When Winfrey asserts that "the underlying message of redemption in James Frey's memoir still resonates with me," and when Seidman affirms that, as a witness to the Holocaust, Wiesel "becomes both priest and prophet" of a "new religion," they suggest that these writers are capable of deriving some sort of metaphysical solace from the painful experiences they underwent. That the desire to detect such moments of redemption in first-person trauma narratives is strong becomes especially obvious in Winfrey's interview with Wiesel in *O, the Oprah Magazine*. In her framing commentary, she writes that "when I talk with Elie about these things, he tells me that he has few answers and many, many questions – yet even in his questions, I hear hope that the human spirit can survive anything. *Anything*" (Winfrey). Winfrey writes this even though Wiesel's answer to her question of whether "every person who did survive" was "proof that the human spirit can triumph over anything" is the following: "It's hard to say. Some people survived because they wanted to, Oprah. I did not [want to survive]. As long as my father was alive, I wanted to live – but only because of him. After he died, between the end of January and April [of the year we were released], I didn't really live."

Wiesel's response does not seem to bear out Winfrey's interpretation, and I suspect that the kind of reading of *Night* she at least implicitly proposes owes more to her own desires and her impression of Elie Wiesel the man than to a careful consideration of the text itself. *Night* is far too radically dark and pessimistic a text to allow us to locate a message of hope at its centre. Yet while both Seidman's straightforward theological reading of *Night* and Winfrey's secularized version thereof do justice to neither the complexity nor the negativity of Wiesel's text, the two commentators are not entirely wrong in detecting moments of transcendence in this harrowing trauma narrative. In fact, I would suggest that *Night* can be read as an extended reflection on the possibility of thinking utopia in times of trauma. The aim of this essay is not to propose such a reading, though. Rather, in what follows, Wiesel's Holocaust memoir serves as a starting and reference point for an extended engagement with the work of Walter Benjamin and Theodor W. Adorno, two Frankfurt School intellectuals who have thought intensively about what it takes not to abandon utopian dreaming in the face of historical catastrophe and trauma.

Trauma and utopia – an odd coupling, perhaps. As writers register and theorists describe, the impact of traumatizing events such as ethnic cleansing, war, rape, torture, or the violent loss of a loved one in many cases forecloses the subject's ability to imagine, let alone lead, the good life and thus denies the central promise of utopia. The historian Dominick LaCapra's characterization of trauma in *Writing History, Writing Trauma* as "a disruptive experience that disarticulates the self and creates holes in existence" (41) is based on that assumption, and so is the definition of "Posttraumatic Stress Disorder" given by the current, fourth edition of the *Diagnostic and Statistical Manual of Mental Disorders* (*DSM-IV*):

> The essential feature of Posttraumatic Stress Disorder is the development of characteristic symptoms following exposure to an extreme traumatic stressor involving direct personal experience of an event that involves actual or threatened death or serious injury, or other threat to one's physical integrity; or witnessing an event that involves death, injury, or a threat to another person; or learning about unexpected or violent death, serious harm, or threat of death or injury experienced by a family member or other

> close associate (Criterion A1). The person's response to the event must involve intense fear, helplessness, or horror (or in children, the response must involve disorganized or agitated behavior) (Criterion A2). The characteristic symptoms resulting from the exposure to the extreme trauma include persistent reexperiencing of the traumatic event (Criterion B), persistent avoidance of stimuli associated with the trauma and numbing of general responsiveness (Criterion C), and persistent symptoms of increased arousal (Criterion D). The full symptom picture must be present for more than 1 month (Criterion E), and the disturbance must cause clinically significant distress or impairment in social, occupational, or other important areas of functioning (Criterion F). (American Psychiatric Association 463)

It is especially the "persistent reexperiencing of the traumatic event," the perseverance of what Freud labelled "repetition compulsion" in *Beyond the Pleasure Principle*, that keeps the traumatized caught up in a present that is haunted by the past to such an extent that its openings towards the future seem to disappear. LaCapra aptly describes the kind of blockage that trauma entails: in "the compulsive repetition of traumatic scenes," the past "is blocked or fatalistically caught up in a melancholic feedback loop" (21). In traumatic re-experiencing, the past and the present collapse and projections into the future are cut short. It is only in working through trauma (as opposed to acting out or compulsively repeating the traumatic scenes) that "one is able to distinguish between past and present and to recall in memory that something happened to one (or one's people) back then while realizing that one is living here and now with openings to the future" (22). As the essays in this volume attest to, much twentieth-century life writing that revolves around experiences of massive physical or psychological pain registers trauma symptoms. Wiesel's *Night* chronicles the multiple psychological effects of deportation and imprisonment in concentration camps: from Madame Schächter's madness (22–30) and the "dumb, motionless, haunted" look of old men (67) to Wiesel's father's "extreme exhaustion" (84) and Akiba Drummer's fate, who "could only repeat that all was over for him, that he could no longer keep up the struggle, that he had no strength left, nor faith. Suddenly his eyes would become blank, nothing but two open wounds, two pits of terror" (72). For these men and women, it would seem almost impossible to imagine a world beyond the present state of displacement, hunger, violence, and death.

Conversely, many writers and theorists imagine utopia as a place (or, more precisely, a non-place) from which those social structures and events which are likely to produce trauma are absent. Herbert Marcuse's definition of utopia as an imagined world that has solved the problem of "the reconciliation of human beings and nature, of non-alienated labour as creative activity, the creation of human relations freed from the struggle for existence" ("Protosocialism" 33) captures this well, as does George Kateb's in *Utopia and Its Enemies*. Utopia, he asserts, allows its inhabitants to live "a life of brotherhood, equality, joy, leisure, plenty, peace, health, and a life of permanent, unrelieved, universal satisfaction" (8). From such a world, potentially traumatogenic social conditions and processes – Kateb highlights war and scarcity – have been removed.

In political philosophy, it is primarily the detractors of utopia who have established causal links between utopia and trauma – though not necessarily in those terms. The two major liberal critics of utopian thinking and practice, Sir Karl Popper and the Austrian-British economist and political philosopher Friedrich August von Hayek, both stress the continuities between socialism and totalitarianism as they pinpoint the destructive potential of social engineering, centralized planning, and collectivism, which they consider to be at the heart of utopian thought and practice. For both, moreover, Friedrich Hölderlin got it right when he wrote that "the state has always been made a hell by man's wanting to make it a heaven" (23). (Hayek uses the quote as an epigraph to "The Great Utopia," the second chapter of his *The Road to Serfdom*.) As Hayek argues, "individual freedom cannot be reconciled with the supremacy of one single purpose to which the whole society must be entirely and permanently subordinated" (211), and a state with a planned economy requires a dictatorial government (91). In line with these observations, he writes this about one of the great utopian socialists: "Where freedom was concerned, the founders of socialism made no bones about their intentions. Freedom of thought they regarded as the root-evil of nineteenth-century society, and the first of modern planners, Saint-Simon, even predicted that those who did not obey his proposed planning would be 'treated as cattle'" (25).

For Popper, it is "aestheticism," that is, "the desire to build a world which is not only a little better and more rational than ours, but which is free from all its ugliness" (1: 145) that lies at the root of utopian violence. Commenting on Plato's assertion that the draughtsmen of his utopia "will not consent to lay a finger on city or individual, or draft laws, until they are given, or can make for themselves, a clean canvas" (Plato 501), Popper writes:

> The artist-politician first has to make his canvas clean, to destroy existing institutions, to purify, to purge. This is an excellent description of all political radicalism, of the aestheticist's refusal to compromise. The view that society should be beautiful like a work of art leads only too easily to violent measures. And all this radicalism and violence is both unrealistic and futile. (1: 146)

Even if we disagree – as I do – with much of what Hayek and Popper write about socialism and utopia, we would do well to recognize that utopian thinking does indeed have a problem with closure. Closure marks the point at which the thoroughly ordered and planned totality threatens to become indistinguishable from a totalitarian order. What I believe needs to be rejected in Popper's and Hayek's accounts is their assertion that totalitarianism is a *necessary* consequence of utopianism. In asserting the necessity of such an outcome, Popper and Hayek subscribe to the same (and mistaken) belief in the complete determination of "really existing utopias" by utopian blueprints that many a utopian subscribes to. Yes, twentieth-century history does bear ample evidence of how the inversion of utopian promises of freedom and equality is always a possibility; but it is not a necessity.

Phrased in terms of the conjunctions between utopia and trauma that I explore in this essay, then, utopians and anti-utopians differ in that the former consider that relationship governed by the law of inverse proportionality while the latter consider it governed by the law of direct proportionality. Yet this by no means exhausts the possibilities. As we take a closer look at the writings of two of the major Frankfurt School theorists, we find that other, more complex links can be established between utopia and trauma. Walter Benjamin and Theodor W. Adorno have both written extensively on the need for utopian thinking in times of trauma. In what follows, I draw on their work to formulate tentative answers to three questions: To what extent are utopian visions of a better world possible under conditions of trauma? What forms can such visions take under such conditions? How are those forms negotiated and produced in Wiesel's *Night* – which I consider a paradigmatic case of twentieth-century life writing that revolves around traumatic experiences?

Benjamin

Benjamin is no utopian thinker in the conventional sense (if, indeed, there is such a sense). Most importantly, he is a fierce critic of progress both as historiographical category and historical force. In the famous ninth thesis of his essay "Über den Begriff der Geschichte" (1940) – a text which in English is usually referred to as "Theses on the Philosophy of History," but whose title is more aptly translated as "On the Concept of History" – Benjamin pictures progress as a violent storm that piles up debris in front of the angel of history, who would like to stay to heal the wounds of the past. But the storm called progress propels him into the future, to which his back is turned:

> A Klee painting named "Angelus Novus" shows an angel looking as though he is about to move away from something he is fixedly contemplating. His eyes are staring, his mouth is open, his wings are spread. This is how one pictures the angel of history. His face is turned toward the past. Where we perceive a chain of events, he sees one single catastrophe which keeps piling wreckage upon wreckage and hurls it in front of his feet. The angel would like to stay, awaken the dead, and make whole what has been smashed. But a storm is blowing from Paradise; it has got caught in his wings with such violence that the angel can no longer close them. The storm irresistibly propels him into the future to which his back is turned, while the pile of debris before him grows skyward. This storm is what we call progress. ("Theses" 257–8)

Through the metaphors of the storm, the debris, and the angel, Benjamin characterizes progress as a destructive force. Here and in other parts of his essay, Benjamin chastises both Rankean historicism and Social Democrats' as well as Marx's understanding of history in terms of progress because it "spells disaster for the proletariat inasmuch as it deprives the working class of the chance to recognize its own struggles in the legacy of oppression that constitutes the historical past" (Gold 1228). For Benjamin, the "hatred" and "spirit of sacrifice" of the working class "are nourished by the image of enslaved ancestors rather than that of liberated grandchildren" ("Theses" 260).[3]

Benjamin's critique of the idea of progress puts him squarely at odds with much of the utopian tradition. As Ruth Levitas points out, for the majority of commentators on utopia from the late eighteenth to the mid-twentieth century,

> the virtue of utopia is that it holds up an ideal, an ideal which encourages social progress – but that progress is seen as properly a gradual process, which the literal attempt to institute utopia would interrupt ... Ideas are

> the motive force in social progress, so that utopia must be taken seriously as a contribution to this – but not too seriously, or evolution and progress may turn to revolution and disaster. (10–11)

While earlier observers – including Oscar Wilde – saw utopia as a catalyst for a progress that could bring either destruction or redemption, Benjamin counteracts the destructive force of progress with the redemptive force of an imagination that unlocks unrealized utopian possibilities of the *past*. Benjamin's utopian imagination, then, is one that returns to those moments where history could have taken a turn for the better – those instances that reveal, as Eneken Laanes puts it in her essay in this volume (chapter 11), "that the course of history could have been different, that there was a moment of choice, a crossroads at which it was possible to decide which road to take." In the "Angelus Novus" passage, "Paradise" is the religious shorthand for such a moment; in thesis XIV, Benjamin names two secular analogues: the French Revolution and the Roman Republic.

Traces of such a backward-looking utopianism can also be detected in *Night*, whose very first sentence introduces a figure whose name evokes hopes for utopian unlocking: "They called him Moshe the Beadle, as though he had never had a surname in his life" (1). Moshe the Beadle is indeed a Moses figure. As the only Jew who returns to Sighet from the first wave of deportation to tell the story of a German massacre, Moshe assumes the role of the prophet who admonishes his fellow Jews to leave the ghetto: "I wanted to come back to Sighet to tell you the story of my death. So that you could prepare yourselves while there was still time. To live? I don't attach any importance to my life any more. I'm alone. No, I wanted to come back, and to warn you" (5). Yet Moshe is not listened to. He is looked upon as a madman and cannot lead his people out of servitude.

Benjamin's utopianism differs from traditional accounts not only in its return to the past but also in its refusal to outline the contours of a better future world. That refusal is partly based on his conviction that the Social Democrats' "focus upon the future … erode[s] the ability of the proletariat to hear echoes of its own struggle in the past, a prerequisite for revolution" (Gold 1228). As such, it is in line with Marx's refusal to write what he scornfully called "recipes … for the cook-shops of the future" (99) in the postface to the first volume of the second edition of *Capital* (1873). More importantly, though, Benjamin's refusal to picture utopia is shaped by the Jewish heritage he draws on extensively throughout his work. As he puts it in a manuscript quoted by Rolf Tiedemann, "those who would ask in what state 'redeemed humanity' finds itself, what conditions must be met for this state to emerge, and when it can be expected, ask questions for which there is no answer. One might just as well ask what the color of ultraviolet colors are" (Benjamin, quoted in Tiedemann, *Studien* 104–5).[4] Benjamin here evokes the old theological topos of the unrepresentability of the wholly other (JHVH in Jewish theology; "redeemed humanity" in Benjamin). Consequently, the angel flying into the future has his back turned to it and sees nothing of it. Yet the main theological context in which Benjamin's refusal to paint utopia must be understood is not the notion of the unrepresentability of the messianic state but that of the proscription against images (*Bilderverbot*) characteristic of Jewish and other monotheistic religions. Formulated in opposition to the polytheistic veneration of images ("idolatry"), the Judaeo-Christian image ban, codified most prominently in the second commandment of the Hebrew Bible (Ex 20:4–5; Dt 5:8–9), is in Benjamin extended to the depiction of utopia.

It is Leo Löwenthal who most consistently links his friend's utopianism to his theological impulses:

> The utopian-messianic motif, which is deeply rooted in Jewish metaphysics and mysticism, played a significant role for Benjamin, surely also for Ernst Bloch and Herbert Marcuse, and for myself. In his later years, when he ventured – a bit too far for my taste – into concrete religious symbolism, Horkheimer frequently said (and on this point I agree with him completely) that the Jewish doctrine that the name of God may not be spoken or even written should be adhered to. The name of God is not yet fulfilled, and perhaps it will never be fulfilled; nor is it for us to determine if, when, and how it will be fulfilled for those who come after us ... The notion of something perhaps unattainable, perhaps unnameable, but which holds the messianic hope of fulfillment – I suppose this idea is very Jewish; it is certainly a motif in my thinking, and I suppose it was for my friends as well – but quite certainly it was for Benjamin a shining example of the irrevocable commitment to hope that remains with us "just for the sake of the hopeless." (232–3)

Reading "On the Concept of History," we realize that Benjamin's utopian hope is invested first and foremost in the past, not the future. The final sentences of the essay make this abundantly clear. In words that call to mind the image ban, Benjamin writes:

> We know that the Jews were prohibited from investigating the future. The Torah and the prayers instruct them in remembrance, however. This stripped the future of its magic, to which all those succumb who turn to the soothsayers for enlightenment. This does not imply, however, that for the Jews the future turned into homogeneous, empty time. For every second of time was the strait gate through which the Messiah might enter. (264)

Drawing on the proscription of images as well as a Jewish understanding of redemption as the "restitution of the ideal condition" or the "restoration of the originary totality" (Scholem 294), these words sum up Benjamin's conviction that visions of a future redeemed humanity bring human beings no closer to that ideal. Such visions are subject to the image ban not solely for religious reasons. They make the "oppressed class" forget the historical role Marx assigned it: that of "the avenger that completes the task of liberation in the name of generations of the downtrodden" (Benjamin, "Theses" 260). Inspired by Marx as well as Jewish messianism, Benjamin resolutely turns to the past, calling for the redemption of those moments in history at which it could have taken an other, better turn. Only thus is the possibility of future redemption kept alive, only thus is the "strait gate through which the Messiah might enter" kept open, and only thus could utopia ever be realized.[5] In *Night*, even once the Jews of Sighet have been deported, first to Auschwitz-Birkenau, then to Auschwitz, traces of such a retro-spective, religious utopianism can still be glimpsed – though not by Wiesel himself, who seems to have abandoned all hopes of deliverance along with his faith: "Some talked of God, of his mysterious ways, of the sins of the Jewish people, and of their future deliverance. But I had ceased to pray. How I sympathized with Job! I did not deny God's existence, but I doubted His absolute justice" (42). Yet to read *Night* as a testimony of one Jew's loss of faith in the face of the atrocities of the Holocaust would be as reductive as reading it as the source of what Seidman calls a "new religion." While the first-person narrator of Wiesel's memoir indeed struggles with his faith, Wiesel himself makes clear in his 1994 memoir *All Rivers Run to the Sea* that

> theorists of the idea that "God is dead" have used my words unfairly as justification of their rejection of faith. But if Nietzsche could cry out to the old man in the forest that God is dead, the Jew in me cannot. I have never renounced my faith in God. I have risen against His justice, protested His

silence, and sometimes His absence, but my anger rises up within faith and not outside it. (84)

Thus, while both Wiesel's and Benjamin's relation to the Jewish faith is complex – a complexity that is fed by their very different experiences of the Holocaust – both speak at least partly from within that faith.

Having said this, I need to acknowledge that my theological-materialist reading of Benjamin's utopianism is by no means uncontroversial. Following the work of Rolf Tiedemann, numerous Benjamin scholars consider "On the Concept of History" the work of a historical materialist whose recourse to religious language has a primarily rhetorical function. Tiedemann was Adorno's research assistant in Frankfurt, and he is the author of the first, influential doctoral dissertation on Benjamin, *Studien zur Philosophie Walter Benjamins* (1963; 2nd ed. 1973). Tiedemann's dissertation, his many additional books and articles on Benjamin, and his editorial co-stewardship of Benjamin's seven-volume *Gesammelte Schriften* (Collected Writings) are indispensable contributions to Benjamin scholarship, and I will frequently refer to Tiedemann's work in this essay. What I do object to, however, is his systematic and undialectical downplaying of the theological dimensions of Benjamin's theses, which goes hand in hand with an overemphasis on their Marxist heritage. In an essay that was added to the second edition of *Studien*, and which has been translated and reprinted in several places as "Historical Materialism or Political Messianism? An Interpretation of the Theses 'On the Concept of History,'" Tiedemann calls Benjamin's theological language a "mask" (202) and even goes as far as identifying the "Messiah" of the sixth thesis as "the proletariat and its science, historical materialism" (187), and asserting that "the Messiah, redemption, the angel and the Antichrist are all to be found in the Theses only as images, analogies, and parables, and not in their real form" (188). Given Benjamin's well-documented, sustained engagement with Jewish metaphysics and mysticism, his twenty-five years of friendship and intellectual exchange with Gershom Scholem – the founder of the modern study of the Kabala; given Benjamin's frequent and explicit references to some of the key issues and topoi in Jewish and Christian theology (e.g., the proscription of images, the Last Judgment, Paradise, the *nunc stans*); and given, finally, Benjamin's assertion that he has "never been able to do research and think in a way other than, if I may so put it, in a theological sense – namely, in accordance with the Talmudic teaching of the forty-nine levels of meaning in every passage in the Torah" (quoted in

Jay, *Dialectical Imagination* 200), Tiedemann's marginalization of Benjamin's theological impulses is difficult to understand.[6] Perhaps, Tiedemann's persistent secularization of Benjamin is influenced by his *Doktorvater* Adorno's assessment of Benjamin's relation to the Jewish religious tradition as one of "unrestrained secularization" (Adorno, "Einleitung" 48) – a characterization that may describe Adorno's own position (as well as the early Horkheimer's) better than it does Benjamin's. In any case, Tiedemann's desire to emphasize the Marxist heritage of Benjamin's thinking to bring it in line with Marx's judgment of religion as "the *opium* of the people" ("Introduction" 131)[7] appears so strong that it has prompted him to overshoot his mark in attempting to delegitimize the non-Marxist elements in Benjamin.[8] In my reading of Benjamin's theses, his recourse to theological language is not a "mask," and the fact that he "could imagine the end of history only as a messianic intervention" is not a sign of his "despair" (151) – as Jeanne-Marie Gagnebin has it. Instead, Benjamin's eschatological vision gives expression to hope in times of despair.

Reading *Night*, we encounter similar visions: "In one ultimate moment of lucidity it seemed to me that we were damned souls wandering in the half-world, souls condemned to wander through space till the generations of man came to an end, seeking their redemption, seeking oblivion" (34). But Wiesel's sentence does not end here. Instead, he adds an utterly pessimistic afterthought "– without hope of finding it" (34). As many traumatic experiences do, Wiesel's first-hand experience of the Holocaust seems to have cut short all visions of a better future. Yet other passages in *Night* speak a different language. Having met Yossi and Tibi, two Czech brothers "whose parents had been exterminated at Birkenau," Wiesel recounts that

> they and I very soon became friends. Having once belonged to a Zionist youth organization, they knew innumerable Hebrew chants. Thus we would often hum tunes evoking the calm waters of Jordan and the majestic sanctity of Jerusalem. And we would often talk of Palestine. Their parents, like mine, had lacked the courage to wind up their affairs and emigrate while there was still time. We decided that, if we were granted our lives until the liberation, we would not stay in Europe a day longer. We would take the first boat for Haifa.
>
> Still lost in his cabalistic dreams, Akiba Drummer had discovered a verse in the Bible which, interpreted in terms of numerology, enabled him to predict that the deliverance was due within the coming weeks. (48)

We do not learn what happens of Yossi and Tibi, but Akiba Drummer is selected for execution. Still, in such scenes, we can glimpse Wiesel's Benjaminian commitment to hope "just for the sake of the hopeless." Unlike at the beginning of his narrative, where he states that "it was illusion" (10) that ruled the Sighet ghetto, Wiesel here does not expose hopes for redemption as false and dangerous chimeras. Instead, he affirms the value of hoping even if Akiba Drummer's specific hopes soon turn to ashes. This commitment to hope against all odds also characterizes "On the Concept of History," which Benjamin wrote in response to the "Treaty of Non-aggression between Germany and the Union of Soviet Socialist Republics" that was signed into effect on 23 August 1939. Scholem famously characterized the theses as representing "the completion of Benjamin's awakening from the shock of the Hitler-Stalin pact" (quoted in Tiedemann, "Historical Materialism" 192). When Benjamin wrote his essay, the Second World War had already begun and the mass murder of European Jews was in its first stages. With the Hitler-Stalin pact, Benjamin's hope in Soviet resistance to fascism vanished, and the essay registers his despair. Indeed, if we follow the majority of Benjamin scholars in considering thesis IX as the heart of the essay, we cannot help noticing the text's bleakness. All history leaves behind is a "single catastrophe," a "pile of debris" that "grows skyward" while the angel of history – who would like to stay to resurrect the dead – is unable to help because the storm that is progress mercilessly thrusts him onward. A pessimist reading of "On the Concept of History" is further corroborated by other passages, including the one in which Benjamin asserts that "the politicians in whom the opponents of Fascism had placed their hopes are prostrate and confirm their defeat by betraying their own cause" ("Theses" 258). The essay's bleakness is also underscored by its place in Benjamin's biography: this was Benjamin's final essay before he committed suicide during an attempt to escape to the United States via Spain. Informed by the police chief of Portbou, a Franco-Spanish border town, that he would be turned over to the Gestapo, Benjamin probably took his own life on 27 September 1940.

And yet I find that the predominant mood of the essay is a different one. For Benjamin, there is hope in a different, non-progressivist kind of historiography that "blast[s] open the continuum of history" ("Theses" 262) to recover both the anger and the utopian desires of those who were defeated and subsequently forgotten in "the triumphal procession" (256) of historicism. For him, the stories the true materialist historiographer tells aim to redeem the struggles of the past with a view towards a better future: "As flowers turn toward the sun, by dint of a secret heliotropism[,] the past strives to turn toward that sun which is rising in the sky of history [*Himmel der Geschichte*]" (255). In the German original, Benjamin writes "*Himmel*," which Harry Zohn translates as "sky," but which could equally well be translated as "heaven." And indeed, as a future that can be realized by way of the present generation's recourse to the past, that rising sun is both a secular and a religious utopia. It is a religious utopia in that it becomes imaginable only in a mystical moment of what Benjamin calls "now-time" or "the time of the now" (*Jetztzeit*). In that moment – a moment that corresponds to the mystical *nunc stans* – the present and the past collapse to enable the realization of a possible future whose seeds the past already contained. Importantly, Benjamin characterizes that realization not simply as an act of redemption, but as one that is part of an eschatological development of history. In Benjamin's words, the historian must "gras[p] the constellation which his own era has formed with a definite earlier one" in order to "establi[sh] a conception of the present as the 'time of the now' which is shot through with chips of Messianic time."[9] Only thus can the historian truly serve humankind, by keeping open "the strait gate through which the Messiah might enter" (264).

And yet, while it is true that Benjamin's utopia is a religious utopia, it is equally clearly the secular utopia of a classless society. This becomes apparent when he identifies "the struggling, oppressed class itself" as "the depository of historical knowledge" (260) and points out that "the class struggle, which is always present to a historian influenced by Marx, is a fight for the crude and material things without which no refined and spiritual things could exist" (254). In thesis XIV, Benjamin adds historical specificity to such claims as he discusses the French Revolution as a realization of ideals that were already present in the Roman Republic: "To Robespierre ancient Rome was a past charged with the time of the now which he blasted out of the continuum of history" (261). In thesis XI, Benjamin even sketches what a future secular utopia could look like. Here, he draws on Charles Fourier's ideas, contrasting them favourably with what he considers the Social Democrats' fetishization of labour and their exploitation of nature in the name of technological progress:

> Compared with this positivistic conception, Fourier's fantasies, which have so often been ridiculed, prove to be surprisingly sound. According

> to Fourier, as a result of efficient cooperative labor, four moons would illuminate the earthly night, the ice would recede from the poles, sea water would no longer taste salty, and beasts of prey would do man's bidding. All this illustrates a kind of labor which, far from exploiting nature, is capable of delivering her of the creations which lie dormant in her womb as potentials. (259)

While twenty-first-century readers will find it difficult to consider the melting of polar ice as part of any utopia, and while we may question the desirability of other elements of Fourier's vision of a better world, this is as close as we get to the blueprint of a secular utopia in Benjamin's essay. Two things must be kept in mind, though. First, this is Fourier's utopia, not Benjamin's. Its main purpose in "On the Concept of History" is to expose the limitations of the Social Democrats' praise of labour and the destructiveness of their calls for the mastery of nature. Thus, we cannot assume that Fourier's vision of utopia corresponds to Benjamin's own. After all, he describes it as merely "surprisingly sound" and does so only in contrast with a vision of the world (Social Democracy) he considers pernicious. Second, the purely secular nature of Fourier's utopia does not tie in with Benjamin's constant intertwinement of theological and Marxist motifs, evidenced, for instance, by his description of now-time as "a Messianic cessation of happening, or, put differently, a revolutionary chance in the fight for the oppressed past" (263). Here as elsewhere, it is in the idea of utopia that historical materialism and theology merge and Benjamin's optimism is given its most powerful expression. Clearly, though, Benjamin's optimism is cautious and fragile, since "the Messiah comes not only as the redeemer, he comes as the subduer of Antichrist. Only that historian will have the gift of fanning the spark of hope in the past who is firmly convinced that *even the dead* will not be safe from the enemy if he wins. And this enemy has not ceased to be victorious" (255). The enemy here is both the Antichrist and the ruling classes. Reading Benjamin's theses, we have to endure that doubleness rather than resolve it in either a purely Marxist or a purely theological reading.

Benjamin's recourse to Fourier also raises the question of the specifics of Benjamin's own vision of a better world. The answer to that question comes as no surprise: he does not provide any of those specifics, for they fall under the theological ban on graven images. Yet this does not keep him from drawing on both religious and Marxist reflections on utopia to provide an optimistic counterpoint to both the essay's and his own bleakness and despair. For Benjamin, it is the utopian imagination that keeps hope alive in times of trauma – even in a text written so shortly before his untimely death.

I am using "trauma" advisedly here, for Benjamin explicitly draws on Freud's trauma theory to describe the effects of modern life on the human psyche. In his essay "The Storyteller: Reflections on the Works of Nikolai Leskov" (1936), Benjamin discusses the waning of storytelling in the traditional sense of an oral act of communication that is based on personal experience. Benjamin identifies two sources of that waning: the First World War, from which "men returned ... grown silent – not richer, but poorer in communicable experience" (84), and the gradual displacement of an older form of communication based on intelligence coming from afar in time or space by a more modern form of communication based on short-lived, self-contained, and immediately verifiable information that feeds on what is new and near (89). In an essay published three years later, Benjamin makes explicit what is only implicit here, namely, that it is the onslaught of sense impressions modern subjects are exposed to in the city and on the battlefield that renders them mute.

In "On Some Motifs in Baudelaire" (1939), Benjamin takes recourse to Freud's theory of trauma to describe the psychological effects of information overflow. For Freud, trauma results when excessive external stimuli pierce a human being's "protective shield," that is, when his or her psychological defence mechanisms fail, leaving the subject's consciousness unable to contain the shocks. Benjamin quotes from *Beyond the Pleasure Principle* to explain that "psychoanalytic theory strives to understand the nature of these traumatic shocks 'on the basis of their breaking through the protective shield against stimuli' [Freud, *Beyond* 29]" (Benjamin, "Baudelaire" 161). Yet while Freud expanded his own theorizing of trauma and the death drive in *Civilization and Its Discontents* to discuss the social-psychological dimension of the First World War, Benjamin takes the notion of "trauma" further than the founder of psychoanalysis himself was prepared to. For Benjamin, modernity marks the historical moment at which "shock experience has become the norm" (162), and Baudelaire is the modern poet par excellence, a "traumatophile typ[e]" who "placed the shock experience at the very center of his artistic work" and "made it his business to parry the shocks, no matter where they might come from, with his spiritual and his physical self" (163). While in "The Storyteller," Benjamin identified the battlefield and a less locatable information overflow as the main sources of traumatic shocks, his Baudelaire essay shifts the focus to the modern city, locating the origins of those shocks in "the metropolitan masses" (165); in technological innovations such as the telephone and photography, where "one abrupt movement of the hand triggers a process of many steps" (174); in "the advertising pages of ... newspaper[s]"; and in "the traffic of ... big cit[ies]" (175).

Clearly, Benjamin's extremely broad use of the notion of trauma is subject to Wulf Kansteiner's critique of more recent, inflationary uses of the concept. Benjamin does subscribe to an "aestheticized, morally and politically imprecise concept of cultural trauma" that "conflate[s] the traumatic and non-traumatic, the exceptional and the everyday" (Kansteiner 194). Yet once we recognize that the First World War is not only a crucial reference point for both of Benjamin's essays but also the main source of those wounds that continued to fester in Germany as Benjamin wrote his texts during the second half of the 1930s, we can historicize his reflections on trauma in ways that make them appear less inflationary. Writing from his Parisian exile, Benjamin could observe Germany sliding into the next historical catastrophe as it imposed its own war-related traumas on others. Benjamin's recourse to the image ban must be understood in this historical context: holding fast to utopian visions of a better world remained an obligation, but to paint utopia under such conditions was not an ethically viable choice.

Adorno

More explicitly than Benjamin, Theodor W. Adorno takes recourse to the theologumenon of the image ban as he explains his own refusal to depict utopia in a discussion with Ernst Bloch, the most prominent utopian related to the Frankfurt School. There, Adorno argues that "the prohibition of casting a picture of utopia" actually works "for the sake of utopia, and that has a deep connection to the commandment, 'Thou shalt not make a graven image!' This was also the defense that was actually intended against the cheap utopia, the false utopia, *the* utopia that can be bought" (Adorno and Bloch 10–11). The stance on utopia that Adorno expresses here is closely aligned with his larger project of negative dialectics as "the ontology of the wrong state of things. The right state of things would be free of it" (Adorno, *Negative Dialectics* 11). From this perspective, utopia functions as a normative ideal that provides a vantage point from which to critique "the wrong state of things." In this, Adorno is in agreement with most of the major theorists of utopia, including Bloch, who in his discussion with Adorno points out that "the essential function of utopia is a critique of what is present" (Adorno and Bloch 12) as well as Karl Mannheim, who defines "the utopian function" as "the function of bursting the bonds of the existing order" (185).

Yet Adorno takes his own critique of the status quo to a more radical conclusion. For Adorno, his world – the world that produced the First World War, the Second World War, and the Holocaust – is so thoroughly debased that utopia must not be depicted. To do so would inevitably produce a false, reified image of reconciliation that betrays hope for a true transcendence of the status quo. The image ban ensures that the difference between empirical reality and a truly reconciled world is maintained by all means. Only thus is the non-identity of utopia preserved, and only thus can utopia perform its main function as a critique of the status quo. In Adorno's own words, "The materialist longing to grasp the thing aims at the opposite [of idealism]: it is only in the absence of images that the full object could be conceived. Such absence concurs with the theological ban on images. Materialism brought that ban into secular form by not permitting Utopia to be positively pictured; this is the substance of its negativity" (*Aesthetic Theory* 207). In Adorno, the *Bilderverbot* ensures that utopia does not provide consolation but instead sharpens our vision of what is wrong with what exists. Elizabeth A. Pritchard cogently summarizes the main thrust of Adorno's recourse to the image ban:

> Adorno inverts our gaze; he does not simply prohibit pictures of the absolute, but would have us assemble pictures of this fallen world from the imagined perspective of the absolute. He is convinced that the divine and/or reconciliation cannot be simply an extension of the status quo. This is not because either is, per se, "wholly other," but because the status quo is hellish. Consequently, Adorno pledges his allegiance to the *Bilderverbot* in order to focus attention on the lived realities of "damaged life," i.e., the antagonistic social relations and material deprivations that make a mockery of any and all depictions of reconciliation. Alternatively stated, Adorno's "inverse theology" entails not the concealment of the divine, but the revelation of our fallen reality. (295)

If Adorno's diagnosis of his post-war world as "hellish" rings true, then that assessment is a fortiori true for the world Wiesel was forced to live in from May 1944 to April 1945. As a testimony to the horrors of German concentration camps, *Night* bears witness to a world that is so radically fallen that it tests and irrevocably alters a young man's faith: "Never shall I forget that nocturnal silence which deprived me, for all eternity, of the desire to live. Never shall I forget those moments which murdered my God and my soul and turned my dreams to dust. Never shall I forget these things, even if I am condemned to live as long as God Himself. Never" (32). Contrary to Oprah Winfrey's reading, *Night* as a whole does not stress the survivor's will to live; it stresses the forces that threaten to and more often than not succeed in crushing that will. *Night* is no exercise in scriptotherapy either: it does not engage in "the process of writing out and writing through traumatic experience in the mode of therapeutic re-enactment" (Henke xii). Instead, it bears witness to a wound that does not close; it testifies to what Wiesel calls the "dark flame" that "had entered into my soul and devoured it" (34).

Adorno's post-war bleakness has its source precisely in the world *Night* describes. Upon returning from his American exile to Germany for good in 1953, he considered it crucially important to remind his fellow Germans of their unmastered past, mainly by way of two essays: "Was bedeutet: Aufarbeitung der Vergangenheit" (1959) and "Erziehung nach Auschwitz" (1966).[10] As he argues in the earlier essay, "National Socialism lives on, and even today we still do not know whether it is merely the ghost of what was so monstrous that lingers on after its own death, or whether it has not yet died at all, whether the willingness to commit the unspeakable survives in people as well as in the conditions that enclose them" ("Working Through" 3–4). Seven years later, Adorno still maintains that "the monstrosity [the Holocaust] has not penetrated people's minds deeply, itself a symptom of the continuing potential for its recurrence as far as peoples' conscious and unconscious is concerned" ("Education" 18). From a social-psychological vantage point, Adorno in both essays probes less the institutional and personnel continuities between the Third Reich and post-war Germany than the survival of an anti-democratic consciousness, that of the "authoritarian personality" he discusses here and in a book of the same title that he co-wrote with Else Frenkel-Brunswik, Daniel J. Levinson, and R. Nevitt Sanford. For Adorno, these authoritarian personalities – the personalities that made Auschwitz possible – continue to be reproduced by a capitalist system that has not only survived the Second World War but has become more firmly entrenched:

> That fascism lives on, that the oft-invoked working through [*Aufarbeitung*] of the past has to this day been unsuccessful and has degenerated into its own caricature, an empty and cold forgetting, is due to the fact that the objective conditions of society that engendered fascism continue to exist. Fascism essentially cannot be derived from subjective dispositions. The economic order, and to a great extent also the economic organization modeled upon it, now as then renders the majority of people dependent upon conditions beyond their control and thus maintains them in a state of political immaturity. If they want to live, then no other avenue remains but to adapt, submit themselves to the given conditions; they must negate precisely that autonomous subjectivity to which the idea of democracy appeals; they can preserve themselves only if they renounce their self ... The necessity of such adaptation, of identification with the given, the status quo, with power as such, creates the potential for totalitarianism. This potential is reinforced by the dissatisfaction and the rage that very constraint to adapt produces and reproduces. ("Working Through" 13)

These words may help explain both Adorno's bleakness – encapsulated most succinctly in his assertion that "the whole is the false" (*Minima Moralia* 50) – and his extremely cautious (and complex) take on utopia.[11] Returning from his American exile, Adorno encountered a Germany he considered to be capable of another Holocaust. For Adorno, the Third Reich had not ended in 1945, at least not in people's heads. The survival of those social conditions that made Germans receptive to fascist ideas ensures that the ideas live on, too. It is against this background that we need to read Adorno's assertion that "utopia is essentially in the determined negation, in the determined negation of that which merely is, and by concretizing itself as something false, it always points at the same time to what should be" (Adorno and Bloch 12). This is Adorno's response to Bloch's characterization of the function of utopia as "a critique of what is present," which I have quoted above. In agreeing with Bloch, Adorno adds a further twist to the notion of utopia as social critique: utopias do not critique the status quo by confronting it with perfect countermodels. Instead, were utopias permitted to be depicted, their falseness, that is, their inability to represent an ideal society, would pass an even more forceful judgment on the status quo as a radically debased world from within which a true utopia cannot even be imagined. This is why he writes in *Aesthetic Theory* that "the Old Testament prohibition of graven images can be said to have an aesthetic aspect besides the overt theological one. The interdiction against forming an image – of something – in effect implies the proposition that such an image is impossible to form" (100). For Adorno, depicting utopia is neither permissible nor possible. Fredric Jameson will later pick up on the latter idea when he asserts that "the true vocation of the utopian narrative" is "to confront us with our incapacity to imagine Utopia" (156).[12]

For Jewish-American writers such as Cynthia Ozick, who ponder deeply on how the Holocaust can be represented, the question of idolatry that Adorno touches upon is also by no means an exclusively theological question. In critic Louis Harap's words, "she [Ozick] interprets the Mosaic commandment against idolatry to mean not only to reject worship of material objects or images, but also not to pursue anything for its own sake apart from moral or religious status. Thus literature enjoyed for its own sake as an aesthetic object is 'idolatry'" (167). Ozick is keenly aware of the burdens placed on all writers by the legacy of the Holocaust, but especially on those who write about the Third Reich. The tales of emotional numbness and madness she tells in *The Shawl* testify to her commitment not to mitigate the horrors of the Shoah in any way. For the greatest part, Wiesel's *Night* shares that commitment: utopia almost exclusively shines through it in the determined negation of the radically fallen world it testifies to: from the babies that are thrown into a fire as Wiesel arrives at Auschwitz-Birkenau (30) to the final blow a German officer delivers on his sick father's head (106). Not only Wiesel as the public figure he is today, but also his early memoir is committed to the possibility of a different, better world, but in *Night*, that commitment is realized almost exclusively in the total rejection of the world that is.

In Adorno's thinking, utopia and trauma meet precisely in his assertion that utopia neither can nor should be depicted. Unlike more recent trauma theorists such as Cathy Caruth, Adorno is keenly aware that his social-psychological analysis of the "collective narcissism" that was first "increased beyond measure" by National Socialism and then "severely damaged by the collapse of Hitler's regime" ("Working Through" 10) is in danger of blurring the distinction between victims and perpetrators.[13] Not only that, it also risks being appropriated by those who seek to absolve the Nazi sympathizers of their guilt:

> At times the victors are made responsible for what the vanquished did when they themselves were still beyond reach, and responsibility for

> the atrocities of Hitler is shifted onto those who tolerated his seizure of power and not to the ones who cheered him on. The idiocy of all this is truly a sign of something that psychologically has not been mastered, a wound, although the idea of wounds would be more appropriate for the victims. (5)

Adorno here uses the term "wound" to talk about both the Germans' unmastered past and the psychological suffering of survivors of the Holocaust and of German military operations of the recent past. The Greek word for wound is *τραυμα*, and the transliteration of that word is "trauma." Trauma originally referred to a physical injury – a meaning that is still in regular use in medical science. Yet "trauma" far more often refers to a *psychological* wound today, and it is that type of wound Adorno speaks of. In his oeuvre, Adorno uses the term relatively seldom to talk about the psychological reverberations of the Third Reich. A full-text search of the CD-ROM edition of the more than 18,000 pages of his *Gesammelte Schriften* yields no more than 26 occurrences of *trauma* and its adjectival and substantival derivatives. And while in some of those cases Adorno uses "trauma" to make sense of the psychological origins of extreme anti-Semitism – which he analyses, at the individual-psychological level, as a symptom of early childhood traumata – only two discuss the social-psychological *effects* of the Third Reich. The first is a passage from Adorno's announcement of *Versuch über Wagner* (1952). There, he describes Richard Wagner as "the classic of the Third Reich" who has become a "national trauma" in the sense that "he is still supposed to represent German culture" while being "inextricable from the outbreak of barbarism" (Adorno, *Versuch über Wagner* 504). The second passage is from *Minima Moralia* (1951), a collection of aphorisms that is aptly subtitled "Reflections from Damaged Life."[14] There, Adorno uses the term in a sense similar to Freud's when he voices his apprehension that "each trauma of the returning combatants, each shock not inwardly absorbed, is a ferment of future destruction" (54). I write "similar to Freud's" because the experience of shell shock by combatants returning from the First World War was one of the phenomena that prompted Freud to theorize trauma in *Beyond the Pleasure Principle* (10–11). Yet neither here nor in his discussion of Wagner is Adorno primarily interested in the war neuroses of individuals, but rather in the social-psychological effects of the Second World War in all of its manifestations. And here as in his discussion of the damage the collapse of the Nazi regime did to Germans' "collective narcissism,"

Adorno expresses his apprehension that the defeated German nation might seek to dress its psychological wounds (once again) by violent means. It is mainly for that reason – the fear that, fuelled by *ressentiment*, fascism may gain further strength – that Adorno takes the "German trauma" very seriously. At the same time, he reminds us of our moral obligation to distinguish between the traumata of the perpetrators and bystanders on the one hand and those of the victims and survivors on the other. Minima moralia indeed.

And yet, despite his despair, and despite his deep concerns about the fragility of a post-war German democracy that is peopled by human beings whose personality he characterizes as "a system of scars" (*Gesammelte Schriften* 8: 24), Adorno holds fast to the utopian vision of a better world. For reasons outlined above, such a vision must perforce remain unspecified, but it forms the uncircumventable foundation for Adorno's social and cultural critique. Indeed, in some places, he actually does sketch the contours of utopia. In his essay "Subject and Object," Adorno perhaps comes closest to picturing a better future world:

> If speculation on the state of reconciliation were permitted, neither the undistinguished unity of subject and object nor their antithetical hostility would be conceivable in it; rather, the communication of what was distinguished. Not until then would the concept of communication, as an objective concept, come into its own. The present one is so infamous because the best there is, the potential of an agreement between people and things, is betrayed to an interchange between subjects according to the requirements of subjective reason. In its proper place, even epistemologically, the relationship of subject and object would lie in the realization of peace among men as well as between men and their Other. Peace is the state of distinctness without domination, with the distinct participating in each other. (499–500)

Martin Jay accurately captures this "most utopian of all" of Adorno's hopes, namely, that "the object will once more regain its rightful place alongside the individual and collective subject in a dialectic of mutually supportive non-identity" (*Adorno* 80). Yet even here, utopia – as a space in which peace is realized as the reconciliation of subject and object, of universal and particular, of reason and nature, of human beings and their other – remains sketchy. And even imagining such a sketchy utopia is only barely permissible (note Adorno's use of an unreal conditional clause in the first sentence). Elsewhere, in aphorism 100 of *Minima Moralia*, Adorno is more concrete in demanding "that no-one shall go hungry anymore," and he envisages a utopia of pure somatic pleasure: "*Rien faire comme une bête*, lying on water and looking peacefully at the sky, 'being, nothing else, without any further definition and fulfilment'" (156–7). Yet while Adorno affirms these minimalist programs, they are prefaced by a characteristic rebuttal of demands for more concrete outlines of utopia: "He who asks what is the goal of an emancipated society is given answers such as the fulfilment of human possibilities of the richness of life. Just as the inevitable question is illegitimate, so the repellent assurance of the answer is inevitable" (155).

That the kinds of strictures Adorno places on the depiction of utopia also inform Wiesel's *Night* comes as little surprise. In fact, Wiesel already at the beginning of his narrative seems to reject utopian dreams outright, exposing them as dangerous illusions. When the Jews of Sighet are transferred to two ghettos, the reader knows that the worst is yet to come. Yet the ghettoized themselves see this very differently: for them, it seems that the utopia of a more secure and more closely knit community has come true:

> The barbed wire which fenced us in did not cause us any real fear. We even thought ourselves rather well off; we were entirely self-contained. A little Jewish republic ... We appointed a Jewish Council, a Jewish police, an office for social assistance, a labor committee, a hygiene department – a whole government machinery.
>
> Everyone marveled at it. We should no longer have before our eyes those hostile faces, those hate-laden stares. Our fear and anguish were at an end. We were living among Jews, among brothers. (9)

The narrator, however, quickly dispels such dreams: "It was neither German nor Jew who ruled the ghetto – it was illusion" (10). Wiesel does more than emphasize the impossibility or moral hazards of painting concrete utopias under traumatic conditions here; he reveals utopian dreaming as a harmful illusion: it is that illusion which keeps the inhabitants of the Sighet ghetto in their place, ready to be deported to Auschwitz-Birkenau. But in other passages, Wiesel affirms the salutary value of hoping against all odds. Even though the initial dream of community is revealed as a false illusion, it never goes away. When Wiesel and his father are transferred from Auschwitz-Birkenau to Auschwitz, they are met by a young Pole in charge of the prisoners. He smiles at the newly arrived and says,

"Comrades, you're in the concentration camp of Auschwitz. There's a long road of suffering ahead of you. But don't lose courage. You've already escaped the gravest danger: selection. So now, muster your strength, and don't lose heart. We shall all see the day of liberation. Have faith in life. Above all else, have faith. Drive out despair, and you will keep death away from yourselves. Hell is not for eternity. And now, a prayer – or rather, a piece of advice: let there be comradeship among you. We are all brothers, and we are all suffering the same fate. The same smoke floats over all our heads. Help one another. It is the only way to survive. Enough said. You're tired. Listen. You're in Block 17. I am responsible for keeping order here. Anyone with a complaint against anyone else can come and see me. That's all. You can go to bed. Two people to a bunk. Good night." The first human words. (38–9)

In a world almost completely deprived of hope, the young man's smile and words gesture at the possibility of different, more humane ways of human interaction. Under the rule of SS guards and considering the enormous physical and psychological tolls imprisonment in a concentration camp takes, such a gesture must by force remain vague and unspecified. But at such moments, not all seems lost. In a later passage, it is again a smile that evokes a world beyond the present world of suffering and destruction. Wiesel wakes up his father on the final death march to Buchenwald:

He started up. He sat up and looked round him, bewildered, stupefied – a bereaved stare. He stared all round him in a circle as though he had suddenly decided to draw up an inventory of his universe, to find out exactly where he was, in what place, and why. Then he smiled.

I shall always remember that smile. From which world did it come? (85–6)

Perhaps, when Benjamin wrote about the present being "shot through with chips of Messianic time," he had moments such as this one in mind. While, for a young Jew whose father is dying on the way to Buchenwald in early 1945, it may be impossible to know where that smile is coming from, in asking that question, he already gestures at a world beyond the unbearable status quo. In this, Wiesel's story resembles that by Palmi Sink, an Estonian woman whose deportation narrative Leena Kurvet-Käosaar discusses in this volume (chapter 7): Sink ends her excruciating story of death and pain "with a call for a happier future not only for Estonians but for all of humankind." In Wiesel, the world beyond may well be that promised by the Judaeo-Christian tradition, but this is not necessarily so. After all, Wiesel's most concrete outline of a better world is much closer to one of Adorno's minimalist secular programs than it is to any notion of religious redemption. Writing about how he hates the regulation of his life by the camp's bell, Wiesel asserts that "whenever I dreamed of a better world, I could only imagine a universe without bells" (69–70). As does Adorno, Wiesel subscribes to the *Bilderverbot* in keeping his visions of utopia either unspecified or minimalist.

In adhering to the ban on images, Adorno forcefully reminds us that "Marx and Engels were enemies of Utopia for the sake of its realization" (*Aesthetic Theory* 322). Consequently, Adorno nowhere in his oeuvre provides a blueprint for a future society. In this refusal, he swims against the main currents of utopian thinking, from Thomas More's *Utopia* (1516) to Heinz Dieterich's twenty-first-century socialism and beyond, in both directions. Adorno's strictures against the depiction of utopia are fed by three sources: Marx's refusal to lay out a detailed plan for a future communist society; the Judaeo-Christian ban on graven images; and, related to the image ban, Adorno's conviction that the all-pervasive nexus of deception (*Verblendungszusammenhang*) leaves no room for imagining a utopia that is worthy of its name. In his unfinished masterpiece *Aesthetic Theory*, Adorno makes clear that his strictures extend beyond utopian theorizing:

> Art is no more able than theory to concretize utopia, not even negatively. A cryptogram of the new is the image of collapse; only by virtue of the absolute negativity of collapse does art enunciate the unspeakable: utopia. In the image of collapse all the stigmata of the repulsive and loathsome in modern art gather. Through the irreconcilable renunciation of the semblance of reconciliation, art holds fast to the promise of reconciliation in the midst of the unreconciled: This is the true consciousness of an age in which the real possibility of utopia – that given the level of productive forces the earth could here and now be paradise – converges with the possibility of total catastrophe. (32–3)

In other words, in a world that is dominated by instrumental rationality and total exchange, art (and, we may add, life writing) that aspires to critique the status quo cannot simply juxtapose it with the image of a better world. Instead, it must adopt a position of negativity towards society by confronting its recipients with an image of despair and by radically dissociating itself from prevalent discourses in an act of communicative refusal. Only thus, in a determinate negation of the world and its forms, can art after Auschwitz perform the utopian function of critiquing "damaged life" by gesturing towards a world that is better than the one we have.[15] This does not prohibit artists and writers from casting occasional glances at a more humane world, but under present conditions, those glances must perforce remain furtive.

Regarding the relation between utopia and trauma, then, there are at least two things we can learn from Adorno's and Benjamin's sustained engagement with both analytical frameworks. The first is a moral and political obligation not to lose hope in the possibility of a fundamentally different and fundamentally better future world, even in the face of a traumatic present. In the final aphorism of *Minima Moralia*, a text that was published eleven years after Benjamin's death, Adorno puts it into words that highlight the theological concerns he shares with his friend:

> The only philosophy which can be responsibly practised in face of despair is the attempt to contemplate all things as they would present themselves from the standpoint of redemption. Knowledge has no other light but that shed on the world by redemption; all else is reconstruction, mere technique. Perspectives must be fashioned that displace and estrange the world, reveal it to be, with its rifts and crevices, as indigent and distorted as it will appear one day in the messianic light. (247)

Clearly, Adorno's recourse to the image ban is more secularized than Benjamin's. David Kaufmann rightly points out that "Adorno … wants to apply theological insights to a world and language that seem too immanent, too mythical. He redeploys the theological to make an ontological point, because a true ontology is impossible in our day" (para. 26). Still, the "messianic light" Adorno writes about is equally clearly not a purely secular notion. While it does not belong to positive theology, it is an integral part of Adorno's "inverse theology" – a term he uses in a letter sent to Benjamin on 17 December 1934 to characterize both his own and his friend's relation to the Jewish tradition (Adorno, "Briefwechsel").[16] In the letter, Adorno speaks of the need to observe "earthly life from the perspective of the redeemed" (90) to expose that which exists in all of its degradation.

Adorno and Benjamin as well as Wiesel also teach us that to think utopia under conditions of trauma is an extremely complex and difficult undertaking that is bound by the image ban and its corollary: to betray neither utopian hope nor utopian critique by constructing blueprints of a future society because, under present conditions, any such undertaking can only produce a false and debased utopia. Yet while all three thinkers are keenly aware that utopia cannot and must not be depicted from within a radically debased world, and while they all understand that to paint utopia would be to betray it to false semblance and consolation, they do not join Marx and Engels in condemning utopias as mere "castles in the air" (Marx and Engels 75). Instead, while refusing to paint utopia in adherence to a partially secularized version of the *Bilderverbot*, they insist on the urgent need for the utopian imagination in times of trauma. Perhaps the inventor of negative dialectics, one of Weimar's last German-Jewish intellectuals, and the author of one of the most significant Holocaust memoirs all sensed, in their different ways, that utopia holds the promise of a relationship to time – and thus to human mortality – that is fundamentally different from that of trauma. To borrow Benjamin's word, in its basic temporal structure, the *Jetztzeit* of utopia is homologous to trauma as I have described it with reference to LaCapra at the beginning of this essay: both in traumatic and in mystical experience, the past and the present collapse. In both, moreover, the flight of time's arrow comes to a "Stillstand" (standstill). And yet the effects are diametrically opposed. While trauma results in a disabling foreshortening of the future, utopia promises, against all odds, to liberate us as it opens the present up to what is to come.

NOTES

1 I would like to thank Rebecca Scorah for her diligent proofreading, Frederike Rathing for her very useful bibliographical research and scanning of anti-utopian texts, Andreas Mauz for good advice on Benjamin, Andreas Hägler and Ridvan Askin for extensive and incisive feedback on an earlier version of this essay, and Andreas Jahn-Sudmann and Kirsten Jahn for sharpening my understanding of Adorno.

2 On the Frey controversy, see also Julia Straub's response to Aija Sakova's essay in this volume (chapter 14).

3 See Maeseneer for a critical take on Benjamin's relation to the question of violence.

4 Whenever possible, I am quoting from already existing English translations of German texts. All other translations from German are mine.

5 In *Spectres of Marx: The State of the Debt, the Work of Mourning, and the New International*, Jacques Derrida stages a rereading of Marx that has affinities with Benjamin's project. In Colin Davis's words, "Attending to the ghost is an ethical injunction insofar as it occupies the place of the Levinasian Other: a wholly irrecuperable intrusion in our world, which is not comprehensible within our available intellectual frameworks, but whose otherness we are responsible for preserving ... For Derrida, the ghost's secret is not a puzzle to be solved; it is the structural openness or address directed towards the living by the voices of the past or the not yet formulated possibilities of the future" (373, 378–9). Yet while Benjamin desires to actualize specific suppressed pasts in the present with a view to the future, Derrida's project is, as many a Marxist critic has remarked (and as Davis also notes), far less openly political in that it considers the ghosts of the past as agents of a more fundamental but also more vague unsettling of present certainties that keeps the present open to what is to come. The future is as indeterminate in Benjamin as it is in Derrida, but the past is not.

6 For a very good overview of Benjamin's engagement with theological issues, see Andreas Pangritz's entry on "Theologie" in the second volume of Michael Opitz and Erdmut Wizisla's supremely useful *Benjamins Begriffe* (Benjamin's Concepts) (Opitz and Wizisla 2: 774–825).

7 Note, however, that Marx in the sentence immediately preceding his famous quote also calls religion "the sigh of the oppressed creature, the heart of a heartless world" and "the spirit of a spiritless situation" ("Introduction" 131). Two things need to be said here. First, the sentimental register Marx uses did not have ironic reverberations; sentimentalism was the predominant literary mode of Marx's time. For an overview of some of the major American literary figures of Marx's time that were buried by modernists and New Critics and resurrected by late-twentieth- and early-twenty-first-century scholars, see my "Resources for the Study of Nineteenth-Century American Poetry: A Selective Guide." The second point that needs to be made is that, in the nineteenth century, opium was widely used for medical purposes and did not have the connotation "delusional." For Marx, then, religion is not the answer, but it does dress the wounds that capitalism inflicts rather than obscuring their cause.

8 For an excellent discussion of "On the Concept of History" that acknowledges the tensions in the essay between its theological and historical-materialist dimensions, see Gerhard Kaiser's "Walter Benjamins 'Geschichtsphilosophische Thesen': Zur Kontroverse der Benjamin-Interpreten," which was originally published in 1972. Since the publication of

Kaiser's essay, he and Tiedemann have been engaged in a long and bitter dispute about the validity of their divergent interpretations. Much of the debate concerning the respective influence of Jewish mysticism and historical materialism on "On the Concept of History" revolves around its first, enigmatic thesis. In it, Benjamin describes a chess automaton that wins its games with the help of a dwarf hidden inside it. As several commentators, including Tiedemann and Kaiser, have pointed out, Benjamin takes the image from Poe's essay "Maelzel's Chess Player," in which he solves the riddle of the chess automaton with which Johann Nepomuk Maelzel "toured the United States in the 1820s and 1830s" (Tiedemann, "Historical Materialism" 189). Benjamin adapts Poe's text to his own needs when he identifies the puppet as "historical materialism" and the dwarf as "theology." In Benjamin's version of the story, the question of which of the two is in control is difficult to answer since, on the one hand, the dwarf "guide[s] the puppet's hand by means of strings," while, on the other, "historical materialism ... enlists the services of theology," which enables it "to win all the time" ("Theses" 253). So who is in whose service; who is in control? Tiedemann answers these questions by asserting that "although philosophy was once considered an *ancilla theologiae*, theology has now become the servant of historical materialism" ("Historical Materialism" 190). Tiedemann goes on to acknowledge that "only when theology and historical materialism have joined forces can the game begin" (190), but he does so only after answering the question of control in favour of historical materialism. The problem with this reading is that it is not borne out by Benjamin's text. The joker of Benjamin's allegory is that the question cannot be answered or, more precisely, that it is the wrong question: the dwarf (theology) and the puppet (historical materialism) control and support one another, in dialectical fashion.

9 Gerhard Kaiser helpfully elucidates the meaning of Benjamin's notion of "chips" (*Splitter*) of messianic time: "Now-time is shot through with chips of messianic time, not simply in the sense that something messianic is already present in now-time, but rather in the sense that, by being blasted out of the continuum of history, now-time is shot through with a chip of the messianic – a chip that painfully brings to consciousness that it is not the whole thing: the messianic is understood as the pain of a presence that is privation and expectation" (56).

10 The following quotations are from the English translations of the two essays, "The Meaning of Working Through the Past" and "Education after Auschwitz," available in Rolf Tiedemann's essay collection *Can One Live after Auschwitz? A Philosophical Reader* (2003).

11 See also Martin Jay on "those desperate affirmations of utopia that seem so out of place against [Adorno's] far more frequent expressions of bleak despair" (*Adorno* 105).

12 See also my discussion of Jameson in "Who's Afraid of Dystopia? William Gibson's *Neuromancer* and Fredric Jameson's Writing on Utopia and Science Fiction" and my review of his *other* opus magnum, *Archaeologies of the Future: The Desire Called Utopia and Other Science Fictions*.

13 For a succinct, fierce critique of Caruth and like-minded proponents of the "cultural trauma" paradigm, see Kansteiner (202–7).

14 "Reflektionen aus dem beschädigten Leben" is better translated as "Reflections from Damaged Life" than as "Reflections on a Damaged Life" because the indefinite article of the latter too strongly invites an autobiographical reading. The question Adorno repeatedly poses in his aphorisms is how reflection is still possible, not only for himself but for humankind in general, from *within* "damaged life," i.e., from within a world over which the Holocaust casts its long shadow.

15 Consequently, for Adorno it is a hermetic text like Samuel Beckett's *Endgame* rather than *littérature engagée* that is still capable of performing the utopian function of art (Adorno, "*Endgame*"). Older, more affirmative forms of utopia are no longer possible from within the world in which Adorno writes *Aesthetic Theory*: "If in the extraordinary biographical chapters of Selma Lagerlöf's *Mårbacka*, a stuffed bird of paradise – something never before seen – cures a paralyzed child, the effect of this vision of utopia remains vibrant, but today nothing comparable would be possible: The tenebrous has become the plenipotentiary of that utopia ... For art, utopia – the yet-to-exist – is draped in black" (178).

16 My interpretation of the passage from *Minima Moralia* draws on Elizabeth A. Pritchard's excellent discussion of Adorno's notion of "inverse theology" (306–14).

WORKS CITED

Adorno, Theodor W. *Aesthetic Theory*. Trans. and intro. Robert Hullot-Kentor, ed. Gretel Adorno and Rolf Tiedemann. Minneapolis, MN: University of Minnesota Press, 1997.

Adorno, Theodor W. "Education after Auschwitz." Trans. Henry W. Pickford. In *Can One Live after Auschwitz? A Philosophical Reader*, ed. Rolf Tiedemann, 18–33. Stanford: Stanford University Press, 2003.

Adorno, Theodor W. "Einleitung zu Benjamins Schriften." In *Über Walter Benjamin*, ed. Rolf Tiedemann, 33–51. Frankfurt am Main: Suhrkamp, 1968.

Adorno, Theodor W. *Gesammelte Schriften*. Digitale Bibliothek 97. Ed. Rolf Tiedemann et al. CD-ROM. Berlin: Directmedia, 2003.

Adorno, Theodor W. *Versuch über Wagner*. In *Die musikalischen Monographien*, vol. 13 of *Gesammelte Schriften*, 7–520. 20 vols. Ed. Rolf Tiedemann et al. Frankfurt am Main: Suhrkamp, 1986.

Adorno, Theodor W. "The Meaning of Working Through the Past." Trans. Henry W. Pickford. In *Can One Live after Auschwitz? A Philosophical Reader*, ed. Rolf Tiedemann, 3–18. Stanford: Stanford University Press, 2003.

Adorno, Theodor W. *Minima Moralia: Reflections on a Damaged Life*. [Reflections from Damaged Life]. Trans. E.F.N. Jephcott. London: Verso, 2005.

Adorno, Theodor W. *Negative Dialectics*. Trans. E.B. Ashton. New York: Seabury Press, 1973.

Adorno, Theodor W. "Subject and Object." In *The Essential Frankfurt School Reader*, ed. Andrew Arato and Eike Gebhardt. London: Urizen Books, 1978.

Adorno, Theodor W. "Theodor W. Adorno and Walter Benjamin, 17. Dezember 1934." In *Theodor W. Adorno, Walter Benjamin: Briefwechsel, 1928–1940*, ed. Henri Lonitz, 90–1. Frankfurt am Main: Suhrkamp, 1994.

Adorno, Theodor W., and Ernst Bloch. "Something's Missing: A Discussion between Ernst Bloch and Theodor W. Adorno on the Contradictions of Utopian Longing." Trans. Jack Zipes and Frank Mecklenburg. In *The Utopian Function of Art and Literature: Selected Essays by Ernst Bloch*, 1–17. Cambridge, MA: MIT Press, 1989.

Adorno, Theodor W., and Michael T. Jones. "'Trying to Understand *Endgame.' New German Critique, NGC* 26, no. 26 (1982): 119–50. http://dx.doi.org/10.2307/488027.

Adorno, Theodor W., et al. *The Authoritarian Personality*. New York: Harper, 1950.

American Psychiatric Association, ed. *Diagnostic and Statistical Manual of Mental Disorders. DSM-IV-TR*. Text revision. 4th ed. Washington, DC: American Psychiatric Association, 2000.

Benjamin, Walter. "On Some Motifs in Baudelaire." Trans. Harry Zohn. In *Illuminations*, ed. Hannah Arendt, 155–200. New York: Schocken, 1986.

Benjamin, Walter. "The Storyteller: Reflections on the Works of Nikolai Leskov." Trans. Harry Zohn. In *Illuminations*, ed. Hannah Arendt, 83–109. New York: Schocken, 1986.

Benjamin, Walter. "Theses on the Philosophy of History [On the Concept of History]." Trans. Harry Zohn. In *Illuminations*, ed. Hannah Arendt, 253–64. New York: Schocken, 1986.

Caruth, Cathy, ed. *Trauma: Explorations in Memory*. Baltimore, MD: Johns Hopkins University Press, 1995.

Caruth, Cathy. "Violence and Time: Traumatic Survivals." *Assemblage* 20, no. 20 (1993): 24–5. http://dx.doi.org/10.2307/3181682.

Davis, Colin. "*État Présent*: Hauntology, Spectres and Phantoms." *French Studies* 59, no. 3 (2005): 373–9. http://dx.doi.org/10.1093/fs/kni143.

Derrida, Jacques. *Spectres of Marx: The State of the Debt, the Work of Mourning, and the New International*. Trans. Peggy Kamuf. New York: Routledge, 1994.

Dieterich, Heinz. *Der Sozialismus des 21. Jahrhunderts: Wirtschaft, Gesellschaft und Demokratie nach dem globalen Kapitalismus*. Berlin: Kai Homilius, 2006.

Freud, Sigmund. *Beyond the Pleasure Principle*. Trans. James Strachey. Standard Edition of the Complete Psychological Works of Sigmund Freud, vol. 18. Ed. James Strachey. London: Norton, 1955.

Freud, Sigmund. *Civilization and Its Discontents*. Trans. James Strachey. Standard Edition of the Complete Psychological Works of Sigmund Freud, vol. 21. Ed. James Strachey. London: Norton, 1961.

Frey, James. *A Million Little Pieces*. New York: Doubleday, 2003.

Gagnebin, Jeanne-Marie. *Zur Geschichtsphilosophie Walter Benjamins: Die Unabgeschlossenheit des Sinnes*. Erlangen: Palm and Enke, 1978.

Gilmore, Leigh. *The Limits of Autobiography: Trauma and Testimony*. Ithaca, NY: Cornell University Press, 2001.

Gold, Joshua R. "The Dwarf in the Machine: A Theological Figure and Its Sources." *Modern Language Notes* 121, no. 5 (2007): 1220–36.

Harap, Louis. *In the Mainstream: The Jewish Presence in Twentieth-Century American Literature, 1950s–1980s*. New York: Greenwood, 1987.

Hayek, Friedrich August von. *The Road to Serfdom*. London: Routledge, 2001.

Henke, Suzette A. *Shattered Subjects: Trauma and Testimony in Women's Life Writing*. Houndmills: Macmillan, 1998.

Hölderlin, Friedrich. "Hyperion, or the Hermit in Greece." Trans. Willard R. Trask. In *Hyperion and Selected Poems*, ed. Eric L. Santer, 1–29. New York: Continuum, 1990.

Italie, Hillel. "Amazon Recategorizes Elie Wiesel's *Night* and 'Memoir.'" Seattle Pi, 18 Jan. 2006. http://www.seattlepi.com/ae/books/article/Amazon-recategorizes-Elie-Wiesel-s-Night-as-1192963.php.

Jameson, Fredric. "Progress versus Utopia; or, Can We Imagine the Future?" *Science-Fiction Studies* 9, no. 2 (1982): 147–58.

Jay, Martin. *Adorno*. Cambridge, MA: Harvard University Press, 1984.

Jay, Martin. *The Dialectical Imagination: A History of the Frankfurt School and the Institute of Social Research, 1923–1950*. London: Heinemann Educational Books, 1973.

Kaiser, Gerhard. "Walter Benjamins 'Geschichtsphilosophische Thesen': Zur Kontroverse der Benjamin-Interpreten." In *Benjamin, Adorno: Zwei Studien*, 1–77. Frankfurt am Main: Athenäum Fischer, 1974.

Kansteiner, Wulf. "Genealogy of a Category Mistake: A Critical Intellectual History of the Cultural Trauma Metaphor." *Rethinking History* 8, no. 2 (2004): 193–221. http://dx.doi.org/10.1080/13642520410001683905.

Kateb, George. *Utopia and Its Enemies*. 2nd ed. New York: Schocken, 1972.

Kaufmann, David. "Adorno and the Name of God." *Flashpoint*, Web issue 1. 1997. 45 pars. http://www.flashpointmag.com/adorno.htm.

LaCapra, Dominick. *Writing History, Writing Trauma*. Baltimore, MD: Johns Hopkins University Press, 2001.

Levitas, Ruth. *The Concept of Utopia*. New York: Philip Allan, 1990.

Löwenthal, Leo. "In Memory of Walter Benjamin: The Integrity of the Intellectual." Trans. David J. Ward. In *An Unmastered Past: The Autobiographical Reflections of Leo Löwenthal*, ed. and intro. Martin Jay, 216–34. Berkeley, CA: University of California Press, 1987.

Maeseneer, Yves de. "Horror Angelorum: Terroristic Structures in the Eyes of Walter Benjamin, Hans Urs Von Balthasar's Rilke and Slavoj Žižek." *Modern Theology* 19, no. 4 (2003): 511–27. http://dx.doi.org/10.1111/1468-0025.00234.

"The Man Who Conned Oprah." The Smoking Gun. 2006. http://www.thesmokinggun.com/.

Mannheim, Karl. *Ideology and Utopia*. London: Routledge and Kegan Paul, 1979.

Marcuse, Herbert. "Protosocialism and Late Capitalism: Towards a Theoretical Synthesis Based on Bahro's Analysis." In *Rudolf Bahro: Critical Responses*, ed. Ulf Wolter, 25–48. White Plains, NY: M.E. Sharpe, 1980.

Marx, Karl. *Capital*. Trans. Ben Fowkes. Vol. 1. 2 vols. Harmondsworth: Penguin, 1976.

Marx, Karl. "Introduction to *A Contribution to the Critique of Hegel's Philosophy of Right*." In *Critique of Hegel's Philosophy of Right*, ed. and intro. Joseph O'Malley, 129–42. Cambridge: Cambridge University Press, 1977.

Marx, Karl, and Friedrich Engels. *The Communist Manifesto*. Intro. Eric Hobsbawm. London: Verso, 1998.

More, Thomas. *Utopia*. 1516. Trans. and ed. Robert M. Adams. Norton Critical Edition. New York: W.W. Norton, 1992.

Opitz, Michael, and Erdmut Wizisla, eds. *Benjamins Begriffe*. 2 vols. Frankfurt am Main: Suhrkamp, 2000.

Ozick, Cynthia. *The Shawl*. New York: Knopf, 1989.

Plato. *The Republic*. Trans. Alexander D. Lindsay. London: Dent, 1908.

Popper, Karl R. *The Open Society and Its Enemies*. 2 vols. London: Routledge, 1945.

Pritchard, Elizabeth A. "*Bilderverbot* Meets Body in Theodor W. Adorno's Inverse Theology." *Harvard Theological Review* 95, no. 3 (2002): 291–318. http://dx.doi.org/10.1017/S0017816002000202.

Scholem, Gershom. *Die jüdische Mystik in ihren Hauptströmungen*. Frankfurt am Main: Alfred Metzner, 1967.

Schweighauser, Philipp. "Resources for the Study of Nineteenth-Century American Poetry: A Selective Guide." In *Teaching Nineteenth-Century American Poetry*, ed. Paula Bernat Bennett, Karen Kilcup, and P. Schweighauser, 315–51.New York: MLA, 2007.

Schweighauser, Philipp. Review of *Archaeologies of the Future: The Desire Called Utopia and Other Science Fictions*. By Fredric Jameson. *Amerikastudien/American Studies* 52, no. 4 (2007): 586–8.

Schweighauser, Philipp. "Who's Afraid of Dystopia? William Gibson's *Neuromancer* and Fredric Jameson's Writing on Utopia and Science Fiction." In *Exploring the Utopian Impulse: Essays on Utopian Thought and Practice*, ed. Tom Moylan and Michael Griffin, 225–42. New York: Peter Lang, 2007.

Seidman, Naomi. "Elie Wiesel and the Scandal of Jewish Rage." *Jewish Social Studies* 3, no. 1 (1996): 1–19.

Tiedemann, Rolf, ed. *Can One Live after Auschwitz? A Philosophical Reader*. Stanford, CA: Stanford University Press, 2003.

Tiedemann, Rolf, ed. "Historical Materialism or Political Messianism? An Interpretation of the Theses 'On the Concept of History.'" Trans. Barton Byg, Jeremy Gaines, and Doris L. Jones. In *Benjamin: Philosophy, History, Aesthetics*, ed. Gary Smith, 175–209. Chicago: University of Chicago Press, 1989.

Tiedemann, Rolf, ed. *Studien zur Philosophie Walter Benjamins*. 2nd ed. Frankfurt am Main: Suhrkamp, 1973.

Weissman, Gary. *Fantasies of Witnessing: Postwar Efforts to Experience the Holocaust*. Ithaca: Cornell University Press, 2004.

Wiesel, Elie. *All Rivers Run to the Sea: Memoirs*. Vol. 1, 1928–1969. New York: Knopf, 1995.

Wiesel, Elie. *Night*. Trans. Stella Rodway. New York: Bantam Books, 1986.

Wiesel, Elie. *La Nuit*. Paris: Les Editions de Minuit, 1958.

Wiesel, Elie. *Un di velt hot geshvign*. Buenos Aires: Unión Central Israelita Polaca, 1956.

Winfrey, Oprah. "Oprah Talks to Elie Wiesel." Interview with Elie Wiesel. *O, the Oprah Magazine*. 15 Nov. 2000. http://www.oprah.com/omagazine/Oprah-Interviews-Elie-Wiesel/print/1.

Wyatt, Edward. "Author Is Kicked Out of Oprah Winfrey's Book Club." *New York Times*, 27 Jan. 2006. A1.

Wyatt, Edward. "Oprah's Book Club Turns to Elie Wiesel." *New York Times*, 16 Jan. 2006. B8.

Wyatt, Edward. "Writer Says He Made Up Some Details." *New York Times*, 12 Jan. 2006. A20.

PART TWO

Auto/biographies as Trauma Narratives

3 Richard Wollheim's *Germs*: Life Writing as Therapy, Despite Theory

JULIA STRAUB

Richard Wollheim's *Germs* is "A Memoir of Childhood": so reads the subtitle of the autobiography of one of the most important philosophers of the second half of the twentieth century. It was published posthumously in 2004, one year after the philosopher's death. Wollheim, who was born in London in 1923, contributed several seminal studies to the philosophical branches of psychoanalysis, aesthetics, and the philosophy of mind with books such as *Sigmund Freud* (1971), *Art and Its Objects* (1968), *Painting as an Art* (1987), and *On the Emotions* (1999). Until 1986, he taught philosophy at University College London, Columbia University, and the University of California, Berkeley and Davis. *Germs* is a very complex memoir in terms of its structure, content, and style. Like many other postmodernist autobiographical texts, it is characterized by a high degree of self-reflexivity, by a consciousness of its own making, and by implicit reflections on the method applied. Wollheim's memoir is sophisticated: it is written by an intellectual who was steeped in linguistic philosophy and psychoanalysis. Hence it seems fair to say that Wollheim is, to a large extent, in control of his childhood narrative: he is able to analyse and question what he is doing, and he does so more or less explicitly. Yet there are blanks in his narrative that point towards the unavailability and irretrievability of memories, either because they are absent, or because they are too inexpressible to be written about adequately. Furthermore, as my discussion of involuntary memory in *Germs* will show, Wollheim's memories can be unruly. Wollheim undertakes what I would call a "mnemonic endeavour," a phrase that suggests a potential incongruence between initial ambition and outcome.

On the one hand, autobiographers and critics compulsively share what Paul de Man called "the need to move from cognition to resolution and to action" (922). On the other hand, autobiographical texts are characterized by "the impossibility of closure and of totalization" (922). This dilemma has been carved into postmodernist forms of autobiography and is reinforced by post-structuralist theories of language and the self. However, *Germs* eventually succeeds in investing the unsaid and the inexpressible with particular significance and thus shows how limitations and challenges to the project of writing one's life can be made fruitful. A good example to illustrate what makes Wollheim's mnemonic endeavour so sophisticated – learned and self-ironic at the same time – is a passage which reflects on his fixation on his body. The body is perceived as a continuous source of ailments, but also as the mirror of physical and even intellectual maturity. Thus, at one point, Wollheim speaks of boundaries that he traversed in his childhood (*Germs* 108), instances of "loss of faith" (109) that he experienced. The most remarkable event occurred on the day when he was allowed to use the bathroom by himself. Wollheim gives a detailed description of what "progress" meant just then. The amount of toilet paper he used, the force with which he pulled the chain to flush – each decision is evaluated in hindsight as a step towards emancipation, towards selfhood. "This small incident," Wollheim writes, "was probably the greatest increase in personal responsibility that my childhood had in store for me. It is what I think of when I hear moral philosophers discuss responsibility" (110).

There are numerous examples of such upfront self-abasement that confront the reader with unexpected insights into the life of a philosopher whose main achievement would not necessarily be thought of as sanitary competence. An educated guess would be to assume that there is a Freudian element to it. And indeed, Freud is present throughout the memoir and on several levels. It is as if Wollheim, the author of a novel called *A Family Romance* (1969), was taking Freud's concept of free association to its literary perfection, ferreting through the remotest corners of his memory, frankly uncovering episodes that others would keep well hidden. Early on in the memoir, the reader learns that many of his stories from the past are the result of therapeutic sessions which the author attended (he mentions "Dr S," who was his "pilot" when sailing "back up the stream of [his] life" [12]). Wollheim was not only a patient undergoing psychoanalysis, but researched and wrote extensively about Freud (he published the aforementioned *Sigmund Freud* and co-edited *Philosophical Essays on Freud* [1982]). Psychoanalysis also shaped his perspective on art history and criticism. The metaphor of the stream in the above quotation implies that the look back into the past is a search not for a linear, but for a cohesive picture of his life. It is an image, Wollheim continues, he "clung to for those strained, pipe-filled sessions, in which the unity that I longed to find in my life seemed to slip further and further into incoherent anxieties" (12). Wollheim did in fact comment on the psychoanalytical dimension of autobiographical writing and the therapeutic assets it held in store for the "patient," the writer. In "On Persons and Their Lives," an essay he wrote in 1980, Wollheim elaborates on the therapeutic aspect of writing one's life, a process which contributes to the formation of personal identity. For Wollheim, self-narration is a process of "working through," a search for continuity and unity of self:

> Anyone who has led a life is a fair object for a biography. But to be the appropriate subject for an autobiography, a person should have lived his life more than most or struggled to make it of a piece. Autobiography … is poised between the writing and the rewriting of a life; and a life may be rewritten so as to impart to that life a unity that it never had – that is, malignly; or it may be rewritten benignly – that is, so as to achieve, even at a late hour, some reconciliation with the past. ("On Persons" 315)

What Wollheim seems to be saying is that even though potentially everybody can write their autobiography, only a life of cohesion, life made "of one piece" – resulting from either the sheer intensity with which it was lived or strenuous efforts to create unity – allows for the most successful kind of autobiographical enterprise. If a person finds himself or herself confronted with broken pieces of his past, he or she will ultimately try to impose unity where there was none in the first place, a process which Wollheim refers to as "malign." It is revealing to see how Wollheim describes "cohesion" as something that has a moral effect, thereby locating the therapeutic benefit of life writing in the attainment of a reconciliation with the past. This reconciliation with the past is a balancing act: it contains a fluctuating degree of variability and improvisation, moving between documentation, that is, the writing of a life, and re-creation – its rewriting, which could be seen as fictional. As Paul John Eakin put it, "Autobiographical truth is not a fixed but an evolving content in an intricate process of self-discovery and self-creation, and, further, … the self that is the center of all autobiographical narrative is necessarily a fictive structure" (*Fictions* 3).

The question of how fictional an autobiographical text may and can be is inscribed in the history and various conceptualizations of the genre. Traditional critics, such as Philippe Lejeune, saw autobiography as a contractual genre whose stability was safeguarded by the identity of the narrating "I" and the author as proper name (*L'autobiographie en France; Le pacte autobiographique*). The prevailing assumption was that the autobiographical text was "a version of the author's own life, anchored in verifiable biographical fact," and that this congruency between recounted life and provable facts was the defining feature of the genre (Eakin, *Fictions* 185). The identity of the writing self and the written self has been conspicuously challenged by the emergence of semi-autobiographical forms, such as autofiction, which consciously seek to escape any such claim to authenticity and blur the line between genres. Critical approaches have similarly opened up to the fuzzier aspects of autobiography. Paul Jay questioned the possibility and necessity, or "illusion" (18) of formal definitions of the genre, arguing that distinctions between fictional and non-fictional forms of autobiographical writing are frail. Paul de Man stated that "empirically as well as theoretically, autobiography lends itself poorly to generic definition; each specific instance seems to be an exception to the norm; the works themselves always seem to shade off into neighbouring or even incompatible genres" (920).[1] Paul John Eakin referred to autobiography as "the slipperiest of literary genres – if indeed autobiography can be said to be a genre in the first place" (*Lives* 2). Entwined with the genre question is that of the referentiality of autobiographic writing. As I will show below, the inadequacy of language to narrate the self coupled with the unreliability of human memory makes autobiography stand on less firm ground than classical definitions would admit. Yet the relation between the self and language (which gave rise to which?) is even more troubled: there is a "self-before-language or a language-before-self set of positions" (Eakin, *Fictions* 191) that tends to polarize our thinking about this complex issue. Different as their approaches are, James Olney's work on narratives of the self, which he views as created through metaphor, as well as Paul de Man's work see the self as an effect of language. For de Man, the self is a linguistic structure and language as its medium defines it: "We assume that life *produces* the autobiography as an act produces its consequences, but can we not suggest, with equal justice, that the autobiographical project may itself produce and determine the life?" (920).

I regard *Germs* as such an interesting text precisely because it is written from the vantage point of a philosopher who knows exactly what debates his own memoir will ultimately be drawn into – and who writes it anyway. Wollheim finds subtle ways of showing his self-conscious concern with the limitations of what he is doing. The subdued form of postmodernist writing about the self he develops makes his memoir special. Postmodernist autobiographical texts tend to flaunt their hybridity, comment on their own making, and play with authenticity. *Germs*, too, self-consciously explores the conditions of its own making and subverts the genre expectations readers may have when buying a philosopher's memoir. However, the rhetorical mode he develops is never too gaudy, flippant, or provocative.

In what follows, I discuss several compositional and formal levels on which *Germs* deviates from established genre conventions, making it a peculiar autobiographical text which challenges prevailing notions of not only what an autobiography is but also what kind of autobiography befits which kind of author. To begin with, *Germs* is an example of a subgenre of life writing, the so-called "philosophical autobiography."[2] This term accords generic status to the more general insight that philosophy and autobiography are intimately related. Thus, Friedrich Nietzsche writes in *Beyond Good and Evil* that "gradually it has become clear to me what every great philosophy so far has been: namely, the personal confession of its author and a kind of involuntary and unconscious memoir; also that the moral (or immoral) intentions in every philosophy constitute the real germ of life from which the whole plant had grown" (13). Stanley Cavell expresses a similar thought when he speaks of a "guiding intuition" which he followed in one of his works, namely, "that there is an internal connection between philosophy and autobiography, that each is a dimension of the other" (vii). Both Nietzsche's and Cavell's observations suggest that the two cannot be kept apart, or that engaging in either of them will evoke traces of the other.[3]

In fact, there are multiple connections between autobiographies and philosophical treatises. Autobiographies have been written by philosophers from the early days onward: there are autobiographical texts by Plato, St Augustine, Boethius, Descartes, Hobbes, Rousseau, Mill, and Nietzsche as well as by twentieth-century philosophers such as Collingwood, Sartre, and Russell. As Thomas Mathien has shown, like any other autobiographical text, most of these texts help the author gain self-knowledge. They can also shed light on the author by illuminating his or her body of work and philosophical views (19). But autobiography also has its philosophical uses in that it provides platforms for moral instruction, consolation, apologies, confessions, and generalized inquiries into human nature (20). Wollheim decidedly deviates from such traditional patterns. In fact, it is hard to find any of these purposes inhering in *Germs*. The most likely function would be that of a confession because of the delicate nature of some of the episodes that he recounts. Yet given the rhetorically refined varnish with which Wollheim covers his anecdotes and the open-heartedness with which he divulges them, their confessional or repentant quality is questionable. In writing his memoir, Wollheim was not interested in monumentalizing his achievement as a philosopher. Quite the contrary: it appears that he was pursuing a very private project, purposefully casting off references to the social roles he would assume later on in his life, the glorious future ahead, the fame, and the accolades that we could expect a philosopher to mention. This is remarkable since memoirs tend to be treated as a separate form of autobiographical writing that lays emphasis on specific periods of a person's life and the author's reflections on his or her public role as well as engagement with other public figures of his or her time. Sidonie Smith and Julia Watson define the memoir in this vein as a "mode of life narrative that historically situates the subject in a social environment, as either observer or participant: the memoir directs attention more toward the lives and actions of others than to the narrator" (198).[4]

In its internal focus and its restriction to an intimate social circle of parents, family, and friends, *Germs* violates such generic expectations. Unsurprisingly for a childhood memoir, it is the parents that are the central points of reference. *Germs* reflects the importance of the intersubjective, relational dimension of individual lives as an important aspect of life writing. Considering the individual as part of a social network adds a new dimension to the understanding of the autobiographical self, which traditionally was seen as an autonomous subject that provided a unilinear account of his (and less so, her) life. What detaches *Germs* further from traditional concepts of autobiography is its lack of temporal linearity and consistent chronology. Instead, it is built on oscillating patterns that create links between several time levels. Thus, what by its title is an account of childhood – an account that conventionally begins either with birth or the onset of memory at the age of two or three and ends with early adolescence – becomes in Wollheim's case an intricately woven tissue of associative memories which connect the boy of eight years with the analytical philosopher and link the little boy traumatized by the killing of two pigeons (41) with the soldier of twenty years, who undergoes the horrors of war and war captivity. While Wollheim excludes certain events from his narration, arguing that they lie "outside the scope of [his] childhood" (206), he nonchalantly jumps forwards in time to incidents that occurred when he was in his twenties, as well as in his seventies (234, 272). In many respects, *Germs* ignores the conventions of autobiography in its most traditional sense as a predominantly male tradition of self-stylization that is characterized by the unfurling of a teleological development, by detached reflections on the self, and by elevated subject matter. Quite the contrary: this memoir is most powerful whenever it points towards silences, to gaps in memory, to what remains unsaid.

One could even argue that *Germs* partakes in a female tradition of life writing given its lack of linearity, its indulgence in the details and small episodes of everyday experience, its deeper emotional engagement, and its stronger social awareness of the intersubjective connections that determine the individual. Most importantly, however, it is Wollheim's preoccupation, or even fixation, with his body that makes *Germs* stand apart from traditional autobiographies in general and philosophers' autobiographies in particular. According to Sidonie Smith, autobiography from its early days and until the twentieth century had become a master discourse which consolidated the Western, bourgeois, male individual (18). The subject of traditional autobiography "reaffirmed, reproduced, and celebrated the agentive autonomy and disembodiment of the universal subject, valorizing individuality and separateness while erasing personal and communal dependencies" (19). What Smith refers to as "disembodiment" needs to be understood as a detachment from the non-identical, the feminine, the body, which the autobiographer has to achieve in order to attain "self-identity and the narrative of a coherent past" (19). The autobiographical self wants to be "unencumbered" and tries to escape from all forms of embodiment. After all, the bourgeois, Cartesian subject pursues a "predominant mode of epistemological engagement with the world ... through the agency of reason" (7) – and at the expense of the body. Contemporary autobiographical criticism acknowledges the significance of the body, its ailments, its diseases, and disabilities for our understanding of consciousness and memory, with the body being revalorized as a "significant component of identity" (Egan 5), thereby challenging the somatophobia which had determined Western philosophy.

In *Germs*, Wollheim's body is of particular relevance for two reasons. First, because his body, perceived and feared as dysfunctional, determined the choices he made in childhood. The presence of illness takes root at such an early age that Wollheim even speaks of the process of writing his memoir, which, he says, stretched over twenty years (123), as a "benign lump" (124). Cast into the role of the "spoiled convalescent" (273) by his overprotective parents, his childhood comes about as spoilt by ill health; peopled by concerned doctors, nannies, and nurses; and tailored to the apparent needs of a chronically ill child (or a child chronically treated as such). Illness became a way of withdrawing from the outside world and its pressures. Most interestingly, the body gets into the way of the pleasures of the mind at the very beginning of the memoir, when Wollheim discovers his home on a summer's morning:

> It is early. The hall is dark. Light rims the front door. The panes of violet glass sparkle. The front door has been left open. Now I am standing outside in the sun. I can smell the flowers and the warmed air. I hear the bees as they sway above the lavender ... I am standing in the sun, my body is tipped forward, and I am walking. Walking I shall trip, and, if I trip, trip without a helping hand, I shall fall ... I am falling, falling ...? When I landed, a large rose-thorn, which had been lying in wait on the gravel path, most probably since the early hours of the morning when it had fallen from its stalk, confronted me, ... and then, like a cold chisel, worked its way up into me ... (9–10)

This passage is interesting for a variety of reasons. First, because it suggests that places of childhood, and especially houses, contain an emotional value which will be conserved throughout one's life. In *Germs*, Wollheim remembers the various houses his family lived in most vividly, internalizing their topography. Opening on a description of the tranquillity and purity of a summer's morning, it depicts Wollheim's fall, his premonition and the fear of losing control of his body and its functions, and the consequent pain, as a thorn pushes itself into the boy's tender skin. Wollheim seems to be saying two things: symbolically, that innocence is always tainted by experience – in this case that of "the fall" – and in this respect this short passage functions as a *mise en abîme* of what he elaborates in the rest of the memoir: that growing older means being exposed to the dangers of life. Yet this passage also hints at the deep dichotomy between the world of the spirit and the world of matter, which permeated his childhood. While his mind is at ease and ready to indulge in the moment and the promises of a new day, Wollheim's body is unreliable and spoils the fun. The body is a main source of embarrassment throughout his life: "I could cite the shame that was to persist through the years of childhood and adolescence and also later at the unreliability of my body, of that constant companion which was to let me down so often and so regularly" (16). Because the body is a recorder of physical experience, particularly of pain once felt, it inscribes itself indelibly into memory. In other words: the way the body experiences life produces memories which will remain permanent and mostly reliable. The body is a fixed point of reassurance.

That bodily sensations are in charge of memory is not a new idea, and the resemblance between Wollheim's associative prose style and that of Marcel Proust lies at hand. In "The Image of Proust," Walter Benjamin describes Proust's concept of *mémoire involontaire* as displayed in *À la recherche du temps perdu* (1913–27) in words that also fit Wollheim's prose style and conception of memory:

> For this very reason, any one who wishes to surrender knowingly to the innermost overtones in this work must place himself in a special stratum – the bottom-most – of this involuntary memory, one in which the materials of memory no longer appear singly, as images, but tell us about a whole, amorphously and formlessly, indefinitely and weightily. (Benjamin 214)

What Benjamin defines as a central quality of *mémoire involontaire* – a concept which Proust turns into the central operating device in his novel – is our unconscious memory of physical, material objects, and the effects of their impressions. As Benjamin states in "On Some Motifs in Baudelaire," experiences that we had unconsciously, whose occurrence we did not consciously notice and cannot retrieve by intellect, that is, by active efforts of remembering, are recalled accidentally by smell, touch, and vision (158). Referring to Freud's *Beyond the Pleasure Principle* (1921), Benjamin explains how what has been experienced unconsciously leaves a memory trace, which, once it emerges into consciousness, erases itself. This has consequences for the writer of autobiographical texts: according to Benjamin, "the important thing for the remembering author is not what he experienced, but the weaving of his memory, the Penelope work of recollection" (202). Consequently, writing about one's life has nothing to do with charting one's acutely and precisely remembered experiences. The decisive aspect is not the authorial act of putting experiences onto paper, but the act of interconnecting memories, the weaving of a web of unforeseeable, unheard-of correspondences. In this endeavour, the writer is at the mercy of fortune, since the ability to write especially about childhood is an accidental gift: our involuntary memory is ungovernable (Benjamin, "On Some Motifs" 159). Proust's "primary task of resurrecting his own childhood" faced exactly this difficulty, making it questionable "whether the problem could be solved at all" (159). Bearing in mind Proust's scepticism as conveyed by Benjamin, it remains important to understand that the concept of *mémoire involontaire* explains the associative quality of Wollheim's prose style, the digressions and the invisible core, the centrifugal and centripetal forces that expand and contract his narration. As a philosophical concept which aims to elucidate mnemonic processes, *mémoire involontaire* also gives a name to the aesthetic characteristics of his writing style, his narrative techniques. It is a further sign of the scholar's sophistication that Wollheim openly alludes to his own *mémoire involontaire*. Thus, his memories of his walks as a young boy in the nearby countryside are unclouded because of the way in which he sensually, that is, by way of vision and smell, perceived the various details of plants, trees, and animals, which created images that "have formed the involuntary backcloth to much thinking in [his] mind" (182). Another example would be the much detested laxative he had to take as part of his medical regimes. The aversion caused by the thick fig syrup, by its colour (and associated with the colour, its smell), would present itself to him again later on in his life "across the cheeks in Giotto, or wherever the shadow of Byzantium falls across Italian painting" (192). Autobiography is about laying bare and interpreting correspondences between different impressions, occurrences, and time levels; autobiography is about (inter)connecting all of these.

However, although Wollheim's prose style acknowledges and reflects certain Proustian qualities, his deeper concerns with memory and its literary representation lie somewhere else, namely, in the limitations that he has to face as the writer of his life. In the final part of this essay, I turn to the limitations of life writing as they are presented in *Germs*, especially with regard to life writing understood as a therapeutic practice that enables closure and resolution. These limitations become visible as we look at the emergence of a leitmotif, that of "germs." The metaphor is used several times in the novel, in three contexts: in reference to anti-Semitism (140), in a description of his mother's obsession with cleaning (170), and with reference to Wollheim's sceptical attitude towards the medium of language (309). Thus, as a metaphor, the term is placed meaningfully and purposefully. It can be seen as an indicator of those aspects of Wollheim's life where memory fails him or where he possibly has it fail him, pointing towards gaps in the reconstruction of his past which either signal absences of memories or blanks that are produced intentionally.

The first time "germs" is used is when Wollheim reports of a distant relative who spoke of synagogues as places where germs can be caught: "In turn [my cousin] talked to me of his mother, an eccentric overbearing lady, who had refused to let the Kaiser see her china collection because he had once visited a Jewish family that she thought of as upstart, and used to tell her children that synagogues were places where one caught germs" (140).

Despite the fact that Wollheim, who was born in 1923, fought in the Second World War, he comments very little on anti-Semitism, the period between the two world wars, and the Holocaust. Wollheim's adolescence in Great Britain coincided with the German Weimar Republic. Yet Wollheim hardly mentions what history would produce just some years later. While war impinged in one way or the other on most (young) people living in Europe at that time, his paternal Jewish roots add an additional level of significance. Wollheim's father's ancestors had converted to Christianity, and he himself was brought up in a decidedly unorthodox environment. His father insisted on an unreligious upbringing of his children and told his sixteen-year-old son Richard to read Freud's *The Future of an Illusion* instead of the Bible (141). The account he gives of his two families in the chapter "My Families" touches upon the loss of distant relatives or their dispersal in the diaspora, but Wollheim remains taciturn with respect to his own feelings about their destinies. When travelling to Germany, he says that he is "totally at the mercy of his sentiments" (282), a statement which he does not elaborate on further, but which gains significance given his war captivity in Germany as a British soldier in 1944 (he did write an essay entitled "Fifty Years," where he depicts his life as a war prisoner and his escape). In a memoir that comments so magnanimously on other, very often delicate things, such deliberate suggestiveness creates a very powerful effect of the unsaid.

The second time "germs" is used is when Wollheim writes about his mother's obsessive cleaning rituals. Following a strict itinerary when cleaning the house, his mother developed a cleaning neurosis:

> But what could only too easily happen, and, if it did, would nullify everything that my mother had done up till that point, was that, while she was working on the large unit, someone in one of the first-floor rooms who hadn't noticed the stage she was at might unthinkingly open a door. And, when I say "open the door," it was enough, on my mother's calculations, for it to be opened the merest crack for the dust, the germs, to be able to creep back … (170)

Wollheim portrays his parents as very different from one another (127). His father was a theatrical impresario, a bookish man of learning; his mother, whose family came from the West Country, was a "showgirl" (161) and later on an actress. Wollheim drops hints at the condition of their marriage and their respective affairs (162, 156). He seems very eager to understand the glue that attracted and kept together his parents, the working principles of their relationship, but even keener to view his parents as individuals a long time after their deaths, as he is approaching his eighties. The difference between his parents is also reflected in the way Wollheim distributes his comments and emphases. His mother's presence in *Germs* stands in contrast to that of his father. While Wollheim writes as much about his mother as he does about his father, he leaves the information he gives about her unqualified, uncommented upon. To give one example: Wollheim writes that his father was a keen reader and that on his bedside table he would find "some Tauchnitz volumes, a work of Freud's in German, a novel by Joseph Kessel in French. My mother had no need for a bedside table" (47). This is a powerful, laconic statement by omission, but because of its suggestiveness, it creates an undertone whose intentionality remains unclear. His mother appears to be the phantom of this memoir. She is surrounded by things unsaid, schematically framed by her son's existing memories. Other examples would be the occurrences of rather blunt statements such as "She did not want to disappoint the world" that ask for further explanation (20). Thus, *Germs*, easy-going and liberated as it is in its depiction of the small details of a boy's everyday life, has its lacunae. It is with respect to the mother–son relationship that the reconciliatory aspect of *Germs* shows most clearly. That we are left with mere speculative interpretation gestures towards one of the ambiguities of life writing: we never know whether the author retains or censors information that he does not want to share or whether, no matter how much he would like to, he cannot write about certain things, because he cannot remember them. Thus, life writing automatically brings up questions of authenticity – of the self, of memories, of language.

This latter point is reflected in the third and final use of "germs" and is related to Wollheim's mistrust of language. As an undergraduate at Oxford, Wollheim comes to realize that "the certainty that I had had interesting experiences, and that one day I would be able to convey their poignancy in words of great precision, [had] died" (53). Wollheim seems to be negating the possibility of a project on which he had been working for decades, that of writing meaningfully about his life (215).

What remains is the possibility, as expressed in the closing paragraph ending with "germs" as the memoir's final word, that in endless processes of saying one thing by saying another, one can convey some truth, in a process of gradual approximization:

> However little there was in the way of truth to the first thing said, there might be more to the second thing said, and eventually, or such was the hope, I would, in saying one thing after another after another after another, each with a grain more of truth to it than its predecessor, come to spill the beans: I might, if only the ear stayed ready, and that was another hope, find myself, with one broad archaic gesture, scattering the germs. (309)

The scepticism which Wollheim develops towards his own activity as an autobiographer makes *Germs* point to a very general, maybe pessimistic conclusion: that life writing is an asymptotic act of striving for certainty and knowledge, but that, while it possibly catches glimpses of truth, it misses it ad infinitum. The metaphor of germs is thus shifted onto a level beyond the autobiographical account since it eventually characterizes words, or more precisely constantly gliding signifiers, as well as the genre of autobiography itself. The psychoanalytical endeavour of using autobiography as a therapeutic measure surfaces clearly in this memoir, yet its success depends, like the entire autobiographical project, on a larger issue. Problems related to the literary representation of the self are interlinked with the psychological aspect of life writing. As Paul Jay puts it, "The whole idea of a cure in psychoanalysis, of course, depends on the subject's ability to fashion a narrative … Thus the recuperative power of the narrative resides not in its factualness but rather in the creative capacity of language itself" (25–6). Wollheim's scepticism towards language affects the curative dimension of his autobiographical project, yet it also underlines the central position that the autobiographical genre in its variety and with all its formal innovations occupies in discourses on concepts of moral, aesthetic, and empirical authenticity unfolding in the second half of the twentieth century. Claims to authenticity, to being real, seem to affect autobiographies in particularly dense ways. Aspects of authenticity bear upon concepts of selfhood and subjectivity as represented and shaped by the act of writing one's life. As de Man suggested, autobiographies work in two directions. Writing one's life means having lived a life, but it also means creating one's life and self: "We assume that life produces the autobiography as an act produces its consequences, but can we not suggest, with equal justice, that the autobiographical project may itself produce and determine the life?" (920). The question of how the self or subjective interiority can be represented linguistically and, as the increasingly popular forms of the autobiographical phototext or intermedial autographics show, visually, brings us back to the question of how authentic autobiographical works need to be in order to count as such, whether authenticity should and can be a criterion at all.[5]

When de Man refers to prosopopoeia as the central trope of autobiographies (926), he acknowledges the deeply rooted, anthropological need to give a voice or a face to the absent. At the same time, he reminds us that we are dealing with a "fiction of the voice-from-the-grave" (927). Wollheim states at some point that over the years he had to learn to accept that "words of great precision" may not be at his command and that the linguistic certainty he had craved as a young man "was to die many deaths, none altogether fatal" (53). It is this persistent trust, against one's better knowledge, in language as a carrier of memories and means of articulating the self, that – coupled with his multiple subversions of genre expectations as well as his unimpaired embrace of the "mnemonic endeavour" I referred to in the opening paragraph – make this memoir an insightful example of how the self can be written about, despite theory.

NOTES

1 See also Leigh Gilmore, who suggests that in order to define autobiography, formalist approaches are doomed to failure. Instead, she regards autobiography as "characterized less by a set of formal elements than by a rhetorical setting in which a person places herself or himself within testimonial contexts as seemingly diverse as the Christian confession, the scandalous memoirs of the rogue, and the coming-out story in order to achieve as proximate a relation as possible to what constitutes truth in that discourse" (3).

2 Shlomit C. Schuster gives a survey of philosophical autobiographies and a list of different examples in the first chapter of her study.

3 See Freadman for a discussion of the complex and dynamic interrelationship between autobiography and philosophy.

4 Leigh Gilmore relates the "boom in memoir" (17) which marks the turn of the millennium to several factors, among them the emergence of

identity-based movements along the lines of gender, race, and sexuality; the interest that the media and mass culture take in the telling of private lives; and market-oriented preferences for the memoir. A fourth reason, which appears to make particular sense in connection with *Germs*, are the consequences of post-structuralist attitudes towards language and the self that allow intellectuals, professors, and philosophers to engage in a discourse of "personal criticism" which allows them to establish a "self" on the page while acknowledging the instability of language systems and the constructedness of any such "I" (17).

5 For an overview of phototexts, see the monographs by Linda Haverty Rugg and Susanne Blazejewski.

WORKS CITED

Benjamin, Walter. "The Image of Proust." In *Illuminations: Essays and Reflections*, ed. and intro. Hannah Arendt, trans. Harry Zohn, 201–15. New York: Schocken Books, 1963.

Benjamin, Walter. "On Some Motifs in Baudelaire." In *Illuminations: Essays and Reflections*, ed. Hannah Arendt, 155–200. New York: Schocken Books, 1963.

Blazejewski, Susanne. *Bild und Text: Photographie in autobiographischer Literatur*. Würzburg: Königshausen & Neumann, 2002.

Cavell, Stanley. *The Pitch of Philosophy: Autobiographical Exercises*. Cambridge, MA: Harvard University Press, 1994.

de Man, Paul. "Autobiography as De-Facement." *MLN* 94, no. 5 (1979): 919–30. http://dx.doi.org/10.2307/2906560.

Eakin, Paul John. *Fictions in Autobiography: Studies in the Art of Self-Invention*. Princeton: Princeton University Press, 1985.

Eakin, Paul John. *How Our Lives Become Stories: Making Selves*. Princeton: Princeton University Press, 1992.

Egan, Susanna. *Mirror Talk: Genres of Crisis in Contemporary Autobiography*. Chapel Hill: University of North Carolina Press, 1999.

Freadman, Richard. "Philosophy and Life Writing." In *Encyclopedia of Life Writing: Autobiographical and Biographical Forms*, ed. Margareta Jolly, 2: 707–10. 2 vols. Chicago: Fitzroy Dearborn, 2001.

Gilmore, Leigh. *The Limits of Autobiography: Trauma and Testimony*. Ithaca: Cornell University Press, 2001.

Jay, Paul. *Being in the Text: Self-Representation from Wordsworth to Roland Barthes*. Ithaca: Cornell University Press, 1984.

Lejeune, Philippe. *L'autobiographie en France*. Paris: Librairie Armand Colin, 1971.

Lejeune, Philippe. *Le pacte autobiographique*. Paris: Éditions du Seuil, 1975.

Mathien, Thomas. "Philosophers' Autobiographies." In *Autobiography as Philosophy: The Philosophical Uses of Self-Presentation*, 14–30. Abingdon: Routledge, 2006.

Nietzsche, Friedrich. *Beyond Good and Evil: Prelude to a Philosophy of the Future*. Trans. Walter Kaufmann. New York: Vintage Books, 1966.

Olney, James. *Metaphors of Self: The Meaning of Autobiography*. Princeton: Princeton University Press, 1972.

Olney, James, ed. *Autobiography: Essays Theoretical and Critical*. Princeton: Princeton University Press, 1980.

Rugg, Linda Haverty. *Picturing Ourselves: Photography and Autobiography*. Chicago: University of Chicago Press, 1997.

Schuster, Shlomit C. *The Philosopher's Autobiography*. London: Praeger, 2003.

Smith, Sidonie. *Subjectivity, Identity, and the Body*. Bloomington: Indiana University Press, 1993.

Smith, Sidonie, and Julia Watson. *Reading Autobiography: A Guide for Interpreting Life Narratives*. Minneapolis: University of Minnesota Press, 2001.

Wollheim, Richard. *Art and Its Objects*. Harmondsworth: Penguin, 1970.

Wollheim, Richard. *A Family Romance*. London: Jonathan Cape, 1969.

Wollheim, Richard. "Fifty Years On." *London Review of Books* 16, no. 12 (1994): 3–6.

Wollheim, Richard. *Germs: A Memoir of Childhood*. London: Black Swan, 2005.

Wollheim, Richard. *On the Emotions*. New Haven: Yale University Press, 1999.

Wollheim, Richard. "On Persons and Their Lives." In *Explaining Emotions*, ed. Amélie O. Rorty, 299–321. Berkeley: University of California Press, 1980.

Wollheim, Richard. *Painting as an Art*. London: Thames and Hudson, 1987.

Wollheim, Richard. *Sigmund Freud*. Cambridge: Cambridge University Press, 1981.

4 Writing Childhood, Writing Lack

MAARJA HOLLO

All life writing is faced with one key question: to what extent does the text represent past events truthfully? Life writing that focuses on painful experiences is faced with an additional, equally important question: to what extent does the recreation of the past through writing have a liberating and healing effect? In the case of Richard Wollheim's *Germs*, however, a third question moves to the centre of attention: the question of genre. In her essay on Wollheim's memoir, Julia Straub notes that it is an example of a philosopher's autobiography, but adds that it does not belong to this subgenre in the strict sense. The reason for this is that Wollheim's reminiscences do not offer philosophically inclined moral instruction, consolation, apologies, or generalized inquiries into human nature. As I see it, though, moral instructions and inquiries into human nature are at the heart of *Germs*. True, moral instructions are expressed through images, and the narrator alludes to demeaning attitudes towards his intellectual and moral competence as a child through imaginative flights that interpolate the stories told. As in all memoirs, Wollheim's reminiscences "do not merely describe the speaker's relation to the past but place [him] quite specifically in reference to it. As assertions and performances, they carry moral entailments of various sorts" (Antze and Lambek xxv). Since the stories woven into the narrative are well wrought in the literary sense, expressive and often also ironic, their moral quality and Wollheim's general observations concerning human nature can easily escape notice.

At the beginning of the last chapter of *Germs*, the narrator characterizes his childhood summers, which were spent mainly in the company of his nanny, as three-part performances, giving the three parts respective titles: "pleasure," "terror," and "routine" (219). In the pleasure category, he includes peep shows that he used to watch on the pier. The narrator, who had a special interest in historical dramas, gives a detailed description of his favourite peep show, the execution of Queen Mary. He explains that as a child, he derived the greatest satisfaction not from the execution itself, but from the knowledge that, for the next viewer, Mary's head would be back on her shoulders again and justice restored. Confessing to his childhood inclination towards Mary, he writes that Elizabeth was "a recurrent figure of loathing," an "enemy of love" (224). What we get here is a moral judgment. Significantly, the theme of enmity towards love continues in the next section, in which the narrator reveals to the reader the meaning of the keyword "terror." In these memoirs, terror is both a symbol of "the deepest, darkest melancholy" (52) and the equivalent of physical loneliness and forgetfulness (225). For Wollheim, the main stimulus for writing *Germs* was clearly the need to write himself free of "the full dismal power" (52) of many childhood experiences, all of which combine to force the narrator to admit, at the beginning of his memoirs, that, in his life, he never owed anything to anyone else (15).

Even if they are given in literary form, the narrator's judgments regarding his parents do not leave much room for interpretation. The narrator sees his father as a reticent man who placed a high value on "freedom from the family" (21); his mother is viewed as a woman who has no intellectual interests whatsoever and is mostly concerned with herself. Wollheim has no warm, tender connections with anyone in his close family circle – neither with his father, mother, nor brother. Early in his life, he "formulate[s] a principle against friends" (90). Thus, Wollheim's book can be read as an attempt to recreate a childhood world lived in almost complete isolation: the author dreams above all of someone who might take the time to listen to his "innermost thoughts" (250). By sharing these retrospectively reconstructed thoughts with the reader, he aims at breaking the silence which separated him from his loved ones all his life, before finding it possible to bid farewell to his childhood and to claim that he has come of age (96). Even here, a moral intention can be recognized. For Wollheim, coming of age is equivalent to becoming worthy of responsibility.

For him, writing one's memoirs represents first and foremost an opportunity to seek reconciliation with the past. Indeed, in her essay, Straub repeatedly mentions the therapeutic purpose of Wollheim's writing, but she avoids the question of whether the narrator's achievement of reconciliation with the past is motivated solely by his wish to overcome scepticisms concerning language and the self, or whether the reason lies rather in much more personal experiences – exclusion, lack of love, solitariness. This latter possibility seems to be corroborated by the author's decision to transmit his reminiscences in a way more closely approximating literature than traditional autobiography. Contra Straub, I argue that *Germs* is a non-traditional piece of writing neither because it falls short of being an autobiography nor because of its experiments in the memoir form, for example, its lack of temporal linearity and of consistent chronology. Rather, what *Germs* foregrounds is an intention to offer the reader a story with aesthetic value, a story that revolves not only about a traumatic childhood but also the possibility of freeing oneself from such a past through storytelling.

The narrator carefully conjures up and attempts to interpret episodes from his past which he claims he can recall most clearly. However, in order to implement the therapeutic function of writing in all of its intensity, the writer must chisel the matter of memory into a narrative with merciless precision. According to the narrator of Marcel Proust's *In Search of Lost Time*, a moment "freed from the order of time" makes us into "the man freed from the order of time" (441), who can perceive time as flowing. If Straub insists on the importance of *mémoire involontaire* to Wollheim's book, I wish to add that involuntary memory is also an act of alleviation that enables the subject to perceive and examine times of hurt.

Allan Hollingurst's characterization of Wollheim's writing style is apt: "In Wollheim's hands the sentence – often half a page long, full of sinuous purpose and subtle qualification – takes on extraordinary interest as he searches for the precise colour and purport of a childhood memory" (9). Wollheim's interest in the precise transmission of memory images does not, however, mean an attempt at factual precision in any sense of correspondence. Rather, he aims at an accurate representation of emotions and feelings. Thus, it seems only natural that even as he confesses that he is unable to speak about several agonizing experiences, the narrator increasingly trusts the language of imagery in the interpretation and judgment of the past. In doing so, he refuses to adhere to the traditional autobiographical format that leads Jaan Kross to claim that, in the ideal scenario, memory material can be presented as a flawless, seamlessly complete bedrock (76). In *Germs*, passages that painstakingly outline memory pictures alternate with highly associative passages, all of which are kept in motion by a wish to trace not only remembering, but also the inner workings of a child's psyche, mental world, and way of configuring his surroundings. Characteristically, the child's attention wanders, and the objects that fascinate him are unpredictable; his creativity generates associations between objects, phenomena, and events that adults would find difficult to connect.

One of Straub's arguments is that Wollheim's book does not belong to the Western tradition of autobiographical writing since he consciously and consistently deals with the relations between the body, memory, and writing. The reasons for this focus are not only his illness, which forced him to take to his bed for weeks when he was a child. Above all, the reason lies in his understanding that genuine closeness with members of his family, something he felt to be absent throughout his childhood, was impossible without experiencing continuous physical contact with them. The longing of a physically shunned child is redirected to the "protective breast" of his caretaker, but also, and with similar intensity, towards the "strong, horse-like bodies" of the dancing girls he glimpses backstage many years later (11). Embodiment is important to the narrator not only because of his illness and his intense need for closeness, but also with respect to gender and sexuality, which were for him "for many early years the most recalcitrant of problems" (239). Indeed, the narrator is plagued by the question of how one makes a decision about one's own gender, as well as about that of others. For Wollheim, gender is not so much a matter of corporeal features but something that can be expressed only through the language of images and which is in turn connected with the possibility (or impossibility) of people understanding one another. For Wollheim, one of the advantages of writing was surely that it enabled him to believe in the possibility of this kind of understanding.

Wollheim's work of mourning takes place alongside the writing process. His amplifications and distillations of his mother's (and his father's) behaviour are significant: by pondering on and interpreting the reasons for his parents' actions, the narrator reopens his wounds and dresses them simultaneously. Straub claims that what Wollheim says about his mother in many cases leaves readers at a loss since the gaps and spaces in the story provide much room for interpretation. Again, this freedom seems to suggest that mourning is at the core of Wollheim's text. The performance of this work of mourning is rendered more difficult because it is the "mourning of a lack," that is, the mourning of relationships and feelings that he never really experienced. There is very little nostalgia in Wollheim's childhood memoir; the few bright pictures from the past are overshadowed by the sadness of a child who believes that his tears belong "exclusively" (262) to his existence.

The child's desire for human warmth finds expression in the narrator's boundless attachment to his dog Nobby. If we believe the narrator, this attachment made it impossible for him to distinguish between love and misery (184). His admiration of his father is not enough to create a warm, trusting relationship with him, and his involvement in his mother's little secrets teases his nerves without laying the ground for a lasting attachment. The narrator is an orphan even though he does not lack parents, and Wollheim shows that spiritual orphanhood can be just as or even more traumatic than actually being deprived of one's parents. Readers of *Germs* can profit much from Straub's reflections on its reworking of the generic conventions of autobiography, but it is just as important to realize that Wollheim's memoir is a trauma narrative that embarks on a difficult process of mourning by way of words.

By way of conclusion, let me return to the question I raised at the outset of this response, the question concerning the truthfulness of the autobiographical text. Straub discusses neither the truthfulness of autobiographical writing nor the question of truth more generally. Instead, she takes Paul John Eakin's discussion of referentiality, which she considers to be entwined with the question of genre, as her starting point, and introduces the notion of "empirical authenticity" at the very end of her article. I would argue that whichever autobiographical text we consider, the main question is neither whether it belongs to a particular genre nor whether it is authentic or referential. Rather, what is at stake is the truthfulness of the narrative. What I mean by truthfulness is the writer's sincere intention to speak the truth about the life that he or she has lived. Such an undertaking is sustained by the belief that it is indeed possible to do so, despite all the obstacles posed by language. As one can see in the final few pages of Wollheim's memoir, it is this impetus to truthfulness that motivates his narration. As *Germs* illustrates, the question of a text's truthfulness or truth is not necessarily tied to the relationship between fictionality and referentiality. Rather, truthfulness is a matter of harmony between the author's intention and the reader's perception. If, according to Straub, Wollheim's text "self-consciously explores the conditions of its own making and subverts the genre expectations readers may have when buying a philosopher's memoir," this does not invalidate his text's claims to truthfulness. Wollheim's self-conscious subversion of readers' expectations does not render any less credible the author's conviction that his text not only expresses the truth about his past but that it will also meet with understanding in the eyes of the reader.

NOTE

1 This article has been written with the support of ESF grant 7354 ("Positioning Life-Writing on Estonian Literary Landscapes") and the TF project "Sources of Cultural History and Contexts of Literature."

WORKS CITED

Antze, Paul, and Michael Lambek. "Introduction: Forecasting Memory." In *Tense Past: Cultural Essays in Trauma and Memory*, ed. Paul Antze and Michael Lambek, xi–xxxviii. New York: Routledge, 1996.

Hollinghurst, Alan. "The Digested Tract." Review of *Germs* by Richard Wollheim. *The Guardian*, 18 Dec. 2004, Features & Reviews 9.

Kross, Jaan. *Omaeluloolisus ja alltekst. 1998. Aastal Tartu Ülikooli filosoofiateaduskonas vabade kunstide professorina peetud loengud.* Autobiographism and Subtext. Lectures Given in 1998 as Professor of Liberal Arts at the Faculty of Philosophy of the University of Tartu. Tallinn: Eesti Keele Sihtasutus, 2003.

Proust, Marcel. *In Search of Lost Time*. Trans. C.K. Scott Moncrieff, Terence Kilmartin, and D.J. Enright. London: Everyman, 2001.

Wollheim, Richard. *Germs: A Memoir of Childhood*. London: Black Swan, 2005.

5 Loquacious Silences: Vikram Seth's *Two Lives* and the German Language

NORA ANNA ESCHERLE

What remains? The mother tongue remains.

Arendt, "Was bleibt? Es bleibt die Muttersprache" 11

Whereof one cannot speak thereof one must be silent.

Wittgenstein, *Tractatus Logico-Philosophicus* 189

At first sight, Wittgenstein's famous sentence seems to imply deliverance: the right, or even the duty not to speak of things inaccessible to the positivist mind. According to Wolfgang Iser and Sanford Budick, however, this is a fallacy. Wittgenstein does not in the least acquit us of "the burdens of the unsayable," but imposes on us "a double responsibility" instead: first, we have "to acknowledge the existence of 'unsayable things'"; second, we must "by means of a language somehow formed on being silent, articulate that which cannot be grasped" (Budick and Iser xii). The essential notion referred to here is that of negativity: the "tacit dimension" and "latent double" (xii) of each spoken or written text – the things unsayable, the things unsaid, the things expressed by not being said, the things perceptible only by their very trace: the silence expressed in their stead.

The contemporary Indian writer Vikram Seth's biography *Two Lives*, which is devoted to Seth's own Indian great-uncle Shanti Behari Seth[1] and Shanti's German-Jewish wife Henny Seth née Caro, shows how the two responsibilities described above are assumed separately by different generations of a family – across cultural as well as linguistic boundaries. The earlier generation, who had experienced traumatic events and was unwilling to articulate them in the aftermath, accomplished the task of acknowledging the existence of things better left unsaid. It was only the later generation, epitomized by Seth himself, that, having experienced the loquacious silences of things unsaid, took on and met the other responsibility of finding a language somehow formed on being silent to articulate that which cannot be grasped. In view of Seth's copious involvement in the actual lives of his biographical subjects and his own manifest presence within the narrative as biographer and as autobiographical subject, the book's title could just as well read "Three Lives": it is as much the story of Shanti's and Henny's lives as it is the story of Seth's relation to his beloved relatives. Thus, *Two Lives* is a piece of life writing – a comprehensive category that includes "writing of diverse kinds that takes a life as its subject" (Smith and Watson 3) – that cannot be sub-categorized neatly: it is neither biography nor autobiography, but both. As much life writing does, *Two Lives* thus "blur[s] the boundary separating autobiographical and biographical modes" as it freely combines the two (7).

Two Lives negotiates other boundaries as well, which are just as meaningful: it is a cross-cultural piece of life writing that not only embraces several generations but also different cultural heritages; it is a piece of life writing that not only cuts across many time lines but also crosses several cultural boundaries and national borders. The three major protagonists of the book "inhabit an intercultural space which may be called tricultural (Anglo-Indian-German)" (Rollason 5). The author and his great-uncle "belong to Indian culture by birth, to British culture thanks to empire, language and residence, and to German culture for family reasons (marriage or great-nephewhood) and having learnt the language," while Henny Seth "is German-Jewish by birth and native language, British by residence and adoptive language, and India-linked by marriage" (Rollason 5). In *Two Lives*, Seth provides what Jan Walsh Hokenson refers to as "the new intercultural perspective [which] surveys cultures from horizontal latitudes and particularly experiences itself at their points of overlap, of bicultural or multicultural interaction" (338).

Fittingly, Seth's narrative starts at the point when he enters his relatives' lives as a seventeen-year-old student coming to stay with them for his years of study at Oxford University. This beginning highlights his personal ties with the people he portrays and opens up the biographical narrative to a distinctly cross-cultural autobiographical mode. Like many forms of life writing, Seth's narrative thus "transfer[s] feelings and attitudes from a person or situation in the past on to a person or situation in the present" (Hughes and Kerr 58), attesting formidably to the "ubiquity of transference in the biographer's work" (Hoddeson 323).

First and foremost, however, Seth's book is the portrait of an unusual partnership whose protagonists are Vikram Seth's great-uncle Shanti and his wife Henny, a German Jew who managed to escape from Nazi Germany while her mother, her sister, and many of her friends were deported and then murdered in concentration camps. The two met in 1931 when twenty-three-year-old Shanti came to Berlin to study dentistry, and finally became a married couple in England, where they both chose to live after the war. Both biographical subjects, Henny as well as Shanti, suffer from trauma, which in both cases is intimately tied up with the Second World War and their alienation from their home countries. *Two Lives* centrally revolves around those traumas. While Henny had to cope with the memory of experiences she had in Nazi Germany and the loss of her family in the Holocaust, Shanti struggled with wounds that stemmed from his service in the British Army Dental Corps during the war. Apart from emotional strain, he suffered from a severe physical affliction: the loss of his right arm during combat nearly ended his career as a dentist, and it took much time and effort on his part as well as the power of persuasion of friends and relatives, especially Henny's, for Shanti to regain his earlier self-esteem and confidence in his abilities.

Vikram Seth reconstructs his relatives' lives mainly on the basis of interviews with Shanti and personal letters written by or addressed to Henny. Unfolding the fate of relationships before, during, and after the Third Reich, *Two Lives* is deeply concerned with different ways of coping with the burden of memory, especially with the burden of things left unsaid. As such, it thematizes the impossibility of living on *with* – but also *without* – remembering, writing, and speaking the past in the present.

In Henny's case, much of the narrative revolves around her inability or, rather, her conscious decision not to talk about past traumatic experiences. Yet her refusal to speak about certain things from the past was not accompanied by a refusal to use her native German language, a language intricately connected to impressions too hurtful to vocalize. Intriguingly, Henny's need for complete silence on issues confronting her with memories of dire experiences was as strong as her desire to maintain contact with her former home and personal past through her mother tongue. Henny's seemingly contradictory ways of behaving

– her silence on traumatic experiences and her unabated indulgence in a language that is inextricably linked with those experiences – bears further scrutiny.

Henny's aversion to speak of, and thus to confront, the memories of traumatic experiences was a major symptom of her survival of the Nazi regime, and the biographer devotes much space to the strategies she employed to cope with her trauma. Yet as powerful as her need for silence was, Henny's need to uphold contact to her former home and personal past through her mother tongue was equally strong. It becomes clear that for the biographer and his subject alike, language has many more functions than that of a means of communication. The German language in particular is crucial not only for Henny's self-fashioning but also for her husband's and, most importantly, for their relationship.

As we read *Two Lives*, Seth himself regularly moves into focus, mainly due to his function as an emphatic listener (and reader) who decides to bear witness to the lives of his two distant relatives, which are marked by cross-cultural experiences and a complex relation to Germany and the German language. The Indian author Seth seeks to do justice to the "in-between-and across-cultures" nature of the biographical subjects' stories by narrating the lives of his Indian great-uncle and his German great-aunt from a decidedly multicultural perspective which interlaces his own multiple cultural and lingual allegiances. The biographer's choice of subject might seem odd at first sight, not least because his Indian origin does not readily suggest a vital interest in German history. Yet even though Seth grew up in India, lacks any direct German or Jewish relatives, and is without apparent relation to Germany or its history, he exhibits a deep concern for Germany's Nazi past and the fate of European Jews.

Seth clearly belongs to that species of writers that Salman Rushdie has termed "inescapably international" (2) in his famous essay "Imaginary Homelands." Like Rushdie and many other Indians writing in English, Seth can be described as having an "identity [that] is at once plural and partial" (15), sometimes "straddl[ing] two cultures; at other times, … fall[ing] between two stools" (15). While this continuously ambiguous and shifting cultural condition may entail hardships, artists and writers have often regarded that condition as an inspiring in-between space which endows them with the capacity to "writ[e] from a kind of double perspective: because they … are at one and the same time insiders and outsiders in [many a] society" (19). Seth, like these writers, has the status of a cultural and "literary migrant" – a status which allows him "to choose his parents" (21) not only in terms of literary tradition but also regarding linguistic preferences and thematic concerns.

Seth's concern is mainly grounded in the fact that he cared much for both his great-uncle and great-aunt and had strong filial feelings for them. Another vital factor in this respect, intrinsically linked with Seth's familial ties to his distant relatives and indeed complementing them, is his own "love-affair" (*Two Lives* 234) with the German language. It is primarily through German that Seth established, maintained, and reinforced links with a culture and a history not his own.

Seth began to work on his book in 1994, five years after Henny Seth's death. At first, to achieve an authentic double portrait seemed improbable since information about his great-aunt would merely be second-hand in the aftermath of her death. His hope to "understand her times through her eyes" seemed futile since, in his grief, her husband had destroyed "anything that reminded him of her" (186). Photographs, letters, and all mementoes of the past were gone when Seth embarked on his project. Beyond that, and still more damaging to Seth's endeavour was the fact that Henny had been a "reticent person" (185). Although Seth and his great-aunt had grown close over the years, she kept vital things to herself and thus remained an unknown person to him in many respects. Seth notes that she "never spoke about her family" and that he only heard from his own parents "that they had all been killed in Germany" (22). Even her husband "did not know how she felt when she heard of the fate of her family" (185). Any book to emerge solely from the interviews he conducted with his great-uncle would clearly have centred on Shanti Seth, and Vikram Seth argued that he "could not justly have called it *Two Lives* unless [Henny Seth's] voice played a role as strong as [her husband's]" (186). This dilemma was solved by the discovery of a cabin trunk in his great-uncle's attic that contained "a file of letters sent to her – and even the occasional carbon copy of a letter sent by her – covering almost exactly the decade of the forties" (187). It is these letters that provided Seth "with an image of [Henny] at least as acute as that of [Shanti]" (187). Seth hesitated to dispose freely of his great-aunt's correspondence, but he overcame his initial qualms for two reasons. First, he argues that "these letters deal with a period of great historical consequence in Germany" and should "help to enrich, through their intimacy, our understanding of the lives of ordinary people caught up in the events of those times" (188). The second reason Seth names is that "every even-handed biography of a completed life has to deal with private matters and has to present its subject as fully as possible, even if the subject, when alive, might have preferred to keep these matters obscured – or at least not open to the world" (188). Her letters made Seth feel able to fulfil his primary purpose, which was to "bring Henny back to life" and "to create ... an image of [Henny] as she had been, only partly as [he] might have envisaged her, but to a great extent as neither he, nor even [her own husband], could have imagined her to be" (188):

> Her friends write to her and through the tone of their words create a sense both of their personality and of hers. She writes to them, speaking in a voice that recreates her presence, and says things she never said to Uncle. She talks with pain and clarity about the very matters I would have found it impossible, had she been alive, to broach. (187)

The general difficulty of understanding and representing his great-aunt's life and personality especially relates to Henny's trauma resulting from her experiences in Nazi Germany and the loss of her family. In her everyday life, she chose to keep almost completely silent about these matters. Such silences would appear detrimental to her healing process if one concurs with psychologists' assertions that, for the healing process to begin, traumatized people need to articulate their painful experiences, be it in speech or in writing (Henke xi). From the biographer's perspective, though, Henny's silence was not total. It was through letters that she came to learn about the fate of her family and finally got to know about their murder by the Nazis. It was in the written words of the letters to her German friends and relatives that she kept going back to the past, questioning, analysing and judging, expressing her grief in written rather than spoken words, fixing them, containing them on paper rather than letting them out into the open to float arbitrarily, dangerously, beyond her control. Henny's speaking out in writing, her "writing out and writing through" (Henke xii) her traumatic experiences in her letters, seems to have counterbalanced, or even enabled, her fundamental silence elsewhere.

Her profound aversion to discussing her experiences and feelings, or even to broaching topics related to the Holocaust, can be seen as an essential strategy for expressing her emotional and mental crises, keeping painful memories at bay.[2] Seth informs the reader that his great-aunt "never spoke to Shanti about the deaths of Ella and Lola," her mother and sister (433). So while Henny chose to discuss and work through the hurtful aspects of her past in letters to friends and distant relatives, she completely abstained from discussing them with her husband. Owing to some "protective or self-protective instinct" (417), she kept her husband in the dark concerning this vital part of herself:

> Once, Shanti said to her, "What a shame that your mother and sister were taken away. If they had survived just a year longer –" before Henny cut him off with "Let's not talk about it." On another occasion, when he tentatively brought up the subject, she said, "Shanti, it's no good going into the graveyard." (433)

Seth learned about the scope of this awkward silence in his relatives' marital relationship through his great-uncle, who admitted to his profound unease and helplessness: "When Henny found out they had died, I only wish she had dropped a tear. She never cried. She would never talk about it, not even to me. She never mentioned their names again" (433). She chose to keep silent about her deepest grief and thus to exclude him from a highly important, if painful, part of her emotional life: "It appears that Shanti did not know how much she had mourned for [her mother and sister], or that her friends received those confidences and that view of her sorrow that were hidden from him" (433). This crucial silence seems to contradict Henny's explanation, in a letter to a friend, why she considered Shanti a suitable, or indeed the best husband she could possibly choose:

> I like Shanti, I value him, and he is particularly close to me because he is the only one here who knew my loved ones and, I could say, also loved them. That is a great deal, that is indeed a very, very great deal, for no other man can understand me, because he can sympathize so very much less than Shanti with what I have inwardly gone through and what will never again be erased. (375)

Maybe Shanti's supposedly intimate knowledge of Henny's plight was the very precondition that enabled Henny's silence. This view is corroborated by Shanti's behaviour: even if he never saw or read Henny's letters in her lifetime, he seems to have been able to read his wife's silences correctly and to know her needs intuitively. For example, Shanti turned off the television set "whenever there was a programme that dealt with the Nazis" (429). Their relationship seemed to work well despite its crucial silences. Speculating on the reasons for Henny's behaviour, Seth suggests two. First, he refers to Henny's express wish, stated in a letter to a friend, that she "want[ed] to make him happy – he deserves it" (375). Seth deduces that Henny very likely considered talking about her grief "to one with suffering on his own" (433) – about which more below – as detrimental to her stated aim. This is corroborated by Henny's response to learning about the vile behaviour of former German friends towards her sister Lola. In a letter to her friend Alice Fröschke, she acknowledges that "all that great sorrow arose in [her] again," and that she felt "so dejected," while later she states that she has not "said a word about this to Shanti" because she "want[s] to keep it from him" (282). The other major explanation Seth suggests for Henny's silence is her need

> to create in her marriage a zone where she could be at peace, a zone where the pain of the past and its tentacles into the present were not allowed to enter. For if she had once spoken of these matters to Shanti, she might well have thought that he could, at any time, have brought them up again, and that she might, without warning, be overwhelmed with resurgent grief. (433)

Seth interprets Henny's decision not to talk to her husband about "matters deep in her heart" (434) as an attempt to safeguard herself, her husband, and hence their marriage from evil things of the past, to deny their power over their present "sense of contentment or even hard-won happiness in life" (434). Both Henny and Shanti at that point acknowledged that some things are better left unsaid.

In a situation where both were exiles in a country that was not their home, among people not speaking their mother tongues, sharing neither their culture nor their memories, Henny and Shanti became refuges for each other, their marital life a kind of fortress from where they sought to exclude everything that could possibly shake the battlements of ordinary middle-class life: "Each found in their fellow exile a home" (403). Their peculiar situation leads Seth to speculate about the nature of their relationship, about their sense of belonging and identity: neither their countries of birth, Germany and India, nor their religions were able to provide them with a sanctuary. Seth states that "what they assuredly were not was what they had been ... Much of what they were they had either shed or let die through attrition and disuse" (401).

Shanti in particular was willing to do anything to preserve the safe harbour of their partnership, giving Henny and her needs top priority in all areas of life. It seems as if his concern for Henny outweighed everything else: his Indian cultural identity, his own mother tongue (Hindi), his connection with his home country, and his family, for which he yearned unabatedly. Henny was highly relieved "to give up her German passport – stamped 'J' – [and] to receive the stiff blue passport issued under the imprimatur of His Britannic Majesty" (401). Perhaps, her husband's declining interest in the affairs of his home country was voluntary, too, but it was also a sacrifice for their relationship.

As becomes clear in the biography, one of the most important factors ruling Henny and Shanti's relationship and their sense of belonging was language, which, according to Seth, is also "a home and confers belonging – not only to the larger culture group and the community, living and dead, who have spoken or written it, but also to the pods and pairs of our intimate lives" (401). As is widely acknowledged in various scholarly disciplines including philosophy, linguistics, sociology, and psychology, language plays a crucial role in processes of identity formation. Marijana Kresic points out that identities are conceivable as "constructs that are negotiated within intra-individual, active and inter-individual, social actions and become manifest in language and other media" (156; my translation). Moreover, at the level of the individual subject, "self-reflection, the constitution of personal identity, of ego-consciousness, ... necessarily proceed[s] in the medium of language" (Hans Bickes, quoted in Kresic 46; my translation).

Werner Hüllen's distinction between *functional* or *communication* languages on the one hand and *identificatory* languages on the other helps us conceptualize the connection between language and identity more precisely. While the former serve primarily as purposeful means of everyday communication in the public sphere or at work and carry relatively little emotional force, the latter – especially native languages or mother tongues – are languages towards which their speakers often develop considerable emotional bonds and loyalty (Hüllen 302–7). In view of theories concerning the formative as well as the expressive power of language, and with respect to personal as well as collective identity, it makes sense to assume that "the speakers' various forms of existence and of living, and consequently also their identities, are realized in different forms of actual speech" (Kresic 251; my translation).

Henny's use of language, with respect both to her trauma and to her bilingual situation, testifies to the significance of such linguistic distinctions. In her case, different aspects of her identity are related to different languages. While her use of the English language seems to be restricted primarily to public and work situations, it was completely different with German. An analysis of her complex, intimate relation to the German language, and of the distinction she made between different contexts of use, sheds light on the concept she had of herself in relation to the language and the identity she ascribed to it.

For Henny and also for Shanti, the identificatory language, the language signifying home, was neither English, the language of the country where they lived for much of their lives, nor Shanti's mother tongue Hindi, which he "over the years lost his ability to speak" (401). Instead, German was "their language" (403). In Henny's case, this comes as little surprise since German was her mother tongue – the type of language most crucial to most people's sense of self:

> Mother tongue, *langue maternelle*, Muttersprache, ... In languages as diverse as English, French, German ..., the name of the mother is invoked to describe that original, originary language, which ... is felt to be intimately bound up with a fundamental, yet difficult to define central core of a subject's identity. (Barossa 398)

With respect to Shanti, this does not apply – or, rather, it applies in a different sense. Shanti, who found a second family and the love of his life in Berlin, adopted Germany as his chosen home, his *Wahlheimat*. In the process, he abandoned Hindi for German as his new primary language. This may come as a surprise since he had lived twenty-three years in India but only five in Germany. Yet those Berlin years had been formative ones – years of achievement through great effort against great odds. They represented his first taste of true independence from his family, some of the happiest recollections of friendship and carefree fun, and warm memories of family life at 60 Mommsenstrasse, his second home. It was these years and this language that brought him and Henny together (422). Thus, he came to supplant Hindi with German as his identificatory language, and German was to remain the primary means of communication in a partnership that was completely void of references to Germany's recent past. For Henny, German had always been an identificatory language; Shanti consciously adopted it for the same purposes. Thus, "the language spoken at 18 Queens Road – when no one else was present – reverted to German" (403).

This is remarkable not only with respect to Shanti, but also with respect to Henny. Her own experiences and the knowledge of her mother's and sister's murder made her positively abhor Germany as the country where the unspeakable had happened, and she was suspicious of Germans in general. Nevertheless, she had taken up contact again with old German friends and acquaintances after the war. Even if it was "difficult and vexed in its own way," Henny seemingly felt obliged to make the effort "to sort out her relations with friends who had shared or been implicated in the sufferings she had undergone" (240). She deeply cared for and highly appreciated her German friends and cherished the German language that seems to have represented home for her.

In intriguing ways, Henny's and Shanti's complex relation to the German tongue returns in their great-nephew's engagement with the language. It is Seth's relation to the German language that testifies most clearly to the presence of processes of transference in this biographer's project. Critics consider transference as an effect of the "biographer's emotional involvement with a [biographical] subject" (Schepeler 112). In Seth's case, this emotional involvement is particularly strong since he not only knew his subjects personally but loved them dearly. During his years of study in London, Henny and Shanti became the biographer's surrogate parents, and he their surrogate son. It was their common understanding and relishing of the German language which greatly deepened the mutual attachment across cultural and generational borders among all three members of this intercultural makeshift family.

At first, Seth shared his great-aunt's love for German. Yet while working on historical sources relating to the Holocaust, he developed a profound aversion to reading the language: "One of the casualties of the process of exploring the material for [*Two Lives*] was my pleasure in the German language" (234). Unlike Hindi and English, the two languages Seth had grown up with, and Sanskrit, which he had chosen as the obligatory third language at school, his relation to German was special from the start, something similar to a forced marriage becoming a love marriage over time. His decision to learn German had been due primarily to an Oxford University requirement that demanded thorough knowledge of a second European language apart from English (10). When his great-aunt offered to teach him her German mother tongue, he was not very enthusiastic about it at first. However, since Seth stayed at his great-uncle and great-aunt's house during his studies, he soon realized that to study a language with the help of a native speaker close by was a highly sensible option. Owing mainly to his great-aunt, who spoke German with him and occasionally also "would sing songs she remembered from her youth" (11), not only did Seth's ability to speak the language increase, but he gradually began to like it:

"After my initial resentment that I had to learn [German] at all and the shock of the genders and declensions, I began to enjoy it, though it was stressful" (10). He also came to realize that to know German considerably deepened his understanding of, and thus his relationship with his great-aunt and great-uncle (11–12). He discerned that, in due time, he "stopped being a guest for Aunty Henny, or a project, but became a sort of companion" (12). Beyond that, his knowledge of German endowed him with yet a different pleasure: the discovery and love of German poetry and music. In poetry, Seth came to favour Goethe, Hölderlin, Morgenstern, Trakl, and especially Heine; in music, he learned to adore Bach and Schubert. His love of German art was also transferred to German people and the country:

> It was an adventure, a love affair under pressure, a concentrated incursion into another world, tied closely to my memories of my first year in England, to reading Kafka's *Letter to My Father*, to singing "Heideröslein" with Aunty Henny in the kitchen, to hitch-hiking across Europe at seventeen, to the landscape of the Danube and the Rhine and the Vierwaldstätter See, to the friendliness of strangers. (234)

His positive relation to the German language and to Germany was severely marred when Seth devoted himself to gaining certainty concerning the fate of his great-aunt's mother and sister. When, during one of his visits to the Yad Vashem archive, Seth read the letter by the Gestapo depicting in a bureaucratic, matter-of-fact manner the circumstances of his great-aunt's sister's deportation to Auschwitz-Birkenau, his body reacted in an intense way. His right knee started to tremble "rapidly and violently" and he was not able to stop it for some time (234). An even more severe effect showed itself when Seth was offered help with the letter by a person who spoke "English with a very strong German accent." Barely able to master his anger, Seth then realized that even the accent of the once highly treasured language had come to embody "sickness and evil" (234). Seth recounts that both speaking and hearing German was "a psychological strain" at that time (452). This affliction proved to be a lasting one. Seth remembers how he could not even read his favourite German poet Heine anymore: "The stench of the language in which I had read the phrases from the Gestapo letter clung to his words as well. Indeed, the consciousness of what the country he yearned for would have done to him made it even more unbearable to read his work" (235–6).[3] Even his sister's marriage to an

Austrian diplomat failed to improve Seth's aversion; instead, it testified to the depth of his affliction: "Even my ties to a beloved brother-in-law could not reconcile me to the language ... Logic and justice told me that this was absurd, but it was as if the language itself forced images upon me that I could neither dissolve nor resist" (237–8). The writing of the biography itself then became a kind of working through, a coming to terms with the German past in order to be able to appreciate its language and its art again: "After some months I forced myself to read the letters that Aunty Henny's friends had written to her after the war, together with her own replies of which she had kept copies. Slowly, ... my ability to read the language recovered; my blind distaste was stilled; and in time even my old love, now both deeper and more troubled, revived" (238). For Seth, the writing of *Two Lives* was what Suzette A. Henke calls "scriptotherapy" (xx). Thus, Seth's own, autobiographical project has affinities with his biographical subject's writing of letters to her German friends and acquaintances, which constituted a therapeutic working through, a healing (or at least coping) through language. Seth's case is different, of course: through his "emphatic responses" (Schepeler 114), that is, through transference, he gains an understanding of his great-aunt's trauma as well as her complex, intense relation to her mother tongue.

The central aspect of *Two Lives*, the one thing that above all connects the two lives of the married couple, and which also takes in the biographer himself, is the complementary status of silence and spoken German in the aftermath of traumatic experiences. Silence not only figures as an invisible wall separating the marriage partners, but also seems to have been the essential precondition that made their marriage the sanctuary both needed so urgently to fend off the ghosts from the past. The German language, however, functions as a complex, multivalent symbol. Henny's relation to the German language powerfully illustrates the close interrelation between language and identity. Although Henny was fluent in English, she primarily lived, felt, and thought in German, her mother tongue. It was intricately bound up with her identity, expressing it and forming it, indeed permeating her entire being. But since German was linked with dire memories and had the overwhelming power to conjure up feelings too painful to endure, she assigned the language's different functions to separate spheres and clearly defined forms. She used its written form to confront painful memories, to analyse and judge the negative experiences of the past; its spoken form served her as a medium of partnership, friendship, and love that allowed her to relate to positive experiences of the past as well as to her life in the present. The very precondition through which the German language could fulfil these positive functions for Henny was again *silence* – the lack of any references in speech to the painful aspects of Germany's past; her and her husband's acknowledgment of the existence of unsayable things.

By writing the biography, Vikram Seth finally breaks this silence: even if he does so in a tongue other than German, the great-nephew represents what had been unrepresentable for his great-aunt. Thus, Seth's biographical writing in English becomes the requisite "language somehow formed on being silent" which finally "articulate[s] that which cannot be grasped." In addition, by telling *Two Lives*, especially by representing the life of his great-aunt Henny and the fate of her family, Seth negotiates his own troubled feelings in relation to Germany, its people, and its language. To a certain extent, *Two Lives* is an example of healing through language also with respect to the biographer: it is Seth's own scriptotherapy. After the personalized, intensive contact with German history had made Seth literally speechless and unable even to read the German language, his resumed work on the biography made him renegotiate his relation to the language which he first learned to love, then to hate, and then – after a hard internal struggle – to love again.

NOTES

1 Vikram Seth was the grandson of Shanti's eldest brother Raj. Raj, who after their father's and grandfather's deaths "took over the role of protector of the family" (61), was loved dearly by Shanti all his life: "Shanti grew to love his brother as one would love a father; indeed, he hero-worshipped him" (61). Obviously, Shanti transferred the great attachment he felt toward his brother Raj onto Vikram, his great-nephew.

2 Seth also mentions physical symptoms of Henny's trauma triggered by her experience of loss, bereavement, and desertion. As his great-uncle tells him, his wife "developed a condition in which her skin was covered with small red spots – urticaria pigmentosa" (416) after she had learned that her sister and mother had been deported and murdered by the Nazis.

3 It seems curious that this problematic – which was extensively discussed by Adorno, Celan, and others – would be such a discovery for Seth. As becomes clear throughout *Two Lives*, Seth chose to draw not on the work of previous writers and thinkers but solely on personal documents,

memories, his own historical knowledge, and his reasoning powers, not only in regard to his retracing of the experiences of his relatives but also with respect to his speculations concerning questions such as "Why did Germany play the central role it did?" (349).

WORKS CITED

Arendt, Hannah. "Was bleibt? Es bleibt die Muttersprache." In *Zur Person: Portraits in Frage und Antwort*, ed. Günter Gaus, 11–30. München: Deutsche Taschenbuch-Verlag, 1965.

Barossa, Julia. "Identity, Loss and the Mother Tongue." *Paragraph* 21, no. 3 (1998): 391–402.

Budick, Sanford, and Wolfgang Iser, eds. *Languages of the Unsayable*. New York: Columbia University Press, 1989.

Henke, Suzette A. *Shattered Subjects: Trauma and Testimony in Women's Life-Writing*. New York: St Martin's Press, 1998.

Hoddeson, David. "Introduction." In *Biography*, ed. D. Hoddeson. Special issue of *American Imago* 54, no. 4 (1997): 323–32. http://dx.doi.org/10.1353/aim.1997.0022.

Hokenson, Jan Walsch. "Intercultural Autobiography." In *Autobiography*. 5 vols. Ed. Trev Lynn Broughton, 2: 335–54. London: Routledge, 2007.

Hughes, Patricia, and Ian Kerr. "Transference and Countertransference in Communication between Doctor and Patient." *Advances in Psychiatric Treatment* 6, no. 1 (2000): 57–64. http://dx.doi.org/10.1192/apt.6.1.57.

Hüllen, Werner. "Identifikationssprachen und Kommunikationssprachen: Über Probleme der Mehrsprachigkeit." *Zeitschrift für Germanistische Linguistik* 20, no. 3 (1992): 298–317.

Kresic, Marijana. *Sprache, Sprechen und Identität: Studien zur sprachlich-medialen Konstruktion des Selbst*. München: Iudicium, 2006.

Rollason, Christopher. "The Multicultural in Vikram Seth's Two Lives: 'History Writ Little' or Global Protagonism?" *Seva Bharati Journal of English Studies* 4 (2008): 56–77.http://yatrarollason.info/files/SETH2LIVESSBJES VERSION.pdf.

Rushdie, Salman. "Imaginary Homelands." In *Imaginary Homelands: Essays in Criticism 1981–1991*, 9–21. London: Granta, 1991.

Schepeler, Eva. "The Biographer's Transference: A Chapter in Psychobiographical Epistemology." *Biography* 13, no. 2 (1990): 111–29. http://dx.doi.org/10.1353/bio.2010.0667.

Seth, Vikram. *Two Lives*. New Delhi: Penguin Books India, 2005.

Smith, Sidonie, and Julia Watson. *Reading Autobiography: A Guide for Interpreting Life Narratives*. Minneapolis: University of Minnesota Press, 2001.
Wittgenstein, Ludwig. *Tractatus Logico-Philosophicus. Intro. Bertrand Russell, trans. C.K. Ogden und Frank Ramsey*. 1922. London: Kegan Paul, 1947.

6 Unsayable or Merely Unsaid?

ENEKEN LAANES

Nora Anna Escherle's exploration of silence resulting from trauma and the attempts to overcome it in the second and third generation in Vikram Seth's double biography *Two Lives* is an extended reflection on matters relating to the representation of trauma.[1] The narrator's great-aunt Henny Caro Seth refuses to talk about her experiences concerning her flight from Nazi Germany and the loss of her family members, who were murdered in a concentration camp. Escherle describes these experiences interchangeably as "the things unsayable, the things unsaid, the things expressed by not being said" (214). At times, she stresses Henny's inability to talk about them; in other passages, she interprets Henny's silence as the result of a "conscious decision" (217).

Escherle's discussion of the "unsayable" is informed by Sanford Budick and Wolfgang Iser, for whom the problem of the unsayable is not specific to traumatic contexts and whose usage of the term is metaphorical. If there is something that *cannot be grasped,* but that has to be *articulated* in a different language, this something is not unsayable in the strict sense of the word. At this point, Escherle's discussion touches on the extensive debate in various disciplines including historiography, philosophy, and literary and cultural studies about the difficulties of representing traumatizing historical events, such as the Holocaust, and of experiences resulting from these events.

The problem that posed itself in the context of historiography, profoundly influenced by the narrative turn, was how to affirm the reality of events such as the Holocaust in order to refute revisionist claims.[2] This need to corroborate facts has led to suspicions concerning artistic representations of the Holocaust in literature and fine art that tend to generalize individual experience and turn it into aesthetic experience.[3]

In the context of personal testimonies about traumatic experiences in various genres (autobiography, memoir, fiction), the problem of representation seems to be posed in a slightly different manner. There is the feeling that, no matter how hard one tries, no narration will ever be able to capture, that is, express, these experiences. This has spawned discourses about the unrepresentability or the unsayability of those experiences. As Wulf Kansteiner has pointed out, in discourses of the "unsayable," which are mainly conducted within literary studies and strongly influenced by deconstructivist thought, the problem of the representation of traumatic experiences is often confused with language's purported inability to represent reality as theorized by deconstructivist thinking (205). Consequently, the problem of the representation of historical traumas such as the Holocaust loses its specificity. The question that arises is whether the burden of the unsayable is unique to individuals who have experienced traumatic events or whether their problems are simply symptoms of a rift between language and reality. Kansteiner's intervention indicates the need to ponder this issue more profoundly. The problem with Escherle's recourse to Budick and Iser's theorization of the "unsayable" is that it runs the risk of confusion outlined by Kansteiner.

In the context of historical traumas relevant to Escherle's discussion, the problem of the unsayable can be understood as a traumatic symptom, but also as the very essence of trauma. For Ernst van Alphen, trauma results from the inability to integrate the events one has lived through into one's structure of experience (42).[4] Behind this idea lies the understanding that experiencing is tied to language. The symbolic order offers modes and frames of representation that enable us to make sense of the world. If language lacks modes of representation for helping us make sense of certain events, these events acquire a traumatic nature. Therefore, the inability to integrate certain events into experience does not result from the extremity of events or the limits of language but from the historically specific symbolic order that lacks modes of representation adequate for expressing these particular events. Language does not fail as such but "as a function of history" (van Alphen 42). For van Alphen, trauma can be mitigated by trying to create forms of representation adequate to the events.

In a related vein, for Jacques Rancière the problem of the representability of historical traumas exists only as a problem of "comparative representability," that is, as the problem of finding suitable means of representation for specific ends. In arguing against inflated use of the notion of the unsayable, he writes that "nothing is unrepresentable as a property of the event. There are simply choices" (129).[5] In terms of Escherle's contribution, the mitigation of trauma proceeds by way of a search for ways of saying the unsayable. In fact, for Escherle, the word "unsayable" simply seems to express the feeling that some events are difficult to represent and that finding suitable means for them is a complicated task.

As far as *Two Lives* is concerned, it is all the more important to use the term "unsayable" with as much clarity and precision as possible because Henny rather refuses than is unable to talk about her past. The things she does not say remain unsaid not because they are unsayable in principle but because she does not want to talk about them or decides deliberately not to talk about them with certain people. Escherle suggests that by not talking about these memories to her loved ones in Britain, she is trying to build a refuge, a garden of peace not discomposed by the past. Thus, Henny's case as represented by Vikram Seth and discussed by Escherle may offer an opportunity to rethink the current understanding of the relationship between talking about historical traumas and working them through.

In this context, Escherle's discussion of Henny's refusal to talk about the past and her continued use of German with her loved ones as seemingly contradictory practices is of particular interest. For Escherle, the paradox lies in the fact that the German language is both Henny's language of love, which she employs only in relation to her husband and their German friends, and intimately related to her painful memories of Nazi Germany: her flight, her suffering, and the loss of her family members. Considering Henny's refusal to talk about her past as an attempt to build a refuge it is possible to see her tenacious use of her mother tongue as part of that process. By using German, she has refused to give the language of her mother and sister, of her childhood and of her love, over to the Nazi regime that had so profoundly marked her life. No matter how the Nazis used this language, what they did *with the help of it* and what they did *to* it in the process, Henny continues to use it stubbornly for her own purposes. However, the language, which is contaminated by the atrocious meanings Nazis gave to its words and phrases, still remembers these atrocities even if it does so in indirect ways and independently of Henny. By using German, Henny speaks her painful past after all, though she refuses to surrender to it by continuing to use the language as the language of love. Thus, she tries to heal not only herself but also her mother tongue.

Escherle relates Henny's different strategies of coping with trauma – in relation to her husband, on the one hand, and in relation to her friends in Germany, on the other – to differences between oral and written modes of expression. She links the oral mode primarily to processes of identity formation and an identificatory use of language. Granted, but it might also be interesting to relate Henny's different strategies of talking and not talking about her feelings to a difference between her addressees as well as to differing social contexts. In the processes of identity formation through narration, oral or written, the role of the person who receives the narration is of utmost importance. As Adriana Cavarero puts it, the self is "constituted by another: *the necessary other*" (84), and her position, her relation to the one who does the telling determines the modalities, the dynamics, and the outcome of the narration in decisive ways.

The role of intersubjectivity is also relevant for narration in traumatic contexts. If one views trauma as a crisis of experiencing, as does van Alphen, the social context during and after traumatizing events acquires a crucial importance for the dynamics of trauma, for it may aggravate or mitigate the belated experience of trauma. Thus, Henny's ability and need to discuss her feelings via letters with her friends in Germany may be related to their shared suffering in Germany before Henny's flight or her addressees' intimate relation to the suffering that her mother and sister went through before their death.

One final interesting question arising from Escherle's reading of Seth's *Two Lives* pertains to the role of the biography and its writing in relation to trauma and to saying things that have been left unsaid by Henny. The writing of the book may be seen as an expression of empathy and responsibility the narrator feels for his great-aunt and great-uncle, which he developed during their shared life in London. But Escherle also discusses the process of transference that unleashes while the narrator immerses himself in the past in order to read Henny's silence. Dominick LaCapra has drawn attention to the dangers of processes of identification and the claims for the status of a traumatized or (surrogate) victim in the case of secondary witnessing (*Writing History* 146). The narrator's aversion to the German language and literature that he develops while reading Nazi documentation in a museum is an interesting case of this kind of transference, which results from an intense occupation with the atrocious past, and the writing of the book may be seen as an attempt to overcome that aversion through the act of working through the transference.

NOTES

1 This article has been written with the support of ESF grant 8530.
2 For pertinent discussions of that problem, see the contributions in Friedlander.
3 For such an approach, see Lang and Langer.
4 Dominick LaCapra specifies the nature of traumatic experience by relating it to the German word *Erlebnis* rather than to *Erfahrung* (*History in Transit* 117).
5 Giorgio Agamben is also suspicious of the word "unsayable" because it mystifies experience and replaces the urgent need to inquire into its specific character by a euphemistic attitude that avoids talking about certain things because of shame or good manners (32).

WORKS CITED

Agamben, Giorgio. *Remnants of Auschwitz: The Witness and the Archive*. Trans. Daniel Heller-Roazen. New York: Zone Books, 1999.

Budick, Sanford, and Wolfgang Iser, eds. *Languages of the Unsayable*. New York: Columbia University Press, 1989.

Cavarero, Adriana. *Relating Narratives: Storytelling and Selfhood*. Trans. and intro. Paul A. Kottman. London: Routledge, 2000.

Friedlander, Saul. *Probing the Limits of Representation: Nazism and the 'Final Solution.'* Cambridge, MA: Harvard University Press, 1992.

Kansteiner, Wulf. "Genealogy of a Category Mistake: A Critical Intellectual History of the Cultural Trauma Metaphor." *Rethinking History* 8, no. 2 (2004): 193–221. http://dx.doi.org/10.1080/13642520410001683905.

LaCapra, Dominick. *History in Transit: Experience, Identity, Critical Theory*. Ithaca, NY: Cornell University Press, 2004.

LaCapra, Dominick. *Writing History, Writing Trauma*. Baltimore, MD: Johns Hopkins University Press, 2001.

Lang, Berel. *Act and Idea in the Nazi Genocide*. Syracuse, NY: Syracuse University Press, 2003.

Langer, Lawrence. *Holocaust Testimonies: The Ruins of Memory*. New Haven, CT: Yale University Press, 1991.

Rancière, Jacques. "Are Some Things Unrepresentable?" In *The Future of the Image*, trans. Gregory Elliot, 109–38. London: Verso, 2007.

Van Alphen, Ernst. *Caught by History: Holocaust Effects in Contemporary Art, Literature and Theory*. Stanford, CA: Stanford University Press, 1997.

7 Voicing Trauma in the Deportation Narratives of Baltic Women

LEENA KURVET-KÄOSAAR

"The arrest and all that suffering – that made you as if numb, as if insane! You were as if not in your own [mental] world any more. You were turned into something like a living lump: you exist and move but your mind has ceased to function" (Roots 224).[1] This is how Aino Roots, an Estonian woman who was deported in June 1941, describes her one-and-a-half months' train journey to Siberia in a cattle car. Aino was deported with her three small children, none of whom survived the journey. The account of the journey to Siberia as well as other painful and excruciating events that Aino experienced also form the core of many other deportation stories of Baltic women. However, what makes Aino's story exceptional is that it makes visible the hurtfulness and traumatic quality of that experience.

With this essay, I seek to facilitate a discussion of the notion of "trauma" in deportation stories of Baltic women who responded to various public calls for personal narratives issued in all three Baltic states during the last twenty years. My analysis will focus primarily on the narrative structuring of these stories and their imagery. Although the majority of women's deportation narratives contain ample illustrations of the experience of violence, injury, and harm that shaped the narrators' lives to a considerable extent and often for prolonged periods of time, the experiences these life writings recount are rarely viewed as self-altering or self-shattering or, in other words, traumatic (Gilmore 6). On the contrary, the reader frequently gets the impression that even though deportation almost always brought about drastic and painful changes in the deportees' lives (e.g., the loss of family members and home, the degradation of their social status, and considerable health damage), this experience did not seem to have had a lasting damaging effect on their psychic frame. Often, the deportation experience is represented as a powerful challenge that is met with the active agency, rebelliousness, dissenting spirit, endurance, and stamina that are viewed as part of the national characteristics of the Baltic states. Only in a few narratives do occasional fluctuations on the level of narrative control and coherence or emotional register emerge that can be interpreted as trauma signals (Benezer 29–44; Vickroy 2–13; Caruth, *Unclaimed Experience* 1–9).

In the late 1980s, when the Baltic states were moving towards regaining independence, several large-scale life-story projects were initiated in all three states.[2] The function and impact of these projects were manifold: bearing witness to various repressions of the Soviet regime; rehabilitating and commemorating the victims; initiating processes of revisioning the past; consolidating Baltic national identities.[3] Today, extensive collections and archives of personal narratives concerning the repressions of the Soviet regime exist in all three Baltic states. Although the narratives do not limit themselves to the experience of the two mass deportations of 1941 and 1949, these events assume central importance, testifying to the repressive, inhuman, and unjust nature of the Soviet regime.[4] The number of narratives by women in this genre is quite high. Women and children were dominantly (although not exclusively) deported to those areas of the Soviet Union where living and working conditions, although varying in harshness, made survival more likely than in labour camps. For that reason, more of them survived to experience the period of the reawakening movement in the late 1980s and early 1990s, when public calls for submitting life stories and oral history projects encouraged and supported the writing and telling about experiences of the Soviet regime, including that of deportation. In later reevaluations of Baltic history, deportation became a topic area to which women could contribute significantly. As an important textual site for testifying to experiences under the Soviet regime, the deportation narrative also harbours at least a potential for women to voice their experience of Soviet repressions.

When looking at the deportation narrative as a site where the female experience of suffering can emerge, it is important to retain an awareness of the impact of the normative frameworks within which these narratives emerged in the late 1980s and early 1990s. Bearing in mind that most deportation narratives tend to highlight – sometimes more overtly, sometimes more covertly – the collective implications of the experience of deportation, thematizing the ways in which not only the authors themselves but the Baltic nations as a whole suffered from the repressions of a violent totalitarian regime, the questions of "the limit of representativeness [and] the compulsory expansion of the self to stand for others" (Gilmore 5) emerge as important issues for readers of the narratives.[5]

This is an aspect of the narratives that gains particular importance from a gendered point of view. As I have argued in "Imagining a Hospitable Community in the Deportation and Emigration Narratives of Baltic Women," what emerges in these narratives is a strong emphasis on communal identification that is characterized by a sense of elasticity and sometimes also transcends the boundaries of national identity (63). As such, it can be related to "the discourse of connectivity" that, according to Judy Long, "does not arise only in response to the challenge of autobiography [but] has deep roots in female culture" (49). In her analysis of Estonian women's deportation stories, Tiina Kirss highlights the importance of interpreting "not only the themes that map women's life-worlds but [also] the impact of gender on the representation of subjectivity and agency," particularly with regard to "how the writing woman sees herself as a self-in-relation," in terms of both the telling of the story itself and the "cultural roles" women either "fulfill or resist" ("Survivorship" 23). Mara Lazda's research on the oral histories of Latvian women deportees also highlights the importance of gender, in particular with regard to women's ability to negotiate "relationships between fellow deportees and their overseers and [to] adapt their concepts of gender norms to establish new relationships in order to survive" (1).

Sometimes even more strongly than those of men, women's deportation narratives make a visible textual effort to prove that despite the extreme harshness and inhumanness of the deportation experience, the goals of the Soviet penal practices – to extinguish national identity, culture, community, and the belief in democratic values – were not realized. While women's deportation narratives by no means bypass the multiple negative effects of deportation, the narrators commonly present themselves as successful survivors. What any careful reader of the deportation stories cannot help noticing in the narrators' self-presentations is the (sometimes rather wide) gap between the harsh and excruciating nature of the experience on the one hand and its impact on the mental frame of mind and outlook of the deportee on the other. In many cases, the composition of the stories seems to be subject to careful selectiveness and (self-)censorship. Women's reticence (including their emotional reticence) to convey the harshest parts of their deportation experience may relate to a conscious decision on their part to highlight neither gender nor the experience of suffering at the expense of national identity.[6]

In her discussion of the personal narratives of three generations of Estonian women (daughter, mother, and grandmother), Kirss highlights that what these women choose to say crucially depends on "culturally significant and historically specific interpretive filters and metanarratives about selfhood, agency, gender, and membership in a larger collective, the Estonian people or nation" ("Three Generations" 114).[7] In a related vein, in her analysis of the patterns of (oral) narrations about the "cultural grammar of terror" (18–19) perpetrated by the Soviet regime in Latvia, Vieda Skultans comes to the conclusion that in cases where the "experiential content was held so bestial as to resist telling," the recourse to cultural metanarratives facilitated the telling of the story as it empowered narrators to "take up center stage as the imaginative recreators of their world" (34). While Skultans's focus is more on the theoretical implications of the use of various cultural resources used for "restoring meaning to lives" (22) than on the traces of the experience of violence and terror itself, she also advances the claim that traumatic experience is often (or mostly) unavailable in the narrative format; the life-story researcher only has access to (narrative) recovery.

It must also be taken into account that, although a well-recognized area of research and theoretical scrutiny, the notion of "trauma" has received only minimal critical attention in the analysis of Baltic history in general and personal narratives concerning the Soviet repressions in particular. As a concept and a therapeutic practice, "trauma" is still only at the beginning of entering Baltic public discourses about the Soviet occupation.[8] Over the past fifteen years, "trauma" has become one of the central conceptual frameworks in historiography, the social sciences, psychology, medicine, and literary studies for tackling the individual and cultural implications of a variety of events, situations, and phenomena that have caused strong long-term suffering that manifests itself in the lives of individuals or groups. Primary among the historical events that have been interpreted within the framework of "trauma" is the Holocaust (Hodgkin and Radstone 98). More recent research in the field of trauma studies indicates a widening of the concept to include, on a more general level, those events in history that can be characterized by the long-term presence of "political terror, systematic oppression, and genocide in former totalitarian and authoritative regimes" (Leydesdorff et al. 10).

The concept of trauma, the origin of which can be traced back to Freud, in particular his study of Jewish history *Moses and Monotheism* (1939), is centred on hurtful, overwhelming, life-threatening, and often catastrophic events or situations that cannot be fully grasped at the moment of their occurrence.[9] There is no (proper) remembrance of these events; memory only manifests itself later via "traumatic re-experiencing" (Caruth, *Unclaimed Experience* 10) that often appears in the form of involuntary and recurring intrusive thoughts, images, backlashes, and nightmares (Caruth, "Recapturing" 4). These symptoms of trauma owe their disturbing and destructive impact largely to the fact that the trauma victim has no access to the primary experience that caused the trauma. Other trauma symptoms include the re-experiencing of the horrors of the past through internal shifts back in time and space, that is, through a collapse of the distinction between past and present (Felman and Laub 14–15); "the numbing of general responsiveness to the external world and a hyper-alertness to certain stimuli" (Leydesdorff 5); and "the loss of various motor skills and a general closing off of the spirit as the mind tries to insulate itself from further harm" (Erikson 184).

At the heart of the concept of trauma lies a dilemma: the verbal unrepresentability of trauma, on the one hand, and the struggle for language "as that which can heal the survivor of trauma" (Gilmore 6), on the other. Scholars who support the idea of healing via an articulation of the traumatic experience have also sought to identify narrative traces of such experience including loss of agency; the failure of the authors to be in control of their narrative; and various difficulties in communicating the experience that include silence, simultaneous knowledge, and denial, dissociation, resistance, and repression (Vickroy 3, 5). In oral narratives, trauma signals such as loss of emotional control, emotional detachment or numbness, repetitive reporting, losing oneself in the traumatic event, and intrusive images have been identified (Benezer 34–5).[10]

The deportation narratives of Baltic women involve many situations and events that can be viewed as traumatic. These include the sudden and violent separation of families; the execution of family members; the death of family members in labour camps and areas of deportation due to poor living conditions; extremely hard working conditions; excessive fatigue arising from malnutrition and poor or non-existent medical assistance; and the prolonged exposure to feelings of fear, terror, and insecurity. Yet the traumatic quality of these experiences is rarely highlighted in the narratives; their emphasis is much rather on personal and collective survival. Within the context of the narratives, the notion of survival itself is seldom reflected upon critically, offering little textual evidence to Cathy Caruth's claim about "the oscillation between a crisis of death and the correlative crisis of life: between the story of an unbearable nature of an event and the story of the unbearable nature of its survival" (*Unclaimed Experience* 7) that she considers to be a central feature of traumatic experience. Possibly, this normative emphasis on survival sets limits to attempts to testify to the traumatic nature of the deportation experience. To represent the deportation experience as traumatic would entail making visible, in one way or another, the difficulty or even the impossibility of subjecthood in the face of the harm and hurt induced by the experience (or the author's inability to grasp the experience altogether). Highlighting such a position would mean admitting to being victimized by the experience, to being (at least partially) unable to cope with it. Such a position is rare in the deportation stories of Baltic women; victimhood is very seldom foregrounded on a personal level. On the more general (communal or national) level, such strategies of identification are acceptable and can be found in quite a few cases.

One example is the narrative of Palmi Sink, who was deported in 1941 at the age of twelve together with her young sister. Palmi concludes her narrative in the following manner: "I didn't know that so many were tortured and killed. That all this big country was full of prison camps ... We were so oppressed and squashed. God forbid that our children and grandchildren or anyone should ever suffer innocently so much and tolerate such pain as our generation did" (Sink 71).

Palmi's narrative is among the few deportation stories that tackle this experience as marked by several painful losses that she still tries to make sense of and, even more importantly, properly mourn in her story. For her, the most important loss she suffered is that of her father, who took care of her and her sister by himself. As far as verbally expressed emotions are concerned, Palmi's narrative is quite exceptional among the corpus of women's deportation narratives. Usually, the authors refrain from expressing emotion, particularly when they render hurtful personal experience (see my discussion of Herta Kaļiņina's life story below). In Palmi's narrative, the key to survival is a strong communal identity that the author maintains (not without a certain effort) throughout her life.[11] The ending of Palmi's narrative elevates communal and relational identity to a more general level: together with her compatriots, she sees herself as the subject of grave injustices on a national scale. In the end, it is not her individual traumatic experience that makes her story worth telling but its compatibility with the broader national suffering. In a sense, though, Palmi also transcends national victimhood by ending her narrative with a call for a happier future not only for Estonians but for all of humankind.

The story of Herta Kaļiņina, a Latvian woman who was deported in 1941, makes visible both collective and individual endurance and survival. In her deportation narrative, she recounts a period when she was suffering from dysentery and severe malnutrition. She recalls one evening when one of the overseers entered the modest shack where her family lived and in a loud voice ordered the inhabitants to start making a coffin as he was certain that the young woman would not survive the night. "There I was," Kaļiņina writes, "just 20 years old, starving and I had to die. I wanted something to eat and then die" (Kaļiņina 81). With the help of extra food from the fellow deportees, however, she stays alive and is soon sent back to work. The narrator briefly discusses the harsh impact her illness had on her mother, but soon shifts her narrative away from the individual and onto the communal level as she weaves together the meaning of her own survival with the Latvian deportee community's collective will to survive: "[While fishing,] it often happened that we would start singing, especially a song in which we expressed our sorrow about having to live in a foreign land and our yearning to return to our homeland, if only to be buried there. We sang through tears. We made a promise to ourselves to survive, come what may, for it couldn't get any worse" (82).[12]

Although Herta's and Palmi's narratives make visible both on an individual and, more importantly, a communal level, that surviving the deportation necessarily also involves crisis situations (Herta's near-starvation) and only partially redeemable losses (the death of Palmi's father as well as several people in Palmi's immediate deportee community), neither of these life stories offer strong textual evidence of traumatic experience. Particularly in Herta's narrative, there is hardly anything that would testify to the self-shattering nature of her experience, to an absence of (full) recall, or to intrusive thoughts or nightmares in her later life. In Palmi's narrative, we can detect only few traces of a recovery from traumatic experience. One point in case is her struggle to cope with and produce a record of her father's death:

> I cannot write any more, as now comes the day when men were taken away. I feel as if this parting is happening right now when I'm trying to write about it. A few days more I would like to spend on the same train with him and that's why I have put away my notebook so that I wouldn't have to write about it as yet. And I even cannot record the pain and loss that we felt back then. (Sink 38)

This is one of the few passages in which the unspeakability of traumatic experience comes to the fore. For the greatest part, though, what is emphasized is pain, loss, and mourning – but not trauma. Palmi's narrative leads us to assume that hardly any of her memories had a permanent and disrupting effect on her present life. Witness her lament for her father ("Our dear dear father! All my life I have tried to follow your teachings. At such an early age we lost you and stayed alone among strangers" [36]) or her utter sympathy for a mother's grief over the death of her little daughter:

> After some days Mrs Suurkivi returned [from the hospital], carrying the blue blanket, but Urve was not in it. There she stood by the furnace and cried, cried in desperation ... Urve had passed away [she said]. Her blue eyes were now closed forever ... I remember ironing last shirts for Urve and crying, and then Liidi went to bury her. Again one of us had passed away. We, however, had to live on. (49)

In such passages, Palmi registers not trauma but deportees' ability to express their feelings and to grieve properly. Such passages testify both to the extreme hurtfulness of the deportation experience and the deportee's ability to react adequately to painful events. Thus, they become testimonies not only of Palmi's survival but also of collective survival.

Many deportation narratives are more laconic than Palmi's in their depictions of the deaths of parents, siblings, and friends. Aino Poom, in a generally optimistic, high-paced narrative that covers a great multitude of topics, addresses her father's death and execution by the officials of the Soviet regime in scant detail and devoid of emotion: "When our father was taken away we did have a difficult time" (10). Somewhat later in the story, she offers a few more bits of information about her father's fate:

> He was taken to the Lasnamäe prison. I never saw him again ... We learned about our father that there was a trial and the sentence from 26.02.1941

> was: to be shot ... My father Evald Ristikivi was shot 24.04.1941 at Pirita-Kose ... 38 bodies were found buried under the floor ... Father's hands were tied with barbed wire, his bones were broken, a rag was shoved into his throat to prevent him from screaming. What sadistic people! ... When my father was shot, he was 39 years old, a big, strong man in his prime. (10–11)

Apart from giving voice to her firm conviction that the Soviet regime inflicted great injustice on her family as well as Estonians more generally, the episode about her father's death does not reveal any emotional response on Aino's part: the narrator limits herself to presenting only the factual knowledge (dates, numerical data). The dates here seem to serve the purpose of guaranteeing the historical accuracy of the narrative and enhancing its testimonial role; they offer hardly any clues as to the narrator's response to her father's death. However, several aspects of Aino's narrative point towards a somewhat different conclusion. Only a few lines after the description of her father's execution, we get the narrator's description of her own deportation together with her two siblings and their mother. Aino was sixteen years old then, the younger of her siblings was only two and a half years old. Her description of the arrest well conveys the shock, the fear, and the feeling of helplessness that the narrator and her family experienced. These two events – the father's execution and the deportation – form the opening section of the narrative, preceded only by a brief paragraph that sums up the narrator's life before the war in a few sentences.[13] This narrative strategy highlights the shocking and traumatic nature of the changes that were brought about in the narrator's life. Her emphasis on the suffering of her fellow Estonians also allows for some space to express her own suffering, if only indirectly.

Despite its firm factual foundation, the episode of her father's execution is ambiguous as far as the author's own response to it is concerned. The reader senses the narrator's unwillingness or inability to convey to the reader her emotional reaction to this event. Aino's chosen mode of narration brings to mind Gadi Benezer's identification of "emotional detachment or numbness" as trauma signals (34–5, 30). The event recounted – in Benezer's case the migration of young Ethiopian Jews to Israel during the period of 1977–85 – "seems to have had a horrifying quality [for the narrator] but [s/he] show[s] no emotions during the narration," which gestures towards the narrator's "forced detachment of the event" (34) from her emotional life. In Aino's narrative, the father's execution is taken up again towards the end, when, in search of justice at the end of the 1980s, the author turns to the Soviet authorities in order to gain access to her father's KGB file. As it turns out, the file does not contain anything that would justify her father's execution. For a moment, the narrative breaks down in the face of unredeemable injustice and the loss Aino has never been able to mourn properly: "[I found] a document with my father's photo ... I could not recognize him, he was a mere shadow of a person. And yet, he was a strong 39-year-old man when he was executed" (Poom 30). But on the whole, the narrative does not leave the reader with the impression that the author was traumatized by the experience of deportation. On the contrary, the reader can only admire the author's stamina, positive frame of mind, and extreme diligence and honesty that earned her the respect of the whole deportee community and testifies powerfully to her successful survival. The (possibly) traumatic quality of the experience becomes visible only at the level of narrative structuring. Her father's inhuman and unjust death both opens and concludes the narrative, being at the closure tied up with another loss that the narrator finds hard to come to terms with: that of the death of her son in the *Estonia* ferry catastrophe in 1994.[14]

As the texts I have discussed so far demonstrate, the deportation narratives of Baltic women rarely present the experience as self-shattering, impossible to come to terms with, or hurtful to the extent that it had continuously disturbing and damaging effects on their present lives. During my research, I have, however, come across a few narratives that are dominated by the gloomy shadow of the experience. In these texts, the authors either self-consciously refuse to offer their readers a coherent testimony to successful survival or are unable to do so. Two narratives in particular represent the experience of deportation as dominated by an erosion of subjecthood that results from either a waning of the moral norms and material standards of human existence or personal losses beyond comprehension and manageability. These narratives were written by Lilija Bīvina, a Latvian woman who served time in a forced-labour camp in the Serenaya Dvina region, and Aino Roots, an Estonian woman who was deported in 1941 and lost three young children during the one-and-a-half month journey to Siberia. Their stories come closest to presenting the deportation experience as a traumatic one.

Lilija Bīvina's deportation narrative consists of a few loosely connected episodes, each of which highlights the erosion or distortion of a norm or standard characteristic of normal human existence.[15] On the one hand, the narrative functions as a series of acts of witnessing that seem to avoid a more specific focus on the narrator's own life. On the other hand, the author is always implicated in the witnessed events. In the narrative, the personal and the collective experience blend together into an indistinguishable entity, bearing evidence to an experience that is excruciating and hurtful to the extent that it nearly dissolves personality and individuality. Lilija herself, unlike most people whom she mentions in her narrative, is a survivor; thus, her narrative might be expected to testify to the ultimate failure of the repressions of the Soviet regime in a particularly powerful manner. However, the narrator, who employs irony as the dominant narrative device, seems to avoid taking up such a position. In an eerily witty and eloquent manner, she stays with the "living mass of corpses," who are nothing but "the mathematical average of a live human being and a corpse" (116–17). In another passage, she looks into the eyes of a mother who has been separated from her children and "in whom everything had died" (124).

These are excruciatingly painful episodes by any means, but it is impossible to gather from the narrative how severe the impact of such or similar experience was on the author's life. The text seems to cut off such lines of inquiry both by way of its self-conscious failure to produce a properly structured deportation narrative and, even more importantly, via the use of irony. Irony is employed as a narrative strategy that enables the recounting of the excruciating memories thanks to the distance it creates between the narrator and the experienced events. Yet the irony is also directed at contemporary (Baltic) readers; it refuses to give us the relief and consolation of a survival story. In Lilija's narrative, her own "escape from a death" does not point to a successful and unproblematic survival but rather seems to testify to trauma's "endless impact on life" (Caruth, *Unclaimed Experience* 7). The survival that Lilija's narrative ironically sketches for her reader is of an "unbearable nature" (ibid.), and its dark shadow looms not only (or not primarily) over the author herself but over the whole nation. "With an ironic smile, our lips would utter the old saying 'the wicked flourish,'" Lilija comments on the overloaded cart that daily transported the deceased to a simple pit that was the substitute for a graveyard (Bīvina 110). Thus, she problematizes the position of the survivors by measuring them (and herself as well) against the ones who did not survive.

Where her narrative touches upon her own experience in the camp, gender is not foregrounded; rather, her focus is on her difficulty (and partial failure) in viewing herself as human to any recognizable extent.[16] Yet this does not necessarily testify to the irrelevance of the category of gender in recounting the experience. In fact, it may be taken as underlining it: feeling ungendered also shows the utter harshness of her experience and the gradual erosion of her capacity to respond to her environment beyond the basic necessities that have to be met in order to stay alive. One of the lengthier episodes in Lilija's narrative, however, addresses the deportation trauma from a markedly gendered point of view. It is the story of Marija, a woman who "had been left with two small children, her home had been burnt down, her husband had been shot and thrown into the flames, and she herself given the burden of ten long years of suffering" (Bīvina 124). As a result, she had lost her mind, her eyes now "gazing fixedly up to the sky, its indifferent, cool blueness blending into the calm immobility of these eyes, a look typical of people who have become insane because of deep despair" (124). Living in "a world of her own," Marija's only concern is an "insane, dark unremitting longing for her children" (124, 126), whose fate is unknown to the narrator, and it is in search of them that she finally escapes from the camp and is shot a few kilometres from it. Although Marija harbours a threat of insanity for Lilija – looking into her eyes, she might risk her own fragile existence – she valorizes her desperate escape attempt as one "blessed by the flames of a mother's love that had not been extinguished by the dark shadow of insanity" (127). Lilija's narrative does not mention her own past, so the reader cannot know whether Marija's story could be an echo of Lilija's own life experience (with the exception that Lilija managed to retain – or recover – her sanity).

The end of Lilija's narrative elevates Marija to a symbol of both national suffering and the suffering of a woman. Although at the beginning of her story, Lilija dwells at length on the inhumane manner in which those who died in the camp were usually buried, now the deportee community arranges a proper burial for Marija: a coffin is made for her from bed-bunk boards, she is dressed in her own clothes, "no government rags were used," and a "faded photograph" of her children, "two smiling imps, a little girl and a boy," is placed in her hand (128). As in Palmi's narrative, the death of a fellow deportee, especially if it occurs in a particularly tragic context, is seen as an event that mobilizes the communal capacity of the deportees. If Palmi, after recounting the episode of the death of a little girl with whom she shared lodgings for a while, asserts the need to go on with one's life, Lilija's narrative ends on a more pessimistic and fatalistic note: "The Holy Grail had spilled at the edge of the eternally impenetrable Taiga" (Bīvina 128). Like the harsh climatic conditions that human force can neither control nor handle, the experience of the people confined to a forced-labour camp remains impenetrable; it cannot be narrativized and smoothly incorporated into the (grand) Baltic narrative of the repression of and liberation from the Soviet regime.

Lilija's narrative, although it does not offer many clues for the reader about the position the author herself adopts towards the episodes recounted, nevertheless highlights strategies that enable the author's survival. Although the dark shadows of the past dominate her narrative, and even though her partial refusal to make visible her own frame of mind in relation to her experience has a strong impact on the reader, her narrative cannot be viewed as offering direct textual proof of her own traumatization by the experience of deportation. Rather, the striking aptness and skilful mode of narration tinted by dark irony suggest a capacity for strong authorial control over the recounted events. At the same time, the narrative offers no clear proof that the author has been able successfully to work through her experience: the narrative contains no references to her present life.

The hurtful weight of past experiences also dominates the deportation narrative of Aino Roots, with whose story I began my essay. Unlike Lilija's life story, Aino's centres around the author's own, gendered experience of trauma as well as her response to it. Aino's story is included in the collection of articles and deportation stories published by the Estonian female student corporation Filiae Patriae in 2004. It is written in the southern Estonian dialect. As the collection brings together the deportation narratives of men and women who belonged to various student organizations, the use of dialect is slightly unexpected. After all, the fact that the author studied at Tartu University (where she was a student at the Faculty of Economics) is sufficient proof that she was able to speak and write in standard Estonian. It is well possible that after returning from deportation and once she resumed the use of Estonian as the language spoken at home, the author may have started using dialect Estonian again, as such language use may have enhanced her communal identity. She emphasizes in her narrative that when she returned to Estonia, many things had changed: "Everything was somehow strange, as if [... things] were [the same and] were not [at the same time]" (Roots 233). In dialect, she may have felt more at home in the Estonia she used to know, and it may be for that reason that she chose to write her narrative in dialect as well.[17]

The central event around which Aino's narrative revolves is the death of her three small children, who were deported together with her. "The children were very very small when we were arrested in 1941," the author recounts, "my little Jaan would have been four in the fall. Little Helga: she was slightly over two years. Ene was really small, an infant only" (220). The narrative mentions the young and vulnerable age of the children several times, as if offering some sort of explanation as to why they did not survive the deportation or, even more importantly, why the mother could not ensure their survival: "No one had so many children [on the train] who were also so small. The youngest was 5 years old. It was easier for the others for this reason" (223). To this, she adds, "The children were so small, I couldn't explain to them what had happened" (223). As we learn, all three children died, either during the one-and-a-half-month journey to Siberia or shortly thereafter (the narrative does not offer any information on how or when they died). The author simply switches from an account of her journey to Siberia – during which she describes feeling like a "human lump [that] exists and moves but where reason has ceased to function" (Roots 224) – to ruminations about the fate of her children:

> I have myself thought if that was a curse or a punishment sent by God but in other ways He has been merciful to me as well. He summoned these children to Himself. What would I have done with those three in Siberia? Would they have ever grown up to become full persons? Their nerves already were damaged when those men came and yelled back then in the middle of their sleep. (224–5)

A few paragraphs later, the author emphasizes that she was never ill during all those years in Siberia, although there were numerous situations that could have damaged her health. Yet she expresses no relief about that. Rather, this aspect of her deportation experience relates to a feeling of guilt, as she was unable to prevent the deaths of her three children. She also emphasizes repeatedly that she did not care much for her life or her well-being during her Siberian years and expresses her gratitude for remaining sane, as "many went nuts there" (225). And yet, the author admits to having no recollection of the time that she spent in a Siberian prison immediately after the death of her children: "I lived as if in a fog," the author writes, adding that after her release she did not feel as "if the reason why she was alive would have become clearer to her as the children were dead" (225).

Of all deportation narratives of Baltic women I have encountered, this one comes closest to representing the deportation experience as traumatic. The whole narrative is shadowed by the dark trace of the author's loss, which is never explicitly narrated. The reader does not learn about the author's disposition or even the scope of her memory pertaining to these tragic events either. Aino's somewhat incoherent narrative is centred around experiences relating to her children: both the three who died and the two who were born in Siberia from her common-law marriage to an illiterate German. The author views the two children who stayed alive as a consolation for the ones who died, yet she also makes clear that her frame of reasoning was not shared by her family, who looked upon the children with whom she returned from Siberia first as an additional burden and, second, as a disgrace. Aino's narrative does not only suggest that there were traumatic experiences from which she has never recovered, but she also comments on a lifetime of emotional isolation that set limits to her ability to recount her story at the end of her life. In her characteristically simple and frank manner, the author makes clear that her losses were unredeemable, that her life would never be the same again, "that deportation is like a shirt upside down, you wear it but it's still the wrong side up" (Roots 236).[18]

The deportation narratives of Baltic women do not easily lend themselves to readings as stories of trauma. Thus, theoretical frameworks around this notion can be applied only with extensive reservations. None of the deportation stories I have discussed fit descriptions of trauma as a hurtful event or situation which owes its disturbing and destructive impact to the fact that the trauma victim has no access to the primary experience that caused the trauma, and which manifests itself later via "traumatic re-experiencing" (Caruth, *Unclaimed Experience* 10). Yet some evidence of the traumatic quality of the deportation experience is present in the narratives. A close analysis of the narrative structuring and emotional register of the stories makes visible several aspects that can be identified as trauma signals: narrative incoherence; bypassing of certain events and situations; omission of the author's emotional response to those events and situations; (self-conscious) failure to produce a properly structured deportation narrative; (partial) impossibility of narrativizing the deportation experience; (emotional) numbness; and a sense of apathy relating to certain events and situations. Each story discussed makes visible both the hurtfulness of the experience and the difficulty of conveying it in the format of a deportation narrative. Thus, they highlight, each in its own manner, the great narrative courage and resourcefulness it takes to reflect on and possibly ease that hurtfulness.

In her 2007 book *Tõrjutud mälestused* (*Memories Denied*), Imbi Paju documents her attempt to "recover the lost time that once surrounded [her] mother and her contemporaries but which now has receded into silence and has been deprived of consolation" and to initiate what she calls "an alleviation of the pain [of history, a movement toward] a calmer and happier memory" (Paju 270). In a different manner, these deportation stories of Baltic women recover that lost time through making visible not only the pain of the past but that of the present as well, teaching the reader to manage living with it. For as much as the stories, each in its own way, try to sketch a trajectory towards a, if not happier, then at least "calmer" and consoling memory, they also testify to the enduring quality of hurtfulness that can never be completely left behind but can only be incorporated into visions of the future.

NOTES

1 This article has been written with the support of ESF grants 7354 ("Positioning Life-Writing on Estonian Literary Landscapes"), 9035 ("Dynamics of Address in Estonian Life Writing") and the TF project "Sources of Cultural History and Contexts of Literature." Unless otherwise indicated, all translations from Estonian are mine.

2 In Estonia, for example, the first call for a collection of personal narratives was published in newspapers in the fall of 1989. In the years 1988–92, the Estonian Heritage Society organized several campaigns for collecting life stories, and a collection entitled *14. juuni 1941: Mälestusi ja dokumente* was published in 1990. In 1995 the Estonian Life Stories Association, which initiated numerous public calls for life stories, was founded. In 1996 a call entitled "My destiny and the destiny of those close to me in the labyrinths of history" was issued that brought in 265 life stories (about 20,000 pages), and a collection dedicated to deportation stories, *Me tulime tagasi* (Tartu: Eesti Kirjandusmuuseum), was published in 1999. Another call entitled "One hundred lives of a century" issued in the same year resulted in the submission of 230 life stories, 65 of which were published in a monumental two-volume anthology, *Eesti rahva elulood, I–II: Sajandi sada elulugu kahes osas* (Tallinn: Tänapäev, 2000, 2003). Another volume, which focuses on life in the Soviet Union, was published in 2003: *Eesti rahva elulood, III osa: Elu Eesti NSV-s* (Tallinn: Tänapäev, 2003). In Latvia, a four-volume series of life

writings about Soviet deportations and labour-camp experiences entitled *Via dolorosa: Staļinisma upuru liecības* (Riga: Preses Nams and Liesma) was published between 1990 and 1995. In 1999 a selection of Latvian deportation stories entitled *We Sang Through Tears: Stories of Survival in Siberia* was published. The National Oral History Archive (NOHA) at the University of Latvia holds almost 3000 life stories (http://www.dzivesstasts.lv). See also Lazda, "Women" (1–12).

3 See also Kirss, "Introduction" (15–17), Kurvet-Käosaar, "Imagining" (59–63).

4 Deportations in the Baltic countries are commonly referred to in terms of two infamous dates, June 1941 and March 1949. The deportation in June 1941 targeted those considered to be anti-Soviet elements within Baltic societies: they included political leadership, government officials, higher civil servants, businessmen, higher ranks of the military, policemen, and prison wardens, and others who were deported together with their families. The 1941 deportation included 45,000 people from all Baltic states (Rahi-Tamm 20). During the transportations to Siberia, men were separated from their families and sent to forced-labour camps, mostly located behind the Polar Circle, where some were executed and many more lost their lives due to extremely harsh living conditions. Although a minority, women holding political or influential social positions were also executed or served time in forced-labour camps. The second wave of deportations that took place mainly in March 1949 was a penal measure undertaken to ensure successful completion of the collectivization of agriculture (40% of the deportees) and to cleanse the Baltic societies of "enemies of the people" (60% of the deportees), including those whose family members or relatives had been arrested or deported before, gone missing, or fled to the West (ibid. 22). It included 95,000 persons from all Baltic states, the majority of whom were women, children, and the elderly (ibid. 23). It was in particular the 1941 deportations – which hit a completely unprepared people for whom such massive repressive measures had been unimaginable – that has crystallized as an icon of the horrors of the Stalinist regime in diaspora memory (Kirss, "Introduction" 14). In addition, one needs to take into account the impact of the Second World War on the condition of the deportees. According to the tentative statistics provided by Anne Applebaum, overall Gulag death rates went up dramatically during the war years, amounting, for example, to 352,560 (24% of all inmates) in 1942 (582). However, it would be extremely speculative and difficult if not impossible to determine the traumatic impact of the deportation in terms of a specific deportation date. As Rutt Hinrikus points out, "One could even refer to the era as having

included a wave of deportations that started in the summer of 1940 and lasted until 1953, when Stalin died" (209). In the post-Soviet popular memory of the Baltic states, the dates were less strictly separated in terms of specific implications. Rather, the word "deportation" came to imply, not unlike Applebaum's conceptualization of the word "Gulag," "the Soviet repressive system itself" (xv–xvi).

5 In particular within the framework of survival, Tiina Kirss refers to *saatusekaaslased* (destiny-companions), "a term that helps us understand an important aspect of the collective level of the deportation experience" ("Survivorship" 17). Among the narratives I have included in my discussion, Palmi Sink's description of the death of the young daughter of Mrs Suurkivi can be interpreted as evoking this term, in this case to undermine both narratives of loss and survival (see my analysis of this episode below). However, Jura Avižienis, in her analysis of a well-known deportation story of a Lithuanian woman named Dalia Grinkevičiūte, has identified marked differences between a loving concern for immediate family members and a tone "verg[ing] on scorn" (192) in descriptions of other fellow Lithuanian deportees. Avižienis argues that while the deportation experience strengthened ethical behaviour towards family, neighbours, and a small circle of friends, it also brought about a "disawoval of moral responsibility toward abstract entities such as community, society, nation, and environment" (192). Among the stories I analyse in the present essay, that of Lilija Bīvina describes a mental atmosphere that is rather similar to that of Grinkevičiūte's story, yet it also registers ethical concerns and empathy for not only the immediate circle of friends and family but also the deportee (labour camp) community as a whole, regardless of their ethnic identity.

6 This reticence seems particularly problematic if it concerns tabooed experiences such as wartime and repression-related sexual violence against women. In her analysis of Russian women's Gulag narratives, Marianne Liljeström comes to the conclusion that "the personal becomes cultural and meaningful and gives the testifiers comfort when 'my voice' is one of many sufferers' voices" (162). According to her analysis, however, female communities of Gulag remembrance can be viewed as becoming "part of a politics of making visible those forms of power that ideologies of 'genderlessness' or of tabooed subjects … had previously concealed" (162). In discussing the deportation stories of Estonian women, Tiina Kirss offers an analysis of a description of "threatened or attempted sexual violence," but maintains that this subject is "broached … in the stories with considerable discretion" ("Survival" 30). The threat and experience of sexual violence is also the focus of exiled Latvian author Agate Nesaule's novel *A Woman in*

Amber and Estonian journalist Imbi Paju's documentary *Memories Denied*. I discuss these elsewhere (Kurvet-Käosaar, "Other Things" 313–31; "Vulnerable Scriptings" 89–114). Although there are indications that taboo subjects such as sexual violence against women are currently emerging into the Baltic public spheres, these changes are too intermittent and gradual to speak of a new politics of remembrance and representation.

7 In this context, Kirss also raises the issue of the ethical stance of the life-story researcher, underlining the need for "a reverence for individual experience *as it has been told and recorded*" (114; my emphasis), proposing as suitable interpretive strategies "questioning rather than pronouncement" and the maintenance of "discretion, tact and reticence as well as the courage of the 'vulnerable observer'" ("Three Generations" 114).

8 See, for instance, Aarelaid-Tart; Kirss, "Three Generations" (132–6); Laanes (433–48); Rein (55–75); and Skultans.

9 Defining the context or event that can cause trauma has been a central and hotly debated issue in discussions of trauma. According to the definition of "post-traumatic stress disorder" (PTSD), published in the third revised edition of the American Psychiatric Association's *Diagnostic and Statistical Manual of Mental Disorders* (1987), trauma is caused by "an event that is outside the range of usual human experience and that would be markedly distressing to almost anyone" (250). Among several others, Erikson and Brown have taken a stand against what they view as a limiting definition. For them, trauma can result from "a constellation of life experiences as well as from a discrete happening, from a persisting condition as well as from an acute event" (Erikson 185). Also, a number of common but nonetheless psychologically destructive events and phenomena (e.g., incest and sexual abuse) should be included among those that are believed to cause trauma (Brown 100–1). Erikson has further argued that it should be the impact, "the *damage done*," not the event itself that should be the focus of trauma research (185).

10 Benezer's list, which he compiled on the basis of oral narratives, includes thirteen different trauma signals; I have only included those that can also be found in written narratives.

11 The strong communal identity that defines Palmi's narrative can also be attributed to the fact that she and her sister were deported without any family members or relatives and became part of different families with whom they shared lodgings during their exile. Palmi's family history is a complicated one, fraught with severe conflicts between her father, who took care of Palmi and her sister by himself, and her mother's brothers, who ultimately got rid of the bothersome relatives by fabricating a complaint

against them that resulted in their deportation. Palmi and her sister were separated from their father during their arrest and never saw him again. Because of her disturbing and violent family history, Palmi may have been more open to form communal networks during deportation and to sympathize more with the fate of the people she came into close contact with.

12 The fact that the collection of Latvian deportation stories in English takes its title, *We Sang Through Tears*, from that passage offers further proof that such strategies of treating deportee's individual hardships and hurtful experiences are strongly favoured within the normative set-up of the deportation narrative genre.

13 The share allotted in the deportation narratives to the time, way of life, and guiding moral principles of the family network as well as society at large differs from narrative to narrative but is usually tackled with enough detail to emphasize the radical change the occupation and repressions of the Soviet regime brought about. Among the overall textual body of deportation narratives, that of Aino Poom dedicates unusually few lines of her narrative to her family's life before the repressions. In that brief section, however, she manages to highlight a number of important aspects of her family's life: a hardworking father who guaranteed a steadily improving standard of life for her family; a happy childhood; the importance of education; and, above all, the important role in the narrator's life of the guiding moral principles of society, such as honesty, love for the native country, and respect for the elders (Poom 9).

14 On 28 September 1994 a ferry commuting between Tallinn and Stockholm sank near the coast of Sweden with 852 people losing their lives. This accident is considered the greatest catastrophe on the Baltic Sea since the Second World War.

15 Lilija Bīvina was sent to a forced-labour camp which was that part of the Gulag penal system used for those found guilty of more severe crimes against the Soviet Union. The year of her arrest and sentencing is not mentioned in the story. Her story is not a deportation narrative in the strict sense of the term. However, the inclusion of Lilija's narrative in the collection of Latvian deportation narratives (*We Sang Through Tears*) shows that forced-labour camp stories are often considered to be part of the corpus of deportation narratives. As the mortality rate in the camps was extremely high, the number of stories in this category is considerably lower than that of deportation stories in the more narrow sense.

16 See also Avižienis (191).

17 I have been in contact with Aino Roots's grand-daughter, who told me that her grandmother had an excellent command of standard Estonian, but

preferred speaking in dialect at home. She would use standard Estonian mainly when they had visitors.

18 The Estonian word *pahupool*, which I translate as "upside down," literally means "the worse side up."

WORKS CITED

Aarelaid-Tart, Aili. *Cultural Trauma and Life Stories*. Helsinki: Kikimora Publications, 2006.

American Psychiatric Association, ed. *Diagnostic and Statistical Manual of Mental Disorders. DSM-III-R*. 3rd rev. ed. Washington, DC: American Psychiatric Association, 1987.

Applebaum, Anne. *Gulag: A History*. New York: Doubleday, 2003.

Avižienis, Jura. "Learning to Curse in Russian: Mimicry in Siberian Exile." In *Baltic Postcolonialism*, ed. Violeta Kelertas, 186–202. Amsterdam: Rodopi, 2006.

Benezer, Gadi. "Trauma Signals in Life Stories." In *Trauma: Life Stories of Survivors*, ed. Kim Lacy Rogers, Selma Leydesdorff, and Graham Dawson, 29–44. New Brunswick, NJ: Transaction Publishers, 2004.

Bīvina, Lilija. "Winter by the White Sea." In *We Sang Through Tears*, ed. Astrids Sics, 109–28. Riga: Jānis Rose Publishers, 1999.

Brown, Laura S. "Not Outside the Range: One Feminist Perspective on Psychic Trauma." In *Trauma: Explorations of Memory*, ed. Cathy Caruth, 100–13. Baltimore: Johns Hopkins University Press, 1995.

Caruth, Cathy. "Recapturing the Past." In *Trauma: Explorations of Memory*, ed. Cathy Caruth, 151–7. Baltimore: Johns Hopkins University Press, 1995.

Caruth, Cathy. *Unclaimed Experience: Trauma, Narrative, and History*. Baltimore: Johns Hopkins University Press, 1996.

Erikson, Kai. "Notes on Trauma and Community." In *Trauma: Explorations of Memory*, ed. Cathy Caruth, 183–99. Baltimore: Johns Hopkins University Press, 1995.

Felman, Shoshana, and Dori Laub. *Testimony: Crises of Witnessing in Literature, Psychoanalysis, and History*. New York: Routledge, 1991.

Freud, Sigmund. *Moses and Monotheism*. Trans. Katherine Jones. London: Hogarth Press, 1939.

Gilmore, Leigh. *The Limits of Autobiography: Trauma and Testimony*. Ithaca: Cornell University Press, 2001.

Hinrikus, Rutt. "Soviet Deportations." In *Carrying Linda's Stones: An Anthology of Estonian Women's Life Stories*, ed. Suzanne Stiver Lie, Lynda Malik, Ilvi

Jõe-Cannon, and Rutt Hinrikus, 207–21. Tallinn: Tallinn University Press, 2006.

Hodgkin, Katharine, and Susannah Radstone. "Remembering Suffering: Trauma and History." In *Contested Pasts: The Politics of Memory*, ed. Katharine Hodgkin and Susannah Radstone, 97–103. London: Routledge, 2003.

Kaļiņina, Herta. "We Sang Through Tears." In *We Sang Through Tears*, ed. Astrids Sics, 71–88. Riga: Janis Rose Publishers, 1999.

Kirss, Tiina. "Ariadne lõngakera: Eesti naiste Siberilood nende elulugudes." In *Paar sammukest 16: Eesti Kirjandusmuuseumi aastaraamat 1999*, 23–31. Tartu: Eesti Kirjandusmuuseum, 1999.

Kirss, Tiina. "Introduction." In *She Who Remembers Survives*, ed. Tiina Kirss, Ene Kõresaar, and Marju Lauristin, 13–18. Tartu: Tartu University Press, 2004.

Kirss, Tiina. "Survivorship in the Eastern Exile: Estonian Women's Life Narratives of the 1941 and 1949 Siberian Deportations." *Journal of Baltic Studies* 36, no. 1 (2005): 13–38. http://dx.doi.org/10.1080/01629770400000221.

Kirss, Tiina. "Three Generations of Estonian Women: Selves, Lives, Texts." In *She Who Remembers Survives*, ed. Tiina Kirss, Ene Kõresaar, and Marju Lauristin, 112–43. Tartu: Tartu University Press, 2004.

Kirss, Tiina, Ene Kõresaar, and Marju Lauristin, eds. *She Who Remembers Survives*. Tartu: Tartu University Press, 2004.

Kurvet-Käosaar, Leena. "Imagining a Hospitable Community in the Deportation and Emigration Narratives of Baltic Women." In *Women's Life-Writing and Imagined Communities*, ed. Cynthia Huff, 59–78. London: Routledge, 2005.

Kurvet-Käosaar, Leena. "'Other Things Happened to Women': World War II, Violence and Discourses of National Identity in *A Sound of the Past* by Käbi Laretei and *A Woman in Amber* by Agate Nesaule." *Journal of Baltic Studies* 34, no. 3 (2003): 313–31. http://dx.doi.org/10.1080/01629770300000111.

Kurvet-Käosaar, Leena. "Vulnerable Scriptings: Approaching Hurtfulness of the Repressions of the Stalinist Regime in the Life-Writings of Baltic Women." *In Gender and Trauma: Interdisciplinary Dialogues*, ed. Fatima Festić, 89-114. Newcastle upon Tyne: Cambridge Scholars Publishing, 2012.

Laanes, Eneken. "Mäletamise lühis: Ene Mihkelsoni *Ahasveeruse uni*." *Keel ja kirjandus* 6 (2006): 433–48.

Lazda, Mara. "Women, Nation, and Survival: Latvian Women in Siberia 1941–1957." *Journal of Baltic Studies* 36, no. 1 (2005): 1–12. http://dx.doi.org/10.1080/01629770400000211.

Leydesdorff, Selma, Graham Dawson, Natasha Burchhardt, and T.G. Ashplant. "Introduction: Trauma and Life Stories." In *Trauma: Life Stories of*

Survivors, ed. Kim Lacy Rogers, Selma Leydesdorff, and Graham Dawson, 1–26. New Brunswick, NJ: Transaction Publishers, 2004.

Liljeström, Marianne. *Useful Selves: Russian Women's Autobiographical Texts from the Postwar Period*. Helsinki: Kikimora Publications, 2004.

Long, Judy. *Telling Women's Lives: Subject/Narrator/Reader/Text*. New York: New York University Press, 1999.

Memories Denied. Dir. Imbi Paju. Tallinn: Allfilm, 2005.

Nesaule, Agate. *A Woman in Amber: Healing the Trauma of War and Exile*. New York: Penguin, 1995.

Paju, Imbi. *Tõrjutud mälestused*. Tallinn: Eesti Entsüklopeediakirjastus, 2007.

Poom, Aino. "Ühe lihtsa eesti naise lugu." In *Me tulime tagasi*, ed. Rutt Hinrikus, 9–31. Tartu: Eesti Kirjandusmuuseum, 1999.

Rahi-Tamm, Aigi. "Küüditamised Eestis." *Eestlaste küüditamine: Mineviku varjud tänases päevas*. Tartu: Korp! Filiae Patriae, 2004. 15–57.

Rein, Eva. "Trauma, keha, mälu ja narratiiv Ene Mihkelsoni romaanis *Ahasveeruse uni*." In *Päevad on laused: Ene Mihkelson*, ed. Arne Merilai, 55–75. Tartu: Tartu Ülikooli Kirjastus, 2005.

Roots, Aino. "Life-Story." *Eestlaste küüditamine: Mineviku varjud tänases päevas*. Tartu: Korp! Filiae Patriae, 2004. 215–36.

Sink, Palmi. "Kannatuste rada." In *Me tulime tagasi*, ed. Rutt Hinrikus, 32–71. Tartu: Eesti Kirjandusmuuseum, 1999.

Skultans, Vieda. *The Testimony of Lives: Narrative and Memory in Post-Soviet Latvia*. New York: Routledge, 1997.

Vickroy, Laurie. *Trauma and Survival in Contemporary Fiction*. Charlottesville: University of Virginia Press, 2002.

8 Trauma Narratives and National Identity

ANNIE COTTIER

Leena Kurvet-Käosaar's essay on the deportation narratives of Baltic women centres on the question of how trauma is or is not expressed in these narratives, and on how they relate to Baltic national consolidations after the end of the Cold War. The deportation narratives have several functions: they bear witness to the repressions of the Soviet regime, they rehabilitate and commemorate the victims, and they initiate processes of revisioning history and of consolidating the Baltic peoples along the lines of national identity. Focusing on the narrative structure and imagery of the stories, she argues that "occasional fluctuations on the level of narrative control and coherence or emotional register emerge that can be interpreted as trauma signals." However, the hurtfulness of traumatic experience is not readily apparent at first glance; the narratives tend to emphasize survival rather than suffering. Although deportation narratives do not bypass difficult experiences, they do reveal a "gap between the harsh and excruciating nature of the experience on the one hand and its impact on the mental frame of mind and outlook of the deportee on the other."

In my response to Kurvet-Käosaar's essay, I focus on her conceptual framework, her analysis of trauma in specific narratives, and her claims concerning the narratives' significance in a national context. I test her claims by bringing them to bear on a different set of stories: the oral narratives by survivors of the 1974 partition of India and Pakistan. Clearly, there are significant differences between the transcribed oral Partition narratives and the written Estonian narratives. Most obviously, oral and written narratives differ fundamentally in the way they are elicited and produced. But the differences between the two sets of narratives are also cultural and historical in nature. Since the end of the 1980s, Estonians who had lived through the deportation to Siberia were encouraged to write down their personal histories by a national call for life writings. In the case of the Indian Partition narratives, Urvashi Butalia's interest in the "'underside' of this history – the feelings, the emotions, the pain and anguish, the trauma, the sense of loss, the silences in which it lay shrouded" (275) triggered her research into and transcription of stories that were told by others.[1] Most importantly, the two sets of texts differ because the motivations of the narrators are different. Kurvet-Käosaar notes that many of the deportation narratives "do not lend themselves to readings as stories of trauma" because "the traumatic quality of these experiences is rarely highlighted in the narratives; their emphasis is much rather on personal and collective survival." Of course, this makes it difficult to analyse traces of trauma in these texts. Of the deportation narratives she studies, Kurvet-Käosaar finds that Aino Roots's story "comes closest to representing the deportation experience as traumatic" because Roots's narrative "does not only suggest that there were traumatic experiences from which she has never recovered, but she also comments on a lifetime of emotional isolation that set limits to her ability to recount her story at the end of her life."

Yet when one takes a look at the trauma signals Kurvet-Käosaar identifies in Roots's and others' oral narratives ("loss of emotional control, emotional detachment or numbness, repetitive reporting, losing oneself in the traumatic events, and intrusive imagery"), one notices that they are fairly similar to those she and other scholars attribute to written trauma narratives: "loss of agency; the failure of the authors to be in control of their narrative; and various difficulties in communicating the experience that include silence, simultaneous knowledge and denial, dissociation, resistance, and repression." Both oral and written trauma narratives exhibit losses of narrative control and specific emotional registers. Moreover, while the motivations of the Estonian writers and the Indian speakers differ, many of the informants express a desire to speak about what happened. In Butalia's words, "While many still found it painful to speak about that time of their lives, there were others who *wanted* their stories to be recorded, they felt that for them the time had come to do so" (Butalia 276). Finally and most importantly, both the Estonian and the Indian narratives consciously seek to inscribe themselves in collective national memory. This is why a comparative "testing" of Kurvet-Käosaar's framework is of particular interest to me: both are accounts by survivors of deeply traumatizing events of the past which continue to haunt a whole nation.

Histories of the Partition mainly focus on the political events that led up to it, and there are only few non-fictional texts on its traumatizing effects. As Butalia notes, the division of families, the endurance of friendships across borders, the coping with trauma, the experience of dislocation and other, sometimes less than glorious aspects of Partition find "little reflection in written history" (7). Sukeshi Kamra adds that "psychological distress, especially for survivors, during and after Partition remains ignored except in fictional, and to a lesser extent, non-fictional testimonials" (165). According to her, "there is indeed a dearth of non-fictional material, which attests to the presence of significant levels of stress in the lives of survivors" (181). Possibly, the disturbing events did not fit in with the national narrative of India as a secular nation that successfully integrates different ethnicities: "The history of violence has been treated in the historiography of modern India as *aberration* and as *absence*: aberration in the sense that violence is seen as something removed from the general run of history: a distorted form, an exceptional moment, not the 'real' history of India at all" (Pandey 27). Indeed, the history of communal violence, including Partition, is, again according to Pandey, given little attention and is written up as a "secondary story ... The history of India since the early nineteenth century has tended to become the 'biography of the nation-state'" (29). Counter-narratives, that is, narratives which undermine the official narratives of history, are apt to be forgotten or remain untold. For those reasons, Butalia's collection constitutes a landmark achievement.

It is not surprising, then, that, unlike in Estonia, there never was a national call for survival narratives in India. The historical context is distinctly different. The Baltic states had been occupied by the Soviet Union, and Baltic women were deported by the political enemy to the Siberian labour camps, which only few survived. In the case of Partition, people who had formerly been neighbours and lived in social communities started killing one another during the months after the declaration of independence and the division of the subcontinent.[2] Killings also occurred within families. This may be one reason why personal narratives of the Partition have not been a matter of public interest in India. Due to the nature of some of the killings (neighbour against neighbour; father against daughter), they would certainly not contribute to any kind of positive narrative of nation building and survival. Certainly, the silences in these Partition narratives do not support a national narrative of survival. Instead, they reveal stories of a forgotten history. Butalia states that "at least where Partition history was concerned, there was a contradiction in the history we had learnt, and the history people remembered" (277). These narratives, then, challenge rather than support the conventional understanding of Partition and its national narratives.

Today, Partition is known through "fiction, memoirs, testimonies, through memories, individual and collective" (Butalia 8). This statement resonates with Kurvet-Käosaar's concerns: Butalia writes that we can know Partition "not only in the texts and memories it has produced but *even through people's reluctance to remember it*" (9; emphasis mine). In Baltic deportation narratives, the textual realization of the "reluctance to remember" can be located in the gap that Kurvet-Käosaar identifies between the harshness of the deportation experience and the survivor's narration of these events. In Indian Partition narratives, we can witness a similar struggle with what *seems* to be absent because it remains unspoken.

In an essay on silence in South Asian women's Partition narratives, Jill Didur focuses on literary texts, arguing that "what [Urvashi Butalia, Veena Das, Ritu Menon, and Kamala Bhasin have] encountered in attempting to document and make sense of survivors' memories of this period is a silence about the actual details of the violence. A similar silence is found in literature that is purported to represent the events of partition and 'abducted' women's experience" (125–6).[3] As Kurvet-Käosaar argues, such silences can be understood as trauma signals. In both the Estonian and the Indian context, this raises questions concerning the relationship between trauma and text. As Butalia observes:

> Words would suddenly fail speech as memory encountered something too painful, often too frightening to allow it to enter speech. "How can I describe this," would come the anguished cry, "there are no words to do so." At such points, I chose not to push further, not to force the surfacing of memories into speech. Tellings begun would thus be left incomplete: I learnt to recognize this, the mixing of time past and time present, the incompleteness, often even contradictoriness, in the stories as part of the process of remembering, to oneself and to others. (18)

In what follows, I focus on the stories told by Basant Kaur, a member of the Sikh community, as examples of oral narratives of Partition which are concerned with killings within communities and families. According to Butalia, "no mention was made of family violence by anyone, neither by the families, nor by the State, nor by historians" (162).

In respect to family-related violence, one of the myths that persists in the established history of Partition was that communities and families had held together in a time of crisis. Generally, violence against women was understood as having been committed by men from "other" communities (153).

One instance of intra-familial violence is Basant Kaur's testimony of the murders of her daughter and other family members by her husband: "My husband, he killed his daughter, his niece, his sister, and a grand-son. He killed them with a kirpan. My jeth's son killed his mother, his wife, his daughter, and a grandson and granddaughter, all with a pistol. And then, my jeth, he doused himself with kerosene and jumped into a fire" (Butalia 158).[4]

In this instance, as well as in another, where she speaks of her daughter's death, she does not reveal any overt emotional reactions, despite the gruesome deaths of her relatives. On the contrary, she factually lists the way her relatives were killed, and which weapons were used. According to Kurvet-Käosaar, one of the trauma signals in oral narratives is emotional detachment or numbness. Arguably, this also applies to Basant Kaur's narrative. When she tells the story of how she and many other women jumped into a well to drown themselves, Basant Kaur does not foreground her emotions either:

> Many girls were killed. Then Mata Lajjwanti, she had a well near her house, in a sort of garden. Then all of us jumped into that, some hundred … eighty-four … girls and boys. All of us. Even boys, not only children, but grown-up boys. I also went in, I took my children, and then we jumped in – I had some jewellery on me, things in my ears, on my wrists, and I had fourteen rupees on me. I took all that and threw it into the well, and then I jumped in, but … it's like when you put roots in a tandoor, and if it is too full, the one near the top, they don't cook, they have to be taken out. So the well filled up, and we could not drown … the children survived. (Butalia 158)

Although her narrative hardly reveals emotions verbally, the fact that she remembers the events very vividly becomes obvious in her detailed account of the "fourteen rupees" she carries on her – a chilling detail. The imagery of this passage is striking: Basant Kaur's metaphoric comparison of the well with a tandoor does not provide comic relief; on the contrary, it strengthens the horrific image of the women down in the well. The final passage describes everyday details (jewellery, money) that can be understood as expressing a clinging to "normal" things in the face of massive violence.

Basant Kaur's account is indicative of unspoken or hidden trauma in its irregular and at times incoherent structure as well as its complete emotional detachment. Interestingly, Kaur refers to how she felt at the time, how frightened she was (159), but she does not mention her feelings about these events today. In the case of the deportation narratives, Kurvet-Käosaar's close reading reveals that the deported women "rarely present the experiences as self-shattering, impossible to come to terms with or hurtful to the extent that it had continuously disturbing and damaging effects on their present lives." Aino Roots's narrative is an exception in that it reveals that, for her, the deportation was indeed a traumatic one. Kurvet-Käosaar argues that this is so because "the whole narrative is shadowed by the dark trace of the author's loss, which is never explicitly narrated ... The reader does not learn about the author's disposition or even the scope of her memory pertaining to these tragic events either."

In conclusion, while Kurvet-Käosaar's conceptual framework can be adapted to discuss trauma in Indian testimonial narratives, significant differences emerge concerning the relation between individual and national narratives. In contrast to many of the Baltic deportation narratives, the Indian narratives do not convey any sense of consolidating national identity. As oral trauma narratives, they reveal aspects of Indian history that had previously not been considered in Indian history books, but have lingered in collective memory for decades.

NOTES

1 Butalia interviewed survivors of the partition and consequently transcribed the interviews. She writes that she has narrativized the interviews by removing the questions posed by the interviewers, and by letting the text run on as one continuous narrative, although no chronological alterations were made (11). She acknowledges the fact that "in transferring words to text, so much is lost: the particular inflection; the hesitation over certain thoughts and phrases, even certain feelings; the body language, which often tells a different story from the words; and indeed the conscious 'shaping' of the interview by the interviewer who is usually in a situation of power vis-à-vis the person being interviewed" (12). Butalia

put down emotional responses in writing, such as "weeping" at certain instances, and pauses in speech are marked by three dots.

2 In the space of only a few months, about twelve million people moved between what is now India and East and West Pakistan. It is now accepted that about a million people died, although estimates vary from 200,000 to two million (Butalia 3).

3 Didur refers to Veena Das's *Critical Events*, Urvashi Butalia's *The Other Side of Silence*, and Ritu Menon and Kamala Bhasin's *Borders and Boundaries*. These scholars have all attempted to "make sense of the silences that punctuate the testimonies of people who lived through these events. Each of these books has a particular interest in thinking through the implications of silences in testimonies by women who were subject to sectarian violence and experienced social alienation as a result of the discourse of contamination that came to inflect their identities. The exceptionally thought-provoking work by this group of researchers has been instrumental in bringing the treatment of so-called abducted women and the activities of the state-sanctioned Recovery Operation (1947–55) to the attention of scholars and the general public" (Didur 125). Didur's argument is that both in the case of (transcribed) survivors' memories and in fiction, "silence serves as a pedagogical purpose in reframing our attitude towards partition history" (126).

4 The kirpan is the holy dagger or sword of the Sikhs, one of the markers of the Sikh religion. Jeth is the husband's brother.

WORKS CITED

Butalia, Urvashi. *The Other Side of Silence: Voices from the Partition of India*. Durham: Duke University Press, 2000.

Didur, Jill. *Unsettling Partition: Literature, Gender, Memory*. Toronto: University of Toronto Press, 2006.

Kamra, Sukeshi. *BearingWitness: Partition, Independence, End of the Raj*. Calgary: University of Calgary Press, 2002.

Pandey, Gyanendra. "In Defense of the Fragment: Writing about Hindu-Muslim Riots in India Today." *Representations* (Berkeley, Calif.) 37, no. 1 (1992): 27–55. http://dx.doi.org/10.1525/rep.1992.37.1.99p00926.

PART THREE

Limit-cases: Exploring the Limits of Telling Pain

9 "Metaphors for the Scots Today": History and National Identity in Scottish Drama after 1945

STEFANIE PREUSS

In A.L. Kennedy's novel *Looking for the Possible Dance*, the narrator formulates "The Scottish Method (for the Perfection of Children)" of which the second clause reads: "The history, language and culture of Scotland do not exist. If they did, they would be of no importance and might as well not" (15). With this statement, the narrator ironically articulates the common apprehension of Scotland's cultural inferiority and marginalization. Contemporary Scottish writers, and dramatists in particular, have sought to disprove this statement by demonstrating that the history, language, and culture of Scotland actually do exist and that they play an important role in constituting cultural and national identity. Drama may not appear an obvious subject in an essay collection concerned with life writing. The present essay suggests, however, that while the novel and the (auto)biography may be appropriate media for narrating individual experiences and traumas, drama is a genre that is particularly suited to recording collective acts of remembering. Although I hesitate to use the term "collective life writing," the collective aspect of a theatre performance makes it a relevant medium of collective remembrance and shared group identities.

Robert Hubbard elaborates on the connection between drama and life writing, mentioning that "biography has frequently been appropriated as material for dramatic representation, in particular a form of history conceived as biography of the powerful" (285). His typology of biographical theatre includes biographical drama (which presents the lives of real-life historical personages), documentary drama, platform performance, literary drama (which depicts the lives of writers), performance art, and community-based theatre. The present essay will focus on examples of two of these forms, namely, documentary and biographical drama, to highlight how theatre is employed in Scotland to function as a means of recording the collective efforts of the nation to remember its history and shape its collective identity.

The title of this essay is adapted from a quotation by the Scottish dramatist Liz Lochhead, who once said that her play *Mary Queen of Scots Got Her Head Chopped Off* was actually "a metaphor for the Scots today" (quoted in Varty 162). This description also fits many other Scottish plays of the second half of the twentieth century, which depict the Scottish past in order to discuss national identity and make claims concerning the condition of Scotland today. These plays notably appeared after the Second World War, when the British Empire was coming to an end. Until the end of the war, the empire had constituted an important object of identification for the Scots and created an overarching British identity.[1] Michael Keating argues that "the Empire allowed Scots to acquire a British identity which was not specifically English and provided outlets for upwardly mobile elements of the population. Scots regarded themselves as one of the mother-nations of the empire and made a disproportionate contribution to the ranks of imperial administrators, soldiers, teachers, doctors and missionaries" (165). When the British Empire went into decline, the Scots lost this potential for identification as Scotland was transformed from a junior partner in the empire into a mere province of England. In Murray Pittock's words,

> After the decline of the "Britains over the seas," Scotland stood (and stands) increasingly alone in a shrinking sphere where the abstract, idealized qualities of Britishness are coming under pressure everywhere due both to the centripetal collapse of the global British ideal and a general Western increase in relativism. At the same time, British society ... became more monolithic, its dependence on key features of English class culture and the political establishment more apparent than ever. (9)

These developments, together with the economic crises and scepticisms concerning Scotland's future in the 1950s, prompted a rise in Scottish nationalism. This went hand in hand with a revival of Scottish literature, which addressed Scottish history and negotiated questions of national identity.

Although Scottish regiments fought in both world wars, and even though Scotland had disproportionately higher casualty rates, contemporary discourse hardly addresses those traumatic experiences. Instead, one strategy of coming to terms with the past is to "forget" Scotland's participation in the empire and to remember earlier history instead, in order to construct a Scottish identity in which the Scots themselves are victims of oppression and colonization. This corresponds to Aleida Assmann's observation that smaller nations tend to remember their tragic defeats rather than their triumphant victories ("Four Formats of Memory"). These defeats are then presented as cultural traumas from which the nation as a whole suffers. Although collective trauma threatens and disrupts social reality, it can also have enabling effects, as Arthur Neal has pointed out: "A national trauma is shared collectively and frequently has a cohesive effect as individuals gather in small and intimate groups to reflect on the tragedy and its consequences. Personal feelings of sadness, fear, and anger are confirmed as appropriate when similar emotions are expressed by others" (4). The cohesive quality of cultural trauma determines its ability to form collective identity, but also makes it susceptible to manipulation. Thus, in Scotland the Highland Clearances are the subject of many literary works and other cultural artefacts,[2] while Scotland's own colonizing efforts are largely excluded from cultural memory. Against historical evidence, Scotland is preferably depicted as a colonized nation.

The establishment of this dominant myth manipulates collective memory and demonstrates that memory and forgetting are inexorably intertwined. Paul Ricoeur has argued in *Memory, History, Forgetting* that "forgetting can be so closely tied to memory that it can be considered one of the conditions for it." In this respect, forgetting is not merely a dysfunction of memory; it is passively and actively cultivated to create "a genuine *ars oblivionis*" (426). Since there is not only destructive forgetting but also "the forgetting that preserves" (442), forgetting also makes memory possible. This observation holds true for individuals as well as collectives. Similarly, Ernest Renan has claimed: "Forgetting, I would even go so far as to say, historical error, is a crucial factor in the creation of a nation" (11). Since national communities require collective memory to coin a common national identity, they need to recount their national history. This account, however, like all narratives, is necessarily highly selective. Thus, as Ricoeur remarks, "the ideologizing of memory is made possible by the resources of variation offered by the work of narrative configuration" (448). It is in this vein that we have to understand selective and at times manipulated memory as a crucial component of the Scottish construction of national identity.

Benedict Anderson defines the nation as "an imagined political community ... It is *imagined* because the members of even the smallest nation will never know most of their fellow-members, meet them, or even hear of them, yet in the minds of each lives the image of their communion" (6). This definition is especially adequate for Scotland's case as it allows for the imagination of a nation without a state. As Stuart Hall elaborates, the nation is imagined through symbolic representations:

> National cultures are composed not only of cultural institutions, but of symbols and representations. A national culture is a *discourse* – a way of constructing meanings which influences and organizes both our actions and our conception of ourselves ... National cultures construct identities by producing meanings about "the nation" with which we can *identify;* these are contained in the stories which are told about it, memories which connect its present with its past, and images which are constructed of it. (292–3)

It becomes clear, then, that memories of a community's past are crucial for the formation of national identity. Anthony D. Smith accordingly defines national identity as "the continuous reproduction and reinterpretation of the pattern of values, symbols, memories, myths and traditions that compose the distinctive heritage of nations, and the identifications of individuals with that pattern and heritage and with its cultural elements" (18).

Writing about cultural memory, Jan Assmann adds that collective identity only exists to the extent that the group members avow it. Collective identity is thus a form of reflexive social belonging. Since any form of identity is a social construct, it is based on a reflexive partaking in a culture and on participation in a shared cultural memory (*Das kulturelle Gedächtnis* 132–4). Assmann argues that just as an individual can only develop and maintain a sense of personal identity by virtue of memory, so too a group can only reproduce its collective identity through memory. The major difference lies in the fact that collective memory lacks a neural basis. This lack is substituted by culture; by a complex of identity-securing knowledge, which is objectified in the shape of symbolic forms such as myths, songs, proverbs, holy texts, and pictures. Cultural memory circulates in those forms of remembrance that are originally a matter of feasts and ritual solemnizations (ibid. 89). Hence, "cultural memory" in Jan Assmann's sense can be defined as "the characteristic store of repeatedly used texts, images, and rituals in the cultivation of which each society and epoch stabilizes and imparts its self-image; a collectively shared knowledge of preferably (yet not exclusively) the past, on which a group bases its awareness of unity and character" ("Kollektives Gedächtnis" 15; translation from Grabes 129). Literature, then, constitutes an important medium of cultural memory that contributes significantly to the construction of collective identities. For Renate Lachmann, literary texts "construct an architecture of memory, into which they deposit mnemonic images based on the procedures of *ars memoriae*" (15). Thus, "literature supplies the memory for a culture and records such a memory. It is in itself an act of memory. Literature inscribes itself in a memory space made out of texts, and it sketches out a memory space into which earlier texts are gradually absorbed and transformed" (15). Texts that are assigned canonical status are of particular relevance for the constitution of cultural identity: as "cultural texts," they gain a binding character for a society as well as additional dimensions of meaning. These texts are selected for transmitting cultural, national, and religious identities as well as the norms and values of a society. Thus, they function as media for the self-portrayal of cultures.[3]

Regarding the question of how literary texts co-construct national identity, scholars mainly focus on narrative fiction. Anderson, for instance, argues that in the eighteenth and nineteenth centuries, beside the newspaper, it was the novel that created the basis for national consciousness and "provided the technical means for 're-presenting' the *kind* of imagined community that is the nation" (25). Most literary scholars likewise see the rise of modern nation-states in nineteenth-century Europe as closely linked to the rise of the novel in general and the historical novel in particular (Craig 9; Brennan 49). Cairns Craig, for instance, claims that "in the work of the historical novelists of the nineteenth century what was being created was a national imagination: an imagining of the nation as both the fundamental context of individual life and as the real subject of history" (9).[4] The significance of the novel for the imagination of the nation lies in the fact that even if it is read privately, every reader is aware that there are thousands of others who perform the same task, even if they do not know one another.

In Scotland, the case is somewhat different. As Scotland developed its own national identity so late, theatre after 1945 played a role at least as important as the novel in creating metaphors for the nation as well as constituting and negotiating collective identity. In contrast to the novel, theatre not only creates an "imagined community" of its audience; it creates a very factual one. As Stephen Greenblatt argues, "The theater manifestly addresses its audience as a collectivity. The model is not, as with the nineteenth-century novel, the individual reader who withdraws from the public world of affairs to the privacy of the hearth but the crowd that gathers together in a public play space" (5). This collective aspect of theatre, notes Pfister, increases the intensity of the reception and "sparks off various socio-psychological group-dynamic processes in which the numerous individual reactions reinforce and harmonise with each other to produce a relatively homogenous group reaction" (38). Theatre thus has the effect of a group experiencing itself as a community that belongs together. In this respect, theatre is closely linked to ritual and can even be described, in Victor Turner's terms, as "one of the many inheritors of ... preindustrial ritual" (12). Through this connection to ritual, theatre functions as an important medium of cultural memory which, in its regular recurrence, provides the mediation and dissemination of identity-securing knowledge and thus the reproduction of cultural identity. Since rituals "dramatize the interplay of the symbolic with the corporeal" (J. Assmann, *Religion and Cultural Memory* 10), drama creates a "connective semantics" among the individual members of the audience. When theatre presents aspects from a nation's history, moreover, and includes the audience through encouraging their participation, the audience members become part of the national community and generate a collectively shared national identity.

Hence, it is no coincidence that after the decline of the British Empire, when Scotland needed to re-negotiate its own identity, drama emerged as a new literary genre. Unlike with other literary genres, there was no serious, professional dramatic tradition in Scotland until the middle of the twentieth century, and still in 1987, David Hutchison wrote that "drama in Scotland is an underdeveloped art form" ("Scottish Drama" 163). The few Scottish dramatists who did exist either wrote for the London stage or were confined to the music hall or pantomime. This changed in the second half of the twentieth century, for several reasons. First, Scottish Arts Council funding provided the means to open new theatres in which new plays could be performed. Second, the decline of Calvinism, which had been hostile to the theatre, opened new possibilities for plays and may also have enabled the emergence of the theatre as an alternative public space for the analysis of morality and conscience (Stevenson, "Home International"). Third, the rise in national sentiment coincided with a recollection of the Scottish vernacular, and theatre provided a venue where this language could be heard and spoken. As Randall Stevenson points out, "with most other media still dominated by standard English, this helped to make the theatre a unique public space at the time – one encouraging national interests to speak in their own voice, national identity to be particularly accented, and collective outlooks to coalesce" ("Border Warranty"). At the same time, the use of one's own language in the theatre produces a corporate feeling among the audience, which implies mutual attitudes, values, and emotions. Language thus becomes a unifying and integrating element that also serves to assert distinction from England. A fourth and final reason for the emergence of Scottish drama after the Second World War was the introduction of Bertolt Brecht's epic theatre into Great Britain in the mid-1950s. Epic theatre provided Scottish dramatists with a model of how to discuss history and today's politics and how to relate the past to the present. Modern Scottish history plays make extensive use of Brechtian alienation effects; they constantly break the fourth wall and involve the audience in the play in order to create a collective consciousness and critical responses to what is presented on stage. To achieve this aim, they often refer to forms of folk culture and popular traditions that are still known to the audience, such as the ceilidh, the music hall, or the pantomime (Folorunso). Thus, it is no coincidence that when modern Scottish history plays emerged, they often did so at the fringes of the Scottish theatre scene.

The mediation and dissemination of knowledge in the Scottish theatre is mainly done via the presentation of Scottish history on stage. Often, the plays written after 1945 address forgotten history, aspects of the Scottish past that had to be suppressed hitherto or were ignored in order to create a common British identity. This is, for instance, the case with the "Radical War" of 1820, in which Scottish workers went on strike in order to call for parliamentary reform. Those events have been dramatized in Hector MacMillan's play *The Rising* (1973) and James Kelman's *Hardie and Baird* (1990). In *Hardie and Baird*, the prologue complains that "neither the two men [i.e., Hardie and Baird, two of the leaders of the insurrection] nor the Scottish Insurrection in general are referred to officially, while within our educational system this part of history, like so many others connected with the Radical movement, remains almost entirely neglected" (109). By revealing and remembering those forgotten events – which came to an end with the suppression of the insurrection and the execution of Hardie, Baird, and James Wilson (another insurrectionary leader) – these plays establish a counter-history and are usable as a "vehicle for asserting the national culture, for marking it off from the English or the joint British one, by demonstrating the existence of a separate history" (Lenz 309). They become metaphors for the struggle for independence, freedom, and justice, and thus function as media of collective remembering and collective identity formation.

Another, even more painful historical memory that was suppressed for the creation of a unified British identity and that was only revived through literary presentation are the Highland Clearances of the eighteenth and nineteenth centuries. After the Jacobite Rising in 1745, great numbers of the Highland population were forcefully and often brutally removed from the land in order to make room for sheep. Together with the prohibition of the Gaelic language and of Highland cultural artefacts such as tartan dress, the forceful evictions eventually destroyed the traditional clan system and its supportive social structure. The Clearances virtually extinguished a culture and, since they inflicted a lasting damage to the social order, they are commonly perceived as constituting a source of cultural trauma.[5] These developments in Scottish history are examined in John McGrath's play *The Cheviot, the Stag and the Black, Black Oil*, which was first performed in 1973 by the socialist 7:84 Company Scotland.[6] The play analyses the exploitation of the Highlands, from the Clearances to the conversion of the Highlands into sporting estates where absentee landlords could go hunting, to the twentieth-century exploitation of Scotland by the oil industry. In his introduction to the play, McGrath explains his motives for dealing with this chapter of Scottish history:

> For years, the Highlands have, to most people, been shrouded in mist. Either the mist of romanticism – the land of solitary splendour, Gaelic twilight, and sturdy, independent, gently-spoken crofters. Or the mists of inevitable backwardness – a land that missed the boat, with no resources and a dwindling population, a land inhabited by lazy, shifty, dreamers who cannot be helped, in which nothing can alter. ("The Year of the Cheviot" vi–vii)

McGrath wanted to clear up that mist and tell a different version of the story by exposing the exploitation of the Highlands by capitalist forces. In order to lend credibility to that version, the play takes recourse to the tradition of the documentary play, incorporating extensive material from primary research such as extracts from biographies, personal letters, newspaper articles, and parish records. Writing about drama in the United States at the end of the twentieth century, Gary Fisher Dawson has argued that "documentary theatre, a dramatic representation of societal forces using a close re-examination of events, individuals, or situations, is just what our suffering society needs at century's end: a difficult theatre art that somehow releases a healing effect" (xii). These observations are also relevant for the Scottish context: they suggest that documentary plays have a similar capacity for collective self-therapy as narrative life writing has for individuals.

McGrath's play starts with the traditional song "These are my mountains." The audience is asked to join in to create a sense of shared Scottish identity. The same song, however, is repeated several times during the play and with each repetition it becomes more obvious that the idyllic Highlands described in the song are merely a myth. The song functions to show how the reality of the Highlands has been suppressed throughout history, and the declaration "these are my mountains" is ironically reversed as it is revealed that the Highlands do not belong to the people but to the ruling classes. This emerges very clearly when Queen Victoria sings her own words to the music:

These are our mountains
And this is our glen
The braes of your childhood
Are English again … (*The Cheviot* 37)

The fictional romanticizing of the Scottish Highlands is also debunked in the scene in which Lord Crask and Lady Phosphate sing a folkloristic song about Scotland:

LADY PH. How I wish that I could paint –
For the people are so quaint
I said so at our ceilidh
To dear Benjamin Disraeli …
LORD CRASK. We love to dress as Highland lads
In our tartans, kilts and plaids –
LADY PH. And to dance the shean trew-oo-oos
In our bonnie, ghillie, shoes –
BOTH. And the skirling of the pi-broch
As it echoes o'er the wee-loch

…

We are more Scottish than the Scotch. (*The Cheviot* 42–3)

This reworking of clichés of Scottish Highland culture reveals the common manipulation of Scottish cultural memory through romanticizing: by regarding the Highlanders as "quaint," picturesque, and charming, Lord Crask and Lady Phosphate demonstrate their condescending and disdainful attitude towards these people. Their claim that in their appropriation of Highland culture they are "more Scottish than the Scotch" ironically comments on popular representations of Scottish culture and their claims to authenticity. At the same time, this romantic eulogy on Scotland reveals the unscrupulous ambitions for power of the ruling classes, for the stage directions tell us:

> They become more serious. They turn their guns on the audience.
>
> LORD CRASK. But although we think you're quaint,
> Don't forget to pay your rent,
> And if you should want your land,
> We'll cut off your grasping hand.
> LADY PH. You had better learn your place,
> You're a low and servile race – ...
> BOTH. ... We'll show you we're the ruling class. (43)

Jäger has pointed out that by putting the folkloristic clichés of the Highlands in the mouths of those who only use the land as a hunting ground and are ready to defend their possessions at gunpoint, McGrath unmasks those clichés as a concealment of the people's oppression (127). As the characters aim their guns at the audience, the audience members become part of the play, which fosters an awareness that they are the people and that it is they who are asked to fight oppression. This involvement of the audience is maintained throughout the play, with many lines being spoken in direct address to the spectators. The audience is also asked to take on a variety of roles, such as a congregation during a sermon, a jury being addressed by a judge, or tenants being talked to by an army recruiter. All these Brechtian moves challenge the audience to relate the historical incidents to its own present situation and to today's means of oppression. Thus, theatre performances participate in the construction of a collective sense of identity.

The links between the past and the present are reinforced when, towards the end of the play, the characters ask, "Have we learnt anything from the Clearances?" (73). They go on to answer their own question:

> When the Cheviot came, only the landlords benefited.
> When the Stag came, only the upper-class sportsmen benefited.
> Now the Black Black Oil is coming. And must come. It could benefit everybody. But if it is developed in the capitalist way, only the multinational corporations and local speculators will benefit. (73)

It becomes obvious that McGrath uses the Highland Clearances and the exploitations of the past as metaphors for today's capitalist exploitation of Scotland. Other Scottish history plays do not present a hidden history of Scotland but offer new interpretations of received and hegemonic versions of the past. This is mainly done by deconstructing the traditional historical narratives and by revealing all historiography as being constructed by historians and shaped by ideologies. Thus, the plays challenge the established conventional images of Scotland. This is, for instance, the case in Liz Lochhead's biographical play *Mary Queen of Scots Got Her Head Chopped Off,* which was first performed in 1987. The play depicts the well-known story of the Scottish queen Mary Stuart and relates it to Scottish conditions today. It portrays Mary – who, of course, stands for Scotland as a whole – as a victim of sexual, religious, and political oppression. The play begins with a question La Corbie, the narrator and ironic commentator on the action, asks the audience: "Country: Scotland. Whit like is it?" (11). Right from the beginning, it becomes clear that the question of Scotland's national identity is an important aspect of the drama. La Corbie then goes on to answer her own question and describes Scotland in pairs of opposites that are symbolic forms by means of which Scotland is discursively imagined as a nation:

> It's a peatbog, it's a daurk forest.
> It's a cauldron o' lye, a saltpan or a coal mine.
> If you're gey lucky it's a bricht bere meadow or a park o' kye.
> Or mibbe … it's a field o' stanes.
> It's a tenement or a merchant's ha'.
> It's a hure hoose or a humble cot. Princes Street or Paddy's Merkit.
> It's a fistfu' o' fish or a pickle o' oatmeal.
> It's a queen's banquet o' roast meats and junkets.
> It depends. It depends … (11)

In this passage, the cultural memory of the Scottish nation is evidently not uniform but pluralist and contradictory. Each member of the nation participates in the construction of national identity, but each imagines Scotland in a different way. Hence, La Corbie invites the members of the audience to create their own images of the nation, only to present her own – which is explicitly marked as subjective: "Ah dinna ken whit like *your* Scotland is. Here's mines" (11). La Corbie mentions the thistle as Scotland's national flower, nostalgia as the national pastime, and the proverbially bad weather, thus calling to mind well-known clichés and images of Scotland.[7] Because of their previous relativization, however, those clichés are identified as only one of many possible images of the Scottish nation – all of whom are equally fictitious. With the help of this insight, the audience is encouraged to question seemingly fixed notions and representations of the nation. No single true image exists.

Like most other Scottish history plays of the time, *Mary Queen of Scots* is mainly a comment on the playwright's own times. The play engages not only with Scotland's marginalization by England, but also with the ways in which women and religious and sexual minorities are oppressed and prevented from gaining access to power. These issues are not only dealt with from a historical perspective; the play insists on their present relevance. This is achieved by way of mediating narrators, anachronisms, overt allusions to the politics of the 1980s, and – in the final scene, which is set in the twentieth century – via explicit presentations of these issues as problems of today. The historical events around Mary Stuart thus function as an allegory of present-day Scotland. Intolerance, oppression of the weaker, misogyny, and religious sectarianism are presented not as a natural state of things, but as conditions that have a history. This is also stressed by Lochhead when she points out that *Mary Queen of Scots* "is really about Scotland, more about the present than the past, how those myths of the past have carried on into the present malaise of Scotland today. [Mary] was around when a lot of the things that rule Scotland today were forming and hardening, you know, misogyny, Calvinism, all sorts of stuff like that" (quoted in Soncini 68).

One of the means by which Lochhead presents those topics as still prevalent is by establishing mediating communications systems within the drama. These are created non-verbally, through props and gestures, as well as verbally, by means of narrative voices and stage directions. These communications systems comment on and connect the historical events with the audience's present concerns. The stage directions, for instance, transcend the usual instructions concerning the performance and staging, which are to a large extent only accessible to readers of the play. This implies an authority that resembles the authorial narrator of some narrative texts. Thus, a sort of narrative voice is introduced that comments on and interprets the events presented on stage. The scene headings, which often constitute ironic assessments of the action, provide examples: headings such as "Rumplefyke" (act 2, scene 2) or "Jock Thamson's Bairns" (act 2, scene 7) identify that narrative voice as Scottish.

La Corbie supplies a narrative voice in more traditional terms. Standing outside the dramatic action, she provides narrative transitions from one scene to the next and also comments and reflects on the action presented on stage. At the same time, however, the internal dramatic action appears as if it had been produced by her, and it is kept going by the cracking of her whip and the snapping of her fingers. For instance, she lets the other characters appear like circus animals in the ring: "*Laughing,* LA CORBIE *cracks whip for* THE ENTRANCE OF THE ANIMALS. *In a strange circus our characters, gorgeous or pathetic, parade*: MARY, ELIZABETH, HEPBURN, DANCER/RICCIO, KNOX, DARNLEY *all dirty and down on his luck. They circle, snarling, smiling, posing. And halt*" (12). Thus, La Corbie mediates between the internal dramatic level and the audience as well as between the historical past and the audience's present. Despite the fact, however, that La Corbie directly observes the historical events presented on stage and occasionally interacts with the other characters, she time and again turns out to be very close to the audience's present. Accordingly, she tells the story of Mary and Elizabeth in the past tense and begins with the conventional initial formula of a fairy tale: "Once upon a time there were *twa queens* on the wan green island" (12). She also repeatedly demonstrates that she has knowledge superior to that of the other characters and that she is able to look into the other characters' futures, thereby demonstrating her time-transcending perspective. With her numerous ironic comments, La Corbie creates a distance between the audience and the events presented on stage and invites the play's spectators to view those events from today's perspective.

By way of numerous anachronistic props, gestures, references, and musical effects, Lochhead also creates non-verbal communications systems that present the historical events as topical. Paper airplanes, typewriters, Polaroid photos, and prams are inventions of later centuries and thus establish a relationship with the audience's present. They mediate between the fictive reality of the play and the real world of the audience. At the same time, their comic inadequacy reveals the fictionality of the play. The presentation of historical events as still relevant today is especially significant in the anachronistic allusions to the Protestant Orange Order, which was founded in 1795, more than two hundred years after Mary Stuart's death. The stage directions at the beginning of scene four of the first act portray John Knox extremely negatively as a member of this radical religious order: "KNOX, *in bowler hat and with umbrella, stands on back pedestal, marching. Two men, stamping, sway a big sheet like a blank banner behind him, swagger on the spot with exaggerated Orangemen's gait. Music and hoochs and ugly skirls.* KNOX *is ranting*" (19). Knox's religious intolerance is thus linked to the discrimination of Catholics and the denominational conflicts between Protestants and Catholics of Irish descent, which still continue today in the West of Scotland.

The most obvious references to the present appear in the last scene of the play, which bears the heading "Jock Thamson's Bairns" – "bairns" being the Scots word for "children." According to the *Concise Scots Dictionary*, the phrase "Jock Tamson's bairns" denotes "the human race, common humanity; a group of people united by a common sentiment, interest etc." This scene heading thus explicitly calls upon the recipients to transfer the action presented on stage to the whole of humanity. Of course, what is presented in that scene provides a rather bleak image of humanity as the characters of the play transform into twentieth-century children who still retain the same patterns of oppression as their historical precursors. The girl Marie, for instance, is excluded from the others' games because of her religion; she is molested because of her sex; and, finally, like Mary Stuart, she is symbolically beheaded. This scene indicates that the prejudices of the sixteenth century are retained today in succeeding generations and that the problems Mary Stuart was faced with in her own time are still prevalent today. The fact that this scene presents children instead of adults emphasizes that such modes of behaviour are unlikely to change in the near future and that foreigners, different-minded people, and women will continue to be victims of social oppression. The numerous references to the present in Lochhead's play confirm that it functions as "a metaphor for the Scots today": an extremely negative and seemingly pessimistic portrayal of Scotland and its future. At the same time, however, the play constantly demonstrates that the conditions presented are not unalterable; they have a history. As such, they are subject to change, perhaps for the better.

My analysis of selected Scottish history plays suggests that by negotiating forgotten aspects of national history and cultural traumas, Scottish drama after 1945 plays an important role in the construction of Scottish collective memory and national identity. It does this mainly by presenting either a hidden past or by providing reinterpretations of received tellings of history in order to show how official versions of history are shaped by ideologies and hegemonic discourses. These revisions of history are almost always openly political. They try to come to terms with the legacies of the past by relating the past to the present so as to show how Scotland remains haunted by the past as exploitation and oppression continue. Playwrights such as McGrath and Lochhead seek to make the audience participate actively in reimagining the nation. Thus, they address spectators as a collectivity, as members of a Scottish nation. In staging cultural traumas, they ask the audience not to forget painful memories but to remember them for the sake of changing present social conditions. Their aim is to change Scotland for the better, and they enlist drama in that service. Thus, even as they stage painful historical events, they contribute to a healing process whose ultimate goal is social change. In the final analysis, these plays end on a positive note. In 1977, David Hutchison complained that "few Scottish dramatists have shown the capacity to move from documentation to metaphor" (*The Modern Scottish Theatre* 149). For contemporary Scottish plays, the reverse is true: in their engagement with history and national identity, they become "metaphors for the Scots today."

NOTES

1 See Linda Colley for an informative tracing of the development of British national identity.

2 See, for instance, Iain Crichton Smith's *Consider the Lilies*, Neil M. Gunn's *Butcher's Broom*, and Fionn MacColla's *And the Cock Crew*.

3 See the introduction to this volume for further discussion of contemporary theories of memory.

4 Ironically, it is a Scot, of all people, who is regarded as the inventor of the historical novel. With his *Waverley* novels, Sir Walter Scott provided the model for other nineteenth-century writers to imagine the nation as a product of history and present history as the expression of national identity (Craig 117). In his novels, Scott promotes a British identity rather than a Scottish one and presents Scottish history as a progression from a barbarian past to a civilized future within an imperial Britain. According to Craig, Scott therefore "carries the burden of having invented a Scotland which displaced the real Scotland in favour of his romantic illusions" (117).

5 See Richards for an account of the Highland Clearances.
6 The 7:84 Company Scotland was founded by John McGrath himself. Its name refers to the unequal distribution of wealth: 7% of the population own 84% of the wealth.
7 For further discussion of the role of nostalgia in identity formation, see also Maarja Hollo's essay in this volume (chapter 19).

WORKS CITED

Anderson, Benedict. *Imagined Communities: Reflections on the Origin and Spread of Nationalism*. London: Verso, 1991.

Assmann, Aleida. "Four Formats of Memory: From Individual to Collective Constructions of the Past." In *Cultural Memory and Historical Consciousness in the German-Speaking World since 1500*, vol. 1, ed. Christian Emden and David Midgley, 19–37. Oxford: Peter Lang, 2004.

Assmann, Jan. *Das kulturelle Gedächtnis: Schrift, Erinnerung und politische Identität in frühen Hochkulturen*. München: Beck, 1992.

Assmann, Jan. "Kollektives Gedächtnis und kulturelle Identität." In *Kultur und Gedächtnis*, ed. Jan Assmann and Tonio Hölscher, 9–19. Frankfurt am Main: Suhrkamp, 1988.

Assmann, Jan. *Religion and Cultural Memory: Ten Studies*. Stanford: Stanford University Press, 2006.

Brennan, Timothy. "The National Longing for Form." In *Nation and Narration*, ed. Homi K. Bhabha, 44–70. London: Routledge, 1990.

Colley, Linda. *Britons: Forging the Nation 1707–1837*. New Haven, CT: Yale University Press, 1992.

Craig, Cairns. *The Modern Scottish Novel: Narrative and the National Imagination*. Edinburgh: Edinburgh University Press, 1999.

Folorunso, Femi. "Scottish Drama and the Popular Tradition." In *Scottish Theatre since the Seventies*, ed. Randall Stevenson and Gavin Wallace, 176–85. Edinburgh: Edinburgh University Press, 1996.

Dawson, Gary Fisher. *Documentary Theatre in the United States: An Historical Survey and Analysis of Its Content, Form, and Stagecraft*. Westport, CT: Greenwood Press, 1999.

Grabes, Herbert. "Constructing a Usable Literary Past: Literary History and Cultural Memory." In *Literary History/Cultural History: Force-Fields and Tensions*, ed. Herbert Grabes, 129–43. Tübingen: Narr, 2001.

Greenblatt, Stephen. *Shakespearean Negotiations: The Circulation of Social Energy in Renaissance England*. Oxford: Clarendon, 1992.

Gunn, Neil M. *Butcher's Broom*. Edinburgh: Porpoise, 1934.
Hall, Stuart. "The Question of Cultural Identity." In *Modernity and Its Futures*, ed. David Held Hall and Tony McGrew, 273–316. Cambridge: Polity, 1993.
Hubbard, Robert. "Drama and Life Writing." In *Encyclopedia of Life Writing: Autobiographical and Biographical Forms*, ed. Margaretta Jolly, vol. 1: A–K, 285–8. London: Fitzroy Dearborn, 2001.
Hutchison, David. *The Modern Scottish Theatre*. Glasgow: Molendinar, 1977.
Hutchison, David. "Scottish Drama 1900–1950." In *Twentieth Century*, ed. Cairns Craig, 163–77. Aberdeen: Aberdeen University Press, 1987. Vol. 4 of *The History of Scottish Literature*. 4 vols. Gen. ed. Cairns Craig.
Jäger, Andreas. *John McGrath und die 7:84 Company Scotland: Politik, Popularität und Regionalismus im Theater der siebziger Jahre in Schottland*. Amsterdam: Grüner, 1986.
"Jock." In *The Concise Scots Dictionary*, ed. Mairi Robinson. Aberdeen: Aberdeen University Press, 1985.
Keating, Michael. *Nations against the State: The New Politics of Nationalism in Quebec, Catalonia and Scotland*. Houndmills: Macmillan, 1996.
Kelman, James. *Hardie and Baird & Other Plays*. London: Secker and Warburg, 1991.
Kennedy, Alison L. *Looking for the Possible Dance*. London: Minerva, 1998.
Lachmann, Renate. *Memory and Literature: Intertextuality in Russian Modernism*. Minneapolis: University of Minnesota Press, 1997.
Lenz, Katja. "Modern Scottish Drama: Snakes in Iceland – Drama in Scotland?" *Zeitschrift für Anglistik und Amerikanistik* 44 (1996): 301–16.
Lochhead, Liz. *Mary Queen of Scots Got Her Head Chopped Off and Dracula*. Harmondsworth: Penguin, 1989.
MacColla, Fionn. *And the Cock Crew*. Glasgow: MacLellan, 1945.
MacMillan, Hector. "The Rising." In *A Decade's Drama: Six Scottish Plays*, 193–251. Todmorden: Woodhouse, 1980.
McGrath, John. *The Cheviot, the Stag and the Black, Black Oil*. London: Methuen, 1981.
McGrath, John. "The Year of the Cheviot." In *The Cheviot, the Stag and the Black, Black Oil.*, v–xxix. London: Methuen, 1981.
Neal, Arthur G. *National Trauma and Collective Memory: Major Events in the American Century*. Armonk: Sharpe, 1998.
Pfister, Manfred. *The Theory and Analysis of Drama*. Cambridge: Cambridge University Press, 1991.
Pittock, Murray. *Scottish Nationality*. Houndmills: Palgrave, 2001.
Renan, Ernest. "What Is a Nation?" In *Nation and Narration*, ed. Homi K. Bhabha, 8–22. London: Routledge, 1990.

Richards, Eric. *A History of the Highland Clearances*. 2 vols. London: Croom Helm, 1982–5.

Ricoeur, Paul. *Memory, History, Forgetting*. Chicago: University of Chicago Press, 2004.

Smith, Anthony D. *Nationalism: Theory, Ideology, History*. Cambridge: Polity, 2001.

Smith, Iain Crichton. *Consider the Lilies*. London: Gollancz, 1968.

Soncini, Sara. "Liz Lochhead's Revisionist Mythmaking." In *A Theatre That Matters: Twentieth-Century Scottish Drama and Theatre*, ed. Valentina Poggi and Margaret Rose, 57–72. Milan: Unicopli, 2000.

Stevenson, Randall. "Border Warranty: John McGrath and Scotland." *International Journal of Scottish Theatre* 3, no. 2 (2002). http://www.arts.gla.ac.uk/ScotLit/ASLS/ijost/Volume3_no2/1_stevenson_r.htm.

Stevenson, Randall. "Home International: The Compass of Scottish Theatre Criticism." *International Journal of Scottish Theatre* 2, no. 2 (2001). http://www.arts.gla.ac.uk/ScotLit/ASLS/ijost/Volume2_no2/3_stevenson_r.htm.

Turner, Victor. "Are There Universals of Performance in Myth, Ritual, and Drama?" In *By Means of Performance: Intercultural Studies of Theatre and Ritual*, ed. Richard Schechner and Willa Appel, 8–19. Cambridge: Cambridge University Press, 1990.

Varty, Anne. "Scripts and Performances." In *Liz Lochhead's Voices*, ed. Robert Crawford and Anne Varty, 148–69. Edinburgh: Edinburgh University Press, 1993.

10 Aspects of Post-Imperial Constructions of Nationhood

EVA REIN

Stefanie Preuss's essay is concerned with the importance of drama for the Scots' reconstruction of national identity once their previous identification with Britishness had entered a crisis with the fall of the British Empire. In her reflections on the relationships between memory, national identity, and culture and her discussion of the role of literature in the development of national consciousness, Preuss makes an important and convincing claim: while most critics consider the novel as instrumental in the rise of nationalism, drama can play an equally significant role. Preuss shows how, in the specific historical, cultural, and political situation of Scotland created by the decline of the British Empire, it was the rise of drama that was inextricably linked with the rise of Scottish nationalism, and it was primarily the theatre that became an important venue for the creation of a collective consciousness. What enabled drama to gain such prominence was its focus on history combined with the specific power of the theatre performance to create a space for the Scottish audience to collectively experience the issues addressed and negotiate a new understanding of their national identity.

Preuss's essay triggered recollections of another rise of nationalism – the Estonian one in the late 1980s – at the decline of another empire – the Soviet Union and its satellite countries. Although Estonia restored its independence only in August 1991, Estonia's decolonization can be said to have begun with Mikhail Gorbachev's policies of *perestroika* (restructuring) and *glasnost* (openness), which were initiated in 1985 and allowed for criticism of the Soviet order at all levels of Soviet society. The years 1987 and 1988 saw an unprecedented public debate on the devastating effects of Soviet economic and cultural policies on Estonia. This debate took place in the media and especially at numerous rallies, where it was often accompanied by communal singing that acquired such proportions and momentum in those years that Estonia's struggle for independence came to be known as the "Singing Revolution." Estonian post-imperial developments were inaugurated with the successful nationwide campaign against Moscow's plans of phosphate mining in northeastern Estonia in 1987. In November 1988, the Supreme Soviet of the Estonian Soviet Socialist Republic adopted the Declaration of Sovereignty by a 90 per cent majority, a crucial event in Estonian history which has been called the starter's shot for the disintegration of the Soviet Union (Made 201).

While the conditions of the rise and fall of the Soviet empire differ from those of the British Empire, there are some remarkable commonalities between the renegotiations of post-imperial national identity in Scotland and Estonia. One of the two most thought-provoking arguments of Preuss's essay concerns her reflections on the Scottish return to a forgotten traumatic past. Preuss shows how, after the decline of the British Empire, Scots in search of foundations for a new national identity neglected their generally advantageous involvement in the British Empire and turned to their forgotten history – the Scottish workers' insurgence of 1820 and the Highland Clearances of the eighteenth and nineteenth centuries – that is, the events that had to be silenced in order to align Scottish with British identity. In these events, the Scots found themselves in the position of the oppressed. Preuss outlines how this return to the past manifests itself most powerfully in Scottish theatre since 1945.

A comparable return to the past was staged in Estonia on the eve of the collapse of the Soviet empire. In the late 1980s, Estonians began to reclaim the history of the independent Republic of Estonia (1918–40), which they had been made to forget under the ideological pressure of the Soviet occupation (1940–91), and unravel the Estonian history, which had been rewritten from the Soviet perspective. This concerns especially Soviet historiography's silencing and garbling of the alternating Soviet, German, and again Soviet occupations of Estonia, including two Soviet mass deportations of large parts of the Estonian population in 1941 and 1949 – an issue whose devastating consequences for individual and national identity are masterfully rendered in Ene Mihkelson's *Ahasveeruse uni* (2001).[1]

It is characteristic of both Scotland and Estonia that what becomes foregrounded in this forgotten and silenced past, as well as in the construction of a post-imperial national identity, are the traumatic events related to oppression and colonization. This raises a series of intriguing questions: why do some nations turn to their traumatic pasts to reconstruct and reassert their identities? What does this reveal about the ways in which nations construct their grand narratives? And what does it tell us about the foundations of national identities? Preuss explains the Scots' focus on selected traumatic aspects via what Aleida Assmann has identified as an inclination of smaller nations to be more concerned with their defeats rather than their victories ("Four Formats of Memory"). While examples which corroborate this claim abound – and Estonia certainly is a case in point – I believe that whether a nation emphasizes tragic or triumphant aspects of its past depends much more on its relations to (an)other nation(s). Moreover, even if smaller nations tend to be subjugated by larger ones, I would suggest that whether nations veer towards one pole or the other has much more to do with the (post-)colonial (power) relations they are or were entangled in. Preuss does make a move towards such a contextualizing inquiry when she shows in her nuanced and insightful reading that a preference to remember Scottish history in a certain way – as a history of the colonized – glossed over the previous Scottish alignment with the empire. Yet after the fall of the empire, this appeared to be a necessary step in renegotiating Scottish identity. As a result, the Scottish began to cast the historically distant defeat of Scotland – the Highland Clearances – as a cultural trauma that became instrumental in the development of a collective identity. While attributing post-colonial status to Scotland without further explanation is controversial, Preuss's discussion of Scottish drama as a literary genre and her analyses of stage performances of representative plays still allows her to claim Scotland's post-coloniality in terms of Linda Hutcheon's observation that "where many nations' identities have been grounded in remembered moments of heroism and glory, a postcolonial nation would be defined (at least, once again, in literary historical terms) by its relation to the lived and recollected trauma of empire and by its reactions to that" (20). Hutcheon's argument is highly pertinent to the post-imperial construction of Scottish and Estonian nationhood. This is so because in both countries it is exactly an engagement with the trauma of empire that binds individuals together and helps forge a new national identity in changing circumstances. While, as Preuss cautions us, the idea of collective trauma is problematic and dangerous, an awareness of sacrifices and sufferings in the past can play an important role in the formation of a nation's sense of self (Renan 19).

The second aspect of Preuss's essay which I found especially insightful and inspiring is her exploration of the instrumental role of forms of cultural performance in the rise of nationalism. The greatest merit of Preuss's contribution lies in her expansion of the repertoire of cultural forms traditionally related to the rise of nationalism: she includes drama in that category and theorizes how plays perform such community-building functions. Thus, her discussion of Scottish theatre creates a framework for addressing and conceptualizing further cultural forms, for example, communal singing at Estonian rallies before the disintegration of the Soviet Union, which has not received due scholarly recognition despite its crucial impact. While theatre did play a remarkable role in Estonia in giving people back their personal and national past and creating a national identity – most notably the tremendous "theatre of memory" of Merle Karusoo, whose numerous theatre projects were based on the life stories of people who had been silenced by the Soviet regime – I argue that the most significant form of cultural performance in the Estonian construction of national identity was communal singing at rallies.

In stating that it is the theatre's affinity to ritual that allowed it to become a significant medium of cultural identity, Preuss makes a point of particular significance for my comparative analysis of Scottish theatre and Estonian communal singing. Preuss's reference to Jan Assmann's conceptualizing of ritual and Anthony D. Smith's definition of national identity is especially useful in this context. As rituals "dramatize the interplay of the symbolic and the corporeal" (J. Assmann 10), the ritual element, which is very much present in both theatre and communal singing, creates a sense of community and provides the collectivity with a shared meaning system by "the continuous reproduction and reinterpretation of the pattern of values, symbols, memories, myths and traditions that compose the distinctive heritage of nations" (Smith 18). In addition, Preuss's analysis of one of the plays dwells on the effect of the theatre event being amplified by involving the audience in communal singing of one traditional and one folkloristic song. While the singing events during the theatrical performance are primarily examples of the Brechtian alienation effect that allow the audience to confront a myth and a cultural cliché, they also serve to create a collective consciousness, which likens them to the communal singing at rallies in Estonia in the late 1980s.

The three largest and most important instances of communal singing took place on the Tallinn Song Festival Grounds in 1988. In early June, during the Old Town Days of Tallinn, a series of communal singing events, known as Night Song Festivals, were spontaneously held every evening, culminating in about 100,000 participants on 10 and 11 June. People flying the Estonian national flags at the events forced the Soviet Estonian authorities to declare the tricolour as the Estonian national colours on 23 June. When Valk called this sequence of song festivals "the Singing Revolution"(Vogt 26) a few days later, the peaceful struggle for the restoration of independence had begun. On 17 June the Estonian Popular Front organized a rally so that people could meet the delegates going to Moscow to attend the Nineteenth Congress of the Communist Party of the Soviet Union. The speeches held were patriotic and supported *perestroika*. An audience of about 100,000 encouraged Estonian delegates to stand up for Estonia. The event acquired the characteristics of a rite as the people collectively sent Estonian delegates to Moscow by way of a ceremony which also included communal singing. In September, the rally "Eestimaa laul" [The Song of Estonia] took place, with alternating political speeches on the stage and communal singing by about 300,000 people. It was during this rally that Heinz Valk pronounced his famous dictum "Ükskord me võidame niikuinii" [Someday we will win anyway] – and he indeed gave the people a utopia, which came true three years later. The rally's ceremonial sense was further strengthened when the night had fallen and the lights had been lit, and the Song Festival Grounds resembled an open-air church with the tall trees forming walls on either side as the audience sang another new national song written by Tõnis Mägi, entitled "Palve" (Prayer) that asks the Creator to protect "Maarjamaa" (St Mary's Land [Terra Mariana]), a historical name for Estonia currently still used in poetic and religious contexts.

Explicitly political in character, these instances of communal singing at rallies had marked elements not only of ritual but also of performance. Their repetitive nature was particularly important, as each event of communal singing became an act of confirmation of Estonian national identity. Furthermore, one can claim that while in Scotland it was theatre that involved audiences in the process of reconnecting with the past, of questioning received notions of one's nation and culture, and of re-establishing a national identity, in Estonia these tasks were performed by communal singing at rallies, which took the proportions, form, content, and functions of the Estonian traditional song festival. The song festival tradition is a crucial context for understanding the implications of communal singing. The tradition began around 1869 and survived throughout the Soviet occupation against Soviet attempts to disrupt historical and cultural continuity in Estonia. Even if its repertoire included compulsory ideological songs under Soviet rule, the Estonian song festival can be seen delete as a *lieu de mémoire* in Pierre Nora's terms – a space where a sense of historical continuity endures – and whose "most fundamental purpose is to stop time, to block the work of forgetting" (19).

The paradox of the survival of the song festival tradition in Soviet Estonia can be explained in terms of a complex relationship of the colonizer and the colonized. In this respect, an anthropological explanation provided by Toomas Gross is especially relevant and illuminating. Gross conceptualizes Estonian song festivals in terms of "a reservoir of memory and a vehicle of collective identity" and "commemorative ceremony" (348). Expanding on Paul Connerton's discussion of how societies remember, Gross brings together Connerton's notion of "commemorative ceremonies" and the repetitive nature of Estonian song festivals to argue that "by repetition, collectiveness is periodically remade. Song festivals were repetitive reminders of the Estonian national awakening in the nineteenth century, distinct cultural and ethnic identity" (348). Gross then analyses the Estonian song festival tradition as a "ritual of intensification" whose function is to "restore social equilibrium by intensifying social interaction" (348). He suggests that the intensification has served both the Soviet authorities and the Estonian people in the sense that, for the former,

> it was a way of making concessions and letting people express their ethnic identity with minimum harm done to the ideological base and political structure. For the participants it was an intensification of the sense of ethnic unity and community by means of collective performance and audience ... For people, song festivals were the moments of "creative effervescence" which ... provided them with a symbolic representation not only of past and present categories, but of utopia. (348–9)

Gross also emphasizes the significance of the very act of singing: in his view, it is not so much the meaning(s) of the lyrics of the songs, but the "social and collective meaning that they acquired at the moment of execution" (349) that is significant. In other words, "it is the performance that can be viewed as an act during which a brief social, ideological and cultural balance is won." Gross aptly calls this sense of "simultaneity and univocality," which is created in communal singing, "a physical realisation of Anderson's 'imagined community'" (349).

Similarly to Gross, Preuss also claims in her discussion of Scottish theatre that "theatre not only creates an 'imagined community' of its audience; it creates a very factual one." Both communal singing and theatre establish a tangible collectivity by individuals assembling in a public space at certain intervals and actively participating in the action. What Preuss points out with reference to Manfred Pfister's and Victor Turner's theorizations of the collective nature of theatre is also true of communal singing: the group dynamics during the event are constitutive in negotiating collective identity (Pfister 38), and the event itself is a development of a pre-industrial ritual (Turner 12). It is the latter connection, Preuss importantly suggests, that makes theatre a significant medium of cultural memory which serves to regularly reproduce cultural identity.

To conclude, with respect to the formation of national identity, collective singing at rallies in late 1980s Estonia functioned on the same premises and in analogous ways to post-imperial Scottish theatre. First, in both cases, the traumas of the (colonial) past, which were conceived as affecting the whole nation, played a considerable role in uniting people and became an important source of collective identity in the re-imagination of the nation. Second, while the decline of two empires – the British and the Soviet – saw the emergence and flourishing of two different forms of cultural performance that arose from different historical, cultural, and political contexts – theatre in Scotland and communal singing at Estonian rallies – these forms not only shared an affinity to ritual that allowed them to become a significant medium of cultural identity in the respective countries, but also served the function of creating a collective consciousness and allowing people to re-imagine, reconstruct, and reassert their national selfhood.

NOTE

1 On *Ahasveeruse uni*, see Aija Sakova's and my own essays in this volume (chapters 13 and 15)

WORKS CITED

Assmann, Aleida. "Four Formats of Memory: From Individual to Collective Constructions of the Past." In *Cultural Memory and Historical Consciousness in the German-Speaking World since 1500*, vol. 1, ed. Christian Emden and David Midgley, 19–37. Oxford: Peter Lang, 2004.

Assmann, Jan. *Religion and Cultural Memory: Ten Studies*. Stanford: Stanford University Press, 2006.

Gross, Toomas. "Anthropology of Collective Memory: Estonian National Awakening Revisited." *Trames* 6, no. 4 (2002): 342–54.

Hutcheon, Linda. "Postcolonial Witnessing." *Neohelicon* 30, no. 1 (2003): 13–30. http://dx.doi.org/10.1023/A:1024150021119.

Made, Tiit. *Ükskord niikuinii* [Someday Anyway]. Tallinn: Argo, 2006.

Mihkelson, Ene. *Ahasveeruse uni.* [The Sleep of Ahasuerus]. Tallinn: Tuum, 2001.

Nora, Pierre. "Between Memory and History: Les Lieux de Mémoire." *Representations* 26, no. 1 (1989): 7–24. http://dx.doi.org/10.1525/rep.1989.26.1.99p0274v.

Pfister, Manfred. *The Theory and Analysis of Drama*. Cambridge: Cambridge University Press, 1991.

Renan, Ernest. "What Is a Nation?" Trans. Martin Thom. In *Nation and Narration*, ed. Homi K. Bhabha, 8–22. New York: Routledge, 1990.

Smith, Anthony D. *Nationalism: Theory, Ideology, History*. Cambridge: Polity, 2001.

Turner, Victor. "Are There Universals of Performance in Myth, Ritual, and Drama?" In *By Means of Performance: Intercultural Studies of Theatre and Ritual*, ed. Richard Schechner and Willa Appel, 8–19. Cambridge: Cambridge University Press, 1990.

Vogt, Henri. *Between Utopia and Disillusionment: A Narrative of the Political Transformation in Eastern Europe*. New York: Berghahn, 2005.

11 Anecdotalization of Memory in Jaan Kross's *Paigallend*

ENEKEN LAANES

In his memoirs *Kallid kaasteelised* (2003, Dear Co-Travellers), Estonian writer Jaan Kross tells the story of a woman who, while sitting in a shelter during a Soviet raid on the Estonian capital Tallinn in spring 1944, "told ... about her life in Germany during the past year and a half, and these were mostly stories of the nights spent in the shelters, anecdotes seen in a talented way" (112).[1] In Estonian, the anecdote is first and foremost a piece of folklore, an entertaining story about third persons that has been heard and is meant to be passed on by oral narration on various social occasions. But in this statement, as in many other passages in his memoirs, novels, and short stories, Kross uses the term to refer to an oral or written narrative form that can be used by a person to represent his or her own experiences and memories. The phrase "anecdotes seen in a talented way" suggests that the anecdote is a way of seeing and narrating that gives the narrated story a special perspective.

Focusing on his autobiographical novel *Paigallend* (1998, Treading Air [2003]), I explore the function of the anecdote in Jaan Kross's poetics of remembering. As in the passage quoted above, "anecdote" in *Paigallend* refers to the process of narrativizing personal memories. As such, it performs several functions. It is generally believed that to write in an anecdotal way means to mediate "between rawer, unformulated experience and more general or formulated truths ... by turning such truths into narrative and character" (Dentith 105). Thus, anecdotes are stories of typicality and general truths. At first sight, this seems to make them unsuitable for representing painful or traumatic memories, which are personal and atypical. Yet in Kross's *Paigallend*, which explores the relationship between life writing and the anecdotalization of memory in fictional form, the anecdote serves important functions precisely in the representation of painful memories. What is achieved by remembering one's past in an anecdotal mode, and what functions does that mode have for the one who remembers? I argue that rather than turning personal memories into stories of typicality and general truths, the anecdotalization of memory is closely related to the formation of subjectivity in life writing.

Kross's work raises the question of life writing in yet another sense. There are a number of autobiographical episodes that Kross tells repeatedly in his many autobiographical novels as well as in his memoirs (which he wrote later, towards the end of his life). Depending on the genre, there are significant differences as to how these episodes are represented. Leigh Gilmore has drawn attention to the contemporary tendency to prefer fiction over autobiography proper to represent the self and tell stories of personal pain. For her, the reason for this diffidence about autobiography lies in the proscriptions it places on self-representation, in particular its legalistic definition of truth telling, which reduces opportunities for representing trauma (Gilmore 3). In Kross's case, his earlier preference for fiction needs to be explored. Analysing the significant differences in the use of the anecdote in his fiction and in his memoirs helps me determine the functions of the anecdote across different genres in Kross's overall life-writing project.

Having written historical novels about eminent figures in the remote Estonian past for two decades, Jaan Kross has turned to twentieth-century Estonian history since the early 1980s. In these texts, he looks at the Estonian past through the prism of his own autobiographical memory. All his later short stories and novels feature political history refracted through his personal memory. *Paigallend* is his third novel in a trilogy that deals with the fate of Kross's generation during and after the Second World War. The first two novels, *Wikmani poisid* (1988, Wikman's Boys) and *Mesmeri ring* (1995, Mesmer's Circle) are based on his memories as a schoolboy at the Westholm/Wikman Gymnasium in Tallinn during the last years of the Estonian Republic and his student years at the University of Tartu during the Second World War, respectively.

Paigallend is the fictional life story of Ullo Paerand, told by his friend and schoolmate Jaak Sirkel (Kross's alter ego). In lectures given at the University of Tartu in 1998, Kross said the following about *Paigallend*:

> When I chose him, that is, Ullo Paerand, to be my protagonist in *Paigallend*, it was – to a certain extent – because I wanted the reader to have an idea how many literary ideas – and not only literary ones – *any* creative ideas

> that Ullo's generation might have had – were crushed under the caterpillar belts of the two – German and Russian – occupations during WWII. As the novel of a generation, it reflects the attitude of Ullo Paerand's generation, which is almost the same as my own – of our generation – to these occupations. In one specific passage, the novel also deals with a case of strong resistance to these occupations. (*Omaeluloolisus ja alltekst* 43)

Kross here characterizes *Paigallend* as a generational novel, a narrative about his generation in the middle of political events that are perceived as collectively relevant. Accordingly, the first half of the novel describes Paerand's and Sirkel's childhood and schooldays at the Wikman Gymnasium. What we get here is a sketch of the formative milieu and the shared values of Kross's generation. The second part inserts Paerand into political history. Working as a civil servant at the state chancery, Paerand witnesses the events leading to Estonia's occupation by Soviet Russia in 1940. During the Nazi occupation from 1941 to 1944, he and Sirkel participate in the resistance movement and witness the failed attempt to restore an independent Estonian state in September 1944. Before the Soviet troops invade Estonia, Paerand attempts to flee the country together with tens of thousands of his countrymen and countrywomen and go to Sweden, but at the last moment he opts to stay home. In order to represent, in formal terms, the emptying out of Paerand's life, his remaining forty years are told in thirty pages of this 330-page novel. Fearing Stalinist repressions, Paerand chooses to spend the rest of his life working as a dyer in a suitcase factory. In 1987, he dies of heart failure in a mental hospital.

The most remarkable structural feature of *Paigallend* is its intricate system of framing and embedded narratives. The text of *Paigallend* is presented as a biographical novel by the author-narrator Sirkel, who is writing it in post-Soviet Estonia in the middle of the 1990s. His novel is based on the notes taken during Paerand's oral testimony, which were given to Sirkel before Paerand's death in 1987. Thus, Paerand's story as told by himself (or, rather, as paraphrased by Sirkel) is framed by two different narrative levels running through the whole text: the dialogic encounter between Paerand and Sirkel during their conversations, and Sirkel's rereading of and commenting on his notes as well as his writing of the novel. In addition, Sirkel includes in his novel Paerand's (literary) texts and frames them with his own interpretations. The complicated relations between the framing and embedded narratives and texts shift the process of remembering and narrating Paerand's story to the centre of the reader's interest. They also make visible the hidden agendas behind Sirkel's biographical undertaking and the ways he shapes Paerand's story.

In this context, the question of transference becomes relevant. Drawing on Freud, Dominick LaCapra defines transference as "implication in the problems one treats, implication that involves repetition, in one's own approach or discourse, of forces or movements active in those problems" (142). In *Paigallend*, the "implication" LaCapra writes about relates to generational belonging. Paerand and Sirkel belong to the same generation, but their fate has been rather different. Having survived the turmoil of the Second World War, and once he has opted for staying in Estonia, Paerand's life fades away and he dies a sorrowful death. Sirkel, however, was deported to Siberia for nine years and then returned to become a successful writer. His biographical undertaking grows out of his feeling sorry for Paerand and so many other members of his generation who were unable to realize their "creative ideas." In interviewing Paerand and in fictionalizing his life, Sirkel is led by transference as he attempts to redeem his friend's life retrospectively.

The temporal relations between the different narrative levels in *Paigallend* are of crucial importance. Paerand tells his story to Sirkel in Soviet Estonia, when remembering the complexities of the Second World War in Estonia and of the Stalinist terror was still a tricky business. He dies before concluding his testimony. While in hospital, he explains to Sirkel that the poison that accumulated in his body from working with hazardous chemicals in the suitcase factory is about to explode because of its reaction with a gas called futurium that started seeping out in 1987. He does not live to see the explosion, which is an explosion of memory: a radical reinterpretation of the history of the Second World War and Soviet Estonia that took place after the collapse of the Soviet Union as well as of the flow of personal memories from that period into the public domain. Sirkel, however, writes his novel about Paerand in the mid-1990s in independent, post-Soviet Estonia. The standard view in memory studies stresses the importance of the present moment for the process of remembering the past. In Sirkel's case, his temporal situatedness after the restoration of Estonia's independence casts a special light on Paerand's story. The events that occur after Paerand's story has ended – especially the collapse of Soviet Union – offer Sirkel an opportunity to rework Paerand's suffering. The main question with which Sirkel seems to be struggling in his biography can be phrased as follows: is Paerand's story – which is full of hopes as well as delusions, suffering, and a rather sorrowful death – redeemed by the restoration of Estonia's independence, which he did not live to witness? Or is it rather Sirkel himself who redeems Paeland's story in and through his biographical novel? The constitutive ambiguity of *Paigallend* – the open question about the meaning of Paerand's life – is reflected in the title metaphor of the novel, "flying in place."[2]

At first glance, the title of *Paigallend* seems to present us with an oxymoron. "Flying" means moving forward; "in place" implies remaining put. However, it is possible to fly and not to move forward. Birds tread in air when strong adverse winds blow. They flap their wings as quickly as they can, but make no progress. If they do not flap quickly enough, the winds may carry them along. The birds may not even understand that they do not move forward. They flap their wings desperately, and only an outside look reveals that they do not budge at all. But flying in one place is not a totally pointless activity. By working hard and spending their energy, the birds at least remain in the air and do not fall down. Seen in this light, flying in place is a kind of achievement. Whether one regards it as a worthy or a pointless activity depends on one's point of view. For some, the birds who, being caught in a gale, hold their ground and tread in air with all their might are heroic and noble. But this desperate struggle may also rouse pity and sympathy. Preventing oneself from falling down does not always make up for the trouble one has taken.

The reception of *Paigallend* in Estonia has more often than not opted for the former reading of both Paerand's life and the entire novel. Paerand, who lives through the tumultuous events of the twentieth century, resembles a bird in a storm. His life is controlled by outside forces, and he must find a way to cope with those forces. He decides to fly in place. Some critics argue that Kross presents this decision in a heroic light.[3] In the framework of such readings, *Paigallend* becomes what Aleida Assmann calls "religious testimony." In a religious testimony, the suffering and death of a religious martyr at the hands of a violent (political) power is rewritten into a death for a higher idea (God), and the passive victim of physical violence is reinterpreted as a symbolic victor (Assmann 87). For Assmann, religious testimony sends a positive message and as such can be used as a foundational story for the consolidation of religious communities. In secular forms, such testimonies of heroic death for a higher cause serve to construct national identities. Many critics have read Paerand's story as an allegory of Estonian political history: for them, the novel becomes a national testimony, and

Paerand's story represents a heroic suffering and death for the nation, to be redeemed by the liberation of the nation after his death.

By pointing out that "the decision to 'fly in place' did not only lead to the loss of a substantial number of tail feathers, but also to the cumulative numbing effect of a quiet despair maintained beneath the face of dignity, a psychological stance that, combined with the toxicity of hazardous workplace chemicals, resulted in psychiatric disturbances and heart failure" (293), Tiina Kirss draws attention to the unredeemable sadness of Paerand's story, which occasionally flashes up in Sirkel's representation of it. Taking my cue from her reading, and stressing the multiplication of narrative levels and voices in *Paigallend*, I claim that Sirkel's reworking of Paerand's "flying in place" as a form of resistance and martyrdom for the sake of the nation is only one of the ways in which Sirkel, troubled as he is by transference, is trying to emplot his story – and even that attempt meets with varying success.

Paerand himself uses another metaphor related to flying in place to describe his situation. In a recurrent dream, he is marched to execution in a procession of executioners and hangers-on. In that procession, he plays the flute "as diligently, as clearly, as fluently, as seriously" (48) as he possibly can, but strangely enough, he is unable to hear his own playing: "it seems that the others can hear me blow the flute, can hear what and how I'm playing it! But in some fateful way I can hear nothing of my own playing" (48). He admits that he is anguished by his "disappointment because of this strange brand of deafness" (48) even more than he is by his imminent execution. Paerand's deafness, his inability to hear his own playing, is related to the fact that he is placed in a specific historical moment. From that position, he is unable to see and judge what his role was at that moment, what function his actions and choices performed, and if, indeed, he acted and played at all. His anguish stems from his uncertainty about what part he played in this turmoil of history. Sirkel's biographical novel is an attempt to alleviate Paerand's anguish by writing him out of this uncertainty and into the unequivocal position of a national martyr. In that endeavour, the anecdotalization of memory serves Sirkel as a poetic device. However, due to the multiple narrative levels, the anecdotalization of memory reveals itself as serving an additional purpose: it restores agency and dignity to Paerand and to other members of his generation through the process of remembering.

In discussing the role of the anecdote in Kross's poetics of memory, we need to distinguish between three different understandings of the term: the anecdote is a form of social memory, a short literary form, and a historiographic device. The anecdote as a short, witty, or piquant story with a twist in the tale belongs to urban lore and is a form of social memory.[4] "Anecdote" in this sense is relevant to Kross's work because social memory is an important issue in *Paigallend*. Kross depicts the events in Estonia during the Second World War through the limited perspectives and knowledge of Paerand and Sirkel, as well as through the stories, rumours, and hearsay collected from their friends and acquaintances. These memories are often covered by Kross's own experience and that of Paerand's prototype, Kross's schoolmate.[5] The stories, rumours, and hearsay are part of social memory, which Kross shares with his readers. Thus, Kross in his novel appeals to a shared community of experience and memory.[6] In order to invoke that community of memory, *Paigallend* retells many anecdotes circulating in social memory, such as the anecdote of a member of an Estonian delegation who searched for a Moscow city map in vain in the late 1930s, only to find a map on his bedside cupboard upon returning to his hotel; or the anecdote of a picture featuring Hitler on one side and Stalin on the other, and which, when hung on the wall, was turned around when that became necessary during the Second World War occupations; or the anecdote in which the rector of Tartu University is mistaken for the porter of the same university and vice versa. Even those narrative units that have been transformed into anecdotes by Sirkel are often triggered by an episode, standpoint, or remark that circulated in generational social memory.

In the German tradition, the anecdote is a literary form, a short story characterized by its focus on a historical or archetypal person, event, human situation, or attitude, but not clearly distinguishable from other short literary forms (*Metzler* 14). Anecdotes are structured as tales that move towards a turning point. This point, which reveals a human trait or some hitherto concealed relationship in one incident, is often presented in the form of a punch line, word play, or paradox. These structural peculiarities of literary anecdotes are present in those stories in *Paigallend* that Sirkel himself calls "novellas" or "anecdotes." The novel's narrative is organized into relatively unified small stories that focus on a single person, event, or incident. Sometimes they are only indirectly linked to the main storyline and are there to delineate the social landscape (one example is the anecdote about Professor Leesment's memory). However, even some of the central episodes in the novel have been shaped as complete tales with an anecdotal point that do not have a comic or bizarre but a tragic or pathetic flavour, such as Paerand's attempt to flee to the West. In my exploration of the specific kind of narrativization of memory that I call anecdotalization, I will briefly analyse two episodes: Paerand's attempt to flee the country and Sirkel's conversation with a KGB major in a Soviet prison camp.

The episode of the attempted flight is a "novella" in its own right, steered towards its final point from the very beginning. After the failure of the attempt to restore Estonia's independence in September 1944, when German troops were retreating and departing from Estonia and the invasion of Soviet troops was imminent, Paerand and his wife Maret bicycle to the northwest coast in order to hire a seat in a boat but unexpectedly decide to turn around and stay in Estonia, driven by a proverbial saying that "even though thousands leave, a million must stay behind" (285).[7]

From Kross's memoirs *Kallid kaasteelised* (2003, Dear Co-Travellers), we learn that the episode of the Paerands' flight goes back to Kross's autobiographical reminiscences of his own flight. Moreover, in his memoirs, which were published after *Paigallend*, Kross retells his story with reference to the novel, that is, he replaces the retelling of some events with long quotations from the novel. In his reminiscences, Kross makes a reference to the punch line at the end of the flight story in *Paigallend*:

> Perhaps all did not go as decently as in the novel called *Paigallend*. The same goes for the statement "even though thousands leave, a million must stay behind." This was on the agenda. But I cannot say that it was foremost on the agenda ... I don't remember now who it was; who first hit the brakes. But I don't believe that the idea that "even though thousands leave, a million must stay behind" was in the foreground of our consciousness. Rather, there was no hope of finding a spot in the stern of a boat. (145)

With this explanation, Kross sheds light on the specificity of narrativization taking place in *Paigallend* and perhaps also on the ways memory works in general. He draws attention to the fact that in the whirlwind of the events, choices are neither made nor interpreted with the help of such slogan-like statements. However, people very often tend to remember them in such forms. The formula "even though thousands leave, a million must stay behind" can be found in the essayistic texts Kross published before *Paigallend*.[8] This means that it is not amplification Kross aims for in his literary text. This formula had long before *Paigallend* helped Kross to impart meaning to his own decision to remain in Estonia. In *Paigallend,* the formula renders meaningful not only the Paerands' choices but also those of other members of Kross's generation who remained home, as well as the lives of those who were born in Soviet Estonia. Maret's afterthought to Ullo's statement that "even though thousands leave, a million must stay behind" includes those who were not yet born. Maret says, "and when all those who are born here have to stay" (285). Ullo and Maret do not stay in Estonia for the sake of their compatriots who cannot flee the country, but for the sake of those who are destined to be born in this country. This is underlined by the continuation of the story of the Paerands' aborted flight. They spend the night at one of the farms on the north coast, where the mistress of the farm describes the current historical situation by saying that "there's not much you can do – some go, others stay, and still others come" (284). Ullo, Maret, and the reader interpret the "still others" who "come" as the advancing Soviet troops. However, the following lines tell us that this interpretation is a misunderstanding: the one who is about to come is not so much the Soviet army as the child to which the farmer's daughter is soon to give birth.

In *Paigallend,* Ullo Paerand's staying in Estonia is not something that happens to a passive subject who has no control over the events or is unable to evaluate them from the outside, as is the case in Kross's memoirs, where staying behind is the result of the lack of a boat to carry them across the sea. Paerand's choice is a choice made by a subject who has agency to make decisions based on ethical principles and a sense of responsibility. This is implied by the way Maret poses the question that led her to decide to stay in Estonia: "Are we doing the right thing, fleeing?" (285). Conversely, Kross's reflections on the events in his memoirs suggest that such questions are not asked when the events happen. And when they are asked, the word "right" signifies pragmatic purposefulness rather than ethical evaluation. And even then, it is impossible to answer such questions when one is caught in the middle of events. It is only retrospectively that fleeing the country becomes a decisive turning point and as such a perceptible moment of decision making in the life of the people who left the country as well as in the life of those who stayed home. This is also so because the fact that the Soviet occupation was going to be permanent only became clear in the light of subsequent events. Thus, the question can also be posed only in retrospect. Moreover, with Paerand's statement in mind, Maret's question could be answered only from Sirkel's temporal situatedness after the collapse of the Soviet Union in independent Estonia. Only then did it become possible to view the decision to stay in Estonia and everything that resulted from that decision as something that was rewarding after all: a million had to stay home in order to guarantee the survival of the nation.[9] The anecdotal narrativization of the flight episode transforms Paerand's decision to stay in Estonia into a mission. While examining Paerand's tragic life story, Sirkel hesitates to answer the question of whether staying in Estonia was "the right decision" from the point of view of his personal fate; in his biographical novel, Sirkel transforms it into the right decision. As it is encoded in the formula "although thousands leave, a million must stay behind," the anecdotalization of the memory of the attempted flight and the decision to stay in Estonia is designed to redeem the suffering that Paerand had to experience once he opted to stay in Estonia.

The story of Sirkel's conversation with a Soviet major at the prison camp does not belong to the main storyline of the novel, but is presented as evidence of Sirkel's personal proximity to the violence and humiliation experienced by his generation. Sirkel is supposed to give an account of his notebook in which he, who works as a felt dryer, has jotted down lines of his poems. During this interrogation, the major inquires as to whether Sirkel's punishment fits his crime – that is, if he had really been in contact with the Estonian national resistance movement during the German occupation. When Sirkel denies his contacts, the major says: "Of course you didn't maintain such contacts. If you had, you'd have received ten years. But you've only been given five" (161). This episode in the novel, which is based on Kross's own experience, has been transformed into an anecdote reflecting the absurdity and brutality of the Soviet regime: people were convicted even if they were not guilty.[10] Whatever the prisoner whose destiny is under discussion might have felt when hearing the major's conclusion – be it perplexity or blind rage – the story in this anecdotal rewriting shows the absurdity of a totalitarian regime. Both in the flight episode and in the prison-camp scene, the anecdotal narrativization replenishes the remembered events with meaning in such a way that the subject position of the person who is remembered or who is doing the remembering is reworked. Anecdotal remembering restores agency and dignity through remembering where the events themselves can no longer be changed.

There is yet another context – the historiography of the second half of the twentieth century – that is relevant to Kross's anecdotes. Although anecdotes in the form of anecdotal evidence found in the archives have always been part of historical research, "objective" historical scholarship developed since the late nineteenth century has never considered the anecdote to be a respectable historical source as it is particular and for that reason not easily subjected to historical generalization. It was precisely for that reason that the anecdote came to the centre of attention of researchers interested in writing histories from below.[11] From the perspective of histories from below, the anecdote seemed to give a voice to those who had been left out of traditional history writing and thus helped undermine history's metanarratives. The anecdote as a miniature story found in the archive that challenges the traditional rendering of an event or period, seems to maintain a touch of the real (Gallagher 49). However, Kross's work shows that details, happenings, and sayings introduced into bigger – and in his case, fictional – wholes are also narrative units that help shape experience in specific ways.

Although the New Historicist critic Joel Fineman shares the idea of the anecdote as adding a touch of the real, he reminds us that the anecdote is a narrative form that shapes reality. Fineman reflects on the aporetic character of the anecdote and argues that the anecdote is a literary form that is structurally similar to the metanarratives of history. Most quintessentially, it can be regarded as the smallest unit of a fact in history writing, a historeme (57). But Fineman emphasizes that, in spite of its similarity to metanarratives, the anecdote has the specific referentiality of a *petit récit*.[12] The anecdote is part of a larger narrative structure, but it is also an opening in this structure, a piercing of that structure. Western history writing is based on historical consciousness, which relies on the laws of historical causality and organizes reality into teleological narratives which have a beginning, a middle, and an ending. In the context of such a story, each event will obtain its special place in the chain of temporality and causality, the place that determines its meaning. Thus, the events and their context determine each other, mutually creating a meaningful whole. Fineman draws attention to the fact that the post-Hegelian critique of metanarratives has shown that this history is really atemporal, because when everything is causally connected and each event has its logical place in a teleological chain, there is no room for chance and therefore no room for history (57). The anecdote is the opening in the totalizing whole that introduces both chance and temporality into that chain:

> The anecdote is the literary form that uniquely lets history happen by virtue of the way it introduces an opening into the teleological, and therefore

> timeless, narration of beginning, middle, and end. The anecdote produces the effect of the real, the occurrence of contingency, by establishing an event within and yet without the framing context of historical successivity, i.e., it does so only in so far as its narration both comprises and refracts the narration it reports. (61)

According to Fineman, the anecdote is not related to the real in the sense that it lends voice to real experience, or describes things as they really happened. What he means by the "real" is chance occurrence, something that disturbs and undermines the totality of meaning. Chance and contingency introduce the idea that the course of history could have been different, that there was a moment of choice, a crossroads at which it was possible to decide which road to take. This theory of the anecdote draws attention to another possible function of the anecdotalization of memory in *Paigallend*. Such anecdotalization takes place when Paerand narrates the June 1940 invasion of the Red Army into Estonia. This scene thematizes the annexation of Estonia, an event with strong connotations of national humiliation in post-Soviet Estonian collective memory because the Estonian government opted for surrender without military resistance. In his story, Paerand hints at the humiliating effect of the event as he explains that he happened to be part of the Estonian delegation that was to witness the invasion of the Red Army only because no one in the government or chancery agreed to participate. Even the way in which he describes General Laidoner, the leader of the Estonian delegation and the protagonist of the invasion anecdote, emphasizes the desperation and humiliation hidden behind outward dignity.

Paerand's story about a journey to the Estonian-Russian border at Narva revolves around a remark made by Laidoner to the invading troops at the opening of the border. At the beginning of the story, Paerand tells Sirkel that he wants to highlight "that characteristic sentence of his, which became famous later by way of rumor, and as a lead-up to which I'm telling you this whole story" (193). Paerand here confesses that the sentence uttered by Laidoner gives meaning to the whole story of the Red Army invasion, which also guarantees that it is worth narrating. Paerand describes the night journey in a special train that carried the commander in chief to Narva, their arrival in Narva, the signing of the agreement by Laidoner and Meretskov, and the troops crossing the Narva border. This story, too, ends in a punch line, a remark uttered by Laidoner. Paerand recounts:

> The drone of the vehicles approached us and could be felt in every cell of your body, the dust raised by the vehicles had not yet reached us, the boys of the border guard stood to attention – then Laidoner turned to his entourage. I was standing three paces behind, between us were Captains Jaakson and Hint with a gap between them, so I saw his mouth move and heard him clearly when he said: "Gentlemen, I hope that what we have built up over the last twenty years [the period of the Estonian Republic, that is, 1918–40] will, if needs be, hold out for another two hundred." (195)

Here, the anecdotalization consists of a poignant remark made during the humiliating events that, in this process of retelling and remembering, introduces a moment of contingency into the chain of events. Only thanks to this sentence does Laidoner, who is forced into a humiliating situation, regain his dignity and agency. The episode ends with an addition Paerand makes to Laidoner's remark: "A claim which, starting from 1945, if you will, you and I have been checking, proving, refuting" (195). While the events were happening, the participants had no agency to change their course. The anecdotal remembering opens up the possibility to act and choose at the moment of remembering: Paerand and Sirkel are the ones who decide by remembering whether Laidoner's remark will find its justification or not, whether it will be proved true or refuted.

In all the cases of anecdotalization of memory discussed above, the anecdote reworks experience in the process of remembering. In all cases, the aim of anecdotal remembering is related to the subjectivity of the one who remembers and, in the act of remembering, both represents his life and writes the life of his friend. Sirkel's and Paerand's anecdotes make visible that Kross uses anecdotalization almost always for representing painful memories of humiliation and suffering that relegate the subject to the position of a passive object, inadequate in the face of overwhelming events. In *Paigallend*, neither Sirkel nor Paerand address their humiliating experiences directly. Instead, they try to recount them in anecdotal ways. Thus, anecdotalization is meant both to cover up the humiliation and to rework it by restoring dignity and agency to the subject. The latter is achieved by organizing memories around anecdotal punch lines, thereby changing the way the events are remembered. Kross's remark regarding the woman who tells anecdotes in a shelter, which I discussed at the beginning of this essay, is revealing in that respect. The anecdotes the woman tells recall the stories of nights spent in a shelter in the past. This means that the narrated experience is linked to the moment of narrating in a particular way. The anecdotal remembering of previous raids, when people faced real fear and risked death, diminishes the horror of not only past nights but also the present one. Thus, anecdotes can help make the emotionally intense experience bearable, to alleviate fear, to restore a sense of self-confidence and agency. In the same way, Sirkel's and Paerand's anecdotes rework the past in the interests of their subjecthood in the present.

As a dialogic novel of memory, *Paigallend* reveals that the main function of the anecdotalization of memory is not to present the anecdotes as moralizing or didactic exempla to be used for the consolidation of collective identities such as a generation or a nation. Rather, the anecdote plays an important role for the subject who does the remembering: it renders painful experiences bearable and therefore memorable in the first place. Rather than representing Paerand's "flying in place" as an allegory of Estonian political history, Kross's dialogic novel makes visible that Sirkel's desperate wish to write Paerand out of his anguish by anecdotalizing the memories of the past grows out of Sirkel's compassion for him and for many other members of his generation. In Kross's own life-writing project, which takes place in his fiction as well as in his memoirs, the anecdote performs a similar function. Kross starts writing his life in fiction by inserting his autobiographical episodes into the lives of his protagonists and by telling them in an anecdotal way. Only after repeatedly retelling, in his fiction, the scenes of humiliation and personal pain hidden behind the shield of anecdote is he able to address them directly in his memoirs. The anecdotalization of his personal memories in fiction has then had a liberating effect on Kross's life-writing project.

NOTES

1 This article has been written with the support of ESF grant 8530. All translations from the Estonian are mine. Quotations from the English translation of *Paigallend* (*Treading Air*) – in some cases modified by me to render the original more closely – are the exception.
2 This is the literal translation of the novel's title, *Paigallend*.
3 See, for instance, Haug and Undusk.
4 The meaning of the anecdote as an informal form of social knowledge can be traced back to its Greek origin, where the term refers to unpublished material or something that has been left out of a manuscript. *Anékdota*

comes from the title of Procopios of Caesarea's collection of short stories, *Anékdota*, which narrates the private life of the Byzantine court that was left out of the official history of Justinian's rule (*Metzler* 14).

5 I thank Ellen Niit and Jaan Undusk for this piece of information.

6 This is implied by Kross's addition of a "List of Political and Cultural Figures" in an appendix to the English translation of the book. This is designed to help those readers who are not part of the shared community of memory addressed by the novel.

7 "A million" refers to the total Estonian population living in Estonia.

8 See, for example, Kross, *Vahelugemised*, 6 (167).

9 For Jaan Kross, his decision to stay led to nine years of imprisonment in a Soviet prison camp. He was incarcerated in January 1946, dispatched to a prison camp, and later exiled in Siberia, from where he returned in 1954.

10 Kross recounts the same episode in his memoirs (*Kallid kaasteelised* 312).

11 For an overview of history from below as a "new way of writing history," see Sharp.

12 The French call the anecdote a little story – a *petit récit*.

WORKS CITED

Assmann, Aleida. *Der lange Schatten der Vergangenheit: Erinnerungskultur und Geschichtspolitik*. München: C.H. Beck, 2006.

Dentith, Simon. "Contemporary Working-Class Autobiography: Politics of Form, Politics of Content." In *Practicing New Historicism*, ed. Catherine Gallagher and Stephen Greenblatt, 94–115. Chicago: University of Chicago Press, 2000.

Fineman, Joel. "The History of the Anecdote: Fiction and Friction." In *The New Historicism*, ed. Aram Veeser, 49–76. New York: Routledge, 1989.

Gallagher, Catherine. "Counterhistory and the Anecdote." In *Practicing New Historicism*, ed. Catherine Gallagher and Stephen Greenblatt, 49–74. Chicago: University of Chicago Press, 2000.

Gilmore, Leigh. *The Limits of Autobiography: Trauma and Testimony*. Ithaca: Cornell University Press, 2001.

Haug, Toomas. "Poliitiline Kross. Paigallennu arvustuse asemel." In *Metamorfiline Kross: Sissevaateid Jaan Krossi loomingusse*, ed. Eneken Laanes, 162–6.Tallinn: Underi ja Tuglase Kirjanduskeskus, 2005.

Kirss, Tiina. "Playing the Fool in the Territory of Memory: Jaan Kross' Autobiographical Fictions of the Twentieth Century." *Journal of Baltic Studies* 31, no. 3 (2000): 273–94. http://dx.doi.org/10.1080/01629770000000111.

Kross, Jaan. *Kallid kaasteelised* [Dear Co-Travellers]. Tallinn: Eesti Keele Sihtasutus, 2003.

Kross, Jaan. *Omaeluloolisus ja alltekst. 1998. aastal Tartu Ülikooli filosoofiateaduskonna vabade kunstide professorina peetud loengud*. Tallinn: Eesti Keele Sihtasutus, 2003.

Kross, Jaan. *Paigallend*. Tallinn: Virgela, 1998.

Kross, Jaan. *Treading Air* [*Paigallend*]. Trans. Eric Dickens. London: Harvill Press, 2003.

Kross, Jaan. *Vahelugemised*. 6. Tallinn: Bibliotheca Baltica, 1995.

LaCapra, Dominick. *Writing History, Writing Trauma*. Baltimore: Johns Hopkins University Press, 2001.

Metzler Literatur-Lexikon: Begriffe und Definitionen. Ed. Günther und Irmgard Schweikle. Stuttgart: Metzler, 1990.

Sharp, Jim. "History from Below." *New Perspectives on Historical Writing*, ed. Peter Burke, 24–41. Cambridge: Polity, 2001.

Undusk, Jaan. "Isiksusest, ajaloost ja häbist: Jaan Krossi lugedes." *Looming* 4 (2005): 597.

12 Meddling with Memory – Negating Grand Narratives

NORA ANNA ESCHERLE

Under the general mutterings of the desire for slackening and for appeasement, we can hear the mutterings of the desire for a return of terror, for the realization of the fantasy to seize reality. The answer is this: let us wage war on totality; be witnesses to the unrepresentable; activate the differences.

Jean-François Lyotard, *The Postmodern Condition* 82

There is no burden I carry, whatever the dead may say. Because I am alive, I can choose what to remember, I can choose what to forget.

Raj Kamal Jha, *Fireproof* 372

In "Anecdotalization of Memory in Jaan Kross's *Paigallend*," Eneken Laanes argues that the anecdotalization of memory has the vital function of retrospectively investing with agency those who were powerless and humiliated in the past, of restoring individual dignity, and, concomitantly, of having a liberating effect on Kross's life-writing project. Laanes names and illustrates three different understandings and uses of the term anecdote – as "a form of social memory," as "a short literary form," and as "a historiographic device." Regarding anecdotes as narrative devices in historiography, Laanes especially appreciates their function as *petits récits* that produce a "touch of the real," as welcome intrusions of the particular, the specific, and the contingent into the totalizing, generalizing grand narratives of history.

In my response, I compare the subversive function of the anecdote as a literary device that represents and reshapes memory in *Paigallend* against the background of official Estonian historiography with the similarly subversive function of magical-realistic elements in Raj

Kamal Jha's *Fireproof* (2006) in relation to the secularist metanarrative of the Indian nation state.[1] Both *Paigallend* and *Fireproof* are historiographical fictional narratives which remember traumatic events. As such, they give an account of things that happened in the Estonian and the Indian past. By narrating them, both novels engage with strategies and purposes of remembering past events, and both antagonize and subvert the authority of those grand narratives that have dictated certain readings of the events – readings which the novels in question either transform, as in the case of *Paigallend*, or disrupt, as in the case of *Fireproof*. These novels differ considerably, however, first, as regards the narrative strategies by which they antagonize the metanarratives and, second, regarding the reasons why and the purposes for which they challenge them.

As Laanes notes, *Paigallend* makes ample use of the anecdote: it "anecdotalizes" the memories of painful and humiliating past events, thereby enabling and propagating a different reading of them which renders the events memorable and worthy of representation for those who suffered from them. In her concluding words, where she refers back to her earlier statement that "the anecdotalization of memory is closely related to the formation of subjectivity in life writing," she suggests that in all of her discussed examples, the anecdote "reworks the experience in the process of remembering" and that anecdotalization is used by Kross "for representing painful memories of humiliation and suffering ... both to cover up the humiliation and to rework it by restoring dignity and agency to the subject." According to Laanes, *Paigallend* aims at redeeming, through the character of Ullo Paerand, those members of the generation of Estonians who stayed behind and contended themselves with spending all their life's energy on "treading air." This act of redemption is accomplished by an engagement with memory, especially with its potential of altering what has been considered true about both the past and the present. In *Paigallend*, where painful and humiliating events are remembered in an alternative way – for example, by accentuating new, unusual perspectives or by referring to positive, meaningful future consequences of the events or the roles taken on by those who suffered from the events – this results in a retrospective reshaping not of the remembered events themselves but of their meaning in the present. Thanks to this, the memory of the events is rendered bearable for their traumatized partakers, and their remembering of what happened and what they endured becomes a worthy, meaningful act.

Like *Paigallend, Fireproof* also deftly meddles with the memory of traumatic, painful, and humiliating events. Jha employs the magical-realist mode in order to enable new, empirically impossible perspectives and to tell what is usually untold. Based on recent Indian history, *Fireproof* is concerned with an outbreak of communal violence in the Indian state of Gujarat that lasted for over three months from February 2002 onward and had devastating effects: "Over a thousand men, women and children were killed, more than 70 per cent of them Muslim" (386).[2] *Fireproof* takes as its starting point the night when the Gujarati violence began, and it tells those aspects of the story which are rarely told: the off-record, muted reports from those who are usually not willing or not able to talk: the traumatized victims and the perpetrators, as well as the dead. The fantastic mode makes accessible the memories, thoughts, and feelings of murdered people, and it opens up a window to the dark recesses of a traumatized murderer's mind. Jha endows the usually powerless victims – dead or alive, but always traumatized – with a voice "by using magical realism to express the 'real' that is 'beyond language' in stories" (Bowers 81). The victims of the atrocities haunt one of the perpetrators, the novel's protagonist Mr Jay, and finally succeed in making him confess to his guilt, which he had conveniently chosen to repress.

In literary works, magical realism frequently performs a similar function as the anecdote does in historiographical narratives: because they enable odd, unusual, usually ignored, or even empirically impossible viewpoints, the narrative techniques of magical realism have the capacity to invest literature with the power to subvert the established truths of grand narratives and to function in ways that are analogous to those of counter-histories. In magical-realistic texts, realistic and unrealistic elements coexist and interact. Such texts are usually based on historically specific socio-political contexts and events, but their otherwise realistic narrative structure is permeated by fantastic elements that originate from myths or dreams. Since magical realism is so well suited "to exploring – and transgressing – boundaries, whether the boundaries are ontological, political, geographical, or generic" (Faris and Zamora 5), it is the narrative mode par excellence for representing and discussing liminal experiences. Faris and Zamora underline magical realism's "assault on the basic structures of rationalism and realism" and argue that it tends to question fundamental truths (6). Not unlike anecdotes, the narrative techniques of magical realism may illustrate the existence of alternative ways to get access to "the truth," or rather, they may undermine positivist notions of truth and instead promote the idea that there are in fact many truths, and manifold ways of access to those many truths: "Magical realism attempts to capture reality by way of a depiction of life's many dimensions, seen and unseen, visible and invisible, rational and mysterious" (Cooper 32). Unlike anecdotes, which lay claim to verifiability and referentiality, magical-realist texts do not claim to be verifiable with recourse to empirical reality (past or present); they are not true in any ordinary, everyday sense of the word, and they do not aim at being perceived as such. In line with Toni Morrison's claim that magic constitutes "another way of knowing things" (342), magical realism can be conceived of as a narrative mode that "allows the expression of a story that goes against what 'authoritative' history … claims" (Bowers 86). In all their different forms and contexts, magical-realist texts "seek to disrupt official and defined authoritative assumptions about reality, truth and history" (ibid. 95) – which likens them to anecdotes and the challenges they pose to established grand narratives of historiography. Hence, magical-realist texts are potentially "subversive: their in-betweenness, their all-at-onceness encourages resistance to monologic political and cultural structures" (Faris and Zamora 6).

In the dominant public discourse in India, the voices of the victims, the stories of the individuals who have suffered from atrocities, are seldom, if ever, heard; more often than not, they are ignored, even suppressed, due to their alleged potential to shake and undermine the fragile secularist peace. As Gyanendra Pandey notes, "the totalizing standpoint of a seamless nationalism" that is cultivated in India – and which perpetuates the grand narrative that the harmonious coexistence of Muslims and Hindus in the secular nation state is the rule, while communal riots are horrible exceptions – ignores, mutes, and stifles those individual voices that would speak of their specific suffering and accuse individual perpetrators (50). Pandey's findings relate to Paul Brass's understanding of communal riots as "grisly form[s] of dramatic production" (15). Brass, a social anthropologist, identifies three phases in that perennial production, namely, "preparation/rehearsal, activation/enactment, and explanation/interpretation" (15), of which the last one is of greatest interest in the context of my response. According to Brass, the essential feature of the third phase is the "process of blame displacement … a process that does not isolate effectively those most responsible for the production of violence, but diffuses blame widely, blurring responsibility, and thereby contributing to the perpetuation of violent productions in the future" (15). Brass notes that the search for the causes of communal riots and the aim of assigning responsibility for the violence, which occur during the interpretation process, paradoxically have the result "to free all from blame and allow the principal perpetrators to go scot-free" (16). If one takes into account the sheer number of atrocities, the trials and convictions of some perpetrators can be called exceptions to the rule of laying blame at the door of an anonymous, amorphous entity called "the mob," which no one can or will hold to account (ibid. 29, 310–11).

The victims in Jha's novel, however, are given the chance to tell their individual stories. It is the dead and the traumatized victims, not the living or those in power, which dominate the representation and interpretation of the events. Their voices are not muted; they are given the space and the occasion to describe the moments of violence they had to experience and to witness. Equally importantly, they do not ask for the reasons or offer any explanation for what the perpetrators did to them or their kin. What they do is describe explicitly what happened, and accuse one perpetrator for committing these crimes. In other words, Jha's novel gives plenty of information about the "how" and also discloses the innuendo of the "who," but it does not give an easy answer to the question of "why." Actually, the novel does not give any reason whatsoever for why or for which purpose the protagonist and his accomplices did what they did. Puzzling as this is for readers of the novel, leaving them without answers is the converse tactic of the standard procedure in the wake of riots. By virtue of this, Jha's novel engages in counter-historiography: it critiques and undermines the usual, officially sanctioned ways of remembering the events and writing the history of communal violence, which, according to Brass, ultimately implies the muting of the victims' voices, the diffusion of responsibility, and the removal of the perpetrators into anonymity for the sake of a dubious, fragile peace.

In *Paigallend*, anecdotalization restores agency to the powerless and "[replenishes] the remembered events with meaning" retrospectively: an existing grand narrative is undermined so that a new way of subjectively remembering the past can emerge – one which redeems the suffering of the "lost generations," restores their dignity, and thus reconciles them with their past and their present. As a result, alternative versions of the past, unpublished or usually muted reports, and impossible perspectives are represented in order to introduce "perceptible moment[s] of decision-making." This is not the case with the use of the magical-realist mode in *Fireproof*. While magical-realist devices are also employed to represent unpublished or usually muted reports and impossible perspectives, they do not introduce moments of choice, restore agency, or replenish meaning. Quite the contrary: instead of rendering the memory of what happened more bearable for those who witnessed the events or only heard about them, instead of replenishing the events with some kind of meaning in order to reconcile the Indian public, and especially the surviving victims, with the recent violent past, *Fireproof* does exactly the opposite. It completely refrains from providing any reason for what happened and thereby insinuates the very pointlessness of the usual arduous search for reasons in the aftermath of communal violence. *Fireproof* negates any attempts at retrospectively investing the violent events with meaning; it aims at representing the "true," unvarnished horror of the atrocities and concentrates on rendering the actual violence, the pain, the humiliation, the suffering, the sadness as drastically as possible, to show the bare helplessness of the victims and to reveal the utter pointlessness of both the violence and the suffering. The uncanny, horrid perspectives and insights enabled by the magical-realist mode of narration achieve an eerie effect of immediacy through strangeness: they apply a shock of unfamiliarity to the reader and confront her with her prior blindness, ignorance, and lack of compassion – effects which have also been attributed to the anecdote (Gallagher and Greenblatt 56). In *Paigallend,* these effects do not appear to be of great importance, and Laanes hardly discusses them in her analysis of the forms and functions of anecdote. In *Fireproof,* however, they are crucially important: immediacy through strangeness, the shock of unfamiliarity, and confrontation with ignorance are powerful functions of the novel's representation of actual violence, individual pain, and individual guilt. They play a decisive role in undermining the authority of the grand narrative of the secularist Indian nation state. *Fireproof* does not create any new metanarrative to replace the old one. Instead, it can be said to make a plea for assigning the victims and their stories their rightful place in the existing grand narrative, which has to be revised and adapted accordingly.

Fireproof does not aim at reconciliation with the recent past; it provides no replenishment with meaning and no redemption of suffering. If anything can restore the victims' dignity, if anything can enable the idea of secularist peace to come true in the Indian nation state, *Fireproof* seems to suggest, the individual perpetrators have to be prosecuted and punished for their deeds and, still more importantly, the stories of individual suffering and confessions of individual guilt have to be given voice and made publicly heard.

Thus, *Fireproof* goes against the grain of the secularist grand narrative of the Indian nation state, which is perpetuated by politicians, historians, and practitioners of the social sciences alike, and which allegedly serves the purpose of maintaining the harmonious coexistence of Muslims and Hindus. Jha's novel shows what the results of Brass's research postulate: riots are no natural disasters caused by anonymous forces; they involve individual human beings on both sides, perpetrators and victims. *Fireproof* shows that anonymity, the repression of responsibility, and blame displacement on a national scale are no solution, but will, as with the traumatized protagonist, eventually result in the blurring of the boundaries between what is real and what is fiction, and thus shake or even destroy the unity and the foundations of the self and of reality.

NOTES

1 See also Annie Cottier's essay on *Fireproof* in this volume (chapter 21).

2 Jha gives these numbers and other particulars concerning the 2002 events in Gujarat in the "Author's Note" to his novel (385–8).

WORKS CITED

Bowers, Maggie Ann. *Magic(al) Realism*. New York: Routledge, 2004. http://dx.doi.org/10.4324/9780203625002.

Brass, Paul. *The Production of Hindu-Muslim Violence in Contemporary India*. Seattle: University of Washington Press, 2003.

Cooper, Brenda. *Magical Realism in West African Fiction: Seeing with a Third Eye*. London: Routledge, 1998. http://dx.doi.org/10.4324/9780203451397.

Faris, Wendy B., and Lois Parkinson Zamora, eds. *Magical Realism: Theory, History, Community*. Durham, NC: Duke University Press, 1995.

Gallagher, Catherine, and Stephen Greenblatt. *Practicing New Historicism*. Chicago: University of Chicago Press, 2000.

Jha, Raj Kamal. *Fireproof*. London: Picador, 2006.

Lyotard, Jean-François. *The Postmodern Condition: A Report on Knowledge*, trans. Geoff Bennington and Brian Massumi. Minneapolis: University of Minnesota Press, 1993.

Morrison, Toni. "Rootedness: The Ancestor as Foundation." In *Black Women Writers (1950–1980): A Critical Evaluation*, ed. Mari Evans, 339–45. New York: Doubleday, 1984.

Pandey, Gyanendra. "In Defense of the Fragment: Writing about Hindu-Moslem Riots in India Today." *Representations* 37, no. 1 (1992): 27–55. http://dx.doi.org/10.1525/rep.1992.37.1.99p00926.

13 Fighting Fear with Writing: Christa Wolf's *Kindheitsmuster* and Ene Mihkelson's *Ahasveeruse uni* (The Sleep of Ahasuerus)

AIJA SAKOVA

What one cannot speak of, one must gradually cease being silent about.

Christa Wolf, *Kindheitsmuster* 262

Memories are a secret language that one must decode. The only meaning of memories lies in the writing hand.

Ene Mihkelson, *Ahasveeruse uni* 268

Though Christa Wolf's *Kindheitsmuster* (1976) and Ene Mihkelson's *Ahasveeruse uni* (2001, The Sleep of Ahasuerus) were published in very different social and political contexts (the GDR and the Republic of Estonia), and with a temporal interval of twenty-five years, the two novels are connected both via their intention to excavate past events, and via their writing in the "remembering mode."[1] This type of writing reveals itself specifically in the authors' avoidance of narrative structure and solid characters. In their stead, the novels stage a highly subjective and personal engagement with the past. This raises the question of whether these novels are autobiographical and, if that is the case, how and to what extent it makes sense to read them as life writing. Any attempt to answer that question in the affirmative must contend with Mihkelson's and Wolf's disclaimers: Mihkelson states that all resemblances between characters in the book and persons or relationships in real life are coincidental (*Ahasveeruse uni* 7); Wolf points out that all characters in her novel are invented by the narrator, adding that if anyone should perceive any similarities between a character and him- or herself, this might be due to the lack of individuation that characterizes the behaviour of many a contemporary (*Kindheitsmuster* 10). Despite or, rather, because of these disavowals, readers are alerted to the possibility that the opposite is the case: they are led to suspect – if not necessarily to believe – that much of what is found in the novels has indeed really happened, or that it plausibly could have happened.[2]

While both authors quite obviously reject autobiographicality as a simplistic assumption, this does not mean that their novels cannot be read – or indeed, should not be read – as life writing understood in a broader sense as "compris[ing] texts that are written by an author who does not continuously write about someone else, and who also does not pretend to be absent from the … text himself/herself" (Kadar 10). After all, Wolf stresses that when writing prose, one should remain truthful "on the ground of one's own experience" ("Reading and Writing" 27). In a similar vein, Mihkelson claims that the origin of her subject matter lies in herself. When I asked her to what extent the content of her novels corresponds to real life, she gave this answer:

> When I write I use my own experience to the extent that I can, and to the extent that it is necessary. Nevertheless, my texts are not autobiographical. The I of my text and my self do not coincide, even when external factors allege it. My personal biography remains the raw material out of which I make something that is not my self. (Sakova 11)

Thus, neither author denies that a significant amount of the lives and experiences of their narrator-protagonists have an equivalent in their own life. For example, we know that Ene Mihkelson's parents were Forest Brethern not unlike those of the narrator of *Ahasveeruse uni*.[3] Likewise, both Christa Wolf herself and Nelly, the childhood-I of the narrator in *Kindheitsmuster*, had to leave their homes in flight of war at the age of sixteen. But why do these writers reject autobiographicality so radically and resolutely if they admit to drawing on their own experiences as much as is necessary and to using their own past selves as prototypes? Is their reticence primarily due to an aversion to psychoanalytic interpretations of their work or is it designed to protect them from being accused of lying about what really happened? In *The Limits of Autobiography*, Leigh Gilmore discusses the thorny issues of truthfulness and authenticity on the basis of Rigoberta Menchú's testimony *I, Rigoberta Menchú*, a book that was marketed as an autobiography but turned out to be filled with facts that the author could not have eyewitnessed. As Gilmore points out, the skirmish over Menchú's autobiography "indicates one reason why not all writers choose autobiography as the mode in which to tell stories of personal pain" (5). The genre of autobiography seems to narrow down the possibilities of both how authors can write and what they can write about, for when reading an autobiography, a reader enters into what Philippe Lejeune calls an autobiographical pact: a contract between author and reader that leads readers to assume that the author, the narrator, and the protagonist are one and the same person and that the story told can be verified as true. It seems as if Wolf and Mihkelson want to avoid this verification and comparison with real life. Moreover, while the genre of autobiography in many cases helps writers insert their lives into the experiential world of a community, Wolf and Mihkelson aim at exactly the opposite: they seek to draw attention to broader social and cultural problems via their own experiences and personalities.

When approaching writing, both authors are concerned with questions of historical truth and guilt; moreover, they are impelled to write and to think because they recognize that what is horrendous in the past is not dead, but rather lives on in people, be it in the form of unconscious fear, bodily suffering, illness, rage, or aggression. Driven by their own pain, they turn back to the past and yearn, by means of various mnemotechniques, to find the trail of what is painful and to give it a name. Thus, memories are a secret language that must be deciphered in order for one to come to a place where the unspeakable is no longer silenced. For both authors, these twin labours – memory work and the excavation of the past – are made possible, first and foremost, through a change of political regime and, second, by a certain temporal distance from the narrated events: writing in 1976, Christa Wolf probes the origins and consequences of the Third Reich; writing in 2001, Mihkelson analyses the deep and lasting impact of the Soviet regime on the Estonian people. The contribution both authors make towards a better understanding of the past is readily apparent, and it is also testified to by the worldwide reception of Christa Wolf's works and Mihkelson's winning of the Herder Prize on 5 May 2006.[4] Yet for Mihkelson's still lesser-known work to make a more tangible contribution to the working through of European history, it is in need of thoroughgoing comparative analyses in the context of kindred works from other literary traditions that negotiate similar themes with similar poetics. In juxtaposing Wolf's and Mihkelson's works, this article develops such a comparative perspective.

Both Wolf and Mihkelson seek to articulate their own childhood pain as well as the horrors that befell their people and their contemporaries.

They seek ways of breaking free from the binds of forgetting and from failures to confront injustice. Indeed, in their novels, forgetting is a breeding ground for evil; the horrors of the past must be opened up and discussed. The time and space to which both Wolf and Mihkelson return in their novels is the time of their childhood. As children, the first-person narrators of both novels had important facts and knowledge withheld from them which strongly influenced their later lives and forced them to revisit their childhood worlds as adults in order to fill in these blanks in knowledge and memory. In both cases, severe personal and family experiences of loss and pain in childhood (loss of parents, leaving home, and experiencing war) serve as catalysts to processes of remembering. Indeed, the pain and the suffering that accompanies those processes are among the most important issues negotiated in the novels. While reading them, one can almost physically sense what the authors were suffering during the writing process. I would even go so far as to claim that without a strong capacity for empathy, one would miss the motive, perhaps even the meaning, of such a novel.

Pain, or the authentic feeling of pain, is the main medium by means of which people can become more sensitive to violent social processes. Pain and loss render one more wakeful and conscious; through them, one may be enabled to see what is wrong with the existing social order. A concise expression of such pain is provided in the eighth chapter of Wolf's novel, which is dedicated to the early, horrible death of the Austrian poet Ingeborg Bachmann. Wolf uses a quotation from Bachmann as the epigraph for the chapter: "With my burned hand I write of the nature of fire" ("Mit meiner verbrannten Hand schreibe ich von der Natur des Feuers" [*Kindheitsmuster* 240]). At the beginning of the chapter, Wolf allows Nelly to recall the day when the National Socialist troops conquered Vienna (Nelly heard the news on the radio). In doing so, she establishes a connection with Bachmann.[5] In the middle of the chapter, narrative time gradually catches up with the historical moment at which Wolf hears of Bachmann's death, and – without explicitly mentioning either Bachmann or her death – she bids farewell to her by means of allusive references to the story "Undine Goes" and the poem "Explain to Me, Love":

> Seldom can one recognize the weight of such a broken hour. It is Friday, the 19th of October 1973, a cool, rainy day, 18.30 in the evening. In Chile the military junta has forbidden the use of the word "compañero." Thus there are no grounds for doubting the power of words. Even when someone,

> whose earnest way of transacting with words you have long held in esteem, no longer needs them, and can no longer make them, who lets herself go, and marks this day with the sentence, Mit meiner verbrannten Hand schreibe ich von der Natur des Feuers. Undine geht. Makes with her hand – her burned hand – the sign for the end. Go, Death, stand still, Time. Aloneness, where no one follows me. It means, with the echo ringing in the mouth, to go further, to be silent.
>
> To be calm? To what end? In order not to be overcome with mourning? Don't explain anything to me. I have seen the salamander go through every fire. No shudder chases him, and he feels no pain.
>
> A farther, earlier, now a more horrendous death (Should I for this short, horrendous time …). A dark thread comes into the pattern. It is impossible to let it fall. To pick it up almost too fast. (*Kindheitsmuster* 260)[6]

Wolf integrates her mourning for Bachmann and her real pain about the Nazi past into her novel. Thus, she inserts elements of life writing – elements that would seem more at home in memories or letters – into her fictional text. If we take Wolf's ethics of writing seriously, both historical events inescapably and deliberately belong to the process of writing; both have sensitized her and sharpened her attentiveness, and they enable her readers to come to a place of insight, where they, too, can speak with the words of Ingeborg Bachmann.[7] Christa Wolf sees the task of the writer as calling people's attention, by means of art and literature, to the realities of historical events, their grounds, and their consequences (*Kindheitsmuster* 493). The living can be differentiated both from the dead and from mere survivors by the responsibility they have to remember and to draw conclusions from their experience (517).

Mihkelson speaks of the responsibility of artists in similar terms: their task is to dig deep, to reach the depths below the surface of the everyday and the superficial, to reach those depths that are not noticed at first glance. In Mihkelson's own words: "The artist opens up the surface to reveal what is beneath it, and his or her responsibility before society lies in thoroughness, the duty to suffer, to hold the tension, which is not possible for those people to experience who are wrapped and hidden behind the demands of everyday living" ("Isiklikust kunstis" 947).

Writers, then, must bring to speech what is painful; they must articulate rather than shy away from the pain that going deeply into violent social processes might entail. This can be done above all through deliberate remembering and recording in writing – which is a particularly pressing task when the past and its horrors continue to live on in the present. Wolf calls this technique of laying bare the continuing influence of the past "Vision": "One suddenly sees what is not to be seen, that which must be there, since it shows itself by its effects. The past in the present, for example. Or the repressed extravagant wish that any minute, no one knows when, it can shoot forth in anyone" ("Reading" 177).

Similarly, Mihkelson states,

> To a large measure, what allows unconsciousness and manipulation to happen originates in the form of stereotypes from earlier times, and this is dangerous to people because it allows unconscious attitudes to continue into the future, one can say that this was the way things were and one cannot know otherwise. When what came before gets buried and people do not talk about it or think it through, then what is buried can begin secretly to move around and to start manipulating people. I believe that if human beings intend to have mastery over their personal, unique lives, they must also investigate this dark chamber, not for the sake of principle, but for the sake of freedom and self-respect. (Sakova 11)

As writers, Mihkelson and Wolf are cognizant of the fact that there are things in their own and in other people's subconscious of which they are not aware, and they are equally aware that one must expend a great deal of effort to get at the concealed aspects of the past. Though it is a laborious and thoroughly painful process, the capacity to remember is necessary, since without it, Mihkelson states, one cannot master oneself. For both Wolf and Mihkelson, drawing close to the past and opening the dark chamber of the subconscious only become possible in and through writing:

> One can either write or be happy ... With "skillful hand," you thought ironically, which should not fear inflicting pain, and even rather do so casually. And so that not just the hand, but also the person it belongs to is trotted out in camouflage and made visible. Thus one earns the right to material which is so constituted as to bring oneself into the picture, while the opening of the garment does not hang too low. (*Kindheitsmuster* 233)

Wolf here highlights once more how important it is for her and for her ethics of writing that authors neither hide away nor pretend to be absent from the text. On the contrary, they should bring to speech how they respond to personal issues as well as social processes. This "bringing oneself into the picture" is certainly a crucial autobiographical strategy, and as such it bears the risks that attend autobiographical projects. In embarking on such projects, writers not only expose themselves before their readers; they can also sink into the past too deeply and be overwhelmed with memories that need to be worked through. Wolf understands very well that writing is dangerous work, because it can inflict pain, on both the writer and the reader. Yet she also realizes that there is no other way: one can either write or be happy.

Just as Wolf's narrator knows how costly her undertaking will be, so Mihkelson's first-person narrator realizes the difficulty of the path of remembering and of getting to the bottom of things. It took her years to finally come to the decision to go back to the village where she was born and ask who her father and his parents were (*Ahasveeruse uni* 9). Further information was in no way easy to find: whenever she digs deeper in her research and reflects on her experience in depth, her mind short-circuits. Her blood pressure rises, she hears a roaring in her ears, and warts grow on her eyelids: "I was made lame, ... my heart stood still and my ears rang" (53); "always, in such moments of observation, the blood pressure would rise" (115); "the pressure numbed the head" (331); and then "the skin warts started to grow on her eyelids" (354).[8] Her body informs her precisely and directly about her psychological state. The intensifying pain and bodily suffering signal to her that she has experienced, seen, or recognized something that has been hidden up to this point:

> Then when she had again been wandering aimlessly and long through Tartu, avoiding the people and places she knows, the pain became dull and docile, and even the colors seemed faded. After the meeting with Kaarel and after the long telephone conversations with Vilma, even nature felt sharp as a knife, but somehow fluid in its knife-bladed gleam, as if the edge of the blade, shining in steady sunlight would finally come to an end somehow, would finally get dull or break, and then they would tell her (she would be told!) that the pain of cutting was like an operation without anaesthetic, but that it was over now, the pain would subside, life would go on, the sky would be blue again and the green grass soft under her feet. That finding out had to be painful, otherwise it would not be something worth wanting. (*Ahasveeruse uni* 335)

Her meeting with the man who quite possibly betrayed her father, and her conversations with her mother Vilma are moments that bring the first-person narrator closer to the truth or at least help her open up hidden horizons of experience. But the more the past opens itself up to her, the more dangerous and painful it becomes. An operation without anaesthesia translates into an ongoing vigilance and perception of what the past has to tell her: "Sickness and sleep make pain sharper, waken the memory, in order finally to fall back into health" (305). Insight and perception, it seems, become possible in those moments of searing pain when her mind short-circuits. The short circuit can be regarded as a metaphor for the narrator's practice of remembering (*Erinnerungspraxis*), because, as she states, the moments of clarity sought after in studying history are the result of short circuits, not of logical deduction (*Ahasveeruse uni* 302).[9] Thus, pain awakens loose and random bits of memories, images, and knowledge that are bound together so that new perceptions become possible. One might say that it is in this way that one goes deeper into experience or memory, that one is enabled to see things that one did not perceive before. Mihkelson herself confirms that she can see more deeply today than she was able to before: "I can perhaps see a few stair steps deeper, or at least I can inquire about the need for seeing deeper. Whether I perceive anything is another matter. But the writer must have the feeling that she or he has reached the maximum capacity or depth as is possible in that moment" (Sakova 11).

Although the writer is referring to her own experience here, one can carry the metaphor across to her writing as well. In *Ahasveeruse uni*, the first-person narrator also sees through to the deepest level accessible to her. A more thorough textual analysis would show how different levels open each other up reciprocally, and how both the narrator and the reader keep falling deeper and deeper, even though they believe they have already arrived at the deepest ground. In her essay "Reading and Writing," Wolf likewise speaks of the issue of depth. Despite the fact that this notion has suffered from imprecision and misuse, and thus is suspect in the eyes of many theorists of the novel, it remains meaningful to her. She concedes that depth is not a property of things, of the material world, but rather an attribute of human consciousness or experience:

> It is an ability acquired through the ages which man not only retained but developed further because it proved useful to him in his life in society. Depth thus depends on us: subjective individuals living in objective circumstances. It is the product of unsatisfied needs, of the tensions and

> conflicts arising from them, and of man's unparalleled efforts to grow beyond himself, or perhaps to reach himself. Such may be the meaning and purpose of depth in our consciousness, so we must not sacrifice it in favor of superficiality. ("Reading" 23)

Depth, then, cannot be measured or witnessed as a textual feature; it only emerges with the help of human consciousness. As Wolf argues, this is possible because of the characteristics of the brain, which is sufficiently differentiated to create a condition whereby "we can deepen the linear dimension of time – its surface, we could say – almost to infinity" ("Reading" 23). The ability to remember (as well as to foresee what is to come) allows people to expand time in their consciousness, that is, to delve into the depths of their experience. Both Wolf and Mihkelson practise this in their novels, and the expression or outcome of this delving into depth is often pain and suffering, the unavoidable accompaniment of the insight that has been realized.

The common psychic pain that both Wolf's and Mihkelson's first-person narrators suffer from is intense fear. As Heino Noor reports, massive acts of violence such as those perpetrated during the Third Reich, at the Gulag Archipelago, and during the Second World War more generally have been means of forcing people to live in a conscious or unconscious state of fear, as a result of which they give up, fall silent, or accommodate themselves (53–4). Yet fear is not only a means, but also one of the most grievous results of these crimes: fear that continues to live on in people on an unconscious level even when the external world is at peace again and there are no real grounds for fear anymore. It is precisely this unconscious fear that drives both authors to write. They want to bring fear to speech, thereby delimiting its power. During her research in the archives, the narrator of *Ahasveeruse uni* recognizes that she has been living with a fear unknown even to herself, and she reflects on how this fear has become immediately relevant to her, even though she feels constrained to be a researcher who stands outside it all:

> I had to be a researcher, and there I was, sitting at the table – but the mysterious pull of heritage and belonging pulled me sharply in and among the documents, so hard that every now and then I could hear my teeth chattering. I had better not even describe the nights, when I had to force myself to sleep, since the archive was only open during the day. Even the hot water in the heating pipes was spying on me. (*Ahasveeruse uni* 367)

Her active engagement with the files on torture as well as the interrogation and extermination of the Forest Brethren and their relatives during the post-war years has adverse effects on the first-person narrator: she herself begins to live in a constant state of fear. Still, working through the past turns out to be unavoidable. She must read the files in the archive, even if instead of unveiling the truth about the death of her father, she finds an entangled family history of betrayal and accusation. In doing so, she understands and accepts that her teeth are not merely chattering from fear; they are gnashing from rage and pain. As a result, she decides not to announce a competition for the "best sketch of a monument to fear." Ultimately, Mihkelson's narrator strives to have some peace and be able to forget, but on the way, an intense preoccupation with painful things seems to be necessary so that one can live in a society where what happened in the Second World War will not be repeated: "With money one can buy success and security, until the next cattle car edict" (375).

Fear of the recurrence of horrible crimes is for both writers an important motive for continuing to transact with their own painful history and that of their respective peoples. Wolf dedicated an entire chapter of her novel to fear: "Ein Kapitel Angst: Die Arche." She explains:

> This is the special kind of suffering called *Angst,* which drives forth a certain kind of product in which you recognize yourself. That's why they deny it. Hope, becoming free. Liberation as a process. As dealing with oneself (self-preoccupation), for which one cannot set aside only one day out of the year. To pursue the pushing back of *Angst* through writing. That territory which has not yet been liberated, but which is occupied by fear. (*Kindheitsmuster* 518)

Wolf's narrator confesses that she is writing because of fear. It is not entirely clear what it is that she is afraid of, though this gradually does become clearer. Just as Mihkelson's first-person narrator resolves to prevent crimes in the future, Wolf's first-person narrator seeks a way of dealing properly with the past and of preserving it:

> Are the only alternatives silence and that which Ruth and Lenka call "Pseudo" (*falsch, unecht, unaufrichtig, unwahr*?).[10] You dispute this with yourself during the night. You imagine: uprightness is not a one-time act of strength, but a goal, a process with possibilities of approaching, by small steps that take one to unknown, today-yet-unimaginable levels,

> from which emerge new ways of speaking more freely and lightly, openly and soberly, about that which is and also about that which once was. (*Kindheitsmuster* 546)

Just as Mihkelson's first-person narrator has no need for a monument, the right way for dealing with the past is for Wolf's narrator not as a single, forceful intervention, but rather a process, for which both writers' works are rich in models and illustrations. Wolf is proposing new discursive modalities not only for an open and sober settling of accounts with the past, but also for envisioning the present, since one cannot live free of worry if one still has skeletons in the closet. Neither can one continue living if one still sees ghosts. In her study of *Ahasveeruse uni*, Eneken Laanes points to the ghosts that the first-person narrator sees not as living people with real lives, but as the long-dead who appear in dreams. Drawing on Derrida's notion of "hauntology," Laanes asserts that ghosts must be accepted and listened to, since the present is not identical to itself; rather, it is tortured by the ghosts of the past as well as the future (Laanes 439–40). Thus, the present is inextricably caught up with the past, and any conceivable liberation from disturbing ghosts can happen only through an encounter with and a naming of what is painful. In Mihkelson's words,

> We need just this act of looking into the face of things, ... the moment, even the hour of suffering with its unmeasurable duration is what we need, so that the faces – even through despair – can regain the living expressions they once lost, so that the traitors, be they dead or alive, can partake of punishment and – forgiveness. (*Ahasveeruse uni* 397)

Dealing with the past, naming agents of violence (traitors, perpetrators, accomplices), and looking into the face of untrammelled truth can allow suffering to make way for forgiveness, which can eventually be followed by a forgetting that is more benign and less toxic than the forgetting which would bypass this process and take place at the price of silencing the unspoken and the unspeakable.

Both Wolf and Mihkelson forcefully remind their readers that fear can be overcome through making conscious, through naming, and through the will to remember. In writing in a remembering mode, they want to get to the bottom of how specific things in the past were possible, and why humans behaved the way they did. For both, this understanding seems to be a precondition for a freer and better life. Wolf begins her

(re)search within the social order; Mihkelson concentrates much more on individuals. In the end, they are pursuing the same goal: Wolf and Mihkelson are united in the belief that society can only work as a community of individuals, and that individuals are the only ones by whom it can be improved and healed.
TRANSLATED BY TIINA KIRSS

NOTES

1 This article has been written with the support of ESF grants 7354 ("Positioning Life-Writing on Estonian Literary Landscapes") and 9035 ("Dynamics of Address in Estonian Life Writing"). Christa Wolf was born in 1929, the daughter of a businessman in Landsberg (Gorzow Wielkopolski), now a Polish city. In 1945 she fled to Mecklenburg with her family. Since 1962 Wolf has been living as a freelance writer in Berlin. Ene Mihkelson was born in 1944 in the county of Viljandimaa. Since her father evaded both the German and the Soviet mobilizations, her parents left their home in 1949 and, fearing deportation to Siberia, hid in the forest. Ene was raised by relatives in northern Estonia and later attended a boarding school in Rakvere (Kruus and Puhvel).

2 As Tiina Kirss points out in her essay in this volume (chapter 1), though Mihkelson herself resolutely resists any psychoanalytic interpretation of her works, "the documentation of the memory seismograph" in her novels invites us to do precisely that.

3 The Forest Brethren (in Estonian, *metsavennad*) were Estonian, Latvian, and Lithuanian resistance fighters who fought against the Soviet occupation and the Soviet regime. Similar groups of partisans were found in Poland, Rumania, and Ukraine. See also Eva Rein's essay in this volume (chapter 15).

4 From 1963 to 2006, the Herder Prize was the Eastern European counterpart of the Western European Shakespeare, Steffens, and Montaigne prizes, and it served "the purpose of nurturing and advancing cultural relations with the countries of Eastern Europe. Recipients have come from Estonia, Latvia, Lithuania, Poland, the Czech Republic, the Slovak Republic, Slovenia, Croatia, Hungary, Rumania, Ukraine, Byelorussia, Serbia, Montenegro, Yugoslavia, Bosnia and Herzegovina, Bulgaria, Albania, Macedonia, and Greece, who have made exemplary contributions to the preservation and broadening of the European cultural heritage. What is essential is creative achievement in the areas of arts and humanities" (Toepfer).

5 Two years before her death, in a 1971 interview, Bachmann said this about the Nazi conquest of Vienna: "There was a precise moment that shattered my childhood. It was when Hitler's troops marched into Klagenfurt. It was something so horrible that it is with that day that my memory begins: through such an early pain, of such an intensity, that I perhaps never felt the likes of it again" (Koschel and Weidenbaum 111).

6 Whenever possible, the author and translator of the present essay rely on English translations of Estonian and German texts. All other translations, including those of passages from Christa Wolf's *Kindheitsmuster*, Ene Mihkelson's *Ahasveeruse uni*, and the author's interview with Ene Mihkelson are Tiina Kirss's. Note that the passage quoted here was omitted from Ursule Molinaro and Hedwig Rappolt's English translation of Wolf's text; this and other truncations were presumably made because of their remoteness from the English-language reader. The German original reads as follows:

"Selten kennt man das Gewicht der eben angebrochenen Stunde. Es ist Freitag, der 19. Oktober 1973, ein kühler, regenreicher Tag, 18 Uhr 30 Minuten. In Chile hat die Militärjunta den Gebrauch des Wortes 'compañero' verboten. Es gibt also keinen Grund, an der Wirksamkeit von Wörtern zu zweifeln. Auch wenn jemand, auf dessen ernsthaften Umgang mit den Wörtern du seit langem zählst, keinen Gebrauch mehr von ihnen machen kann, sich gehenläßt und diese Tage zeichnet mit dem Satz: Mit meiner verbrannten Hand schreibe ich von der Natur des Feuers. Undine geht. Macht mit der Hand – mit der verbrannten Hand – das Zeichen für Ende. Geh, Tod, und steh still, Zeit. Einsamkeit, in die mir keiner folgt. Es gilt, mit dem Nachklang im Mund, weiterzugehen und zu schweigen.

"Gefaßt sein? Worauf denn? Und von Trauer nicht übermannt? Erklär mir nichts. Ich sah den Salamander durch jedes Feuer gehen. Kein Schauer jagt ihn, und es schmerzt ihn nichts.

"Ein ferner, früher, nun denn: schauerlicher Tod. ("Sollt ich die kurze schauerliche Zeit ...") Ein dunkler Faden schießt in das Muster ein. Unmöglich, ihn fallen zu lassen. Ihn aufzuheben beinah zu früh" (*Kindheitsmuster* 260).

Note that Christa Wolf here mentions 19 October 1973, though Bachmann died on 17 October. It is possible that Christa Wolf did not learn of Bachmann's death until two days later; this, however, is only a conjecture.

7 In Bachmann's own words, "Thus it cannot be the task of the writer to avoid pain, to erase its tracks, to cheat it. To the contrary, he must accept it,

and once again make it clear, so that we can see it. Then we can all come to sight" (75).

8 High blood pressure is one of the most widespread lifelong psychosomatic illnesses suffered by those oppressed during the Second World War in Estonia (Noor 57).

9 Laanes reaches a similar conclusion in "Mäletamise lühis."

10 Roughly, the German words *falsch*, *unecht*, *unaufrichtig*, and *unwahr* translate as fake, artificial, disingenuous, and untrue in this context.

WORKS CITED

Bachmann, Ingeborg. *Die Wahrheit ist dem Menschen zumutbar: Essays, Reden, Kleinere Schriften*. Munich: Piper, 1981.

Gilmore, Leigh. *The Limits of Autobiography: Trauma and Testimony*. Ithaca, NY: Cornell University Press, 2001.

Kadar, Marlene. "Coming to Terms: Life Writing – From Genre to Critical Practice." In *Essays on Life Writing: From Genre to Critical Practice*, ed. M. Kadar, 3–16. Toronto: University of Toronto Press, 1992.

Koschel, Christine, and Inge von Weidenbaum. *Ingeborg Bachmann: Wir müssen wahre Sätze finden. Gespräche und Interviews*. Munich: Piper, 1991.

Laanes, Eneken. "Mäletamise lühis: Ene Mihkelsoni *Ahasveeruse uni*." *Keel ja Kirjandus* 6 (2006): 433–48.

Lejeune, Philippe. *Le pacte autobiographique*. Paris: Éditions du Seuil, 1975.

Menchú, Rigoberta. *I, Rigoberta Menchú: An Indian Woman in Guatemala*. London: Verso, 1993.

Mihkelson, Ene. *Ahasveeruse uni* [The Sleep of Ahasuerus]. Tallinn: Tuum, 2001.

Mihkelson, Ene. "Isiklikust kunstis." *Looming* (Tallinn) 6(1971): 947–8.

Noor, Heino. "Tervisele tekitatud püsikahjud." In *Valge Raamat: Eesti rahva kaotustest okupatsioonide läbi 1940 – 1991.*, 52–66. Tallinn: Eesti Entsüklopeediakirjastus, 2005.

Sakova, Aija. "Et olla õnnelik, peab olema ärkvel. Intervjuu Herderi preemia laureaadi Ene Mihkelsoniga." *Sirp*, 12 May 2006: 11.

Toepfer, Alfred. "Preise bis 2006." Alfred Toepfer Stiftung, 2006. http://www.toepfer-fvs.de/preise-bis-2006.html.

Wolf, Christa. *Kindheitsmuster*. Munich: Luchterhand, 2002.

Wolf, Christa. *Lesen und Schreiben: Essays, Aufsätze, Reden*. Darmstadt: Luchterhand, 1983.

Wolf, Christa. "Reading and Writing." In *The Author's Dimension: Selected Essays*, trans. Jan Van Heurck. Chicago: University of Chicago Press, 1995.

14 The Stigma of the Autobiographical

JULIA STRAUB

Aija Sakova's essay is concerned with the ghosts of the past and their return, brought about by the act of writing; the inescapability of memories; and the painfulness inherent in processes of remembering and life writing. Her juxtaposition of one of the most renowned and remarkable works in twentieth-century German literature, Christa Wolf's autobiographical novel *Kindsheitsmuster*, and a gem of Estonian life writing, Ene Mihkelson's *Ahasveeruse uni* – both of which focus on the author's childhood – reflects the paradox residing in the act of writing about trauma: it is a potentially curative measure, that is, a means of coping with atrocious experiences, but it also has the power to tear open such wounds. Furthermore, Sakova shows that there is something like a moral imperative to remember that reaches beyond individualistic purposes usually ascribed to the genre, such as self-objectivization and self-stylization or mere navel gazing. Both of the autobiographical novels she discusses suggest that it is one's individual as well as humanity's collective duty not to let certain things slip into oblivion. The second feature these texts share, according to Sakova, is that they explicitly deal with the discomfort which writing about one's life can cause. To this, she adds that the unease which accompanies the writer's task also affects the reader. It is in the line of convergence of these two aspects that Sakova's central concern in her essay, namely, the unavoidable painfulness of memory residing in the act of writing about one's life, surfaces most clearly. As Sakova demonstrates, both novels are as much about the remembered events they depict, the horrors of the past – in Wolf's case the catastrophic build-up of the Third Reich, in Mihkelson's case the impact of Soviet occupation on the Estonian people – as about the afterlife of these atrocious events, which can, if at all, only be controlled with enormous efforts and provided there is a willingness to face the ghosts of the past. The painfulness of reliving traumatic events does not only light up in processes of remembering and the subsequent putting down of these memories on paper, but they haunt the writers in psychological and tangible, physical ways, that is, in the form of bodily ailments often caused by and connected to intense emotional stress or fear. "Fear" is a central focus of Aija Sakova's article: coming from various angles and caused by a variety of factors, fear seems to be bound up with writing about trauma in autobiographical contexts. My response focuses on the ways in which "fear" runs through Aija Sakova's contribution and aims to further our understanding of why Mihkelson and Wolf are hesitant to see their texts typologized as autobiographies. In other words, I probe the stigma that seems to adhere to the autobiographical genre.

Sakova's article compellingly investigates the processes of remembering and writing about traumatic experiences as fear-ridden phenomena: fear is the engine that sets free the energy to cope with trauma by writing, and fear is a force which imposes the ethical imperative to write against oblivion and to keep these horrors from continuing. Yet Sakova is aware that there is a danger inherent in writing about trauma, for "writers not only expose themselves before their readers; they can also sink into the past too deeply and be overwhelmed with memories that need to be worked through." I would like to take this idea further and at the same time postulate a challenge to the assumption that life writing has a curative or restorative effect per se. The writer who is faced with trauma, his own or that of others, commits a balancing act which could go horribly wrong. Philip Roth includes a passage in *Exit Ghost* (2007) which characterizes the writing about trauma in a thought-provoking, since less reconciliatory or optimistic, way:

> When Primo Levi killed himself everyone said it was because of his having been an inmate at Auschwitz. I thought it was because of his *writing* about Auschwitz, the labor of the last book, contemplating that horror with all that clarity. Getting up every morning to write that book would have killed anyone. (151)

The striking aspect of this line of reasoning is that it depicts the act of writing about traumatic experiences as ultimately more harmful and challenging than living through the horrors which produced the trauma. In this understanding, writing offers no healthy working through of the past, no prospect of recovery. The contemplative quality of life writing is here shown as the cruellest kind of suffering since it confronts the writer with the scope and immensity of the committed cruelties, which only become clear if seen from what is an allegedly safe vantage point of spatial and temporal detachment. This is an argument which should keep us from any hasty conclusions regarding the painful, yet wholesome effects of writing about trauma. While it can bring about reconciliation and healing in many cases, it provides no universal, easily available cure. One thus has to fully acknowledge the danger of self-annihilation which Wolf and Mihkelson – and any other writer in their situation – face. They brave it, since remembering and writing are experienced by both as their moral duty, even if the consequences for their own lives may be disastrous. As is said at one point in Sakova's essay, not to write, not to remember would mean to look away, to become a mute witness and thus an accomplice, and thereby to help prepare a potential breeding ground for a reiteration of events which should never be repeated. Hence, Wolf and Mihkelson's texts, regardless of their different historical contexts, point towards the humanistic ends of life writing in its broadest sense since the individual suffering which these works narrate refers back to moments of collective traumatization and memory. While being accounts of private traumatic experiences, they thus function as testimonies or voices for those who cannot reflect on or express their suffering for themselves (any longer).

There is a further question connected to the idea of "fear," one which Sakova raises but ultimately fails to answer. *Why* do Wolf and Mihkelson "quite obviously reject autobiographicality as a simplistic assumption"? In other words, why is there a stigma of the autobiographical, which makes these two authors, like many others, prefer to stick to the novel as the safer category? Why do they not want their texts to be thought of as autobiographies, if, as Sakova points out, they are very much present in their texts, that is, if the autobiographical elements are perfectly obvious? Undoubtedly, genre labels "narrow down the possibilities of both how authors can write and what they can write about," as Sakova puts it. Autobiography opens up a contractual dimension of the reader–author relationship which could be seen as an infringement on imaginative licence. After all, the umbrella of the novel allows for refractions, distortions, digressions, and transgressions which are the prerogative of fictional writing. Referring to a work of literature as autobiographical implies an adherence to factuality which threatens to straightjacket the imagination of a writer. Furthermore, factuality might exactly not be the means by which trauma can be dealt with on a literary level, as it basically means that gaping wounds are bluntly pointed at, without the interceptive buffer of fictionalizing strategies.

It is interesting that Wolf and Mihkelson, by virtue of their disavowal of the genre of "autobiography," opt for the inverse strategy chosen by some authors who turn to the genre of life writing in the hope of thereby securing a wider readership and concomitant financial rewards. A far-reaching scandal was caused, for example, by the failure of the publishers of James Frey's *A Million Little Pieces* (2003) to unambiguously identify it as a "novel" from the beginning. By not acknowledging the fictional components of this book, they broke the contract set up with its buyers and readers, eliciting a public outcry of dismay and disappointment.[1] Many other examples could be brought into play that illustrate the dovetailed relationship between life writing and fiction, a relationship which is so intricate that it can hardly ever be fully elucidated. Yet maybe this is not even called for.

Are these sufficient reasons to explain why autobiography is a troubled genre that inspires a certain wariness in authors? I would like to introduce another, related reason to account for Mihkelson's and Wolf's reluctance to consciously embrace the autobiographical mode, apart from their being scared of losing their imaginative freedom and enduring psychoanalytic interpretations, or being suspected of not telling the truth. Jacques Derrida's work on Friedrich Nietzsche and his afterlife provides my point of departure. In *Otobiographies* (1982), Derrida fuses the problematic notions of historical authorship, authority, and the function of the reader in ways that might be useful for an exploration of Mihkelson's and Wolf's sceptical attitudes towards the autobiographical. Eventually, autobiographical writing means putting oneself "on the line," as Derrida puts it (6). The author's proper name or signature establishes a contract between the reader and the author: the author lives on his own credit, that is, by signing the text with his name he becomes complicit with his own mortality. The author's signature represents "a nominal contract which falls due only upon the death of the one who says 'I live' in the present" (10–11). The autobiographical contract will only come into effect when the reader returns to the author, whose life will be validated, that is, the contract sealed, by virtue of the reader's reaffirmation of the author's life. According to Derrida, the genre of autobiography, in its most misunderstood sense, results in an "impossible protocol ... for reading and especially for teaching," revealing the "ridiculous naiveté, ... [the] sly, obscure, and shady business" that lies "behind declarations of the type: Friedrich Nietzsche said this or that, he thought this or that about this or that subject" (14). Thus, autobiographies can be corrupted by the reader unlike any other text. Their critical and popular afterlives are likely to impose closure upon texts that should remain open for reiterated reception processes, for repeated affirmation, defying definite interpretation. Early in her essay, Sakova writes about the empathy which is required of Wolf's and Mihkelson's readers, and she thereby also characterizes the recipients' position as essentially vulnerable. Readers cannot withdraw behind a safe curtain which separates their lives from those of others, or their reality from that presented in the book they are reading. For readers of *Kindheitsmuster* and *Ahasveeruse uni*, this means that they have to leave their comfort zone and become aware of the urgency of the authors' concerns, and their relevance to anybody's, including their own, existence. But the reader bears another responsibility and is not just the helpless recipient, constantly on the verge of being affected. He has to keep his reading of autobiographies dynamic. Thus, if authors baulk at the label "autobiography" for their work, however obviously autobiographical it may be, then this maybe happens because they are afraid of what readers will do to it. They fear the irreversible seal of interpretation which we may stamp on the texts, and themselves.

NOTE

1 On Frey, see also Philipp Schweighauser's essay on Adorno, Benjamin, and Elie Wiesel's *Night* in this volume (chapter 2).

WORKS CITED

Derrida, Jacques. *The Ear of the Other: Otobiography, Transference, Translation: Texts and Discussions with Jaques Derrida*. 1982. Ed. Christie V. McDonald. Trans. Peggy Kamuf. New York: Schocken Books, 1985.
Frey, James. *A Million Little Pieces*. New York: Picador, 2003.
Mihkelson, Ene. *Ahasveeruse uni*. Tallinn: Tuum, 2001.
Roth, Philip. *Exit Ghost*. London: Jonathan Cape, 2007.
Wolf, Christa. *Kindheitsmuster*. Munich: Luchterhand, 2002.

15 The Search for the Lost Parent in Joy Kogawa's *Obasan* and Ene Mihkelson's *Ahasveeruse uni* (The Sleep of Ahasuerus)

EVA REIN

We are the Issei and the Nisei and the Sansei, the Japanese Canadians. We disappear into the future undemanding as dew.

Joy Kogawa, *Obasan* 131–2

We are omitted from history if we do not speak out.

Ene Mihkelson, *Ahasveeruse uni* 66[1]

The Japanese-Canadian writer Joy Kogawa's *Obasan* (1981) and the Estonian writer Ene Mihkelson's *Ahasveeruse uni* (The Sleep of Ahasuerus, 2001) were written and published roughly during that decade in the histories of Canada and Estonia in which the silenced and traumatic chapters of the two countries' pasts began to be addressed. Canada's adoption of a policy of multiculturalism in 1971 and Estonia's restoration of its independence in 1991 paved the way for the emergence of narratives about previously marginalized individuals and groups. In many cases, these narratives were authored by marginalized individuals themselves. The functions Kogawa's and Mihkelson's novels perform are similar to those of (auto)biographies that engage with the same historical events and situations: they provide a space in which the traumatic pasts can be addressed, and they aim for a recognition of the narratives that come out of those pasts and their insertion into the story of the nation. At the same time, the stories these writers tell differ significantly from coming-to-voice narratives of trauma as we know them from more conventional forms of life writing. Apart from being works of fiction, or, rather, precisely because they are fictions, both novels thematize and embody the ongoing struggle between telling and not telling, between remembering and forgetting, between constructing a life story and refraining from doing so. And in staging that struggle, Kogawa and Mihkelson comment on life writing from a metaperspective.

While Kogawa's and Mihkelson's novels contain autobiographical elements, they are not autobiographies. They are trauma novels that emphasize transgenerational haunting, and they are historiographic metafictions that mix fact and fiction.[2] Still, *Obasan* and *Ahasveeruse uni* are also life writings in a specific, broad sense of the term. Discussing life writing by French women since 1968, Kathryn Robson identifies "the quest for self-expression, to 'break out of silence,' be it via fiction, autobiography or hybrid forms of both" as a "dominant theme of these texts" (14). Robson's characterization of her texts, all of which centrally revolve around individual and collective traumas, also applies to Kogawa's and Mihkelson's novels: "These texts are not … offered up as straightforward, 'raw' testimonies to lived traumatic experiences, or even as autobiographies; instead, they are self-consciously stylized and fictionalised, concerned less with telling a story of trauma than with exploring, and exploding, the limits of what can be told" (14). In Robson's view, the choice of fiction over autobiography is particularly appropriate for trauma narratives: "Where autobiography implies a knowing subject who can claim and narrate his or her own experience, trauma renders such (self)knowledge impossible; and questions how we can be sure of the 'truth' and of the reality of experience and memory" (15). *Obasan* and *Ahasveeruse uni* stage precisely those epistemological difficulties. In these texts, too, "the relation between 'life' and 'writing' can never be taken for granted," and they also "do not simply narrate [lived] experience as such; instead they foreground the very question of how such experience can be narrated" (15). It is in that sense that both Robson's texts and those I discuss can be described as "life writing" – a term that serves Robson "to trouble the fraught relation between 'life' and 'writing'" (15).

Already in the first chapters of *Obasan* and *Ahasveeruse uni*, as the middle-aged female protagonist-narrators begin their stories in the narrative present, it becomes clear that both novels are haunted by the past. In *Obasan*, Naomi Nakane is wondering why Uncle Isamu has been taking her on an annual trip to the coulee for the past eighteen years without ever revealing its purpose to her (4). Only later will she learn that this had been done to commemorate her lost mother. In *Ahasveeruse uni*,

M. Reiter visits the village of her birth and early childhood in order to interview the people who had known her lost father when an elderly woman called Endla suddenly asks M. whether her father was shot by an Estonian (24). The ghosts of Naomi Nakane's mother and M. Reiter's father epitomize a silenced and suppressed chapter of both their daughters' personal histories and that of the nation. Kogawa's *Obasan* and Ene Mihkelson's *Ahasveeruse uni* both deal with the Second World War and its aftermath. More specifically, through the story of the protagonists, the novels focus on the experience of large groups of people who became exiles in their own homeland as a result of a succession of events triggered by the war. In the wake of Pearl Harbor (7 December 1941), Japanese-Canadians were labelled a "yellow peril" by Canadian authorities and became targets of persecution and internments carried out on the grounds that Japanese-Canadians might prove disloyal to Canada. After the incorporation of Estonia into the USSR on 6 August 1940, the Soviet authorities began to purge Soviet Estonia by raids and mass deportations of people considered "unfit elements" of Soviet society. Among the victims were private farm owners, whom the Soviets stigmatized as *kulaks* (rich peasants). The power elites of Canada and Estonia considered these groups "enemy aliens" and "enemies of the people," respectively. In the process of realizing the racist plan "to solve (once and for all?) the 'Japanese problem'" (Miki 39) in Canada and to "liquidat[e] the *kulaks* as a class" in Estonia, the two countries' authorities not only removed the "enemies" physically from society, but also silenced their voices in official historiography.[3] Thus, in both nations, efforts were made to wipe whole groups of people from collective memory. *Obasan* and *Ahasveeruse uni* can be read as fictional attempts to write these groups back into history and to remind us that social catastrophes have a profound long-term impact not only on the survivors but also on their children. While physically absent from the protagonists' lives, the lost parents haunt their daughters in both novels. What haunts them with particular force are the gaps created by the silences and secrets of the survivors.

The terror of the Second World War and its aftermath resulted in a nightmare whose grip was tightened by oppressive legal measures taken long after the war was officially over. The wartime policy of the dispersal of Japanese-Canadians disintegrated their families and destroyed their close community, and it rendered them both outsiders and insiders of Canadian society – an utterly perplexing state for many. In Estonia, families and communities were torn apart, and further divisions ensued due to people's different allegiances during the alternating wartime Soviet and German occupations and the half-century of Soviet domination. Under those circumstances, and as a result of the protective silences and willed amnesia of the surviving family members and relatives, Naomi's mother and M.'s father were also erased from their daughters' family histories. In the narrative present of both novels, the daughters become aware of the depth of their identity crisis when they realize that they have been cut off from their historical, cultural, and social heritage. Both protagonists yearn for a physical and emotional reconnection with their lost parent and seek to gain knowledge about the earlier generation's life so as to alleviate their own sense of dispossession. At the outset, Naomi and M. hope that by learning about the personality, the ethnic and cultural background, and the fate of their lost parent, they can resolve their own identity crisis. Yet while both embark on a quest, their narratives diverge from the traditional Ulyssean quest plot to foreground cultural intertexts that enable them to establish an imaginative relationship with their lost parent.

Naomi's and M.'s condition is characterized by what Cathy Caruth calls being "possessed" by a traumatic event ("Trauma" 4–5), a state that manifests itself in the daughters' recurrent dreams and compulsive thoughts relating to the lost parent and the circumstances of the parent's disappearance. Caruth's observation that "history, like trauma, is never simply one's own, that history is precisely the way we are implicated in each other's traumas" (*Unclaimed* 24) is highly pertinent to Kogawa's and Mihkelson's exploration of their protagonists' attempts to know the past in the present. Naomi and M. are possessed by the loss of their parent because they have not been able fully to experience the event when it happened, nor have they been able to assimilate it at a later stage. What further complicates the daughters' situations and access to the past of their parents is their generational position in relation to the time of the social catastrophe. As survivors of the internment (in Naomi's case) and the raids (in M.'s case), both protagonists suffer from traumas of their own. At the same time, they are the children of survivors whose few personal memories of the events that shaped their parents' lives are filtered through an infant's limited perspective. This likens them to what is known as the "generation after" in Holocaust studies. Ernst van Alphen has pointed out that the traumatized survivors' children, who do not have their own memories of the Holocaust, grow up surrounded by the silences and cryptic remarks of their parents, or by excessive retellings of camp memoirs, and that in both cases, the children suffer from their parents' inability to relate to them, which creates a discontinuity in the relationship between generations (477–8).

Being raised by foster parents who never explain to them the context of their silences and cryptic remarks, Naomi and M. have no access to the world in which either they or their biological parents lived during the atrocities. In both protagonists' narratives, there are multiple references to survivors hiding information about the lost parent. For decades, Naomi has heard the survivors whispering, "Kodomo no tame. For the sake of the children" (*Obasan* 26). In vain does she ask Aunt Obasan about the fate of her mother: "The greater my urgency to know, the thicker her silences have always been. No prodding will elicit clues" (55). Similarly, relatives withhold information concerning her father to protect M. from Soviet repressions: "It is better if you do not know what happened to your father ... then it is not possible to elicit anything from you even in the case of coercive interrogation" (*Ahasveeruse* 107). While it is obvious that part of the foster parents' and the relatives' silence is protective, there is a highly problematic side to that silence: in addition to their own traumas, Naomi and M. have unawares inherited another trauma from the survivors – the unexplainable secret concerning the circumstances of the lost parent's death. Some theorists speak of the transgenerational transmission of trauma in such cases: "An individual, who is usually a parent, transmits a traumatic or shameful event that he keeps secret, in silence directly into the unconscious of his child through cryptic language and behaviour" (Rashkin 435).

Naomi's and M.'s experiences show that the children of survivors have a paradoxical and vexatious relation to the social catastrophe – they both know and do not know about it. Eva Hoffman argues that in order to make sense of these cryptic messages and silences, the children of survivors need to start contextualizing and conceptualizing them. She elaborates on the marked differences between the survivors of the Holocaust and their children, explaining that the survivors are eventually able to narrate their memories with the help of narrative frameworks provided by fiction and film, memoirs, and the testimonies of others. For the generation after, memory work proceeds in the opposite direction: "While the adult world asks first 'what happened,' and from there follows its uncertain and sometimes resistant route toward the inward meaning of the facts, those who are born after calamity sense its most inward meanings first and have to work their way outwards toward the facts and the worldly shape of events" (16). One of the crucial questions that arises for Naomi and M. is – to borrow the images of dismemberment that plague them – whether and how an amputee, cut off from her parents, her heritage, and the anchors of memory that would help her make sense of the past, can cope with loss. According to van Alphen, "the hampered indexical relationship between past and present, between event and its memory" can be "restored thanks to the help of others, or culture as such" (486). In the case of the children of survivors, van Alphen adds, we cannot really speak of memories in the strict sense of the word; yet this is not to say that these children completely lack an idea of their family's past (486). In fact, as Vieda Skultans has observed, some people who are too young to have their own memories of a war, can still "remember" it, which points to "the fact that [such memories] are not private property" (18).[4] As Skultans points out, personal narrative accounts rely on shared stories about the past and use various cultural resources "to make sense of the past and incorporate it into a personal history" (27). Apart from survivors' accounts, these cultural resources may include literary and historical texts that people have been exposed to at school as well as a host of other texts accessible in cultural space.

Naomi and M. especially turn to documentary sources available in private and public archives. The documents found there not only allow them access to the time in which the lost parent lived; the knowledge they gain from them plays a crucial role in their quest. Naomi reads materials received in Aunt Emily's parcel after her uncle's death. These include official letters; newspaper clippings; Aunt Emily's diary, which consists of her letters to Naomi's mother; her manuscript of the Nisei struggle for freedom;[5] and various additional documents. For Naomi, old family photographs are also of great importance. M. reads reports, witness testimonies, and other texts from several archives, including that of the security forces, to which she only gains access after the restoration of Estonia's independence. She also orders archival photographs of her father and mother and listens to the memoir of Kaarel Kolgamets, who recalls the years he spent in the forest together with M.'s parents who had become Forest Brethren to avoid being deported to Siberia once M.'s father had been proclaimed a *kulak* by the Soviet authorities.[6]

In the narratives, the numerous documents Naomi and M. read are presented in the form of paratextual insertions. As Linda Hutcheon points out, such insertions perform a double function in historiographic metafiction: they provide the events of the story with a historical context; at the same time, they reveal that the historical context itself is discursive, that is, that it is made up of representations (84). Importantly, Naomi and M. are not passive readers of those documents. On the contrary, they begin to interpret them critically and become aware that the past is made up of numerous versions that are often in disagreement with one another. These multiple versions of the past serve to draw attention to what Hutcheon calls the "textual nature of the archival traces" (75). She explains that "archival traces are by no means unproblematic in their different possible interpretations. Historiographic metafiction's self-conscious thematising of the process of fact-producing also foregrounds this hermeneutic problem" (75). Hutcheon adds that postmodern fiction is characterized by "a contradictory turning to the archive and yet a contesting of its authority" (77). It is exactly this simultaneous affirmation and contestation of the archive that characterizes Naomi's and M.'s searches for knowledge about their lost parents. During these quests, it becomes painfully clear that texts do not merely mirror the real; they shape it. As *Obasan*'s Aunt Emily puts it when she comments on the Canadian government's policy of labelling Japanese-Canadians the "yellow peril": "None of us ... escaped naming. We were defined and identified by the way we were seen" (139).

Kogawa's novel shows how Japanese-Canadians were constructed both as the enemy and as a model minority during the Second World War. Naomi becomes aware of the harsh segregation after Pearl Harbor when she reads Aunt Emily's diary of letters addressed to her elder sister in Japan, Naomi's mother: "Signs have been posted on all highways – 'Japs Keep Out'" (103). However, a propaganda article published in a Canadian newspaper that Naomi finds in Aunt Emily's package testifies to an opposite discourse on Japanese-Canadians. The article features "a photograph of one family, all smiles, standing around a pile of beets. The caption reads: 'Grinning and Happy'" and is offensively titled "Find Jap Evacuees Best Beet Workers" (231). Naomi's disaffection with both images imposed on her ethnic community is best exemplified when she says, "And I am tired, I suppose, because I want to get away from all this ... I want to break loose from the heavy identity, the evidence of rejection, the unexpressed passion, the misunderstood politeness" (218). Naomi's narrative points to Canada's serious racism problem, which takes less obvious but equally dangerous forms in the age of multiculturalism. *Obasan* calls for the need to explore racism in the foundations of Canada as well as in the social, political, and cultural frameworks that continue to support it in the country today. In a similar vein, M.'s narrative in

Ahasveeruse uni reveals the way in which the Forest Brethren are constructed as both enemies and heroes from within different ideological discourses during the occupation and after the restoration of independence. While going through the security forces' files dating from the period in which her father perished, M. insightfully observes that, depending on what was necessary and useful for the Soviet authorities, different documents represent the interrogated suspects in differing ways: "In the protocols, the interrogated are often presented like children whose lies the wiser person sees through, while in reports the same men have been described as bandits who pose a threat to the whole nation and whom it has been necessary to besiege with a carload of soldiers" (392). A series of photographs from the security forces archive that show some Forest Brethren in a less than favourable light eventually makes M. herself aware that treating them as a homogeneous group is not justified. However, her critical reasoning is cut short by a threatening remark from a character called the Archivist, who calls her a troublemaker for not allowing the survivors and their children to live in peace. Obviously, her archival research and interviews have led to results that make her dangerously knowledgeable in the eyes of those for whom too much is at stake. M. realizes that she is swimming against the tide of public opinion with her questioning of the Forest Brethren's behaviour. Only after Estonia regained independence did they come to be regarded as heroes who kept alive ideals of freedom and national independence during the Soviet occupation. While this is definitely true for some of them, M. discovers that the motives of the individual Forest Brethren could vary from escaping Soviet repressions to collaborating with the Soviet security forces. M. muses with bitter irony, "We need a different picture and view. We need the lie that men fought for the fatherland to their last breath. And the women oiled the guns, were faithful companions to the men, soldiers anyway" (*Ahasveeruse* 282). M.'s narrative obstructs the introduction of new lies before the old ones have been challenged. These lies serve the cause of the newly independent nation's fragile selfhood, which does not yet allow for a critical look into the complexities of its recent past. M.'s story highlights the need for an Estonian equivalent of *Vergangenheitsbewältigung*,[7] but it also shows why it is difficult to begin the process when the critical distance from the previous social formation is missing, and when the position, choices, and deeds of many individuals and institutions appear in a completely different light from the perspective of the present.

M.'s and Naomi's searches do not provide them with concrete answers to their questions about their lost parent's past, but leave them with a number of contradictory accounts. During their quests, both encounter the complex legacy of their heritage. As their narratives evolve, the protagonists gain insights into the discourses that have defined their families and themselves as other, shaped the destiny of their parents, and continue to shape their own identities in the present. More specifically, this narrative present is, in Naomi's case, 1970s Canada, whose official narrative of progress presents it to Canadians and the rest of the world as the first country to have adopted a "multiculturalism policy" and, in M.'s case, 1990s Estonia, whose official discourse renders all of Estonian history in terms of a centuries-long struggle of ethnic Estonians against various oppressors that has reached a desired and rightful closure with the restoration of Estonian independence. Neither protagonist can identify with that master narrative and its underlying ideology, whose aim is obviously to sustain the nation's collective identity and image at home and abroad. This is so because Naomi's and M.'s complex legacies cannot be fitted into another sweeping success story of the nation. Such a story would silence their little narratives for the common good.

In addition to the stories told by survivors and the archive, Naomi and M. draw on a multiplicity of additional cultural resources and intertexts: the Bible, Christian and (in *Obasan*'s case) Buddhist religion, works of literature, research papers, parables, legends, fairy tales, and songs – from folk music to national anthems. According to Skultans, the significance of such cultural resources "lies primarily in the power which they give to individuals to organize their experience rather than in any direct access to the past" (27). Skultans emphasizes that the ways in which individuals tap into these cultural resources differ from person to person, and she adds that they are tailored to personal needs (27). This is also true for the two novels' most important intertexts, which the protagonists enlist in their attempts to establish a meaningful relationship with their lost parent: Fyodor Dostoevsky's parable of the Grand Inquisitor in *Obasan* and the legend of Ahasuerus/the Wandering Jew in *Ahasveeruse uni*. These intertexts deserve a closer look.

In *Obasan*, the Grand Inquisitor makes his appearance in the middle of Naomi's dream and turns it into a nightmare as she is taking a nap during Uncle Isamu's wake. In Dostoevsky's *The Brothers Karamazov*, the Grand Inquisitor has Jesus jailed and silences him, only to let him go when Jesus kisses him on his lips.[8] In Naomi's dream, the Grand

Inquisitor questions Naomi's mother: "His demand to know was both a judgement and a refusal to hear. The more he questioned her, the more he was her accuser and murderer. The more he killed her, the deeper her silence became" (273–4). Naomi considers the behaviour of the Grand Inquisitor as deeply short-sighted and flawed, and she suggests how her mother should be approached instead: "What the Grand Inquisitor has never learned is that the avenues of speech are the avenues of silence. To hear my mother, to attend to her speech, to attend to the sound of stone, he must first become silent. Only when he enters her abandonment will he be released from his own" (274). By interpreting the implications of the figure of the Grand Inquisitor for herself, Naomi reaches a crucial moment in her understanding of her mother's silences, and she realizes that she has made the same mistake as the Grand Inquisitor: "Her tale is a rose with a tangled stem. All this questioning, this clawing at her grave, is an unseemly thing. Let the inquisition rest tonight. In the week of my uncle's departure, let there be peace" (274). Naomi begins to realize that by having doubted and questioned her mother and by demanding a response without really wanting to know what her mother would have to say, she has herself silenced her mother in much the same way that the Grand Inquisitor silenced her in the nightmare and Jesus in the prison of Dostoevsky's novel. Naomi realizes that her judgment of her mother's silence as useless to herself was a mistake, and she concludes that her mother's silence was a loving silence. For Naomi, the intertextual figure of the Grand Inquisitor – a figure that embodies individuals and institutions that abuse power, manipulate their victims, and silence them – is an important means by which she rethinks her relation to her lost mother.[9]

In *Ahasveeruse uni*, the figure of Ahasuerus appears as a Jewish man in a dream that M.'s father, Meinhard, allegedly had. In Mihkelson's fictional world, we learn about that dream from the memoir of the Forest Brother and national hero Kaarel Kolgamets, who claims that both he and Meinhard had a prophetic dream before Meinhard's death in the Battle of Kolga: "Kaarel had been informed in the dream that he would be left hanging by his hair attached to a log thrown over a ravine, and in Meinhard's dream a man of Jewish descent had given him a passport as a present" (148). When M. finds that Kaarel quotes Meinhard's dream verbatim from his memoir, she begins to doubt its veracity: "Why exactly a man of Jewish descent, it had started hammering in her head, what kind of passport. Travel passport! Does Kaarel want to announce – was it announced to Meinhard in the dream! – that such a long journey would be awaiting him that he should need a passport for that? ... What kind of journey would be waiting for a Forest Brother in the February of 1953?" (148). M., who knows that "Meinhard's name remained free for someone else" (148), begins to suspect that the actual patterns were the reverse of what she is told and that it was Kaarel himself who was going to travel. This scene problematizes the official version of Meinhard's death as recorded in the archive of the security forces. It highlights that there may have been at least one additional reason for killing Meinhard – not only because he was a Forest Brother, but also because his death would provide a new identity for Kaarel. And indeed, M. later learns from official documents that when Meinhard was shot dead, his identity was stolen by Kaarel, who turns out to be a Soviet agent disguised as a Forest Brother who had accompanied Meinhard to the farm at Kolga, where the shooting occurred. When M. learns this, she realizes that her father shares the fate of Ahasuerus, the legendary figure of the Wandering Jew who is condemned to live until the end of the world for insulting Jesus on his way to crucifixion: "As if the organizers of the raid had known in that spring of the year 1953 that a time may come when Kaarel, too, needs defence. There is no way of demanding anything from the dead person, and her dead father will live in these documents to the end of times" (200).[10]

Since 1884, the legend of Ahasuerus has been published in Estonian several times under different titles (Sildre and Laur).[11] In its Estonian versions, the legend contains a modification that is relevant for Mihkelson's novel. In Estonian folklore, "the punishment of Ahasuerus entails eternally rolling a stone up a high mountain, only to go after it again to the base of the mountain" ("Ahasveerus"). Through this link with the Greek Sisyphus myth, Mihkelson's use of the Estonian version of the legend of Ahasuerus foregrounds the punishment that has befallen M.'s father. In *Ahasveeruse uni,* it is not clear what exactly may have earned Meinhard his punishment. Part of this vagueness stems from the fact that the crimes he may have been considered as being guilty of were not really those he could have been responsible for – for example, he could not choose the country he lived in when it became occupied territory. Neither did he have any say when he was drafted into the German army, nor could he prevent being declared a persona non grata – a *kulak* – by the Soviets. His "crime" may have been his loyalty to the ideal of Estonian independence and his resistance to the Soviet ideology and occupying powers. And yet, Meinhard's punishment is handed down to his daughter in the sense that M., too, resembles an Ahasuerus who can find neither peace nor home. In search of her lost family history, M. wanders throughout Estonia and other European countries in search of a home in the physical as well as the psychological sense. One could read M.'s "punishment" in terms of a transgenerational transmission of trauma, but when she incorporates the Sisyphus intertext into her own narrative, her notion that she has inherited her father's punishment undergoes a significant transformation. Earlier in her narrative, M. argued that with the restoration of Estonian independence, her "body lost the innocence of resistance" (27). Until then, she considered herself a victim of choices made for her by the occupying regime (26). Now, M. assumes responsibility for her father and herself as she thinks of herself rolling not just a stone but a "stone of voice." She thinks, "I must continue – now her voice rose again – as if the stone of voice had to be lugged up a mountain again, I must continue to the end, so that the thump of the bodies rendered nameless could be heard a little bit farther than the beats of my own heart that is growing tired" (211). M. is determined to break the silence surrounding the circumstances of her father's death as well as other similar cases, and to struggle against collective amnesia to challenge official historiographies that are revealed as deeply problematic. That her goal is extremely hard to achieve is implied by the Sisyphean intertext of endless struggle. Yet the activity itself provides consistency that can bring about change: "It is me who is my father, it is me who is his future" (330).

In assigning multiple new meanings to the intertexts and cultural resources they draw on, the protagonists of Kogawa's and Mihkelson's novels bridge the gap between the historical knowledge they accumulate from the archive and the torturing inexplicability of their parent's disappearance. In their slow and intermittent moves from forgetting to remembering, Naomi and M. incorporate and weave these cultural intertexts into their narrative to articulate their own multiple, shifting, and contradictory subject positions, while at the same time giving an identity to their lost and silenced parent. As they raise questions concerning the fate of collective and cultural memory in Canada and Estonia, these daughters rethink not only their sense of self, but also their relation to their family, their community, and their nation. Their quests end neither in a full recovery of essential selfhood nor in a Ulyssean homecoming: while the eloquent hero of Homer's epic recites parts of his story before a large audience, Naomi and M. struggle to break the silence and find a voice, telling their stories in silence, with nobody to listen to them. In telling the stories of their lives, they repeatedly sift through the same material the way an archaeologist digs the ground. In the process, they both draw on and contest the authority of the archive, explore the limits of what can be told about the self and others, and come to realize that unless the stories of all those whose experiences were similar to those of their lost parent are told, the past will become irretrievable while continuing to exercise its power over present and future generations.

NOTES

1 All translations of Ene Mihkelson's *Ahasveeruse uni* are mine. I would like to thank Linda Hutcheon for her valuable comments on an early version of this essay and her encouragement of my comparative research project.
2 The vexed question of the genre Ene Mihkelson's novel belongs to is also discussed by Aija Sakova in her essay in this volume (chapter 13).
3 Raun explains that "liquidation of the *kulaks* as a class" was an official slogan of the supporters of Stalin's ideas (178).
4 Skultans's argument is grounded in the tension between her own awareness of "the nature of Soviet history: its rigid and monopolistic view of history which was at odds with individual experience" (17) and her insight that "personal memories are inscribed on a palimpsest which still bears the imprint of other earlier memories" (18). I am indebted to Tiina Kirss for pointing me to the work of Vieda Skultans, which has been instrumental to the development of my argument in the present essay.
5 "Nisei" refers to the second generation of Japanese-Canadians.
6 "Forest Brethren" refers to anti-Soviet guerrillas.
7 The German term *Vergangenheitsbewältigung* names a collective process of coming to terms with the (violent) past.
8 In Dostoevsky, the passage in question focuses on a poem Ivan thinks up about an encounter between Jesus and the Cardinal Grand Inquisitor in sixteenth-century Spain, when the Inquisition was at its worst. Jesus's visit unsettles the Grand Inquisitor to the point that he has him taken to the prison in the house of the holy court. Later, the Grand Inquisitor visits his prisoner and, after scrutinizing him, asks: "'Is it you? You?' Receiving no answer, he quickly adds: 'Do not answer, be silent. After all, what could you say? I know too well what you would say. And you have no right to add anything to what you already said once'" (250). After a long accusatory speech in which he challenges the convictions and decisions of Jesus, the Grand Inquisitor expects Jesus to reply, even criticize

him, but Jesus remains silent, and then answers by suddenly kissing the Inquisitor on his lips. While the Grand Inquisitor has earlier threatened to burn Jesus alive, he now lets him go, without, however, reconsidering his views.

9 Kogawa's recourse to Dostoevsky's parable has further important implications. When the Grand Inquisitor rationalizes the necessity of taking away freedom from people for their own good, his rhetoric is strikingly similar to that of Canada's Prime Minister Mackenzie King (1921–6, 1926–30, 1935–48), who justified the confiscation of the property of Japanese-Canadians and the dispersal of their community by claiming that these were a "protective measure only" taken by the Canadian government for the good of Japanese-Canadians themselves (Miki 43). Moreover, the "shiny skin cap" (273) of the Grand Inquisitor in Naomi's dream/nightmare is that also worn by Old Man Gower, a character who repeatedly molested Naomi and told her to hide the deed from her mother (72–3).

10 The intertext of Ahasuerus is based on a German pamphlet entitled *Kurze Beschreibung und Erzählung von einem Juden mit Namen Ahasverus* that was published in 1602. The pamphlet reworks a Christian legend in which the character who has insulted Jesus on his way to crucifixion has to live until the end of the world. The pamphlet, in which the Wandering Jew is given the name of Ahasuerus, spread throughout Protestant Europe quickly and in various translations ("Wandering Jew").

11 According to Tiiu Reimo, there is a legend dating back to the middle of the sixteenth century of a man who roamed Livonia (the historical name of the area that overlaps with the territory of present-day Estonia). The protagonist of Mihkelson's novel, in fact, quotes a passage from Reimo (para. 25–8) in her narrative (150–3). Thus, the Reimo intertext becomes another cultural resource relevant to M.'s research into the implications of the cryptic story of her father's disappearance as told by Kaarel.

WORKS CITED

"Ahasveerus." At Rahvapärimuse leksikon. Ed. Mare Kõiva. Eesti Kultuuriloo ja Folkloristika Keskus. 2007. http://haldjas.folklore.ee/leksikon/?list=all.

Caruth, Cathy. "Trauma and Experience." In *Trauma: Explorations in Memory*, ed. C. Caruth, 3–12. Baltimore: Johns Hopkins University Press, 2004.

Caruth, Cathy. *Unclaimed Experience: Trauma, Narrative, and History*. Baltimore: Johns Hopkins University Press, 1996.

Dostoevsky, Fyodor. *The Brothers Karamazov*. Trans. Richard Pevear and Larissa Volokhonsky. Intro. Malcolm V. Jones. London: Random House, 1997.

Hoffman, Eva. *After Such Knowledge: Memory, History, and the Legacy of the Holocaust*. New York: Public Affairs, 2004.

Homer. *The Odyssey*. Trans. Robert Fitzgerald. Intro. Seamus Heaney. London: Random House, 1992.

Hutcheon, Linda. *The Politics of Postmodernism*. 2nd ed. New York: Routledge, 2005.

Kogawa, Joy. *Obasan*. New York: Anchor Books, 1994.

Mihkelson, Ene. *Ahasveeruse uni* [The Sleep of Ahasuerus]. Tallinn: Tuum, 2001.

Miki, Roy. *Redress: Inside the Japanese Canadian Call for Justice*. Vancouver: Raincoast Books, 2004.

Rashkin, Esther. "The Haunted Child: Social Catastrophe, Phantom Transmissions, and the Aftermath of Collective Trauma." *Psychoanalytic Review* 86, no. 3 (June 1999): 433–53. Medline:10550869.

Raun, Toivo U. *Estonia and the Estonians*. 2nd rev. ed. Stanford: Hoover Institution Press, 2001.

Reimo, Tiiu. "Baltica leide Briti raamatukogus." *Tartu Ülikooli Raamatukogu aastaraamat* (Tartu) 1997: 197–210.

Robson, Kathryn. *Writing Wounds: The Inscription of Trauma in Post-1968 French Women's Life-Writing*. GENUS: Gender in Modern Culture 4. Amsterdam: Rodopi, 2004.

Sildre, Urve, and Tiiu Laur, eds. "Igavene juut" and "Rahva- ja Naljajutud. Kogumikud." At Mineviku menuraamat: Väga ilusad, hirmsad ja armsad lood. Eesti Rahvusraamatukogu. 2004. http://www.nlib.ee/html/expo/menurmt/rahva.html.

Skultans, Vieda. *The Testimony of Lives: Narrative and Memory in Post-Soviet Latvia*. New York: Routledge, 1998.

van Alphen, Ernst. "Second-Generation Testimony, Transmission of Trauma, and Postmemory." *Poetics Today* 27, no. 2 (2006): 473–88. http://dx.doi.org/10.1215/03335372-2005-015.

"Wandering Jew." *Encyclopaedia Britannica*. Encyclopaedia Britannica Online. 2008. http://www.britannica.com/EBchecked/topic/635269/wandering-Jew.

16 Making the Silence Speak: A Critical Discussion of Trauma Transmission and Identity Formation

STEFANIE PREUSS

"There is a silence that cannot speak. There is a silence that will not speak." Thus starts the proem to Joy Kogawa's novel *Obasan*. Both novels discussed by Eva Rein, *Obasan* and Ene Mihkelson's *Ahasveeruse uni* (The Sleep of Ahasuerus), are texts about silences and finding the voice to make those silences speak. Rein shows how secrets and silences concerning their parents haunt the protagonists of both novels – Kogawa's Naomi Nakane and Mihkelson's M. – and she stresses the importance of personal and familial heritage for their constructions of identity. She argues convincingly that both protagonists hope to resolve their identity crises and overcome their own traumas by learning about the fate of their lost parent. Yet while "trauma" and "identity" are the two key terms in Rein's essay, they remain relatively under-theorized. My response aims at complementing Rein's analysis with a theoretical discussion of trauma and identity that subjects the notion of "transgenerational transmission of trauma" to critical scrutiny and results in a different interpretation of the two novels.

Since both "trauma" and "identity" are often used in a non-specific, colloquial way, it is necessary to explain what Rein means by them. She argues that the protagonists of both novels suffer not only from their own traumas as survivors of the internment of Japanese Canadians during the Second World War and the Soviet raids on Estonian *kulaks*, respectively, but also from inexplicable silences about their parents' deaths. Yet if we take recourse to the American Psychiatric Association's definition of trauma as the "direct personal experience of an event that involves actual or threatened death or serious injury, or other threat to one's physical integrity; or witnessing an event that involves death, injury, or a threat to another person; or learning about unexpected or violent death, serious harm, or threat of death or injury experiences by a family member or other close associate" (*DSM-IV* 463), it becomes doubtful whether one should speak of trauma with regard to Naomi's and M.'s suffering. Although Naomi and M. have witnessed and survived the great social catastrophes of their countries, they have not personally experienced the threat of death or serious injury.[1] Moreover, it is only late in their lives and quests that they learn about the fates of their parents, and so these incidents cannot account for their psychological distress. The two protagonists of the novels, Naomi and M., are haunted by their own as well as their nation's pasts, but they are not presented in the novels as suffering from symptoms of post-traumatic stress disorder.

According to Rein, "in addition to their own traumas, Naomi and M. have unawares inherited another trauma from the survivors – the unexplainable secret concerning the circumstances of the lost parent's death." Although Rein mentions the notion of a transgenerational transmission of trauma only in passing, it deserves a closer critical look here, since she uses the term without reflecting on it critically. The concept is based on the work of Esther Rashkin, who maintains that through a parent's silence and repression of unspeakable events, the children of survivors inherit traumas, that is, they suffer from their parents' experiences being transmitted to their unconscious memories as well as from their parent's inability to relate to them. Although Rein does not claim that the protagonists of *Obasan* and *Ahasveeruse uni* have biologically inherited their parent's traumas, her essay implies that Naomi and M. suffer from the transgenerational transmission of those traumas to their own unconscious. I believe that the theoretical assumptions that underlie such an argument need to be subjected to critical scrutiny and confronted with different theoretical paradigms. More specifically, sociological concepts of identity formation and the theory of narrative identity allow us to account for Rein's findings without taking recourse to the controversial notion of the transgenerational transmission of trauma.

While Rein rightly identifies the complicated relation of the second generation to the social catastrophe, the concept of the transgenerational transmission of trauma is highly problematic. Although there is some neurological evidence that the experience of a traumatic event can alter the brain's heritable genetic material (Binder et al.; Stein et al.), Rein does not describe genetic transmissions of trauma but social and discursive ones. According to her understanding of secondary traumatization, which can be traced back to psychological studies of the children of Holocaust survivors, the parents' trauma is passed on to their children through the older generation's words and actions. Thus, the trauma is repeated in the minds and bodies of the second generation, who did not themselves experience the events but were exposed to their parents' reactions to them. In the introduction to his *International Handbook of Multigenerational Legacies of Trauma*, Yael Danieli argues in the same vein: "Children of survivors seem to have consciously and unconsciously absorbed their parents' Holocaust experiences into their lives. Like their parents, many children of survivors manifest Holocaust-derived behaviors, particularly on the anniversaries of their parents' traumata" (5). Likewise, Nanette Auerhahn and Dori Laub maintain that "children of survivors are witnesses to the Holocaust – to a reality in which aggression surpassed anything predictable or even imaginable – for they cannot but be profoundly affected by it despite their, at times, outward silence, for their innermost psychological structures are shaken by Holocaust knowledge" (38).

It is my contention that, in its insistence on secondary traumatization, the concept of the transgenerational transmission of psychic lives overuses the notion of trauma and renders it effectively meaningless in relation to the real victims of traumatic experiences. Children of survivors may suffer from severe psychological problems that are undeniably related to the atrocities their parents have had to endure, but these problems are more likely due to the parents' inability to cope with their parental role than being direct psychic effects of the parents' traumatic experiences themselves. As Wulf Kansteiner points out, the parents' disturbed behaviour and their inability to deal with their traumatic experiences often cause them to become negligent parents, and this neglect may be a major cause of the second generation's psychological problems. Therefore, Kansteiner argues, these psychic problems should rather be compared with those of other children whose parents cannot cope with their parental role (125). Ernst van Alphen argues similarly when he writes about the children of Holocaust survivors that they "can be traumatized, but their trauma does not consist of the Holocaust experience, not even in indirect or mitigated form. Their trauma is caused by being raised by a traumatized Holocaust survivor" (482). Thus, to call the second generation "witnesses," as Auerhahn and Laub do, and to compare their psychological stress to that of the survivors is to play down the latter's traumatic experiences and their suffering. Inflationary uses of "trauma" make victims of us all and dissociate the term from its clinical-psychological sense as "trauma" becomes a mere metaphor for memories of pain or violence.

For the protagonists of the two novels discussed by Rein, however, the situation is notably different. Because of the absence and death of their parents, they have been raised by foster parents and can hardly remember their biological mother or father. Thus, it is neither their parents' traumatic experiences nor being raised by traumatized parents that has caused Naomi's and M.'s identity crises. Rather, they suffer from an inability to reconcile their various and contradictory experiences to form a stable and coherent self-image. As an alternative to the concept of the transgenerational transmission of trauma, I propose the notion of "postmemory," which has been introduced by Marianne Hirsch "to describe the relationship of children of survivors of cultural or collective trauma to the experiences of their parents, experiences that they 'remember' only as the stories and images with which they grew up, but that are so powerful, so monumental, as to constitute memories in their own right." As Hirsch explains, postmemory "characterizes the experience of those who grow up dominated by narratives that preceded their birth, whose own belated stories are displaced by the stories of the previous generation, shaped by traumatic events that they can neither understand nor recreate" (8). Accordingly, neither Naomi in *Obasan* nor M. in *Ahasveeruse uni* have inherited their parents' traumas. Rather, the silence around their parents' disappearance as well as the fragmented stories and their ignorance of their absent parents have prevented Naomi and M. from establishing stable identities for themselves. As Rein correctly maintains, both suffer from identity crises that are caused by their inability to relate to their parents as well as by their dissociation from their communities and historical and familial heritage. For those reasons, they can neither form communicative memories nor fashion a stable sense of self.

Just like "trauma," however, the concept of "identity" needs to be defined more precisely in order to make productive use of it in this context. In various disciplines including philosophy, sociology, and psychology as well as in colloquial usage, "identity" has been defined inconsistently. Moreover, the concept has undergone a remarkable change over time. Modern reflections on identity began with Enlightenment thinkers, who conceived of a person's identity as an unchanging centre of the self that was based on that person's consciousness. Thus, John Locke in the 1694 edition of his *Essay Concerning Human Understanding* writes: "For, since consciousness always accompanies thinking, and it is that which makes every one to be what he calls self, and thereby distinguishes himself from all other thinking things, in this alone consists personal identity; i.e., the sameness of a rational being: and as far as this consciousness can be extended backwards to any past action or thought, so far reaches the identity of that person" (449). This traditional conception of identity, which is similar to its colloquial usage, is based on the idea that every person has an essentially stable, coherent, and unified core that defines his or her subjectivity.

In the course of the nineteenth and twentieth centuries, however, the individual began to be seen as no longer autonomous but as shaped by existing social forces and structures. From a sociological perspective, subjects were conceived of as being shaped in the interaction between the self and "significant others" within social networks. George Herbert Mead states that the self "arises in the process of social experience and activity, that is, develops in the given individual as a result of his relations to that process as a whole and to other individuals within that process" (135). In Mead's understanding of subjectivity, the self is composed of the "I" and the "me": "The 'I' is the response of the organism to the attitudes of the others; the 'me' is the organized set of attitudes of others which one assumes. The attitudes of the others constitute the organized 'me,' and then one reacts toward that as an 'I'" (175). While Mead acknowledges that a person can be split into several "selves" when talking to different people, he still assumes a unified identity as the "normal" case (142–3).

This conception notably changed with the emergence of post-structuralist thought. Stuart Hall maintains that "the subject, previously experienced as having a unified and stable identity, is becoming fragmented; composed, not of a single, but of several, sometimes contradictory or unresolved identities" (276–7). The idea of an autonomous, stable identity is replaced by the notion of a provisional self whose identity is constructed through social discourse. Thus, identity is constantly changing. Hall adds that no individual constructs a single identity for him- or herself: "The subject assumes different identities at different times, identities which are not unified around a coherent 'self.' Within us are contradictory identities, pulling in different directions, so that our identifications are continuously being shifted about" (277). This fragmentation of identity is the result of a rapidly changing world in which globalization and social change produce scepticism towards traditional models for identification such as profession, gender, nationality, religion, and class, and provide a number of new ways of constructing identity.

Identity, according to Jan Assmann, is a matter of consciously reflecting an unconscious self-image (130). Assmann defines individual identity as an image, created and maintained in the consciousness of the individual, of those characteristics that differentiate the individual from all ("significant") others, enabling the individual to become conscious of his or her individuality, uniqueness, and irreplaceability (131). Identity can thus be explained as a social and discursive construction that enables individuals to reconcile the different environments and social contexts with which they are faced and to create an image of a unified self. Despite the disparity of experiences and contexts, however, "coherence is crucially important for human beings' everyday identity work" (Keupp et al. 59). Since identity is a matter of memory and remembrance, and since a remembered past is expressed through narration (Assmann 89, 75), a person's different and fragmented identities must be combined by a unifying narrative. As James C. Mancuso has maintained, we create and construct our whole life and our relations to the world in narrative structures. If this fails, an identity crisis can be the result.

In contrast to Rein, I propose that this is the case with Naomi and M. in the two novels. M. is unable to reconcile her identity as the daughter of a Forest Brother with the contradictory facts she reads about them; Naomi is torn between her Japanese and her Canadian identity:

> The girl with the long ringlets who sits in front of Stephen said to him, "All the Jap kids at school are going to be sent away and they're bad and you're a Jap." And so, Stephen tells me, am I.
>
> "Are we?" I ask Father.
>
> "No," Father says. "We're Canadian."
>
> It's a riddle, Stephen tells me. We are both the enemy and not the enemy. (*Obasan* 84)

Through the absence of the protagonists' parents and the silence around them, their self-narrations are disrupted; Naomi and M. are unable to reconcile their identities. As a result, they are unable to form a coherent self-image – a fact that becomes evident, for instance, in the characters' names: Naomi's nickname "Nomi" is a homophone of "no me" (Pogner 109) and can thus be read as a sign of her identity crisis. Similarly, the reader never learns the protagonist's first name in *Ahasveeruse uni*. Through their search for the lost parent, both protagonists aim at creating a coherent past for themselves in order to fashion their individual identities. They want to know who they are and where they come from. The question Naomi is asked by the father of one of her students, "Where do you come from?" (8), thus becomes the key question for both novels.

Both protagonists try to resolve their identity crisis by attempting to learn about the personality, the ethnic and cultural background, and the fate of their lost parent. When this fails, they have to resort to other means of establishing continuity and coherence. They manage to fill the missing gaps in their history with their own narratives and use cultural intertexts such as religious myths or literary texts as substitutes for the resources they lack. Thus, both characters employ narration as a tool for constructing identity understood as "the story that the modern I constructs and tells about the me" (McAdams 63). Narratives have the capacity to accommodate the different, and sometimes contradictory, aspects of identity into a coherent and unified self-image and thereby establish a consistent narrative identity. According to Paul Ricoeur, "the narrative constructs the durable character of an individual, which one can call his or her narrative identity, in constructing the sort of dynamic identity proper to the plot (*l'intrigue*) which creates the identity of the protagonist in the story" (77). We give meaning to our life story by "constructing more or less coherent, followable, and vivifying stories that integrate the person into society in a productive and generative way and provide a purposeful self-history" (McAdams 63).

The concept of narrative identity can account not only for Naomi's and M.'s identity crises, but also for their usages of cultural intertexts to bridge the gaps in their own biographies. Lacking the necessary knowledge of their families' pasts, Naomi and M. are unable to tell their stories of origin straightforwardly. Because they have no access to conventional models for narrating their lives, they turn to established cultural intertexts. As Rein notes, Naomi draws on Dostoevsky's story of the Grand Inquisitor, and M. draws on the legend of Ahasuerus. But rather than merely providing the means for a better understanding of their parents, as Rein's essay implies, these cultural texts also offer the narrative framework for the protagonists' constructions and narrations of their own identities. Naomi and M. make these intertexts function as substitutes for their family narratives and use them to establish the sense of origin and continuity that they need to form a coherent individual identity. The cultural intertexts help them recreate the past, make sense of it, and incorporate it into their own life stories. With the help of these texts, Naomi and M. are ultimately able to frame their personal experiences and put them into a consistent narrative. Thereby, they not only gain deeper insights into the legacies of their family heritage and are able to form new and meaningful imaginative relationships with their lost parents, but they are also able to resolve their own identity crises. The theoretical discussion of trauma and identity, and particularly the concept of narrative identity, thus leads to a different interpretation of Kogawa's and Mihkelson's novels. Although both novels engage with collective and cultural traumas, they are not "trauma novels that emphasize transgenerational haunting," as Rein maintains. Rather, in their insistence on personal life writing and memory, they are novels that focus primarily on subjectivity and the narrative construction of individual identity. This perspective is able to account for the importance narration and cultural intertexts hold for the formation of identity in both novels; it can explain how the protagonists in *Obasan* and *Ahasveeruse uni* have made the silence speak.

NOTE

1 While Naomi in *Obasan* has experienced sexual assault, this is not discussed by Rein.

WORKS CITED

American Psychiatric Association, ed. *Diagnostic and Statistical Manual of Mental Disorders. DSM-IV-TR.* Text revision. 4th ed. Washington, DC: American Psychiatric Association, 2000.

Assmann, Jan. *Das kulturelle Gedächtnis: Schrift, Erinnerung und politische Identität in frühen Hochkulturen*. Munich: Beck, 1992.

Auerhahn, Nanette C., and Dori Laub. "Intergenerational Memory of the Holocaust." In *International Handbook of Multigenerational Legacies of Trauma*, ed. Yael Danieli, 21–41. New York: Plenum, 1998.

Binder, Elisabeth B., R.G. Bradley, W. Liu, et al. "Association of FKBP5 Polymorphisms and Childhood Abuse with Risk of Posttraumatic Stress Disorder Symptoms in Adults." *Journal of the American Medical Association* 299, no. 11 (2008): 1291–1305. http://dx.doi.org/10.1001/jama.299.11.1291. Medline:18349090.

Danieli, Yael. "Introduction: History and Conceptual Foundations." In *International Handbook of Multigenerational Legacies of Trauma*, ed. Y. Danieli, 1–17. New York: Plenum, 1998.

Hall, Stuart. "The Question of Cultural Identity." In *Modernity and Its Futures*, ed. David Held Hall and Tony McGrew, 273–316. Cambridge: Polity Press, 1992.

Hirsch, Marianne. "Projected Memory: Holocaust Photographs in Personal and Public Fantasy." In *Acts of Memory: Cultural Recall in the Present*, ed. Mieke Bal, Jonathan Crewe, and Leo Spitzer, 3–23. Hanover: University of New England Press, 1999.

Kansteiner, Wulf. "Menschheitstrauma, Holocausttrauma, kulturelles Trauma: Eine kritische Genealogie der philosophischen, psychologischen und kulturwissenschaftlichen Traumaforschung seit 1945." In *Handbuch der Kulturwissenschaften*, vol. 3, ed. Friedrich Jäger and Jörn Rüsen, 109–38. Stuttgart: Metzler, 2004.

Keupp, Heiner, et al. *Identitätskonstruktionen: Das Patchwork der Identitäten in der Spätmoderne*. Reinbek: Rowohlt, 2008.

Kogawa, Joy. *Obasan*. New York: Anchor Books, 1994.

Locke, John. *An Essay Concerning Human Understanding*. 1694. Vol. 1. New York: Dover, 1959.

Mancuso, James C. "Constructionism, Personal Construct Psychology and Narrative Psychology." *Theory & Psychology* 6, no. 1 (1996): 47–70. http://dx.doi.org/10.1177/0959354396061004.

McAdams, Dan P. "The Case for Unity in the (Post)Modern Self: A Modest Proposal." In *Self and Identity: Fundamental Issues*, ed. Richard D. Ashmore and Lee J. Jussim, 46–78. New York: Oxford University Press, 1997.

Mead, George H. *Mind, Self and Society: From the Standpoint of a Social Behaviorist*. Chicago: University of Chicago Press, 1934.

Mihkelson, Ene. *Ahasveeruse uni* [The Sleep of Ahasuerus]. Tallinn: Tuum, 2001.

Pogner, Helga. *Maxine Hong Kingston und Joy Kogawa: Autobiographisches Erzählen in einer multiethnischen Gesellschaft*. Trier: Wissenschaftlicher Verlag, 1998.

Rashkin, Esther. "The Haunted Child: Social Catastrophe, Phantom Transmissions, and the Aftermath of Collective Trauma." *Psychoanalytic Review* 86, no. 3 (June 1999): 433–53. Medline:10550869.

Ricoeur, Paul. "Narrative Identity." *Philosophy Today* 35, no. 1 (1991): 73–81.

Stein, Murray B., K.L. Jang, S. Taylor, et al. "Genetic and Environmental Influences on Trauma Exposure and Posttraumatic Stress Disorder Symptoms: A Twin Study." *American Journal of Psychiatry* 159, no. 10 (Oct. 2002): 1675–81. http://dx.doi.org/10.1176/appi.ajp.159.10.1675. Medline:12359672.

van Alphen, Ernst. "Second-Generation Testimony, Transmission of Trauma, and Postmemory." *Poetics Today* 27, no. 2 (2006): 473–88. http://dx.doi.org/10.1215/03335372-2005-015.

PART FOUR

Fictions of Loss and Trauma

17 (Re-)Visions of the Buried Self: Childhood Trauma and Self-Narration in Margaret Atwood's *Cat's Eye*

CHRISTA SCHÖNFELDER

Margaret Atwood's 1988 artist novel *Cat's Eye* narrates in much detail the life story of Elaine Risley, a Canadian painter in her fifties. Back in Toronto, the place of her childhood, for a retrospective of her paintings, the protagonist-narrator Elaine finds herself haunted by childhood memories and feels compelled to confront anew her painful past. Switching back and forth between past and present, the narrative dramatizes Elaine's quest for identity and self-narration. Setting up the autodiegetic narrator Elaine as the fictional autobiographer, *Cat's Eye* explores in depth the impact of childhood trauma and its complex repercussions in adulthood. In other words, Atwood's novel puts centre stage the interrelations between trauma and self-narration; it could be read as a "limit-case" in Leigh Gilmore's sense, that is, as an example of the numerous "contemporary self-representational texts about trauma [that] reveal and test the limits of autobiography" (14). The fluidity of generic boundaries is here closely connected with the slipperiness of trauma. Like many trauma critics, Dolores Herrero and Sonia Baelo-Allué in their recent essay collection *Between the Urge to Know and the Need to Deny* warn us against thinking of trauma as a "stable and immobile notion" (12), asserting that trauma inherently "remains open and undecidable" (13). This openness and instability of trauma tends to manifest itself in generic slippages, as Atwood's *Cat's Eye* well exemplifies. The text is a multilayered exploration of life writing and trauma, which has autobiographical resonances[1] *and* can be read as a particularly rich exploration of life writing through the ways it constructs Elaine's trauma narrative as a fictional autobiography. Thus, I explore here how *Cat's Eye* engages with key concerns of life writing and how – in spite of, or rather precisely because of, its structures of fictionality and literariness

– it reflects on the genre in important ways.[2] As Gilmore asserts, "the limits tell us what the genre alone cannot" (10).

Cat's Eye problematizes the act of autobiographical narration in the face of trauma in several ways, foregrounding trauma's profound impact on identity and memory, as well as the complex relations of trauma and narration, which are at the heart of much contemporary trauma writing and trauma theory. The narrative calls attention to the complexities of self-narration through its highly visual negotiation of the psychology and poetics of trauma. A cluster of objects, images, and themes circling around a variety of forms of vision – marbles and paintings; dreams and memories; the haunting gaze of Elaine's peers; distortion, loss, and retrieval of vision – play a key role throughout the text.[3] Not only does Atwood's emphasis on the visual highlight the powerful impact of trauma, it also points to trauma as the "unspeakable" and "untellable" and stresses the complexities of self-representation. The autobiographical project staged in *Cat's Eye* oscillates between the desire for a unified picture and narrative of the self and a sense of the self breaking down into a series of multiple and fractured self-images.

Reading Atwood's *Cat's Eye* as a trauma narrative, I argue for an interdisciplinary approach: bringing trauma theory from literary and cultural studies into a dialogue with psychiatric and clinical-psychological approaches to trauma allows us to illuminate trauma writing from new perspectives. As Herrero and Baelo-Allué emphasize, "No disciplinary economy can exclusively account for the traumatic" (12); trauma invites the crossing not only of generic but also of disciplinary boundaries. A dialogue across disciplines may in fact help us perceive some of the blind spots of each trauma theory. For example, in literary and cultural studies, the term "trauma" tends to be overused, as is particularly the case with Cathy Caruth's highly influential trauma theory. If trauma merely becomes the symptom of a general cultural condition that is characterized by an increasing and painful awareness of the limitations of language, representation, and history, that is, if trauma essentially becomes a cultural trope representing postmodernity, it is reduced to something rather ordinary and loses its meaning.[4] Psychiatric and clinical-psychological trauma theory offers very precise and differentiated concepts of trauma and its after-effects, allowing for detailed analyses of characteristic symptoms caused by trauma. It can help us reinvestigate and rethink certain key concepts of literary and cultural studies, for example, those related to conceptualizations of identity. Moreover, psychological trauma theory can give us insights into certain aspects of trauma, especially recovery, which are crucial to many autobiographical as well as fictional trauma texts, but which are largely eclipsed by Caruth and other cultural trauma theorists. As Roger Luckhurst rightly points out, "There seems to be a flat contradiction between cultural theory that regards narrative as betraying traumatic singularity and various therapeutic discourses that see narrative as a means of productive transformation or even final resolution of trauma" (82).[5] It is precisely this tension that I want to make fruitful for my discussion of self-narration and recovery in *Cat's Eye*.

On the other hand, to speak with Laurie Vickroy, "literary and imaginative approaches [to trauma] provide a necessary supplement to historical and psychological studies" (*Trauma and Survival* 221). It seems that the literary imagination, with its complex processes of fictionalization and symbolization, can create a space in which experiences that appear to defy confrontation and verbalization as well as existential dimensions of the human condition – especially threatening experiences of vulnerability or mortality – can be tackled and explored from multiple perspectives. Staging the process of writing the self and writing trauma within structures of fictionality, literary trauma narratives and limit-cases have the potential to push dimensions of self-reflexivity to a degree that life writing in the more narrow sense may lack. They also tend to consciously expose the essential paradox that characterizes trauma narratives in general: they attempt to communicate that which seems to resist ordinary processes of remembering, representation, and comprehension. Highlighting trauma's intricate, or even impossible, position in the symbolic order, Caruth suggests that trauma demands a mode of representation that enacts or performs trauma through repetitions and conveys its impact through gaps and silences, that is, through repeated breakdowns of language and collapses of understanding. As Vickroy puts it, "Trauma narratives go beyond presenting trauma as subject matter or character study. They internalize the rhythms, processes, and uncertainties of traumatic experience within their underlying sensibilities and structures" (*Trauma and Survival* 3). While drawing on Caruth, Vickroy, like Whitehead, re-perspectivizes the ways in which trauma fiction negotiates the unspeakable, untellable, and incomprehensible aspects of trauma. Vickroy and Whitehead acknowledge the challenges trauma poses to narration and representation, but simultaneously assert that writers have found ways to represent trauma that convey these complexities while still fostering understanding. Here, Dominick LaCapra's theory of trauma writing is apposite. LaCapra regards it as problematic to restrict possibilities of writing about trauma to two extremes only (as Caruth implicitly does): on the one hand, narratives characterized by the "phantasm of total mastery, full ego identity, definitive closure" (which Caruth rejects) and, on the other hand, writing determined by "endless mutability, fragmentation, melancholia, aporias, irrecoverable residues or exclusions" (LaCapra, *Writing History* 71) – which is the main focus in Caruth's readings. LaCapra postulates that there is a kind of trauma narrative located somewhere between these two poles; like Vickroy and Whitehead, he has in mind the kind of narrative which acknowledges that it cannot make the phenomenon of trauma fully known and yet is capable of illuminating some aspects of it.

Cat's Eye, through its foregrounding of both the crises caused by trauma and the struggles for recovery, as well as through its complex exploration of the interrelations between trauma and self-narration, can clearly be said to belong to this category of trauma narratives. The project of life writing staged in the text revolves heavily around childhood trauma and its lasting impact. The beginning and core event of Elaine's traumatic past is a harrowing experience at the age of nine. Forced to play the role of beheaded Mary Queen of Scots, Elaine is put into a hole by her three girlfriends Cordelia, Grace, and Carol. The girls then cover the hole with boards and mud and cruelly abandon Elaine. Elaine experiences this moment with the feelings of "fear, helplessness" and "horror" that the standard psychiatric handbook, the *Diagnostic and Statistical Manual of Mental Disorders* (*DSM*), identifies as the emotions determining a traumatic experience (*DSM IV* 464): "When I was put into the hole I knew it was a game; now I know it is not one. I feel sadness, a sense of betrayal. Then I feel the darkness pressing down on me; then terror" (107). Elaine both experiences and remembers this traumatic moment as a moment of darkness, of a darkness so intense that obscured vision turns into blindness. Trying to remember this experience years later, Elaine states, "I have no image of myself in the hole; only a black square filled with nothing" (107). The moment of trauma is, thus, introduced as a moment where the subject literally and figuratively loses sight of herself and her environment. Speculating further that this moment may be a "time marker that separates the time before it from the time after," marking "the point at which [she] lost power" (107), Elaine emphasizes the trauma of the black hole, whose importance is also underlined by the section title "Deadly Nightshade," as an intense crisis and rupture in her life story.

The narrative of Elaine's childhood unfolds along a series of further cycles of interpersonal trauma. Following the initial traumatic event, the trio of girls start to torment Elaine psychologically by continuously observing all her actions and by constantly telling and showing her that something is "wrong" with her and that she needs to be "improved" (116). Since Elaine believes the girls' affirmations that they are her best friends, she quietly accepts the ongoing and painful humiliations. She desperately strives for, but never obtains, their approval and affection and, therefore, increasingly suffers from severe self-doubt and a permanent fear of acting the wrong way. The narrative suggests that these constant mind games are as traumatizing for Elaine as the experience of being trapped and abandoned in the dark hole. Even more than their verbal attacks, it is the relentless gaze of the other girls that Elaine experiences as profoundly disturbing and threatening, to such an extent that even the eyes of her first "girl-shaped" doll fill her "with creeping horror" (128).

Elaine's description of the phase following her traumatic experiences clearly conveys the powerful impact of the traumatizing gaze. The narrative particularly highlights her suffering from "psychic numbing," that is, from profound emotional apathy, which is generally regarded as one of the most common symptoms of post-traumatic stress disorder (PTSD).[6] Elaine loses interest in school and games, experiences a persistent loss of energy and feels how her "body is stiffening, emptying itself of feeling" (154). The leitmotif of the cat's eye, which plays a prominent role throughout the text, is also closely connected to processes of psychic numbing and emotional detachment. Elaine uses her cat's eye marble as a defence mechanism, internalizing its cold, unemotional vision: "I can see people moving like bright animated dolls … I can look at their shapes and sizes, their colours, without feeling anything else about them" (141). The narrative, as Karin Gerig emphasizes, plays with the homophones "I" and "eye"; Elaine reduces her subjectivity, her "I," to the unemotionally gazing "eye" (219). Elaine herself puts it thus: "I am alive in my eyes only" (141).

What is crucial to note, then, is that *Cat's Eye* stages both the process of traumatization and Elaine's post-traumatic crisis through a powerful emphasis on the visual: the omnipresent, traumatizing gaze results in the trauma victim's distorted vision. The theme of a distorted, emotionless vision culminates in Elaine's experiences of what psychiatrists call "dissociation," that is, experiences of depersonalization and derealization, which make individuals perceive the reality of their self and of their environment in abnormal ways (Herman 109). Elaine emphasizes how she recurrently feels as if her self was split into two or experiences her consciousness as split off from her body: "I'm seeing all this from above, as if I'm in the air, somewhere near the GIRLS sign over the door, looking down like a bird" (172). The narrative suggests that Elaine's repeated retreat into a distorted and detached vision of herself and others is the only way of enduring – or escaping – the emotional distress caused by her trauma; yet at the same time, this vision results in a highly problematic disconnection – or dissociation – not only from her social environment, but also from her own emotions and subjectivity. The emphasis on dissociation is symptomatic of a concern that runs throughout the text: the traumatized subject and its fractured ways of seeing.

The concern with seeing and being seen also plays a central role in the text's representation of trauma's long-term effects as closely intertwined with processes of socialization and gender formation. As Sharon R. Wilson points out, while here the "main Gaze is that of female bullies," its origin "is still patriarchal, hierarchical and conformist" (182–3). The girls' constant observation and judgment stands for society's omnipresent controlling gaze and continues to haunt Elaine throughout her life. She remains caught up in the deeply internalized belief of her wrongness even as an adult. Many episodes in her life story revolve around anxieties about clothes and appearances, or around her conflicted gender identity and her difficult relationships, especially with women. *Cat's Eye* thus emphasizes that long-term exposure to trauma in childhood can leave particularly deep and persistent traces. As Herman puts it, "Repeated trauma in adult life erodes the structure of the personality already formed, but repeated trauma in childhood forms and deforms the personality" (96). Elaine's life narrative suggests precisely such a "deformation" of personality; the self-blame that she displays as a child is a pattern of reaction that can be traced throughout her life story, showing her "life-long insecurity about her identity" (Staels 180). In Elaine's own words, "I have done something wrong, something so huge I can't even see it, something that's drowning me. I am inadequate and stupid, without worth. I might as well be dead" (372). This theme of self-blame – a form of mental self-destructiveness and at the same time another form of distorted vision – is complemented by the theme of physical self-destructiveness; Elaine's narrative records different forms of self-injury, which culminate in a suicide attempt. Crises of identity, thus, in several ways figure as a prominent topos throughout Elaine's life narrative. The text thereby raises key questions about trauma and self-representation, encouraging us to reflect on what it means for autobiographical subjects whose identity and sense of self are severely disrupted by trauma to record their self in writing.

Foregrounding the impact trauma has on identity, *Cat's Eye* also calls attention to the ways in which trauma memory complicates and challenges processes of autobiographical narration. Atwood's novel thereby explores a set of issues that are crucial to many fictional and non-fictional trauma narratives alike. As many trauma specialists point out, trauma memories differ significantly from ordinary memories and are encoded and recorded in special ways. While ordinary memories are integrated into existing cognitive schemes and consciousness, memories of trauma seem to resist such integration (van der Kolk 282). As Ehlers and Clark put it, trauma memory is "poorly elaborated and inadequately integrated into its context in time, place, subsequent and previous information and other autobiographical memories" (325). As a result, trauma victims tend to experience difficulties in intentionally recalling memories of the traumatic event. As psychiatrist Ronald J. Comer asserts, this amnesia or "loss of memory" may affect some or all memories of the disturbing period of time or even "exten[d] back to times long before the upsetting period" (177). In addition, trauma victims often vividly and involuntarily re-experience parts of the traumatic past through intrusive memories, that is, through images and other sensory impressions that appear suddenly and against the individual's will, with striking force and immediacy (Ehlers and Clark 324).

Through a nuanced psychology of trauma memory, *Cat's Eye* also alerts us to the ways in which the specificities of remembering trauma complicate the act of writing one's life. The text depicts Elaine's memory crisis as a complex dynamic of both major forms of memory disturbance – intrusions of the traumatic past and symptoms of amnesia. Back in Toronto, Elaine is frequently assailed by intrusive memories of her childhood tormentor Cordelia:

> Now that I am back here I can hardly walk down a street without a glimpse of her, turning a corner, entering a door. It goes without saying that these fragments of her – a shoulder, beige, camel's-hair, the side of a face, the back of a leg – belong to women who, seen as a whole, are not Cordelia. (6)

This passage conveys the extent to which Atwood has Elaine re-experience distorted fragments of the past in the present. The most striking instance of an intrusion, which calls attention to the "extreme vividness" and overwhelming force with which trauma victims tend to experience intrusions (van der Kolk 282), is once again centred on Cordelia. In a bout of depression, Elaine suddenly hears "the voice of a nine-year-old child" that urges her, with overwhelming clarity and power, to commit suicide (374). Atwood has her protagonist surrender to this voice – Cordelia's voice – and cut her wrist (though she is then rescued by her husband), which emphatically conveys the power intrusions can possess even decades after the traumatic event. Elaine's cry, "Get me out of this, Cordelia. I'm locked in. I don't want to be nine years old forever" (400), is both a cry of despair and a cry of protest, expressing how much Elaine feels entrapped in her past. In other words, her life narrative expresses a pattern of circularity, with the past oppressively dominating the present.[7]

Cat's Eye also depicts Elaine's paintings as closely connected to such intrusive memories, signalling once again the heavily visual nature and uncontrollable quality of trauma memories. Elaine is bewildered to find that her paintings focus on a number of objects whose significance and context she fails to recognize: "I know that these things must be memories, but they do not have the quality of memories. They are not hazy around the edges, but sharp and clear. They arrive detached from any context; they are simply there" (337). These images and objects, which the reader perceives as bound up with Elaine's childhood, seem to "come from the involuntary and unconscious well of traumatic memory" (Vickroy, "Seeking Symbolic Immortality" 134). The passage emphasizes Elaine's confusion about the way she simultaneously remembers and does not remember, highlighting the disturbing sense of having images and visions of the past which appear disconnected from one's autobiographical narrative. In other words, it captures the bewildering interplay of the "*elision* of memory" and the "*precision* of recall" characteristic of trauma memory (Caruth, *Trauma* 153; emphasis in original). Elaine's memory crisis, then, also involves a disrupted sense of time. She repeatedly experiences the past as part of the present, finding herself, in the words of Ehlers and Clark, in a "state of being 'frozen in time'" (334). This post-traumatic disrupted sense of time is reinforced textually by the sections of the narrative, often flashbacks, that are narrated in the present tense and focalized internally, that is, through the perspective of the experiencing rather than the narrating self. The controlling distance associated with an autobiographer who retrospectively records earlier versions of the self here repeatedly breaks down.

Trauma overrides ordinary structures of remembering and narrating the past.

A further obstacle that Atwood has Elaine face in the process of autobiographical narration revolves around lost or buried memories, around the sense of gaps in her life story: "I've forgotten things. I've forgotten that I've forgotten them ... I've forgotten all of the bad things that happened" (200–1). She later recalls her being trapped in the dark hole vaguely as a moment of intense fear and agony, and the trauma's aftermath is also nothing but a dark void in her memory: "Shortly after this I became nine. I can remember my other birthdays, later and earlier ones, but not this one" (108). Sensing that some experiences are entirely deleted from her conscious autobiographical memory, Elaine perceives this loss of memory as a threat, lamenting that "time is missing" (201). The gaps in her memory also confront Elaine with the unsettling question of her memory's general unreliability. Lacking the sense of a coherent autobiographical narrative, Elaine feels disconnected "from earlier versions of her 'self'" (King 87), while, paradoxically, also feeling caught up in the past and her past selves due to her vivid and violent intrusions.

Cat's Eye expresses, then, how intensely distressing the experience of trauma memory's main paradox – the bewildering state between knowing and unknowing – can be for an individual, and how memory disturbances can exacerbate post-traumatic identity crises. As Elaine states: "My life is now multiple, and I am in fragments" (316). In other words, Elaine's vision of her self and of her past is one of fractures, fragments, and distortions; her lasting crises of identity and memory complicate the act of self-narration. The autobiographical project that makes up the core of the novel is fraught with tensions and obstacles typically caused by trauma. Yet the narrative not only thematizes the crises resulting from trauma, but also foregrounds the trauma victim's struggle to overcome these crises and find ways to recovery. The text shows that the alienation, fragmentation, and disintegration in the aftermath of trauma create a longing for reconstitution, a yearning to regain a sense of coherence in self and life. In this context, it is crucial to take a closer look at the novel's approach to questions of identity.

In its emphasis on identity as lacking stability and unity, *Cat's Eye* may be said to call to mind post-structuralist identity theories that challenge notions of a unified self and a stable and coherent identity and conceptualize identity as constructed, malleable, and discontinuous. More specifically, the novel in some ways evokes Judith Butler's theory of the performativity of identity as put forward in her seminal study *Gender Trouble*. The protagonist-narrator not only regards identities as multiple and fluid – "I vary. I am transitional" (5); "There is never only one, of anyone" (6) – but also repeatedly muses over the power of disguise and performance, associating different clothes and appearances with different identities and versions of her self: "I pull on my powder-blue sweatsuit, my disguise as a non-artist, and go down the four flights of stairs, trying to look brisk and purposeful. I could be a businesswoman out jogging, I could be a bank manager, on her day off" (19). Elaine does indeed seem to recognize the power of the performative, reflecting, for example, on the "opportunities for disguise and concealment" facial hair provides to men and pondering on the subversive potential such a "costume" could offer her (20). Yet in *Cat's Eye*, the performative is not celebrated as offering potential for resistance, agency, or power, as it is in Butler, but figures as a tool the traumatized subject resorts to in her struggle for identity. Instead of playing with the creative and subversive potential of appearances and other performative acts, Elaine essentially yields to gender norms, social pressure, and expectations, feeling forced to adapt her actions and appearance to various group identities. The narrative demonstrates that Elaine's identity is malleable and changing, but also conveys how draining this continuous process of redefining and reconstructing her identity is. Thus, Elaine enacts the performative in Butler's sense, though only in its most negative and constraining variant. For traumatized individuals such as Elaine, who struggle too much for control over their selves and actions to play with fluid subjectivities, the performativity of identity emerges as a problematic concept and practice. When the self threatens to fall apart, the novel implies, the potential for agency, change, and resistance that critics like Butler associate with the collapse of notions of the unified self is completely lost. *Cat's Eye* does not celebrate the positive, creative, or subversive potential of subjectivities as malleable, multiple, and fluid, but foregrounds the disturbing, threatening, and often severely destabilizing effects of instability and fragmentation. What it emphasizes is, on the one hand, that "trauma is a disruptive experience that disarticulates the self and creates holes in existence" (LaCapra, *Writing History* 41) and, on the other, that these holes trigger the desire to restore a stable existence and a unified self.

In other words, the novel's negotiation of identity issues suggests that the theoretical challenges to the notion of a unified and permanent identity do not necessarily mean that the individual's psychological need for such an identity (or the illusion thereof) has also disappeared. According to psychologist Klaus Grawe, the so-called consistency principle is in fact the most constitutive principle of psychic functioning; it subsumes the basic psychological needs for control, stability, and coherence (386, 421). Grawe maintains that trauma severely undermines or violates consistency – through the threat to a stable identity and stable relationships, and through memory disturbances (426) – and that the psychic system, destabilized by trauma, instinctively strives to restore consistency.

The theme of a trauma victim's struggle to regain a sense of consistency plays a crucial role in *Cat's Eye*. The autobiographer Elaine does indeed seem to be driven by the urge to regain a sense of stability and control over her identity and memory. She longs to fill the gaps in her memory, to substitute the dark void with images: "I close my eyes, wait for pictures. I need to fill in the black square of time, go back to see what's in it" (144). *Cat's Eye* hence powerfully communicates that "in the face of mounting amnesia, there is an urgent need to consciously establish meaningful connections with the past" (Whitehead, *Trauma Fiction* 82). Throughout the narrative, Elaine's need for consistency manifests itself in her attempt to (re-)construct a coherent life story of the fragments of the past. It suggests that for traumatized individuals, the process of narration is essentially an attempt to bring together the shattered pieces of their identity and to establish meaningful connections between past and present. Constructing the autodiegetic narrator as the fictional author of her own life story, the novel is structured around the "book metaphor," in the words of Hannes Fricke (240), a recurrent narrative framing device in contemporary trauma fiction (though "author metaphor" would probably be the more appropriate term). The novel here also resonates with the claim put forward by many trauma psychologists that self-narration may enable trauma victims to integrate the trauma into the story of their life and thereby slowly come to terms with their traumatic past.

Cat's Eye is thus a fictional exploration of what Suzette Henke calls "scriptotherapy," "the process of writing out and writing through traumatic experience in the form of therapeutic reenactment" (xii). By staging this practice of writing within the frame of fictionality, the text consciously reflects on the potential and the limitations of life writing. As Cooke emphasizes, *Cat's Eye* "speaks to the form as much as it speaks from or within it," encouraging readers to rethink their assumptions about the genre (162). Atwood's trauma narrative explores in depth if and how the act of writing one's life can function as a means of self-therapy for a traumatized individual. It certainly evokes the idea of scriptotherapy; but at the same time it repeatedly alerts us to the ways in which trauma seems to resist language and (re-)integration. With its fragmentation on various narrative levels, its gaps and disruptions of chronology and temporality, and its frequent shifts in focalization and unstable subject-positions, the novel foregrounds the complexities of narrating trauma and thereby complicates psychologists' theories of self-narration as a form of re-establishing consistency, on the one hand, and discussions of the narration of trauma in non-fictional life narratives, on the other.

One way in which *Cat's Eye* complicates the trope of writing as self-therapy is in its emphasis on visuality. Psychological trauma theory commonly conceptualizes trauma memory as a highly visual or sensory, and in any case decidedly non-narrative, form of memory, and regards the transformation or integration of trauma memory into narrative memory as an integral component of recovery. *Cat's Eye*, however, challenges this opposition of the visual being associated with trauma and the verbal being associated with recovery by juxtaposing the act of rewriting one's life story, as discussed above, with the act of *revisioning* the past. A key component of Elaine's revisioning are her paintings, many of which centre on an image of her traumatic past. When she assembles all her previous paintings in her first retrospective, this parallels her piecing together into a narrative fragments of her life and self. *Cat's Eye* thus suggests that the verbal and the visual may both play a central role in the process of coming to terms with a traumatic past, without clearly privileging either. It is significant that the narrative heavily emphasizes the visual in two key scenes concerned with recovery, revolving around visions rather than stories of the past; yet these visionary moments occur in the final chapters of the novel and hence, it could be argued, only after the transformation of trauma memory into narrative memory. Processes of revisioning and rewriting seem closely connected.

The first of these moments of Elaine's revisioning of her traumatic past occurs when Elaine and her mother look through a collection of objects that are assembled in an old trunk which has not been opened for years. Among these objects, Elaine finds the cat's eye marble she had as a child, which marks a key moment in her life narrative: "I look into it, and see my life entire" (398). The text constructs this scene as a moment of revelation and insight, but what, precisely, Elaine "see[s]" in her marble remains an open question. Does the marble – which is deeply inscribed with memories of her traumatic childhood – complete the picture of her life by triggering long-forgotten memories that were buried in amnesia? Or does she finally "see [her] life entire," in the sense that these regained memories change her view of her whole life? Should we interpret this vision as an example of how memories of trauma can be "frozen in time" and preserved intact over decades, or does the novel represent it as a moment in which Elaine gains access to nothing but "a world of inevitably distorted vision," as Earl G. Ingersoll asserts (19)? I want to suggest that Elaine's claim to "see her life entire" in the marble metaphorically stands for the dream at the heart of the autobiographical project, the dream of a unified picture of self and life. Yet by having Elaine refrain from verbalizing this vision any further and merely stating its occurrence, Atwood seems to signal that this sense of unity is an illusion. As Shari Benstock states, "Autobiography reveals the impossibility of its own dream: what begins on the presumption of self-knowledge ends in the creation of a fiction that covers over the premises of its construction" (11). The image of the self that the autobiographical self creates seems to be inevitably distorted and fractured.

The visionary moment of the cat's eye marble is followed by a second vision soon after, which is embedded in another key scene that highlights the precariousness of self-narration even further. Back in one of the main sites of her traumatic childhood, a ravine, Elaine re-experiences her traumatizing relationship with Cordelia in a very intense, vivid, and visual way. However, her vision of Cordelia as her tormentor and of herself as the victim suddenly transforms into a new vision, where she and Cordelia have swapped places: "I am the older one now, I'm the stronger. If she stays here any longer she will freeze to death; … I reach out my arms to her, bend down, hands open to show I have no weapon. *It's all right*, I say to her. *You can go home now*" (419). Elaine's gesture of helping Cordelia embodies a symbolic vision of reconciliation that expresses her readiness to finally forgive her main childhood tormentor, which is reinforced by the fact that this final section of the novel is entitled "Bridge." It is crucial to see that through this key moment, which is constructed as an epiphany, Atwood's literary trauma narrative essentially privileges a vision of the self that is based on the individual's imagination rather than on the "truth" of the past. *Cat's Eye* thereby implicitly points to the limitations of the demand of truthfulness long imposed on the genre of autobiography. Elaine's visionary moment, in spite of its being based on the imagination rather than on actual experience and memory, clearly marks a turning point in her life story and trauma narrative. This seems to be the moment when Elaine finally regains a sense of consistency and reintegration. This fictional autobiography thus indirectly voices a plea for the potential of the imagination in the face of trauma.

Cat's Eye, then, explores a combination of different paths to recovery for a traumatized individual, based on self-narration and self-representation, on memory and the imagination. In spite of the hopeful notes that characterize the text's negotiation of issues of recovery, this trauma narrative should not be read as a literary example of what LaCapra critically terms a "fetishistic narrative" determined by an "imaginary, illusory hope for totalization, full closure and redemptive meaning" (*Representing the Holocaust* 193). Elaine's life narrative throughout conveys that the process of overcoming the crises caused by trauma is long, arduous, and intricate, depicting "scriptotherapy" as a complex process. Furthermore, her "story also acknowledges gaps and losses which cannot be restored" (King 63). On a plane to Vancouver, watching two elderly women who seem "amazingly carefree," Elaine suddenly realizes that she misses "something that will never happen" (421); she sadly muses that she and Cordelia will in all probability never be friends in old age and seems to doubt if she will ever experience a close friendship with any woman. The optimism of Elaine's symbolical vision about Cordelia is thus somewhat muted by melancholic undertones. I conclude with King that "Atwood's novel ends on a note of cautious and qualified optimism" (92). Implying that Elaine is ready to accept her traumatic past as part of her life story, the novel highlights processes of (re-)integration, reinterpretation, and recovery, but at the same time refrains from depicting both Elaine's narrative and her sense of self as fully "'complete' and resolved" (92). Once again, this fictional autobiography thus alerts us to the limits of the genre of life writing. As Howells similarly argues, the fact that the novel registers "incompleteness in the construction of 'subjecthood'" points to the more general "limits of autobiography and its artifice of reconstruction" (216). Until the very end, in spite of its foregrounding of recovery processes, the text reminds us of the complexities of self-narration and self-representation in general and under conditions of trauma in particular.

Cat's Eye centres on a complex and multifaceted depiction of trauma and its after-effects. Framed like a fictional autobiography, the text reflects on the genre of life writing in numerous ways. Similarly to the texts Gilmore discusses in *The Limits of Autobiography*, Atwood's trauma narrative demonstrates how "an engagement between self-representation and the representation of trauma lies at the heart of this limit testing" (15). Through its extensive and nuanced exploration of the psychology of the traumatic and the post-traumatic, which, I suggest, can be brought into particularly sharp focus by way of an interdisciplinary dialogue, *Cat's Eye* highlights how trauma tends to push processes of self-narration and self-representation to its limits; it explores how trauma-related crises of identity and memory function as considerable obstacles to autobiographical narration. Through a powerful emphasis on visuality, the novel points to the "narrative/anti-narrative tension at the core of trauma" and registers its characteristic "shock impact" that "issues a challenge to the capacities of narrative knowledge" (Luckhurst 79–80). Interestingly, however, the text, in contrast to psychological trauma theory, emphasizes visuality also in connection with recovery. While *Cat's Eye* depicts processes of self-narration as a potential means of recovery, thus evoking the idea of scriptotherapy, Elaine's life narrative juxtaposes rewritings and revisionings of the traumatic past, thereby highlighting the complexities of overcoming a post-traumatic crisis. On the one hand, the novel emphasizes the autobiographical subject's desire for wholeness, unity, and consistency, the attempt to "see [her] life entire"; on the other hand, it suggests that autobiographical visions of the self will, ultimately, remain fractured, incomplete, or distorted. The narrative stages this tension par excellence through the leitmotif of the cat's eye marble, which implies that it is only the power of the imagination which may allow for the subject's vision – or illusion – of unity and wholeness. The cat's eye marble, which encapsulates both the text's literariness and its emphasis on visuality, symbolically exemplifies how Atwood's trauma text simultaneously reflects on the genre of life writing and moves beyond it. *Cat's Eye* is a complex negotiation of the tensions between trauma, self-narration, and self-representation that highlights both the potential and the limitations of narrative in the face of trauma.

NOTES

1 Ingersoll offers an overview of the ways in which *Cat's Eye* resonates with Atwood's own biography and concludes: "*Cat's Eye* is the revision and completion of a manuscript she began in her mid-twenties … and finished

as she approached her fiftieth birthday. Despite Margaret Atwood's disclaimer that the novel is not autobiographical, it is a text performing itself as a text, a text of the author's own struggle to achieve selfhood as a woman and as an artist" (26). Moreover, as Jessie Givner argues, Atwood seems to deliberately destabilize boundaries between fiction and life writing, notably through an "incessant play between naming and misnaming, facing and defacing, figuration and disfiguration" that runs through the text (56).

2 Sidonie Smith and Julia Watson define the term "life writing" as follows: "An overarching term used for a variety of nonfictional modes of writing that claim to engage the shaping of someone's life" (197). "Life writing" is, thus, used in a more inclusive sense than "autobiography."

3 For a more general discussion of the importance of vision and blindness in the works of Margaret Atwood, see Wilson.

4 For similar criticisms see, for example, Leys and Kansteiner.

5 Neither the trauma narratives Caruth discusses in *Unclaimed Experience* nor her theoretical framework seem to allow for languages and visions of integration and healing. Whitehead reads Caruth's trauma theory in a similar light when she emphasizes that Caruth "articulates concerns that the traumatic 'cure' implies a dilution of the experience into the reassuring terms of therapy" and concludes that "there is, then, a distinct tendency in recent theorizations of trauma towards an anti-therapeutic stance, a scepticism regarding the inherent value of telling one's story" (*Memory* 116–17).

6 The *DSM-IV* distinguishes between three main categories of symptoms: first, different ways of re-experiencing the traumatic event; second, avoidance of stimuli associated with the trauma, often combined with "psychic numbing"; and third, symptoms of anxiety or increased arousal (464, 468).

7 Osborne's discussion of the novel also highlights structures of circularity, but reads them primarily as a characteristic of recent examples of the female Bildungsroman in contrast to the tradition of the male Bildungsroman with its linear structures.

WORKS CITED

American Psychiatric Association, ed. *Diagnostic and Statistical Manual of Mental Disorders. DSM-IV-TR*. 4th ed. Text revision. Washington: American Psychiatric Association, 2000.

Atwood, Margaret. *Cat's Eye*. London: Bloomsbury, 1989.

Benstock, Shari, ed. *The Private Self: Theory and Practice of Women's Autobiographical Writings*. Chapel Hill: University of North Carolina Press, 1988.

Butler, Judith. *Gender Trouble: Feminism and the Subversion of Identity*. New York: Routledge, 1990.

Caruth, Cathy. *Unclaimed Experience: Trauma, Narrative, and History*. Baltimore: Johns Hopkins University Press, 1996.

Caruth, Cathy, ed. and intro. *Trauma: Explorations in Memory*. Baltimore: Johns Hopkins University Press, 1995.

Comer, Ronald J. *Fundamentals of Abnormal Psychology*. 4th ed. New York: Worth Publishers, 2005.

Cooke, Nathalie. "Reading Reflections: The Autobiographical Illusion in *Cat's Eye*." In *Essays on Life-Writing: From Genre to Critical Practice*, ed. Marlene Kadar. Toronto: University of Toronto Press, 1992.

Ehlers, Anke, and David M. Clark. "A Cognitive Model of Posttraumatic Stress Disorder." *Behaviour Research and Therapy* 38, no. 4 (2000): 319–45. http://dx.doi.org/10.1016/S0005-7967(99)00123-0. Medline:10761279.

Fricke, Hannes. *Das hört nicht auf: Trauma, Literatur und Empathie*. Göttingen: Wallstein, 2004.

Gerig, Karin. "Ein Knick in der Optik: Visualität und weibliche Identität in Margaret Atwoods Cat's Eye." In *Geschlecht–Literatur–Geschichte I*, ed. Gudrun Loster-Schneider, 213–34. St Ingbert: Röhrig Universitätsverlag, 1999.

Gilmore, Leigh. *The Limits of Autobiography: Trauma and Testimony*. Ithaca, NY: Cornell University Press, 2001.

Givner, Jessie. "Names, Faces and Signatures in Margaret Atwood's *Cat's Eye* and *The Handmaid's Tale*." *Canadian Literature* 133 (1992): 56–75.

Grawe, Klaus. *Psychologische Therapie*. Göttingen: Hogrefe Verlag für Psychologie, 1998.

Henke, Suzette. *Shattered Subjects: Trauma and Testimony in Women's Life-Writing*. Basingstoke: MacMillan, 1998.

Herman, Judith Lewis. *Trauma and Recovery*. New York: BasicBooks, 1992.

Herrero, Dolores, and Sonia Baelo-Allué, eds. *Between the Urge to Know and the Need to Deny: Trauma and Ethics in Contemporary British and American Literature*. Heidelberg: Universitätsverlag, 2011.

Howells, Coral. "*Cat's Eye*: Elaine Risley's Retrospective Art." In *Margaret Atwood: Writing and Subjectivity*, ed. Colin Nicholson, 204–18. New York: St Martin's Press, 1994.

Ingersoll, Earl G. "Margaret Atwood's *Cat's Eye*: Re-Reviewing Women in a Postmodern World." *Review of International English Literature* 22, no. 4 (1991): 17–27.

Kansteiner, Wulf. "Testing the Limits of Trauma: The Long-Term Psychological Effects of the Holocaust on Individuals and Collectives." *History of the Human Sciences* 17, nos. 2–3 (2004): 97–123. http://dx.doi.org/10.1177/0952695104047299.

King, Nicola. *Memory, Narrative, Identity: Remembering the Self.* Edinburgh: Edinburgh University Press, 2000.

LaCapra, Dominick. *Representing the Holocaust: History, Theory, Trauma.* Ithaca: Cornell University Press, 1994.

LaCapra, Dominick. *Writing History, Writing Trauma.* Baltimore: Johns Hopkins University Press, 2001.

Leys, Ruth. *Trauma: A Genealogy.* Chicago: University of Chicago Press, 2000.

Luckhurst, Roger. *The Trauma Question.* New York: Routledge, 2008.

Osborne, Carol. "Constructing the Self through Memory: *Cat's Eye* as a Novel of Female Development." *Frontiers: A Journal of Women Studies* 14, no. 3 (1994): 95–112. http://dx.doi.org/10.2307/3346682.

Smith, Sidonie, and Julia Watson. *Reading Autobiography: A Guide for Interpreting Life Narratives.* Minneapolis: University of Minnesota Press, 2001.

Staels, Hilde. *Margaret Atwood's Novels: A Study of Narrative Discourse.* Basel: Francke Verlag, 1995.

van der Kolk, Bessel A. "Trauma and Memory." *In Traumatic Stress: The Effects of Overwhelming Experience on Mind, Body, and Society*, ed. Bessel A. van der Kolk, Alexander C. McFarlane, and Lars Weisaeth, 279–302. New York: The Guilford Press, 1996.

Vickroy, Laurie. "Seeking Symbolic Immortality: Visualizing Trauma in *Cat's Eye.*" *Mosaic* 38, no. 2 (2005): 129–43.

Vickroy, Laurie. *Trauma and Survival in Contemporary Fiction.* Charlottesville: University of Virginia Press, 2002.

Whitehead, Anne. *Memory.* London: Routledge, 2009.

Whitehead, Anne. *Trauma Fiction.* Edinburgh: Edinburgh University Press, 2004.

Wilson, Sharon R. "Blindness and Survival in Margaret Atwood's Major Novels." In *The Cambridge Companion to Margaret Atwood*, ed. Coral Ann Howells. Cambridge: Cambridge University Press, 2006. http://dx.doi.org/10.1017/CCOL0521839661.013.

18 Grasping Patterns of Violence

AIJA SAKOVA

In her essay on autobiographical narration in the face of trauma in Margaret Atwood's *Cat's Eye,* Christa Schönfelder not only draws on literary and cultural theories of trauma and life writing, but combines them with approaches derived from psychiatric and clinical-psychological studies, particularly with regard to post-traumatic stress disorder (PTSD).[1] This interdisciplinary approach gives the reader good insights into not only the after-effects of traumatic experiences but also the ways in which painful memories can be confronted in and out of literature and what impact they can have on one's identity. Written in a quasi-autobiographical mode, *Cat's Eye* strongly foregrounds identity-formation issues and is in this sense closer to life writing than to a novel. Yet ultimately, the generic boundaries of *Cat's Eye* are difficult to determine, which is why it makes sense to read it, as Schönfelder does, as both a "trauma novel" and a fictional autobiography. At its heart is a traumatic childhood experience or, rather, traumatic childhood experiences, a difference that is worth stressing since I read *Cat's Eye* differently from Schönfelder and consider a different episode the traumatic core event of the narrator's life.

The traumatic experiences result in an ambivalent and complicated relationship between Elaine, the narrator-protagonist, and Cordelia, who was not only Elaine's childhood tormentor but also the girl Elaine considered her best friend during high school. After years of living separated from her former girlfriends, the psychological violence Elaine endured as a young girl seems forgotten. But the past returns to haunt her.

The temporal trajectory of Elaine's traumatic re-experiencing is, as Schönfelder notes, not linear; instead, time is composed of transparent layers laid on top of one another: "You don't look back along time but down through it, like water. Sometimes this comes to the surface, sometimes that, sometimes nothing. Nothing goes away" (*Cat's Eye* 3). All of Elaine's memories seem to be down there somewhere, but since she does not remember them consciously, they do not come to the surface whenever she wants them to. Her memories lie like small stones or shells at the bottom of a lake. Some of them appear larger or more distinct from above, and some of them cannot be perceived at all. Their image rises up unbidden, and all she sees and experiences are blurred spots. As soon as she tries to get hold of one, the water turns muddy again. These water metaphors, which Atwood resorts to again and again, emphasize that memories cannot simply be retrieved the way one takes an object out of a container. The process of remembering is erratic, fragmentary, meandering, and difficult.

While Schönfelder accuses Cathy Caruth's trauma theory of inflating trauma to a cultural condition – and thus something so widespread it is in danger of becoming ordinary – I argue with Caruth that it is exactly the lack of full consciousness of the traumatic experience that returns to haunt the traumatized: "What returns to haunt the victim … is not only the reality of the violent event but also the reality of the way that its violence has not yet been fully known" (6). The traumatic experiences are things that have not been acknowledged as such by Elaine and for that reason return to haunt her. Thus, it is not only the experience of violence that traumatizes Elaine, but also her inability to name it as such. As Schönfelder emphasizes, Atwood has her protagonist-narrator suffer from trauma-induced amnesia as well as intrusive memories, both of which can be grasped via water metaphors – amnesia as the inability to see through to the bottom of the lake; intrusive memories as bubbles that rise to the surface as if out of nowhere. Thus, it comes as little surprise that Atwood herself frequently uses metaphors of freezing in cold water and drowning to describe Elaine's experiences and state of mind. Surprisingly, Schönfelder does not elaborate on these central water metaphors.

In Schönfelder's reading, the core event of Elaine's traumatic past is a harrowing experience at the age of nine, when her girlfriends abandoned her in a dark hole. Schönfelder also understands the constant verbal attacks and mind games that follow this initial event as traumatizing. However, it is also possible to consider a related later episode, which Schönfelder does not discuss in any detail, as the most traumatic event of Elaine's life. In this scene, she almost freezes to death as she attempts to collect her hat from the icy surface of a creek at the bottom of a ravine (185–9). Cordelia threw the hat down there and ordered her to pick it up. In her adult life, it is the memory of that specific moment which Elaine is forced to return to over and over again. This, it seems to me, constitutes Elaine's pivotal traumatic experience, an experience whose recollection almost drives her to suicide later on, when she hears a voice, "not inside [her] head at all but in the room," that commands her "to do it," that is, to commit suicide: "*Do it. Come on. Do it.* This voice doesn't offer a choice; it has the force of an order. It's the difference between jumping and being pushed" (373). This last sentence takes us back to the core traumatic episode. Back then, she was oppressed by Cordelia to such an extent that she did not see any alternative to obeying her order and going down into the ice-cold ravine. In the later episode, too, Elaine seems to be freezing as she is driven to move around fast – to move the way people in danger of freezing to death are supposed to do to keep the blood circulating (373).

Significantly, the core traumatic scene returns in an alternative version at the end of the book. In Elaine's childhood visions, it was an imaginary Virgin Mary who saved her from the bottom of the ravine by reassuring her that she could "go home now … It will be all right. Go home" (201). Now, as the narrative ends, Elaine uses exactly the same words as she imagines the juvenile Cordelia at her mercy:

> There is the same shame, the sick feeling in my body, the same knowledge of my own wrongness, awkwardness, weakness; the same wish to be loved; the same loneliness; the same fear. But these are not my own emotions any more. They are Cordelia's; as they always were.
>
> I am the older one now, I'm stronger. If she stays here any longer she will freeze to death; she will be left behind, in the wrong time. It's almost too late.
>
> I reach out my arms to her, bend down, hands open to show I have no weapon. *It's all right*, I say to her. *You can go home now*. (419)

Schönfelder reads this episode at the very end of the narrative as a symbolic vision of reconciliation that expresses Elaine's readiness to forgive her main childhood tormentor, but she does not connect the passage with the earlier, parallel passage, in which the Virgin Many speaks almost identical words to Elaine: "It will be all right" and "you can go home now" (189). I agree with Schönfelder that the final scene gives expression to some sort of reconciliation, but I do not concur that it happens through forgiveness.

In my reading, Elaine experiences in this ultimate vision some sort of closure neither by reconciliation, nor by way of revenge, nor by re-living or remembering the traumatic experience itself, but by grasping what really happened back in her and Cordelia's childhood. In this scene, Elaine begins to understand that Cordelia herself was tormented by her father, and that the only way that she knew how to express her pain and anger was to inflict pain on her friend. To the adult Elaine, this insight offers some sort of redemption and allows her to confront her own painful memories. Elaine now grasps that the patterns of physical and psychological violence that Cordelia's father inflicted on his daughter, and that Cordelia subsequently inflicted on Elaine, live on in herself, in both the way she herself used to humiliate juvenile Cordelia and in how she as an adult cannot escape the commanding voice of a younger Cornelia.

Even if I read *Cat's Eye* differently, I agree with Schönfelder that it makes much sense to read it as a "trauma novel" that shows how traumatic experiences can be acted out, worked through, and incorporated into one's life story without achieving complete resolution or closure. But I am not convinced that this fictional autobiography should be read as an attempt to (re-)construct a coherent life story from the fragments of the past, and I do not think it offers a good example of scriptotherapy. Finally, I miss in Schönfelder's essay a more sustained discussion of the paired scenes of freezing and drowning that I situate at the heart of Atwood's fictional autobiography/trauma novel as well as of the water metaphors and images of freezing and drowning that are associated with them.

NOTES

1 This article has been written with the support of ESF grants 7354 ("Positioning Life-Writing on Estonian Literary Landscapes") and 9035 ("Dynamics of Address in Estonian Life Writing").

WORKS CITED

Atwood, Margaret. *Cat's Eye*. London: Virago, 1990.

Caruth, Cathy. *Unclaimed Experience. Trauma, Narrative, and History*. Baltimore: Johns Hopkins University Press, 1996.

19 Nostalgia and Redemption in Bernard Kangro's Joonatan Novels

MAARJA HOLLO

But when a man has come to look at the land of his past, what can he think about if not his past?

Milan Kundera, *Ignorance* 90

The question posed by the narrator of *Ignorance* about one of the novel's main characters is the key question for all those exiles returning to their homeland and attempting to overcome the contradiction between a ruptured past and an estranging present.[1] Paradoxically, this undertaking can be hindered by both an absence and an "excess" of nostalgia. In the first case, being back in the homeland is uncomfortable and shameful because memory selectively calls up episodes from the past that one has tried to forget while providing nothing that moves the soul; in the second case, nostalgia blurs the vision of the present as it resists the pressure of time and relentlessly repeats and fixates fragments of the past which are connected to the "past homeland": the tastes, the smells, and the voices of its places. These fragments, however, are distorted, since nostalgia has rendered them more beautiful and sublime in order to make an intolerable present bearable.

This essay explores the connections between remembering and nostalgia in situations of exile on the basis of the first and third novels of Estonian writer Bernard Kangro's Joonatan trilogy.[2] Since the Joonatan novels are autobiographical in nature, and since they also contain reflections on the reasons and conditions of autobiographical writing, I limit my investigation to the problematics of autobiographical writing in these works, arguing that the reasons for the unavoidability of the autobiographical that permeates Kangro's oeuvre lie in his condition and status as a writer in exile.

Since the dweller in exile lives in two times and places simultaneously, the kind of remembering that happens in exile can give rise to a drama of memory that "consists in the perpetual failure of memory to re-create the experience of the homeland, doubled by its failure to forget those experiences and thus liberate the psyche from that painful duality; finally, this double failure is generally capped by the refusal to forget" (Radulescu 190). Indeed, in cases of political exile, the drama of memory makes itself felt both on individual and collective levels as the refusal to forget becomes an imperative for the whole national community. In exile, individual memory not only serves to preserve the integrity of the subject; it must also fulfil a responsibility towards those compatriots who were left behind and those who have lost their homeland.

The Second World War has been considered twentieth-century Europe's greatest catastrophe; it created so new and unprecedented a situation that historians are justified in talking about the destruction of a whole geographical and cultural community – old Europe. More than thirty million people were left homeless at the end of the war. About 70,000 to 90,000 Estonians had to leave their homeland in the autumn of 1944, driven by fear of the red terror (Kumer-Haukanõmm 18).[3] Those who remained in the homeland began to be reshaped into Soviet citizens who were separated from the so-called free world by the Iron Curtain for more than half a century. By the fall of 1944, history had wiped off the map a young state that had barely reached maturity.

For the Estonian writers who remained in their homeland, the Soviet occupation meant either the beginning of a long period of internal exile or an adaptation to the official ideology that led to a diversity of writing strategies. Thus, it has been claimed that we can talk about a doubled or bifurcated literature of the Soviet period as "Soviet literature and Estonian literature" (Olesk 344). Of course, this is an arguable distinction, since "Estonian literature" was subject to the same strict censorship as "Soviet literature," though it dared to take greater aesthetic liberties while avoiding politically sensitive issues. Those writers who had chosen exile were limited by the small size of their target readership and its preference for certain themes and ways of writing that were often related to national ideology. In an overview of literary works published during the first fifteen years of exile, that is, up to 1959, Kangro noted that "it is remarkable how few novels have at their centre philosophical, psychological, or religious problems, or some other aesthetic goal autonomous of us and of the specificity of our times ... Maybe Estonian writers have been too confined by their circle of readers" ("Sada raamatut" 300). Besides making a judgment about the general aesthetic weakness of these literary works, Kangro's comments also point in another direction – to the need for literary creation to reach beyond the boundaries of the national language so as to overcome provincialism and become part of world literature.

Bernard Kangro, one of the twenty-one writers who left Estonia for Sweden in the autumn of 1944, is considered one of the father figures of Estonian literature, as well as the consummate man of letters in Estonian literary space. His literary contribution is staggering in its volume and diversity, spawning sixteen novels, seventeen collections of poetry, short stories, plays, essays, studies, criticism, overviews, letters, memoirs, and a short autobiography.[4] In the present essay, I focus on Kangro's novels, which can usefully be regarded as limit-cases of autobiographical writing. Indeed, the novels are more interesting with respect to the problematics of autobiography than those two texts in his oeuvre that were overtly written in the autobiographical genre. In *The Limits of Autobiography*, Leigh Gilmore defines limit-cases as texts which "confront how the limits of autobiography, multiple and sprawling as they are, might conspire to prevent some self-representational stories from beginning to be told at all if they were subjected to a literal truth test or evaluated by certain objective measures ... In swerving from the centre of autobiography toward its outer limits, [the authors] convert constraint into opportunity" (14). According to Gilmore, limit-cases also present themselves as testimonial projects, though the events of which they speak do not belong to "the protocols of legal testimony" (146). The purpose of such testimonial projects is not just punishment of the guilty, but a different kind of justice, afforded the author through the practice of narrating his/her story. The possibility of finding justice and thereby liberating oneself from the burden of the past is one of the central issues of Kangro's Joonatan novels. Another autobiographical element of these novels is their paratextual framework, which the author deems necessary as a means of shaping the interpretive space surrounding the novels and through which he also defines himself in relation to the protagonist.[5] According to the author, the eponymous protagonist of the Joonatan novels originated in a troubling dream in which Kangro found himself, as Joonatan does in the writer's fictional world, a stranger in a familiar city, where no one remembered him, and where he could not even recall his own name. In addition to the impulse of telling a story from his own life, Kangro is interested in the reasons and conditions of self-narration – an inquiry that involves investigating exile as a state of mind and the ways in which the process of remembering is represented. It is also in this sense that the Joonatan novels are fictional negotiations of life writing.

The first book of Kangro's Joonatan trilogy, *Joonatan, kadunud veli* (Joonatan, the Lost Brother), was published in 1971; the second, *Öö astmes X* (Night to the X Power), in 1973, and the third volume, *Puu saarel on alles* (A Tree on the Island Still Stands), in the same year. The trilogy was preceded by a six-part cycle of novels about Tartu. The unusual poetics of that cycle put to the test fixed notions of the possibilities and necessities of the novel in conditions of exile, notions which by this point had become stabilized in the cultural community of Estonian exiles. In these earlier texts, Kangro showed that there were other novelistic possibilities beside constrictive and dark realism. The very search for such alternatives indicated shifts that were taking place in his spiritual and intellectual needs; even before finishing the final novel of the Tartu cycle at the end of the 1960s, Kangro had found himself afflicted by a dark night of the soul. This oppression of spirit was intensified by his realization that the decline and disappearance of the old world was unavoidable. A collection of poems emerging from this period of crisis, *The Trees Walk Farther Away* (1969), contains the lines "I wait for the birth of a miracle / But at my deepest core there is impenetrable darkness" (*Kogutud luuletusi* 155). Though these lines also anticipate spiritual liberation, a letter Kangro sent to the homeland in 1968 further confirms his nadir mood: "I do not even know what I want, or where I want to go. Maybe nothing and nowhere. To Võrumaa of course. But Võrumaa has been locked up and the key has been broken" ("To Valmar Adams" 11).[6]

Kangro's home in the southeastern part of Estonia remained locked up in a very real sense, right up to the end, but it was not locked to the imagination that gave his life shape in verses and longer prose works. Kangro's response to his internal crisis was, to use his own words, to yield to inspiration and start a new novel. As in the Tartu cycle, Kangro delves into the past, but *Joonatan, kadunud veli* – the book that emerged out of that process – does not belong to the type of nostalgia genre that asks no questions about memory and the act of remembering; rather, there is a very deliberate, self-conscious, and deep dedication to problems of memory and the past. While Kangro's poetry seems to oscillate perpetually between "heroically self-instilled hope and increasingly

Sunday memories of home" (Ristikivi 249), the Joonatan novels stage not only a search for solace in the comfortless reality of exile – which is characteristic of most nostalgia literature written in exile – but above all an attempt to understand a present illuminated by the future. For Kangro's protagonist Joonatan, remembering is therefore both a nostalgic and a metanostalgic journey in time that allows him to know that he can "move on and back, go and come again" (*Joonatan, kadunud veli* 158).

The notion of "nostalgia" was first theorized in the seventeenth century by the Swiss physician Johannes Hofer, who described it in his doctoral dissertation as a new sickness that was spreading among mercenary soldiers. It was only at the beginning of the twentieth century that nostalgia ceased to be conceptualized as an illness. The term then began to denote a feeling, and "nostalgia" was set free from the negative connotations it had carried to date (Ritivoi 27). For our purposes, the relation of nostalgia to remembering and life writing is of particular importance. Since "memory is ... both source and authenticator of autobiographical acts" (Smith and Watson 16), Kangro's literary representations of nostalgic memories bring issues concerning traumatic remembering into sharp focus. Traumatic memories cannot be weighed on the scale of truth and falsehood. Rather, they indicate ways in which an individual interprets his past and the intensity of the loss which has been suffered.

The pathological consequences of exile are often interpreted as manifestations of psychological crises or traumas. Cuban-born American sociologist Rubén G. Rumbaut talks about exile as a dialectic of loss and reconstruction that entails prolonged psychological agonies. Rumbaut defines the essence of exile as a convergence of two simultaneous processes: "Psychosocially, it involves an arduous process of dislocation and relocation, uprootedness and new growth, anomie and adaptation ... The exile is challenged to resolve dual crises: a 'crisis of loss' (coming to terms with the past) and a 'crisis of load' (coming to terms with the present and immediate future)" (338). Kangro's Joonatan novels exemplify this convergence of crises: on the one hand, they testify to a refusal to accept the loss of the homeland; on the other, they are an attempt to overcome this refusal so as to find a way into the future. In his novels, Kangro shows that homecoming as an imaginary journey can be just as pivotal a task as it is in empirical reality.

Homecoming has been regarded as the most universal topos of exile literature: most exiles seem to have experienced recurrent dreams of it.

Yet as Piotr Kuhiwczak points out, the exile who actually returns to his homeland may experience contradictory feelings instead of unequivocal acceptance or celebration. He adds: "Literary accounts of returning are equally rare, and those available have few common characteristics. Some are subdued, others more expressive, but in no case do they measure up to the pathos and sublimity of departure" (38). Since he is received like a brother who arrives among his own after a long absence, Joonatan's return does not fit these generalizations. In the final part of Kangro's trilogy, *Puu saarel on alles*, Joonatan's return even attains a sublime stature when it is imbued with a religious meaning by way of the intertext of Dante's *Divine Comedy*: the journey to the occupied homeland is compared to a trip to hell that is followed by purification on an island.

Joonatan is an exiled writer and museum worker who returns to his homeland neither remembering nor wishing to remember anything about the war years or the time immediately preceding his flight. Two of Joonatan's dreams that he had abroad are connected with his return home. Both contain similar elements – a secret arrival in the homeland, pursuit, arrest, a trial, and a verdict – which together materialize his fears concerning homecoming and confirm their direct connection with a sense of guilt, albeit one that does not become completely conscious. Joonatan justifies his return to the homeland with his wish to search for his self and for lost time or, in other words, to search for a confirmation of the "correctness" of his memories. Joonatan's memory trip is impelled by nostalgia, but at the same time he fears the loss of even those images of the past that he has preserved in his memory. It is interesting that Joonatan prefers not to talk about himself, saying, "I have nothing particular to tell" (97). Instead, he allows seventeen of his former classmates to talk: among them there are ideologues of the regime, resistance fighters, disillusioned ones, and those who have simply adapted. Symbolically, Joonatan's gesture is highly significant since it gives voice to those who in reality would only have been able to speak of their painful past in a whisper, in a circle of close friends. Each classmate remembers Joonatan differently, but their reminiscences do not arouse in Joonatan any urge to remember times past. Joonatan's memories have become very ambiguous, in his own words, like excerpts "from an old movie, seen long ago and long ago forgotten" (33). During his sojourn in the homeland, Joonatan restores his past through the memories of his schoolmates. However, this is of little help in establishing clear outlines for Joonatan as a character, since his own retrospectives and explanations are missing – elided, eclipsed, or unarticulated. Perhaps his memory gaps are also the reason why Joonatan finds no real rapport with any of his classmates.

Joonatan wants to believe that the images of the past retained in his memory will not fade or disintegrate as long as he ignores the present moment. The longer he stays in his hometown, however, and the more classmates he converses with, the clearer it becomes to him that it is impossible completely to separate the present and the past. He realizes that, strangely enough, the nostalgic images of the past that he seeks to corroborate "at home" prevent him from understanding both the present and himself within that present. This is expressed by both Joonatan's inner speech and his discussions of memories and remembering with his classmates. One of these classmates, Edgar Kiideon, now the director of a psychiatric clinic, admits to Joonatan that liberation from memories makes a person happy, since "the past is burdensome. Especially when memory becomes intense, deforming present-day reality, and one's clear sense of one's situation" (71). Clearly, Joonatan does not agree with such a concept of happiness, which fits only too well with the official ideology; Joonatan's own purpose is not forgetting, but the opposite – finding out the truth, and seeking happiness through "reconciled memory" (Ricoeur 496).

However, it is paradoxical that in Joonatan's case, the preconditions for reconciled memory include not only commemoration but nostalgia: without experiencing nostalgia, he would have no access to his own past. According to Janelle L. Wilson, nostalgia can be an interpersonal form of conversational play, the ideologization or mystification of the past as well as a cultural commodity. Alongside these elements, another level exists, which Wilson describes as "an intrapersonal expression of self which subjectively provides one with a sense of continuity" (19). Joonatan's relation with nostalgia can be seen as an example of this last, intrapersonal level. This level of nostalgia does not only signify passive caressing of soul-nourishing images of the past, but is also "a builder of memory and memories, a creator of meaning and order, which performs a cathartic function in the human life course, a manifestation of cleansing and focusing" (Kukkonen 5). Thus, the task of nostalgia is the conferral of meaning on events of the past, parts of which are elevated through this process to a special status, while others fade altogether. This gathering of images, which resists the orderly sequencing of events, is in turn the basis for a unique memory and identity.

In *The Future of Nostalgia*, Svetlana Boym points to this function of nostalgia when she distinguishes two different types. The first of these, "restorative nostalgia," "puts emphasis on *nostos* and proposes to rebuild the lost home and patch up the memory gaps." Boym writes that this kind of nostalgia is usually not considered nostalgia at all, but rather is a synonym for truth and tradition. In restorative nostalgia, the "two main narrative plots are the restoration of the origins and the conspiracy theory," according to which "home" is in constant danger of besiegement, and requires defence against the enemy (43). The second type, "reflective nostalgia," is oriented towards personal narrative. As distinct from restorative nostalgia, which tries to gain victory over time by spatializing it, reflective nostalgia temporalizes space and can be ironic, even joking. Since reflective nostalgia "has a capacity to awaken multiple planes of consciousness" (49–50), it may also be labelled "creative nostalgia."

In addition to Boym's two types of nostalgia, which are arguably valid only for certain experiences of exile, one should perhaps also introduce a third one to account for the context of post-war Estonian exile. This third type of nostalgia is based on a more complex intertwining of personal memory and the political imperatives of collective memory. It contains elements of both restorative and reflective nostalgia, but does not summarize the two mechanically. Instead, it shows a synergy of personal and collective dimensions, a synergy that results in personal narratives that are so completely intertwined with the narrative of national destiny that every impulse or need to draw such boundaries is immediately overruled.

Joonatan seems to be the kind of nostalgic in whom the marks of restorative and reflective nostalgia are combined: he has not come back to the homeland to rebuild anything, but rather to find reconciliation with the past. At the same time, he feels the need to do something to benefit his occupied country, unconsciously expressing the idealistic view that it is possible to resist the cultural expansion of the occupation regime with the resources and values of European culture. Joonatan resolutely tells one of his classmates, the writer Siim Öösalu, that "Europe is unconquerable – European culture, however ambiguous such a concept is. It will persist despite everything. There is nothing that could replace it" (*Joonatan, kadunud veli* 184).[7]

Nostalgic images of the past affect those who look back like half-epiphanies that interrupt the continuity of time in memory (Annus 331). Joonatan does not want to succumb unreflectively to the seduction of nostalgic remembering; the lures and spells of nostalgic memories prevent him from understanding the reality of the present, including the changes wrought by the occupation in people and places. On the way to the parsonage to visit his schoolmate Bruno Moorkop, a pastor, Joonatan's nostalgic backward glance at his home is interrupted by his own voice:

> I leaned my back against the post and closed my eyes. But as soon as I did so, I saw, with frightening clarity, our farmhouse, the yard, the storehouse, the view from our gate up to the distant hills, shimmering blue through a light haze, my home hill and the white trunks of the birch trees rising from it. – No, I must not succumb to it, I warned myself, and opened my eyes. (58)

Such interruptions take place throughout the first novel of the trilogy, and, as is characteristic of nostalgic remembering, the static fragments of the past are animated by memories of tastes, colours, and voices. "The taste of marzipan apples, the beehives under the trees … the evening light, the glowing edge of the sky; farther off a wagon rattles, there is singing, the dogs are barking in the distance … Half-running I fled from these images – I must not succumb to memories!" (143). The distant hill shimmering through a light haze, the white trunks of the birch trees, and the beehives are, of course, significant, but they are not the only components of Joonatan's nostalgic picture of the past. An important place in it belongs to Mirjam – the girl of Joonatan's dreams and those of all of his classmates. Mirjam is a mystification, created by Joonatan himself, the quintessence of his own and his classmates' youthful fantasies, which in the final novel of the trilogy, *Puu saarel on alles*, is embodied as Dante's Beatrice through a pair of characters named Silvia and Ingeborg. The brighter, more romantic, and unearthly pole of Beatrice is embodied by Silvia, with whom Joonatan had a romantic-platonic relationship in his youth. Reminiscing together with her unleashes a tide of nostalgic images of the past, which are interrupted by his painful recognition that at some point in his life, he made "a fateful mistake" (53). Whether Joonatan here alludes to an unspecified decision related to Silvia, to leaving his homeland, or to a third possibility known only to himself remains unclear. By contrast, Ingeborg represents the darker, more unpredictable side of love ("Ingeborg – that was not an easy chapter" [175]), calling forth those episodes of the past that Joonatan does not want to remember. There are many allusions in the text to Ingeborg's suicide attempts, which Joonatan was mixed up in. Her later madness – she has been away in a place "from which one does not return unchanged" (67) – is the reason why his reunion with her results in troubling thoughts, questions, and doubts. Nevertheless, it is to Ingeborg that Joonatan entrusts the key that opens "the locks of memory" before leaving the island. Although Ingeborg does not become what Beatrice was for Dante, the saviour and "means by which purification takes place," she is transformed into one of the "eternal images" (Williams 147) in the last part of the trilogy, an eternally loving guardian angel who cares for Joonatan throughout his stay on the island, even though Joonatan fears her on account of her ostensible madness.

However, Joonatan is not only the lost brother, but also the prodigal son who has come back to the homeland to seek information about the fate of his father Taavet. Questions about what happened to his father weigh on Joonatan, but the opportunity to ask them does not come until he talks to Valde Tiivoja, one of his classmates. It turns out that Valde does not know what really happened to Joonatan's father; yet he does venture several rumours about him that allude to the possibility that Joonatan himself might have been responsible for his father's arrest.

Joonatan seeks more detailed information about his father from another classmate, the prison warden Richard Vissel, who, knowing Joonatan, senses that he has not come just to visit, but with an additional agenda. Theirs is one of those reunions that turn into a chilly talking past one another: both Joonatan and Richard are unwilling to bring to light many of the past events connected with betrayal. Before leaving, Joonatan does, however, hear that his father was executed by a firing squad "for treason and acts of hostility toward the people" (86). The story of betrayal does not come to a resolution, and Joonatan is not satisfied with Richard's fatalistic statement "We are nothing but pawns in the hands of historical processes" (87). Coming from a representative of those in power, it belies resignation, but also absolves those who betrayed others from responsibility for their deeds. Joonatan later hears more about his father's fate from his writer-classmate Siim Öösalu and also, on his following day on the island, from a character named Jeesus. Needing to have certainty about his father's fate reintroduces the question of Joonatan's own guilt. It turns out that Siim was sentenced to forced labour because of letters received from Joonatan; once again, Kangro's protagonist is forced to realize that it is easier to live with the imagination than with the burden of truth. Similarly to Richard, Siim also sarcastically suggests that in this state it is much more beneficial to forget and accept than it is to remember: "The question of guilt – we have gotten past that long ago. That is an outdated idea in our new society" (*Joonatan, kadunud veli* 187). The problematics of guilt and innocence become especially sharply relevant in the conversations between Joonatan and his school brothers, which force Joonatan to solve moral dilemmas that he did not anticipate: on the one hand, he feels guilty for leaving his homeland behind and thus does not have the right to judge those who stayed behind; on the other, his classmates, especially those in opposition to the regime, seem to expect him to confer clear moral judgments on the events of the past as well as those of the present. Thus, the historian Peeter Kallikorn asks Joonatan for his position with respect to the desirable relationship between compromise and resistance, but Joonatan does not have a ready answer. He is also disturbingly reminded of the forthright words of "stray intellectual" Artur Agask: "You come from another world, and you have stayed there too long. You do not know anything about our problems. Problems for which there is no solution in sight. Only one escape route is left" (*Joonatan, kadunud veli* 170–1).

Like other nostalgia texts, the Joonatan novels are characterized by the special attention they devote to places, buildings, and interiors. Joonatan's narrative indicates that the overall impression of the town and its buildings has changed very little. The house where Joonatan rented a room in his school days, the schoolhouse, even the one-time best restaurant in town, the Grand, have seen very little wear. According to Joonatan's descriptions, it is as if nothing had really changed. Thus, his nostalgic remembering carries on the bright spirit of the time of the first Republic of Estonia. Seen through Joonatan's eyes, even his school brothers themselves seem much the same. Yet even though much of the real effects of the occupation on people remain incomprehensible to him, Joonatan cannot help being tormented by his feelings of guilt concerning his rejection of his homeland – feelings that are both personal and collective for an exile like him. The final novel of the trilogy, *Puu saarel on alles*, which tracks the second day of Joonatan's journey, speaks of ways in which this guilt could be redeemed. Since most of the action in this text once again takes place in Joonatan's inner world and is related from his perspective, different dimensions of time meet and mix. Compared to the first volume, more importance is accorded to figures of thought. To understand the third part of the trilogy, one must grasp the stable, recurring images from Dante's *Purgatorio*: the island, the tree, and Joonatan's Beatrice – Mirjam. The novel's religious dimension is also emphasized by the co-presence of cathartic and redemptive forms of nostalgia. If Joonatan, who has recently read the *Divine Comedy*, thinks of Mirjam as his Beatrice, his former bench mate Laur Paomees becomes his Virgil figure, rescuing him at the last minute from the clutches of those who have come to arrest him. In keeping with the reference to internal exile implicit in his name ("Man of Refuge"), Laur is a mysterious character. He belongs neither to the collaborators nor to those who actively oppose the regime. On their first meeting, Joonatan finds no rapport with him at all, but later he finds out that Laur has suffered a great deal, since he made an attempt to escape, was caught, and was punished harshly. "[We are] dead only in the spiritual sense," Laur tells Joonatan, and asks the rhetorical question: "What would put an end to the dictatorship here? Will anyone come to help us?" Then he gives his own answer: "We can only rely on ourselves" (242).

Towards morning, Laur takes Joonatan to the island. There, Joonatan finds himself in a strange and at the same time familiar house in which he meets Mirjam. More precisely, he meets "Mirjams" in his former home. Its isolation and boundedness make the island a safe and intimate, but also an oppressive place, where he feels a sharp need to be released from his own limits and to forget the constraints of his body. Being on the island stimulates Joonatan's creative powers, and he begins to daydream, fantasize, and remember. However, the island is not only totally isolated but also completely open – open in all directions, though its openness actually works mostly in one direction. Just as is characteristic of the islands of classical utopias, in which the inhabitants are informed about the outside world, though the island itself remains a secret to those on the mainland, so in Kangro's novel the island is a refuge for Joonatan from the servants of the totalitarian regime, a patch of freedom in a reality defined by strict rules and regulations. At the same time, news is brought to him about events in the outside world by Jeesus, one of the leaders of the resistance movement, as well as by Ingeborg. As a symbol, the island can also be interpreted as a nesting place, an ordered, holistic world that provides a sense of security, anchoring for the exile a piece of "*terra firma* in this restless, shifting world" (Kangro, "Tükike tõelisust" 68).[8]

"The spirit of the times (*Zeitgeist*) is in the final analysis always the spirit of place, which bursts out of the depths of a place, dispersing over many places in the course of time," writes Madis Kõiv in an essay on Kangro (344). Kõiv goes on to claim that, for Kangro, intuitions of space are stronger than intuitions of time. The Joonatan novels support this argument in every way, since the places described there begin their lives in a space-time continuum not necessarily accessible to the uninitiated. In Kangro's novels, places come alive through the memory of objects that have remained there. Accordingly, the house on the island is not only a shelter for Joonatan but also a place of initiation, the site of a ritual of dedication, where "commands of things are made known" (355). Joonatan rediscovers his past home in the attic of this house, which reminds him strongly of the attic of his home farmhouse: here he finds familiar objects, smells, and beloved childhood toys, which call up clear memory images. From childhood on, the attic had been a mysterious place for him, prone to inexplicable rearrangements of objects. At one point, Joonatan cannot find his way out of it, but after that, all temporal and spatial obstacles disappear, and Joonatan is being interrogated in a clinic. Somewhat later, it becomes clear that this episode had been one more among Joonatan's dreams or hallucinations, since once his thoughts clear up, he finds himself back in the house on the island.

The most emotional aspect of this episode is Joonatan's rediscovery of his childhood toys. For the first time during his whole period spent in his homeland, he is reminded of his mother. For Joonatan's journey back home, this meeting is crucial and definitive: it is not clarification of the circumstances surrounding his father's death that take him closer to home, but rather the brief flashing image of his mother passing before his eyes: "I saw her there for a moment, standing there at the end of our road under the row of trees, where she had come to see me off. Looking back I saw her still standing there, her hand raising her apron to her eyes. Every time I left – for school, university, the war, the wide world" (*Puu saarel on alles* 141). The coming to life of the figure of the mother in Joonatan's nostalgic memory – forever sending off, eternally waiting – signifies his coming to terms with the past, as well as his liberation from it, and it is this visionary moment that presages his liberation from the identity of the prodigal son and his restoration of the identity of the true son.

Joonatan is reinvested with a son's identity after both his parents have accepted him as their son. In the case of his mother, this happens through the mediation of nostalgic memory; in his father's case, through commemoration. As soon as Joonatan hears from Jeesus that due to rearrangements in the power structures at the top, leaving the island is no longer dangerous, Joonatan bids farewell to Mirjam/Ingeborg and hurries to the old cemetery near the town to search for his father's grave. The cemetery is a place of eternity where time and life seem to stand still. Everything is possible in the time of eternity, even the raising of the dead and Joonatan's reunion with his mother. Indeed, Joonatan meets an old woman who takes him for her son, and Joonatan does not think it ethically sound to break the woman's illusion. While giving his hand to the woman, he thinks to himself that this could have been his mother's hand, the hand that he never clasped. Through this initiation, Joonatan receives confirmation of his identity as a son, and is received as one of his own.

Joonatan received his name from his father, who, being a devout man, had taken it from the Bible. In turn, Joonatan's name has directed him to the Bible: "It became clear to me that there was some connection between my name and that thick book, and I tried to find out for myself what this was. My attempt failed that time, but through it I discovered the Bible" (*Puu saarel on alles* 196). Joonatan supposes that his father wanted to give his life direction through that name, but that having understood this action as an evocation of magic potential, he had decided to die for Joonatan "so that the word would be fulfilled" (196). While Christ redeemed humankind, Joonatan's father Taavet went to his death for his son. Joonatan's sins and crimes have thus been atoned for, opening for him the gate to his home, the opportunity to truly arrive.

Arrival as a completely blissful, incomparable feeling of fulfilment had already revealed itself to Joonatan in his earlier nostalgic daydreams and fantasies about his home. This is a state of pure being that requires no justification or explanations: "Everything retreats and settles, the world becomes simple and understandable. There are no more problems, everything has been set right, all is well just the way it is. And everything just is – clear, obvious, calm" (167). When he arrives at his farmstead, Joonatan has a similar experience: "I stood quietly, holding my breath. The house was there, it was just standing there, nothing more" (248). That this is indeed the end of Joonatan's journey, his arrival on the threshold of paradise, is confirmed by the remembrance of the tree growing on the island.

Joonatan's homecoming is one of the core symbols of the novels. It signifies the overcoming of many contradictions and internal doubts connected with remembering, all of which Joonatan encounters on his complicated journey of memory. Neither Kangro nor, by implication, Joonatan would have begun that journey without the stimulus of nostalgia, guilt, and feelings of loss. Through his novels, Kangro engages with his personal fate as well as the past and present realities of his homeland. Significantly, that engagement happens not in a strictly autobiographical mode but through a work of fiction that incorporates autobiographical elements. As limit-cases, Kangro's Joonatan novels enable a freer negotiation of the past. On the one hand, Joonatan is able to reconcile his memories on a personal level, as marked by the island and the cemetery as symbols of the different stages of his memory work. On the other hand, reconciled memory is not achieved at the level of the occupation as a historical reality. Thus, as far as the protagonist is concerned, there is no definitive resolution for the drama of memory. The contribution of the Joonatan novels to the literature representing traumatic experiences is rather that, in an unusual literary way, they "expose conditions in which alternative forms of knowledge about justice are compelled to appear" (Gilmore 147). One of the keys to understanding the Joonatan novels is to consider the date and context of their publication. The need to write in an autobiographical mode does not merely testify to Kangro's unwillingness to come into conflict with the expectations of his readership – expectations which he thoroughly understood, and with which he always had to reckon as a publisher. More importantly, Kangro chose to write in a mode that hovers between autobiography and fiction out of a need to put himself to the test, both in the ethical and the aesthetic sense.

NOTES

1 This article has been written with the support of ESF grant 7354 ("Positioning Life-Writing on Estonian Literary Landscapes") and the TF project "Sources of Cultural History and Contexts of Literature."

2 In addition to being a prolific writer, Bernard Kangro (1910–94) was the editor of the literary and cultural magazine *Tulimuld* and the linchpin of the Eesti Kirjanike Kooperatiiv, one of the major diaspora publishing houses. His activities gave impetus to literary life, and he remained an ongoing participant in that process through his creative work. Thus, it is understandable that no exhaustive and synthesizing study of his work has yet been written.

3 This figure includes those who were living abroad before the war, those who chose to remain abroad, and those who perished in the attempt to escape.

4 Kangro's autobiography is entitled *This Is Bernard Kangro's Mortal Life, Composed by Himself, for the Purpose of Remembering and Teaching a Lesson and Just for a Laugh.* Published only in 1992 in the newly independent

Estonia, the text gives a brief overview of the author's life from his birth to the year 1966 and is dense with facts and interspersed with occasional reflections on literature and writing.

5 In "Ühe triloogia sünnilugu," Kangro explains the starting points of his Joonatan trilogy, referring to the impulse that lies behind his writing of the first novel of the trilogy as the need "to live through," a phrase that he uses repeatedly when describing his own creative process (363, 364).

6 Kangro probably began corresponding with Valmar Adams in the middle of the 1950s, but the first surviving letter dates from 1961. Besides Adams, Kangro corresponded with several writers under official publication bans, such as Uku Masing, August Sang, and Betti Alver, who like Kangro himself had belonged to the literary grouping *Arbujad* (the Soothsayers) before the war.

7 Joonatan has written a book entitled *The Myth of Europe: Essays on Europe's Past, Present, and Future* in which he stresses, among other things, that the bipolarity of mysticism and logic is and will remain the basis of European culture. This claim says a great deal about Joonatan's own mentality.

8 Apart from Dante's *Purgatorio*, the text significantly refers to another island. On the wall of a room in the island house, Joonatan sees Arnold Böcklin's painting *Isle of the Dead* (1880) in what seems to be an ironic prolepsis, since Joonatan soon finds out that he has been pronounced dead by mistake. This does not rule out the possibility that the painting is a reference to Joonatan's task, meaning that he has to stay on the "isle of the dead" long enough to go through the purgatory of remembering. In addition to this, the allusion to Böcklin's painting foregrounds the split between Joonatan's nostalgic yearning for the Mountains of Longing and the real purpose of his purification. There are many further references to the *Purgatorio*, especially in the opening chapters of *Puu saarel on alles*. While, in preparation for purgatory, Dante is dressed in reeds as a mark of humility, Joonatan prepares to enter the houses of memory by means of Mirjam's linden leaf. In canto 9 of the *Purgatorio*, immediately before Dante enters purgatory, colour symbolism appears: the steps leading to the gates of purgatory are three different colours, symbolizing the three sacraments of Penance: "contrition of the heart, confession by the lips, and satisfaction by works" (Sinclair 128). In Kangro, the first of the three steps, made of white marble, is described with a quotation from Dante as "so mild and clean" and speaks of the sincerity of Regret; the second step, made of dark stone, represents the effort of Confession; the third step, made of red quartz, points to Joonatan's zeal to become a better person through the lessons of love (129). Joonatan stands doubting

at the gate, the white colour of which is "bleached and faded" (23). The stones lining the street leading up to the house were also white at one time, but with time have become "patchy or completely grey" (26). It is also no coincidence that there are "red-patterned curtains" (26) at the window, and that a single amaryllis blooms there. Joonatan enters the house with the help of Mirjam, in whom he recognizes the one-time girl of his dreams. Though, like Joonatan himself, Mirjam has changed with time, she succeeds in convincing him that she is really the same Mirjam whom he dreamed about, and who has become flesh and blood on the island thanks to Joonatan's faith.

WORKS CITED

Annus, Epp. *Kuidas kirjutada aega* [How to Tell Time]. Tallinn: Underi ja Tuglase Kirjanduskeskus, 2002.

Boym, Svetlana. *The Future of Nostalgia*. New York: Basic Books, 2001.

Gilmore, Leigh. *The Limits of Autobiography: Trauma and Testimony*. Ithaca: Cornell University Press, 2001.

Kangro, Bernard. *Joonatan, kadunud veli* [Joonatan, the Lost Brother]. Lund: Eesti Kirjanike Kooperatiiv, 1971.

Kangro, Bernard. *Kogutud luuletusi: Aastaist 1927–1989. II köide* [Collected Poems from the Years 1927–1989. Volume II]. Lund: Eesti Kirjanike Kooperatiiv, 1991.

Kangro, Bernard. *Öö astmes* X [Night to the X Power]. Lund: Eesti Kirjanike Kooperatiiv, 1973.

Kangro, Bernard. *Puu saarel on alles* [A Tree on the Island Still Stands]. Lund: Eesti Kirjanike Kooperatiiv, 1973.

Kangro, Bernard. "Sada raamatut: Kokkuvõtteid ja mõtisklusi" [One Hundred Books: Summaries and Reflections]. *Tulimuld* 4 (1959): 289–303.

Kangro, Bernard. "To Valmar Adams." Estonian Cultural History Archives: The Files of Valmar Adams. 56 letters from 26 October 1968 to 9 April 1991. File 344, folder 20: 18, p. 11.

Kangro, Bernard. "Tükike tõelisust" [A Piece of My Reality]. In *Minu noorusmaa: Koguteos 24. autorilt* [The Land of My Youth: Anthology of 24 Authors], ed. Valev Uibopuu, 69–77. Lund: Eesti Kirjanike Kooperatiiv, 1964.

Kangro, Bernard. "Ühe triloogia sünnilugu" [The Story of the Birth of a Trilogy]. *Keel ja Kirjandus* 6 (1988): 363–6.

Kõiv, Madis. "Genius Loci." In *Luhta-minek* [Going to the Bottom], ed. Aare Pilv, 341–57.Tartu: Ilmamaa, 2005.

Kuhiwczak, Piotr. "When the Exile Returns." In *Literary Expressions of Exile: A Collection of Essays*, ed. Roger Whitehouse, 31–45. Lewiston, NY: Edwin Mellen Press, 2000.

Kukkonen, Pirjo. "Nostalgian Semiosis" [The Semiosis of Nostalgia]. In *Nostalgia: Kirjoituksia kaipuusta, ikävästä ja muistista* [Nostalgia: Writings about Longing, Sadness, and Memory], ed. Riikka Rossi and Katja Seutu., 13–44. Helsinki: Suomalaisen Kirjallisuuden Seura, 2007.

Kumer-Haukanõmm, Kaja. "Eestlaste Teisest maailmasõjast tingitud põgenemine läände" [The Flight of Estonians to the West due to the Second World War]. In *Suur põgenemine 1944. Eestlaste lahkumine läände ning selle mõjud. 22. oktoobril 2004 Tartus toimunud rahvusvahelise teaduskonverentsi artiklite kogumik* [The Great Exodus of 1944: The Flight of Estonians to the West and Its Influences], ed. Kaja Kumer-Haukanõmm, Tiit Rosenberg, and Tiit Tammaru, 13–37. Tartu: Tartu Ülikooli Kirjastus, 2006.

Kundera, Milan. *Ignorance*, trans. Linda Asher. New York: HarperCollins, 2003.

Olesk, Sirje. "Kirjandusest kahes ruumis" [On Literature in Two Realms]. In *Eesti kirjanduslugu* [Estonian Literary History], ed. Epp Annus et al., 343–4. Tallinn: Koolibri, 2001.

Radulescu, Domnica. "Theorizing Exile." In *Realms of Exile: Nomadism, Diasporas, and Eastern European Voices*, ed. D. Radulescu, 185–203. Lanham, MD: Lexington Books, 2002.

Ricoeur, Paul. *Memory, History, Forgetting*. Trans. Kathleen Blamey and David Pellauer. Chicago: University of Chicago Press, 2004.

Ristikivi, Karl. "Pagulus – teema variatsioonidega" [Exile: Theme with Variations]. In *Viimne vabadus* [The Final Freedom], ed. Janika Kronberg, 249–53. Tartu: Ilmamaa, 1996.

Ritivoi, Andreea Deciu. *Yesterday's Self: Nostalgia and the Immigrant Identity*. Lanham, MD: Rowman & Littlefield, 2002.

Rumbaut, Rubén G. "The One-and-a-Half Generation: Crisis, Commitment, and Identity." In *The Dispossessed: An Anatomy of Exile*, ed. Peter I. Rose, 337–43. Amherst: University of Massachusetts Press, 2005.

Sinclair, John D. "Note." In Dante Alighieri,*The Divine Comedy*, vol. 2, *Purgatorio*, 127–9. New York: Oxford University Press, 1977.

Smith, Sidonie, and Julia Watson. *Reading Autobiography: A Guide for Interpreting Life Narratives*. Minneapolis: University of Minnesota Press, 2001.

Williams, Charles. *The Figure of Beatrice: A Study in Dante*. London: Faber & Faber, 1943.

Wilson, Janelle L. *Nostalgia: Sanctuary of Meaning*. Lewisburg, PA: Bucknell University Press, 2005.

20 Renegotiations of Longing and Belonging: Exile, Memory, and Nostalgia

CHRISTA SCHÖNFELDER

Maarja Hollo's essay explores issues of exile and homecoming, and of memory and nostalgia in a trilogy of novels written in exile by Estonian writer Bernard Kangro and published between 1971 and 1973. Hollo repeatedly emphasizes that Kangro's novels – which are, like a number of texts discussed in this collection, "limit-cases" in Leigh Gilmore's sense – closely connect the experience of exile to a "drama of memory," that is, various conflicts and crises of memory. The exile's "drama of memory" revolves around tensions between the pain of remembering and the impossibility and refusal to forget – with nostalgia functioning as a complex mediator of these tensions. Roberta Rubenstein in *Home Matters* claims that "narratives that engage notions of home, loss, and/or nostalgia confront the past in order to 'fix' it, a process that may be understood in two complementary senses. To 'fix' something is to secure it more firmly in the imagination and also to correct – as in *revise* or *repair* – it" (6).[1] I want to respond to Hollo's discussion of nostalgia and remembering in the context of exile and homecoming by exploring the protagonist Joonatan's memory journey as a complex negotiation of these two ways of "fixing" the past, which I, with Rubenstein, regard not as opposites, but as complementary. To investigate further the meanings and the implications, as well as the interrelations, of these two modes of approaching the past, I also draw on psychological and sociological studies. Like Aleida Assmann and Harald Welzer, and Svetlana Boym and Janelle L. Wilson, among others, I regard interdisciplinary perspectives on memory and nostalgia as particularly fruitful.

The first type of "fixing" the past can be described as closely related to the desire to secure the past and corroborate memories, but also to rely on the past as a source of comfort and consolation. In Joonatan's case, this mode or practice of remembering is evoked particularly with regard to his urge to indulge in nostalgic memories, in daydreams and fantasies of his home and homeland. This desire for nostalgia can be related to an important psychological function of nostalgia that Wilson investigates extensively. Wilson maintains that nostalgia may significantly contribute to a "coherent" and "consistent" sense of identity and self (8): "Nostalgia may facilitate *continuity of identity*, allowing people, through narrative and sometimes vicarious experience, to 'place' themselves in time and space" (61). Nostalgia may thus be a particularly important mode of remembering for trauma victims, who tend to suffer from a disrupted sense of consistency with regard to the self and the past.[2] For Joonatan, the experience of exile is one of the primary factors causing such ruptures of consistency. As Sue Gee emphasizes, "For the exile or émigré, the past is literally another country" (11). Hence, the combination of temporal and spatial distance and dislocation inherent in the experience of exile seems to create a strong need for "fixing" the past and firmly "placing" oneself both spatially and temporally.

However, this first mode of approaching and "fixing" the past also connects to a dimension of nostalgia that has often been regarded as dysfunctional, associated politically with a regressive or reactionary attitude and psychologically with a problematic absorption in the past. It is the dimension of nostalgia that Kimberly Smith describes as a "mental escape from the *present to the past* – a past colored by false, unreliable imaginings" (512), and that Svetlana Boym calls "a romance with one's own fantasy" (xiii). This dimension of nostalgia may also be the reason why nostalgia – interestingly a notion that originally emerged from the realm of the pathological, signifying a disease – sometimes tends to evoke a certain "dis-ease."[3] It is part of the critical, in Hollo's terms, "metanostalgic" potential of Kangro's novels that the protagonist recognizes this seductive, problematic aspect of nostalgia. Joonatan realizes that too much indulgence in nostalgic remembering may not be psychologically beneficial and stabilizing but would, in Wilson's terms, "impair a functioning identity by causing one to fail to live in the present" (157). In this sense, Wilson continues, "nostalgia could lead to a stifling or constraining of self; the proverbial person who is stuck in the past" (157). It is precisely this fear of nostalgia separating him from the present that Joonatan expresses. A different anxiety about nostalgia relates to the past rather than the present: nostalgia implies a very selective way of remembering, based on cherishing certain memories and evading or erasing others. As Robert Hemmings asserts, "Nostalgia and trauma operate from the same liminal space between memory and forgetting" (3). For Joonatan however, it is a key concern *not* to forget, and Kangro's novels, like many other texts explored in this collection, are texts that essentially work against oblivion.

While alerting us to these dangers of pushing too far the first type of fixing the past, Kangro's novels suggest that a combination with the second type of fixing that Rubenstein refers to may allow for a different – a functional rather than dysfunctional – psychology of nostalgia and remembering. This second type shifts the emphasis from "securing" to "revising," involving an active and critical engagement with the past. This type of engaging with the past is closely connected to a key issue with regard to memory that is implicitly present in Hollo's reading, but that could have been spelled out more clearly. Hollo repeatedly emphasizes that Kangro's novels foreground individual and collective, personal and political dimensions of remembering. Yet, the novels highlight a third dimension, namely, the interpersonal dimension of remembering. The way in which Joonatan lets a strikingly large number of his former schoolmates talk about the past when he is back in his homeland clearly points to this essential characteristic of memory that has been explored extensively in recent years – the fundamentally interpersonal, that is, the social or communicational, nature of memory. The emphasis on the interpersonal also highlights that what is at stake in Joonatan's memory journey is, to use two key terms by Rubenstein, not only "longing," but also a renegotiation of his sense of "belonging" (6).

Social psychologist Harald Welzer maintains that both collective and individual pasts are built and continuously rebuilt in a constant and ubiquitous process of social practice ("Gedächtnis und Erinnerung" 164–5). Welzer conceptualizes the self as involved in a continuous process of synthesizing and synchronizing, striving to make its own stories, beliefs, and feelings about the past and the past self compatible not only with the present self, but also with the memories of others, their narratives of the past, and related value judgments and feelings.[4] Kangro's novels foreground these interpersonal dimensions of remembering especially through the emphasis on "memory talk" (Welzer) between the returned exile and those who stayed behind.[5] The different ways in which Joonatan is separated or alienated from those who remained at home – through time, a very different array of experiences, a different relation to his homeland, and so on – function as considerable obstacles to the compatibility of memories. The communication about the past is also hampered by Joonatan's memory gaps and, even more importantly, by issues of guilt. Joonatan suffers from a sense of guilt and betrayal towards his father, as well as towards his homeland, and, on top of that, discovers that one of his classmates was sentenced to forced labour because of letters he had received from Joonatan. Through the interpersonal problems involved in Joonatan's return, Kangro's novels, as Hollo notes, bring to mind Piotr Kuhiwczak's point that the exile's return to the homeland tends to be experienced as difficult or ambiguous (37). Yet while "memory talk" is depicted as complicated and painful, it is crucial to see that it nevertheless plays a key role in Joonatan's attempts at fixing and re-confronting the past. After all, "belonging," far more than "longing," is a "relational, reciprocal condition that encompasses connection and community" (Rubenstein 4). In other words, memory talk is one kind of memory practice that prevents Joonatan from overindulging in sentimental longing and a problematically one-sided form of nostalgic remembering.

The contrast between the two poles but also the need for both are also symbolically represented in the two female figures that are important to Joonatan's process of homecoming: Silvia stands for a kind of romantic, blissful nostalgia, while Ingeborg stands for the need to confront the dark, painful aspects of the past too. Moreover, the novels' representation of Joonatan's homecoming connects the emphasis on women that played a key role in his past to a powerful emphasis on place and space. The Joonatan-trilogy foregrounds the power of places that are deeply inscribed with individual memories and personal meaning, such as his former school, his old farmstead, and his father's grave – places that we, in analogy to Assmann's German term *Gedächtnisorte*,[6] can call *memory places*. The text, however, puts particular emphasis on one rather special memory place which is imbued with intertextual references to Dante: a house on an island, the place where Joonatan meets the women of his past and which in his imagination also becomes his former home. This house – which, similarly to the cemetery he visits soon after, is both a *Gedächtnisort* and a heterotopia in Michel Foucault's sense ("Of Other Spaces") – triggers his memory journey back into his childhood and through its special aura brings back – for the first time after his return – memories of his mother. Experiencing a strikingly vivid flashback of his mother, Joonatan symbolically recovers his identity as a son. This exemplifies how individual places of memory, both real and imaginary, play a fundamental role for Joonatan in the symbolic completion of his homecoming and his gradual coming to terms with the past.

The heterotopic space of the island is closely connected to the redemptive function of nostalgia that Hollo highlights. At the same time, through the emphasis on highly symbolic tokens of memory, namely, childhood toys, and the mother, the text evokes one more dimension of nostalgia, one related to structural rather than historical trauma. As Rubenstein maintains, "Nostalgia, or homesickness, whose meaning remains so closely allied with it, is the existential condition of adulthood. While 'exile' is a freighted term within the context of postcolonial awareness, we are all, – regardless of gender, homeland, or place of origin – exiles from childhood" (4–5). The novels' emphasis on this dimension of homesickness, the adult's nostalgia for childhood, may be said to signal simultaneously the impossibility of an actual homecoming and the importance – and redemptive potential – of homecoming in a figurative or spiritual sense. It is then also telling that in the cemetery Joonatan meets an old woman who believes him to be her son. The text here seems to set up a connection between nostalgia and utopia, resonating with Wilson's assertion that nostalgia can be interpreted as "a longing for a utopia, projected backwards in time" (37). In fact, Joonatan's acceptance of this mother figure can be read as a gesture that is nostalgic and utopian at the same time, enacting a "longing for belonging" that is directed both backwards and forwards in time, towards his past and future, real and imagined, identities as a son.

Kangro's novels, then, signal that nostalgia should be regarded as encompassing more than, in Wilson's terminology, simply a "living in the past"; nostalgia may also entail "an active engagement with the past, and a juxtaposition of past and present" (157), involving the process that Kangro labels "liv[ing] through." Nostalgia emerges as a mode of remembering that may well combine the two complementary senses of "fixing" the past and thereby allow the subject to experience a symbolic recovery of home and to "mediate – and traverse the gap between longing and belonging" (Rubenstein 6).[7] After all, as Hemmings asserts, any nostalgic "look[s] to the past to make sense of the present" (5). Moreover, through the heterotopias of island and cemetery, spaces that allow the protagonist to experience different layers of time accumulated into one place, and simultaneously spaces of transformation and purging, the text may be said to enact a kind of homecoming that is, paradoxically, oriented towards both the past and the future. Thus, ultimately, this could seem to suggest that in the aftermath of trauma – here, the trauma of exile – we may not only have a need for nostalgia, but also a certain need for utopia – as Philipp Schweighauser argues in his contribution to this volume – and that both can serve important functions in the complex process of coming to terms with the past.

NOTES

1 Rubenstein's study explores a selection of texts by twentieth-century British and American women writers; yet a number of her general reflections on home and homesickness and related issues are very relevant in this context too.

2 For a more extensive discussion of the psychological notion of "consistency," especially with regard to trauma and identity, see my essay in this volume (chapter 17).

3 See Wilson (8). On nostalgia as a disease, particularly a disease "of the Swiss on foreign service," see for example Ida Macalpine and Richard Hunter (499–500). Kimberly Smith also calls attention to the history of nostalgia, i.e., how it developed from a mental disorder to an emotion, through a gradual process of demedicalization.

4 On this approach to autobiographical memory see also Welzer and Markowitsch.

5 Welzer draws on the notion of "memory talk" as conceptualized by developmental psychologists such as Katherine Nelson, who explores the ways in which parents talk to their young children about the past and how the children, through these processes of "memory talk," gradually acquire the narrative structures of autobiographical remembering. What Welzer emphasizes, however, is that "memory talk" is not only crucial from developmental perspectives, but in fact continues to play a key role throughout adult life; he considers different forms of "memory talk" or "conversational remembering" as important social practices and a lifelong process (*Das kommunikative Gedächtnis* 16).

6 Assmann draws on Pierre Nora's well-known notion of *lieux de mémoire*, but also develops it further and reconceptualizes it. In *Erinnerungsräume*, she suggests a distinction between different types of *Gedächtnisorte*, including *Generationenorte* (places of generations), *heilige Orte* (sacred places), *traumatische Orte* (sites of trauma), and other places of memory.

7 Rubenstein suggests that narrative enactments of nostalgia may have important functions not only for the characters but also for the authors themselves: "Through nostalgia, authors provide their characters with a vehicle for discovery or transformation of consciousness. For the authors themselves, narrative nostalgia provides opportunities to work through

mourning, to revisit and revise the emotional sites of loss" (164). The same may be said to apply to Kangro, whose Joonatan trilogy in complex ways reflects on the author's biography.

WORKS CITED

Assmann, Aleida. *Erinnerungsräume: Formen und Wandlungen des kulturellen Gedächtnisses*. Munich: C.H. Beck, 1999.

Assmann, Aleida. *Der lange Schatten der Vergangenheit: Erinnerungskultur und Geschichtspolitik*. Munich: C.H. Beck, 2006.

Boym, Svetlana. *The Future of Nostalgia*. New York: Basic Books, 2001.

Foucault, Michel. "Of Other Spaces." Trans. Jay Miskowiec. *Diacritics* 16, no. 1 (1986): 22–7. http://dx.doi.org/10.2307/464648.

Gee, Sue. "The Country of Writing." In *Literary Expressions of Exile: A Collection of Essays*, ed. Roger Whitehouse, 9–29. Lewiston, NY: Edwin Mellen Press, 2000.

Hemmings, Robert. *Modern Nostalgia: Siegfried Sassoon, Trauma and the Second World War*. Edinburgh: Edinburgh University Press, 2008.

Hunter, Richard, and Ida Macalpine. *Three Hundred Years of Psychiatry 1535–1860: A History Presented in Selected English Text*. London: Oxford University Press, 1963.

Kangro, Bernard. *Joonatan, kadunud veli* [Joonatan, the Lost Brother]. Lund: Eesti Kirjanike Kooperatiiv, 1971.

Kangro, Bernard. *Öö astmes X* [Night to the X Power]. Lund: Eesti Kirjanike Kooperatiiv, 1973.

Kangro, Bernard. *Puu saarel on alles* [A Tree on the Island Still Stands]. Lund: Eesti Kirjanike Kooperatiiv, 1973.

Kuhiwczak, Piotr. "When the Exile Returns." In *Literary Expressions of Exile: A Collection of Essays*, ed. Roger Whitehouse, 31–45. Lewiston, NY: Edwin Mellen Press, 2000.

Nelson, Katherine. *Language in Cognitive Development: Emergence of the Mediated Mind*. Cambridge: Cambridge University Press, 1996.

Rubenstein, Roberta. *Home Matters: Longing and Belonging, Nostalgia and Mourning in Women's Fiction*. New York: Palgrave Macmillan, 2001.

Smith, Kimberly K. "Mere Nostalgia: Notes on a Progressive Paratheory." *Rhetoric & Public Affairs* 3, no. 4 (2000): 505–27. http://dx.doi.org/10.1353/rap.2000.0019.

Welzer, Harald. "Gedächtnis und Erinnerung." In *Handbuch der Kulturwissenschaften*, vol. 3, *Themen und Tendenzen*, ed. Friedrich Jaeger and Jörn Rüsen, 155–74. Stuttgart: Metzler, 2004.

Welzer, Harald. *Das kommunikative Gedächtnis: Eine Theorie der Erinnerung*. 2nd ed. Munich: Beck, 2008.

Welzer, Harald, and Hans J. Markowitsch. "Towards a Bio-psycho-social Model of Autobiographical Memory." *Memory* (Hove, England) 13, no. 1 (2005): 63–78. http://dx.doi.org/10.1080/09658210344000576. Medline:15724908.

Wilson, Janelle L. *Nostalgia: Sanctuary of Meaning*. Lewisburg, PA: Bucknell University Press, 2005.

21 Haunted Whispers from the Footnotes: Life Writing in Raj Kamal Jha's *Fireproof*

ANNIE COTTIER

Raj Kamal Jha's novel *Fireproof* (2006) is concerned with the communal riots in the Indian state of Gujarat in 2002.[1] It is not the first fictional text to raise the issues of communalism and Hindu nationalism, which rose to prominence in the 1980s and 1990s and have become increasingly visible presences in Indian English literature ever since. In recent years, writers such as Shashi Tharoor in *Riot* (2001), Vikram Seth in *A Suitable Boy* (1993), Rohinton Mistry in *Family Matters* (2002), and Gita Hariharan in *In Times of Siege* (2003) have examined issues of Hindu nationalism, cultural identity, and communal violence. *Fireproof* does this too. However, it does it with a particularly innovative focus on the trauma and testimony of those who cannot speak: the dead, two children too young and too traumatized to tell their tales, and objects who witnessed the murders and are called upon to speak and testify against the perpetrators of violence. Jha's use of fragments of life writing serves to stress the urgency of the victims' plights and underlines their right to expression as well as their right to protest against their murders. Jha's literary text participates in an ongoing discussion of communalism. Its contribution to that discussion is valuable not only because of its differentiated and multilayered narrative, but also because it does what only fiction can do: it invents, narrates, and authenticates testimonial accounts of those who have already died and of those whom trauma prevents from speaking.

Communal Violence in India

The Gujarat riots, the most recent outbreak of communal violence in India on a large scale, occurred in 2002. In the first chapter of *Fireproof,* the narrator states the number of people who died in the riots: about a thousand men, women, and children, 70 per cent of them Muslim, were killed, ostensibly as revenge for the death of fifty-nine Hindu passengers in an attack on a train by a Muslim mob (*Fireproof* viii). The killings that occurred between February and mid-June 2002 affected mostly Muslims and were "carried out on a scale and ferocity reminiscent of the genocidal massacres that occurred during the partition of the Punjab in 1947" (387).[2]

Judith Brown defines communalism as "a privileging of religious identity above other identities in the political arena, which in turn bre[eds] violence and threaten[s] the very existence of an inclusive and national body politic" (46). Sandeep Shastri puts it even more succinctly when she describes communalism as an ideology which "exploits religion for crass political ends" (107). One example is the Hindutva movement of Hindu nationalists, which subscribes to a fiercely anti-Muslim politics. As Paul Brass points out, the Bharatiya Janata Party (BJP), which ruled the state of Gujarat (as well as India) at the time of the 2002 riots, has successfully "launched numerous Hindu-oriented campaigns since Independence in which the Muslims have been portrayed directly as obstacles to the achievement of national aspirations or have been clearly assumed to be the main obstacle" (7). Although the BJP no longer rules on a national level, it has profited greatly from the consolidation of Hindu communal sentiment and is still one of the leading Indian parties. In *Fireproof*'s "Author's Notes," it becomes clear that Jha links Hindu nationalist groups (specifically the Vishwa Hindu Parishad, the World Hindu Council) as well as the BJP to the unprecedented rise of violence against Muslims, adding that there was "clear evidence in many cases that the police, if not complicit, looked the other way as the massacres went on" (386). At the end of the introduction to the novel, we read that "all of what follows is fiction" (viii), a statement which suggests that what is written earlier on in the introduction (as well as in the concluding "Author's Notes," which are set off from the main text) is fact, and as such gruesomely true. At the same time, it is important to note that the "fictional" part of Jha's text does not make accusations against any political or religious group, or any particular people. In line with this, the main focus of the novel is not on the perpetrators but on the victims of violence and the dead, who have had no voice in the public discourse surrounding communal violence.

Narrative and Generic Complexity

Fireproof has an intricate narrative structure that does justice to the complexity of the painful events it deals with. In Jha's novel, the different narrative levels correspond to the different levels at which memory work takes place. While the beginning of the story is told in a realist mode, recurring surrealist intrusions into plot and imagery – which are strongly reminiscent of magic realism – bring about a gradual change of mode, and the narrative ends in an imaginary, fantastic realm. This change in mode is closely linked to the structure of the novel, which encompasses the footnotes, from which the dead whisper their complaints, and the dramatic eyewitness accounts of three inanimate objects, rendered in email attachments. The complexity of the novel's structure is further heightened by the insertion of photographs in the text.[3]

The first textual level consists of the main narrative told by Mr Jay, the protagonist-narrator. His narrative is at times fragmented, broken by dreams and memories. The second and third levels of the text (the footnotes and the email attachments) function as testimonial witness accounts. The footnotes are short fictional autobiographical narratives in which the anonymous dead tell the story of how they lived and how their deaths came about. On the third level, fictional biographical narratives in the form of email attachments are sent to Mr Jay by Miss Glass, the leader of the dead. They tell the plight of Shabnam and Tariq, both children, and of Abba, an old man, during the riots. This tripartite narrative structure is further complicated by Jha's mixing of genres: the climactic final part is rendered in dramatic form, with the narrator commenting on this "drama of the absurd" (330).[4] The narrative and generic complexity of *Fireproof* challenges readers to put the pieces together by themselves, and it is only towards the very end of the novel that the issues it engages with fully become clear: trauma, memory, testimony, and guilt in the light of communal violence.

The plot, in all brevity, is this: Mr Jay, a nondescript young man, took part in the riots as a torturer and killer, one of the four anonymous ABCD. Led by the ominous Miss Glass, the dead – who form a community outside the city on fire – decide to avenge their deaths and call their killers to justice. Mr Jay is the first person they lure into their realm. At the hospital, where he is waiting for the birth of his child, they convince him that the baby Ithim is his son. Ithim is given to Mr Jay by the dead because its mother, who was murdered, wanted it to experience life for just one day. Although it is grossly deformed, Mr Jay loves it as if it were his own child. Only at the end of the story, when the plot is resolved, does it become clear that Ithim is actually a foetus, torn from its mother's womb by the four rioters, ABCD. With the promise of a place where Ithim will get better, Miss Glass takes Mr Jay on a fantastic journey through the city. He is unknowingly led, step by step, to a land under water, where he is judged and found guilty on the basis of eyewitness reports by three objects: a watch, a towel, and a book.

Fictional Testimonies

Eyewitnesses and acts of testimonial witnessing are central in *Fireproof*. In integrating such figures and forms of life writing into his novel, Jha draws on postmodern narrative strategies, including the use of textual fragments and the blurring of the boundary between fact and fiction. Postmodernism's challenge to dualist thinking as well as its destabilizations of truth, totality, and objectivity have had much impact on theorizations of not only fictional negotiations of life stories but also of life writing in the more narrow sense. Marlene Kadar, for instance, questions the distinction between autobiography and fiction and concludes that "in the end, life writing problematizes the notion of *Literature*. Without wanting to deny *Literature*, life writing allows us to see it, too, as only one possible category of special writing" (12). To this, Merle Tönnies adds that life writing has been "openly appropriated by the domain of fiction" (305). Observations such as these have led to a more encompassing questioning of the opposition between fiction and nonfiction as exemplified by Sidonie Smith and Julia Watson's definition of "life writing" as "a general term for writing of diverse kinds that takes a life as its subject. Such writing can be biographical, novelistic, historical" (3). With regard to *Fireproof*, the question that poses itself is what functions its biographical and autobiographical elements perform.

First and foremost, these elements serve to give subalterns a voice. Second, they serve a testimonial function. In their tone of urgency and their documentary mode, they speak to a public, thus testifying to the distinction Doris Sommer makes between "the private and lonely moments of autobiographical writing" and testimonies, which are "public events" (118). Fictional testimonies such as *Fireproof* can perform that public function in special ways: they can convey suffering otherwise unarticulated (Young). This function of fictional testimony becomes relevant for the dead, who have been robbed of the right to speak. In an interview, Jha states that he "wanted to let them whisper their stories, uninterrupted. Imagine if each person in Gujarat had the tools that [we] have: a laptop, a broadband, a good turn of phrase, access to TV stations. Think of the discourse then" (Sing, para. 8). But the same testimonial function also becomes relevant for the children Tariq and Shabnam, who are too young and too traumatized to talk about the events they have been submitted to. Their experiences are rendered by the object-narrators Watch, Towel, and Book in the email attachments. As Book states, he and his fellow objects "are here to speak the unspeakable" (345). With regard to the speakability of the unspeakable in general and the presence of the dead in Jha's novel, Heonik Kwon's reflections on ghosts of war in Vietnam as "a powerful means of historical narration" (2) are apposite. Kwon relates ghosts to a "historical evidence (and a cultural witness) of war-caused violent death and displacement in human lives" (5). Like ghosts of war, the dead in *Fireproof* bear witness to acts of violence. Fictional as their voices are, they serve to inscribe the experience of violence into Indian historiography.

The Footnotes

In the footnotes of *Fireproof*, the desire of the dead to avenge their own death as well as the suffering of those who survived comes to the fore. In fact, as it turns out, it is the dead who are in charge of the narrative, not Mr Jay. At best, he tells the story for them. In their closing statement, they tell the reader:

> This is Mr Jay's story. We made no changes in his narrative, not one word. Except for his name. For if we remain unnamed, it's only fair that he should, too. But then, Miss Glass said, he is our central character, anonymity could be seen as dissembling, even disrespect. So we called him Mr Jay. (379)

In their opening statement, the dead announce that death is not an excuse for inaction, that grief should not become a substitute for sloth, and that it is time for some justice. "This is the story of how we went about it," they write. The "narrator, however, is not one of us but one of the living. He is a man waiting for news of the birth of his first child, his wife in the operating theatre. In a hospital in the night where we lay dead and dying in the city on fire" (6). The dead are the real (if fictional) authors of this story, who use Mr Jay as a narrator for their own ends.

As Shoshana Felman and Dori Laub have noted, to give testimony is to "impart … carnal knowledge of victimization" (101). In the footnotes of *Fireproof*, the dead give testimony in that sense. They not only tell their own stories, talk about their families, their worries, and regrets, but also bear witness to their own deaths:[5]

> I am Doctor, I was forty-four years old. I have a wife and three children, two sons, fifteen and thirteen, and a daughter, ten years old … I would have survived the fire … had it not been for the driver of the van, they stopped him, they asked him who we were, what our names were, and he told them, if he had lied, if he had made up two Hindu names for us, they would have let us go, I doubt they would have forced two doctors in uniform to undress … Of all patients in this city almost ninety-nine percent were Hindu but then these things don't matter, a mob doesn't think, you can't argue with a thousand people at one time … then the flames slipped in through the window, I hear Head Nurse scream, her face the last thing I saw through smoke, she trying to cover it with her shawl. (117)

All footnotes are rendered as dramatic monologues and follow a similar pattern: the dead first state who they are and what their situation in life was, then narrate what happened on the day they died, and finally describe their death, which mostly occurred by fire. Taken together, the footnotes form a choir of lament which builds up an exceptionally strong textual presence by way of repetition. With each new testimony, the personal narratives of individual voices build up a collective narrative which expresses a collective identity.

The whisperers from the footnotes remain nameless, yet all characters in the biographical narratives have Muslim names. Considering that a high percentage of the victims of the Gujarat riots were Muslims, that is not surprising. As names often indicate religious affiliation in India, their importance in the context of communal violence cannot be overestimated. In not divulging their own names, the dead in *Fireproof* choose to hide their (religious) identity, whose revelation can, as Doctor's story reveals, prove deadly. With some exceptions, the dead identify themselves by their professions and by their social and familial status instead: they are doctors, head nurses, daughters, husbands, and so on: "If you insist on at least one piece of identification, you may call us by the roles we play" (3). Miss Glass, the leader of the dead, also remains nameless until Mr Jay names her, although ultimately the name is her own choice (95).[6] With the exception of Mr Jay, the perpetrators who torture and kill Tariq's, Shabnam's, and Abba's families also remain anonymous: they are referred to simply as ABCD. One could read Jha's suppression of the religious identities of the dead as a secularist reminder that religion must not serve as a means of identification. However, I would argue that such elisions rather testify to a desire to represent, to speak for other victims as well, and to suggest that anyone can be caught up in the role of victim or perpetrator. If, as Kwon suggests, ghosts contribute to historical narration because they represent the positions of those who are no longer here, then the dead who narrate their lives and deaths in Jha's footnotes also contribute to the writing of history. In so doing, they are freed from the subaltern position of voicelessness even as they bear testimony to their own death.

The Email Attachments

Whereas the dead narrate their own stories and manipulate Mr Jay's narrative, the stories of the three survivors are told by three objects: Towel, Book, and Watch. The towel is the one that Abba's daughter-in-law is strangled with (214); the schoolbook belongs to Tariq (183); and the watch is that of Shabnam's father (198). These inanimate objects witnessed not only the murders of family members but also the suffering those killings inflicted on the survivors. Their testimony will incriminate Mr Jay as one of the perpetrators ABCD. Interestingly, while the voices of the dead cry out assertively from the footnotes, the survivors are not first-person narrators. Their stories are told for them by objects because they are too young and too disturbed to tell them by themselves: Tariq can remember "only a few things" (175), and Shabnam also lacks the words to express what she has seen, because "all she has are her feet and her arms, her knees and her elbows clawing through the fire and the fog" (198). In Mr Jay's trial, Miss Glass explains the importance of Book, Watch, and Towel: "They are here because they are eyewitnesses and they are earwitnesses. And unlike us, people who were killed, these three are objects. That's why their story will be objective. And their words will, therefore, carry more weight" (333).[7] While Miss Glass's play on "object" and "objective" is obviously tongue in cheek, the point she makes about the objectivity of thoroughly fictionalized speech acts is in line with the novel's overall project of authenticating fictional voices. As eyewitnesses, these objects lend additional credibility to the victims' tales. That credibility is further enhanced by Jha's decision to give these victims not only names – which sets them apart from the nameless dead – but also stories that are more individualized than those we find in the footnotes. Thus, it is objects that turn these victims into subjects.

While the victims of the riots either testify themselves to what was done to them, or have their stories narrated by witnesses, the voices of the perpetrators remain comparatively silent. Mr Jay succeeds in suppressing his past deeds until his murderous traits and his guilt manifest themselves in violent nightmares (257–64). But it is only when the dead call him to trial and Watch, Towel, and Book incriminate him with their eyewitness accounts that his guilt becomes fully palpable. When he attempts to rejoin his wife and newly born child, he sees a "black, cold and limitless" gap, "like the universe itself," opening itself up at his feet, and he falls into it (373). He sees his victims in their injured state and hears "words that until then I hadn't spoken, not once even thought ...: I am guilty" (374). It is only upon admitting his guilt that he is forgiven by the dead and is able to rejoin his family. However, the baby Ithim, whom he loved, will always be in his mind when he looks at his own child, thus reminding him of his gruesome deeds. Miss Glass says: "Every time he looks at his own baby, which we have learnt is safe in the hospital, he will remember this one ... A story of his love that carries, within it, the story of his hate. That, I guess, is justice. Not the best, not the cleanest, but I think it's as good as we, the dead, can get" (358).

Conclusion

Jha's use of fragments of life writing raises the question of what it means to bear witness to violence. In its innovative exploration of traumatic experiences in the face of communal violence, *Fireproof* demonstrates that fictional texts can contribute meaningfully to our understanding of the audibility of subaltern voices. By giving a voice to and authenticating the voices of both survivors of violence and the dead, *Fireproof* gives us new insights into the effects of communal violence in Indian history. *Fireproof* is indeed haunted, by whispers from the dead which come to haunt the living with voices of regret and with a desire for both revenge and a perpetrator's acknowledgment of wrongdoing.

NOTES

1 Raj Kamal Jha is the author of *The Blue Bedspread* (1999), which won the Commonwealth Writers' Prize for Best First Book (Eurasia), and *If You Are Afraid of Heights* (2003). Jha lives in New Delhi, where he works as the managing editor of the *Indian Express*.

2 Communal riots in India occurred on a large scale in the 1940s, in the years before and the months after the partition of India in 1947, when the state of Pakistan was created. Approximately one million people died in riots in 1947, when many millions crossed the new border in both directions. For further discussion of Partition-related violence, see my response to Leena Kurvet Käosaar's essay in this volume (chapter 8). In the years that followed Partition, it seems that the secular policy of the state managed to keep the number of communal riots low. During the riots in the 1980s and 1990s, hundreds of Muslims were killed in a communal riot in Bhagalpur in 1989, and in 1992 the Babri Mosque in Ayodhya was destroyed by Hindu communals. As a consequence, thousands of Muslims were again targeted in Surat, Ahmedabad, and Bombay (Butalia 7).

3 Gabriele Rippl has pointed out that Jha's use of three press photographs documenting the destructions after the riots constitutes a new form of literary expression about issues which are usually difficult to communicate and to understand: issues of guilt, violence, and trauma (14).

4 There are additional theatrical aspects to the novel. There is an opening and a closing statement (a prologue and epilogue) in which the dead clearly state that they are defined "by the roles we play" (3). In this performance, the leader of the dead, Miss Glass, takes on the role of director as she manipulates Mr Jay into coming to the land of the dead, where he is forced to sit in the audience of a play in which he is accused of being one of the killers. She also directs the other characters, who call her their "angel" (381), and appears in two of the footnotes. Miss Glass withholds her life story by saying that she "is not going to give [us] a personal profile of her grief" because she has "a lot of work to do" (131). In chapter 19, she shushes an audience of the dead by saying, "We will all be quiet now, no more distractions, no more whispering in these footnotes, let Mr Jay's story move towards its end, smooth and unhindered" (293).

5 In their expression of plight, which is told in a linear narrative, these fictional testimonials are reminiscent of the testimonials in Butalia's *The Other Side of Silence: Voices from the Partition of India*.

6 Obviously, the first association Miss Glass's name calls up is "glass," a transparent and reflecting material that is also breakable and thus vulnerable. Glass also melts at a certain temperature, which connects it to the fires of the riots. Most pertinent to me seems the reflecting quality glass possesses, for, metaphorically speaking, Miss Glass holds a mirror up to those guilty of cruelty. It is of course tempting to speculate that Jha's choice of name may also refer to Jacques Derrida's *Glas*. The French noun *le glas* means death knell, and death is one of the major topical interests in *Glas*.

7 Photographs function as another form of testimony in *Fireproof*. Young writes that "as a seeming trace or fragment of its referent that appeals to the eye for its proof, the photograph is able to invoke the authority of its empirical link to events, which in turn seems to reinforce the sense of its own unmediated factuality. As a metonymical trope of witness, the photograph persuades the viewer of its testimonial and factual authority in ways that are unavailable to narrative. One of the reasons that narrative and photograph are so convincing together is that they seem to represent a combination of pure object and commentary on the object, each seeming to complete the other by reinforcing a sense of contrasting functions" (57–8).

WORKS CITED

Brass, Paul. *The Production of Hindu-Muslim Violence in Contemporary India*. Seattle: University of Washington Press, 2003.

Brown, Judith M. *Nehru*. Harlow: Longman, 1999.

Butalia, Urvashi. *The Other Side of Silence: Voices from the Partition of India*. Durham, NC: Duke University Press, 2000.

Derrida, Jacques. 1974. *Glas Totenglocke*. Trans. Hans-Dieter Gondek and Markus Sedlaczek.. Paderborn: Fink, 2006.

Felman, Shoshana, and Dori Laub. *Testimony: Crises of Witnessing in Literature, Psychoanalysis, and History*. New York: Routledge, 1992.

Hariharan, Gita. *In Times of Siege*. New York: Vintage, 2003.

Jha, Raj Kamal. *Fireproof*. London: Picador, 2007.

Kadar, Marlene. *Essays on Life Writing: From Genre to Critical Practice*. Toronto: University of Toronto Press, 1992.

Kwon, Heonik. *Ghosts of War in Vietnam*. Cambridge: Cambridge University Press, 2008.

Mistry, Rohinton. *Family Matters*. London: Faber and Faber, 2002.

Rippl, Gabriele. "Erzählte Fotos: Foto-Text-Beziehungen in Raj Kamal Jhas Roman *Fireproof.*" *Fotogeschichte: Beiträge zur Geschichte und Ästhetik der Fotografie* 108 (2008): 11–17.

Seth, Vikram. *A Suitable Boy*. London: Phoenix, 2004.

Shastri, Sandeep. "Secularism, Fundamentalism and Communalism: An Attempt at Understanding the Indian Experience." In *Fundamentalism and Secularism: The Indian Predicament*, ed. Andreas Nehring, 99–117. Madras: Gurukul Lutheran Theological College, 1996.

Sing, Jai Arjun. "The Jha Interview." Interview with Raj Kamal Jha, 3 Dec. 2006. *Jabberwock*, 28 Nov. 2007. http://jaiarjun.blogspot.com/2006/12/jha-interview.html.

Smith, Sidonie, and Julia Watson. *Reading Autobiography: A Guide for Interpreting Life Narratives*. Minneapolis: University of Minnesota Press, 2001.

Sommer, Doris. "'Not Just a Personal Story': Women's Testimonios and the Plural Self." In *Life/Lines: Theorizing Women's Autobiography*, ed. Bella Brodzki and Celeste Schenk, 107–30. Ithaca: Cornell University Press, 1988.

Tharoor, Shashi. *Riot*. New Delhi: Penguin Books, 2003.

Tönnies, Merle. "Radicalising Postmodern Biofictions: British Fictional Autobiography of the Twenty-First Century." In *Fiction and Autobiography: Modes and Models of Interaction*, ed. Sabine Coelsch-Foisner and Wolfgang Görtschacher, 303–14. Salzburg Studies in English Literature and Culture 3. Frankfurt am Main: Peter Lang, 2006.

Young, James E. *Writing and Rewriting the Holocaust: Narrative and the Consequences of Interpretation*. Bloomington: Indiana University Press, 1988.

22 What Only Fiction Can Do

LEENA KURVET-KÄOSAAR

In her discussion of the Indian writer Raj Kamal Jha's *Fireproof* (2006), Annie Cottier concentrates on the role of the novel's fictional testimonial accounts, which, in Cottier's opinion, make a significant contribution to the discussion of communalism and Hindu nationalism in Indian literature by granting a testimonial voice to "those who cannot speak": the dead, children who are too young to tell their tales, and inanimate objects.[1] Such testimonial voices, Cottier emphasizes, are "authenticat[ed]" by specifically fictional means that, at the same time, contribute to public discourses regarding communal violence. Cottier also highlights the depiction of communal violence in Jha's novel as a contribution to "the writing of history," in particular with regard to Heonik Kwon's consideration of ghosts of war in Vietnam as "a powerful means of historical narration" (Kwon 2). Cottier's argument thus proceeds from outlining the significance of *Fireproof* in Indian literature, to emphasizing its role in public discourses regarding communal violence, to concentrating on one particular type of public discourse, that of historiography. At the same time, Cottier retains a focus on the importance of the fictional capacities of the novel that is apparent in the framing of her discussion of *Fireproof* in relation to life writing, in particular with reference to ways in which life writing blurs the boundary between fiction and nonfiction.

Thus, on the one hand, Cottier discusses Jha's novel as part of historical discourses concerning communal violence. On the other, her analysis highlights the novel's fictionality. This certainly raises questions concerning the interrelationship of historicity and fictionality, a subject area that has received extensive critical attention.[2] Taking as my starting point Dominick LaCapra's discussion of the relationship between historiography and fiction and the possibilities of the latter of making (historical) truth claims, I wish to explore the ways in which *Fireproof* participates in historical discourses not through blurring the boundaries between non-fictional and fictional discourses, but, instead, through consolidating them.

In *Writing History, Writing Trauma* (2001) and a number of additional writings, LaCapra adopts a critical stance towards the historiographic approach that he refers to as "radical constructivism," which, in his view, minimizes the referential dimension or the role of truth claims in historiography and reduces the past to the telling of the (historian's) text (*History* 29) or substitutes the past with the text altogether (*Writing* 10).[3] However, LaCapra considers of equal importance the need to view critically the more dominant, positivistically inclined historiographical research paradigm – which he refers to as "documentary or self-sufficient" – mainly because of the processes of extreme objectification such a paradigm may entail (1, 5). LaCapra nevertheless strongly emphasizes the need to retain a number of elements of the "positivist" paradigm, including "contextualization, clarity, objectivity, footnoting," and, most importantly, the recognition of "making truth claims based on evidence" as a central premise of historiography (5). However, the documentary or, at its worst, the "objectionalist" research paradigm also has several problematic and dangerous features (sharp object/subject differentiation, objectification of the other, dominance of and uncritical belief in causal explanation, exclusion of the dialogic nature of historiographic research) to which the constructivist paradigm can be viewed as offering (at least potentially) productive alternatives (4–5).

The importance of avoiding the impasses of the self-sufficient research paradigm becomes especially important in the case of historical events or series of events of an extreme and traumatic nature such as the Holocaust, which are "highly 'cathected' or invested with affect and considerations of value" (*Writing* 18–19). In particular with events of such nature, fiction can play an important role in providing insight, at times via the use of formal devices that underline the fictional texts' departure from "ordinary reality" (185–6). Also, fiction can give "a plausible 'feel' for experience and emotion" that cannot be achieved easily by the use of "restricted documentary methods" (13). Without claiming to take the place of historiography or problematizing historiography as a discipline, art (fiction) can complement historiography by offering "significant insights" or interfering with it, suggesting, for example, "possible lines of inquiry for the historians" (15). Truth claims would be the premise of both modes of interaction between art and historiography just as art can be submitted to critical questioning based on "historical knowledge and research" (15).

In what follows, I offer a brief reading of the framing strategies of *Fireproof* in its opening and closing sections as they relate to the historical event depicted (the Gujarat riots). The novel presents the reader with the categories of fiction and fact (or art and history) and probes their interrelationship on its very first pages: "All of the above is fact," Jha writes about his description of the Gulbarga Housing Society, which was set on fire by a mob in March 2002 and in which thirty-eight residents "burnt alive" (viii); about the name by which it became known in the media (the Gulbarga massacre); about the number of victims of the Gujarat riots; about the ostensible triggering event of the riots; about the title and publisher of a child's book laying in the yard of the burnt building; about the poem on page 43 of that book; and about the lack of information concerning the number of children killed in Gulbarga. As the section is set off from the rest of the text (spatially as well as by a different pagination format), the speaking voice in the section is difficult to identify. It is not identical with the narrator(s) of the rest of the novel, nor can it be categorized as the author's own voice. In addition, the section contains a laconic yet emotionally intense description of the burnt remains of the Gulbarga apartment complex. Then, the reader is told: "All of what follows is fiction" (ix).[4] Although the opening section is not exclusively documentary, it seems to have been important to the author to lay the categories – fact and fiction – bare for the reader. Jha, it seems to me, does not do this with the intention to erase the borderline between the two, but by emphasizing the role of each in the production of knowledge.

In LaCapra's terms, *Fireproof* clearly aims at making truth claims regarding the Gujarat riots – claims that are based on an understanding of the role (and responsibility) of art in relation to a historical event of extreme and traumatic kind. It does so via the construction of a markedly fictional experience that cannot be recovered via documentary methods (*Writing* 13), but which provides "a more expansive space … for exploring the modalities of responding to trauma" (185). The opening section as well as the "Author's Notes" (385–8) at the end of the novel highlight the limited information and the ongoing work concerning the event on various levels (such as, for example, court cases concerning the riot). According to Cottier, this is where fiction steps in to provide a take on communal violence that is different from journalistic, legal, historical, and other discourses: in the opening section of her essay, she states that

Jha's "contribution to [the discussion of communal violence] is valuable ... because it does *what only fiction can do*: it invents, narrates, and authenticates testimonial accounts of those who have already died and of those whom trauma prevents from speaking" (my emphasis). Cottier's insistence on the unique role of fiction, is, however, overshadowed in her later discussion by her emphasis on the blurring of the boundaries between fiction and nonfiction.

The central plot thread of *Fireproof* is the trial of Mr Jay by the dead, and the closing of the novel suggests that the murderers of each victim of the massacre should be tracked down and made to admit their guilt: "Miss Glass ... has unfinished business ... Go after the others, she says. I will have to start with each one of you, she says, all of those who could only whisper in this story, as a footnote ... One by one, I will do all one thousand" (380).

The "Author's Notes," which follow the closing of the novel, include detailed statistical data about the court cases concerning the riots and also refer to possible corruption in the hasty closing of many cases for lack of evidence as well as the prominent role the Supreme Court of India has played in "pushing the state's institutions to deliver justice," including an order to reopen all the cases (386). Jha's praise of the Supreme Court of India in handling the cases regarding the riots suggests that, on the legal level, he prefers justice to be done in the form of a conviction of the guilty. Legal justice, however, differs considerably from the kind of justice that is served within the novel itself. Mr Jay, upon admitting his guilt, is not punished, but, on the contrary, pardoned and returned to his healthy baby son instead of the severely deformed Ithim, who, as it turns out, is actually the fetus torn from the womb of a woman murdered during the massacre. Yet, as Cottier points out, the ramifications of his actions will have an enduring presence in his memory, and this haunting memory is the justice that is served in the novel.

Presenting the reader with various possibilities of achieving justice, Jha underlines the capacity and also responsibility of fiction in the face of traumatic events. While presenting his interpretation of the events as neither a definitive account nor a story of closure, Jha underlines fiction's capacity for eliciting empathy, for enabling a kind of understanding that cannot be achieved in the same manner through other kinds of discourse, and for giving a voice to victims of violence that would otherwise remain unheard (children and the dead). The novel as a whole, or, to be more exact, all of the text that the reader is presented with in *Fireproof*, underlines the role of different discourses pertaining to the Gujarat riots that inevitably interact with and inform each other without, however, ultimately erasing the borderline between factuality and fictionality or art and histor(iograph)y.

NOTES

1 This article has been written with the support of ESF grants 7354 ("Positioning Life-Writing on Estonian Literary Landscapes"), 9035 ("Dynamics of Address in Estonian Life Writing") and the TF project "Sources of Cultural History and Contexts of Literature."

2 Most importantly, Cottier evokes the work of the New Historicists, especially that of Hayden White and Louis Montrose. For White, the explanatory status of historical narratives owes a great deal to its interpretive (in other words, inferential and speculative) component (51). That component, according to White, is so pre-eminent that historical narratives should be regarded as "*verbal fictions*" that share more similarities "with their counterparts in literature than with those in the sciences" (82). Louis Montrose advances a similar position by emphasizing the doubly meditated nature of history, on the one hand, and the "social embedment" of "all modes of writing," on the other (20).

3 LaCapra identifies Hayden White and Frank Ankersmit as the key practitioners of this approach.

4 The generic status of *Fireproof* is confirmed on the inside of the back cover of the blurb, where it is presented as Jha's third novel, although the word "novel" appears neither on the cover of the book nor on the title page.

WORKS CITED

Jha, Raj, Kamal. *Fireproof*. London: Picador, 2007.

Kwon, Heonik. *Ghosts of War in Vietnam*. Cambridge: Cambridge University Press, 2008.

LaCapra, Dominick. *History in Transit: Experience, Identity, Critical Theory*. Ithaca: Cornell University Press, 2004.

LaCapra, Dominick. *Writing History, Writing Trauma*. Baltimore: Johns Hopkins University Press, 2001.

Montrose, Louis A. "Professing the Renaissance: The Poetics and Politics of Culture." In *The New Historicism*, ed. Aram Veeser, 15–36. New York: Routledge, 1989.

White, Hayden. *Tropics of Discourse: Essays in Cultural Criticism*. Baltimore: Johns Hopkins University Press, 1985.

Afterword: Ethical and Political Aspects of Life Writing and Remembering

MARGIT SUTROP

This volume of essays is the fruit of a stimulating cooperation between philosophers and literary and cultural scholars of the Universities of Tartu and Berne.[1] July 2006 found us sitting around a table at the Bernese Department of English, where we began a conversation around a shared interest in memory and life writing. Each participant had an hour to present a paper and to field questions. The conversation continued for two days in an atmosphere of generous hospitality, and that meeting laid the groundwork for a shared topic that would bridge two very different cultural situations: Switzerland, a welfare society, peaceful, stable, and multicultural; and Estonia, a vulnerable transition society and recently re-established democratic state, a third of whose population is Russian-speaking in the aftermath of a half-century of Soviet military occupation. Similar to other post-communist countries, Estonia had witnessed a "biographical turn" since the disintegration of the Soviet Union. This was a manifestation of the necessity to rehabilitate memory, which in the totalitarian Soviet Union had been surrounded and permeated by taboos. One of the outcomes of that turn were campaigns sponsored by memory institutions to collect oral and written life stories, including life-story "writing competitions." The popular response to those calls was strong and extensive; the writings foregrounded those chapters of the past that had been restricted or altogether banned from representation.[2]

It was no wonder that the common topic we found was memory and the construction of individual and collective identities under twentieth-century conditions of political repression and war. Since our interdisciplinary research covered different cultures and historical epochs, we could count on expertise from a wide spectrum of fields. Yet it did seem challenging to us to compare diverging forms of life writing, and we were fully aware that our own experience made us see these texts from different viewpoints. For the Swiss scholars present, any discussion of trauma and the past automatically took place against the background of the Holocaust. But since they are also scholars of British and American literature, other cultural fields in Europe, North America, and beyond entered the picture. This enabled the group not only to elaborate on the dramatic and traumatic events of the Second World War, but also to link those events to other times and cultures. The project we formulated connected research frameworks in cultural memory with theoretical models from literary and cultural studies, and our double focus on life writing and trauma memory held out the promise of opening new comparativist vistas without pretending that societies with disparate histories could be approached in identical ways.

As Rippl, Schweighauser, and Steffen explain in their introduction, our contributors rely on a broad notion of life writing that includes auto/biographies revolving around traumatic experiences, autobiographically inclined fictions of loss and trauma, as well as limit-cases that trouble the fact/fiction divide. In what follows, I address the ethical dimensions of life writing in what may be deemed an "age of memoir," with a special focus on non-fictional texts. In doing so, I explore the various functions and uses of such writing.

The Ethics of Life Writing

In his seminal book *The Ethics of Life Writing* (2004), Paul John Eakin discusses the cultural phenomenon of "life writing" in the following terms:

> Autobiographies and biographies crowd the shelves of bookstores today, prompting columnists and reviewers to tell us that we live in an age of memoir, fostered by a pervasive culture of confession in the media. Life histories are also getting a lot of attention in many academic disciplines and professional practices, including medicine, history, anthropology, psychology, and journalism, as well as literary studies. Spurred by these developments, critics have coined an umbrella term, *life writing*, to cover the protean forms of contemporary personal narrative, including interviews, profiles, ethnographies, case studies, diaries, Web pages, and so on. (1)

Almost immediately, Eakin's definition strikes one as fraught with a host of thorny ethical issues – which he fully recognizes and identifies.

The first of these is the issue of truth telling. Life writing both is an act and has a content, and on both levels two questions arise: first, how much personal information should be revealed intentionally; second, to what extent are such revelations unwitting and unconscious? What further complicates the issue is the emergence of new media that make the boundary between the personal and the public increasingly fluid and porous. As Eakin points out,

> Life writers are criticized not only for not telling the truth – personal and historical truth – but also for telling too much truth ... Life – and life writing – in the information age has meant the transmission of more and more personal information, often quite intimate, with less and less restraint. People may protest the loss of their privacy, but with an assist from computers and cell phones in these wired and wireless times, they are conducting much of their private lives in public places; as see-all, tell-all Web sites proliferate, a lot of people log on and look. (3–4)

Self-narration that expresses life plans necessitates and presumes a person who is both politically free and able. For those who have emerged from life under a totalitarian regime, being able to think through and tell the stories of their lives freely now is in itself a sign of freedom. It has been claimed that for those who survived the Holocaust, the freedom to reflect on and tell their stories opens up possibilities not only to remember, but also to forget, to heal, to make peace, and even to forgive. Charles Taylor (1989) has argued that narrative is what allows us to understand the direction and meaning of our lives. This implies that storytelling, identity, and morality are intimately and inextricably connected, and that ethics is not merely one possible perspective on life writing but constitutive of its very practice. Indeed, asking the question of what a good life is, and how we become or fail to become the sort of people we want to be is at least implicitly inscribed in the texture of most life writing. In other words, "narrating the self" generates and records a continuous history of the narrator's orientation in moral space.

Truth telling belies the question of fact and fiction in life writing, and this concerns not only the writing self, but also the ethical boundaries of how to speak about others, particularly about those with whom our life narrative is tightly interwoven. We might say that we trespass on the privacy of other people by writing about them. On another level, our concepts of the human being and of human possibilities are at stake. Are we autonomous individuals or interpersonal subjects, inextricably connected with others? No one's life is a life for themselves alone. Carol Gilligan (1982) has claimed that a life is a network in which we are interwoven with others' lives by a diversity of threads and knots. What we say about our own life always touches those around us. Of course, the question is not only whether or not we are allowed to talk about others, but what we should or should not say about them. By selecting an event that we begin to narrate, we extract and sever it from the flow of life, and it is unavoidable that in its new context, we give it a specific meaning. Thus, it can easily happen that a person we refer to in the telling remembers what happened completely differently and does not agree with what we have said or written about him or her. Even if one wants to tell things "as they actually were," we are bound by the act of storytelling. As Eakin and others have pointed out, each time one writes a life story, one tells it differently, not only because we make different selections and probe different levels of detail on each occasion, but also because we construct a different kind of whole depending on the storytelling situation and the readership/audience. In view of these constitutive, often very thorny restrictions, it is fair to ask:

Why Has There Been a Life Writing Boom? Under What Social Conditions Does It Happen at All?

In his excellent essay "Õigus biograafiale: Teksti ja autori isiksuse tüpoloogilisest suhestatusest" ["The Right to Have a Biography"], Juri Lotman points out that, for a long time, not everybody had a right to a biography. That right was granted exclusively to prominent people. Though his study focuses on Russian cultural history, the questions Lotman raises are pertinent to the life-writing boom in other times and places. What happens when biography is no longer entrusted to sanctioned carriers who conserve the memory of the famous? What happens when the baton is handed to the less prominent, even to "little people"? In the two-volume collection of one hundred Estonian life stories generated from popular collection campaigns and published in 2000 (Hinrikus, *Eesti rahva elulood, I–II*) – a collection that was later supplemented by a third volume (Hinrikus, *Eesti rahva elulood, III*) – the organizers of life-story competitions quoted from Lotman's essay, extending the "right to biography" to all the contributors to the competition – as well as to those who (still) remained silent. Since the biographical turn, everybody's memories have been considered valuable.

Despite an explosion of work on memory in historical and cultural studies, relatively little has been published on the functions of life writing. These functions can be grouped under two headings: first, those that relate to the individual; second, those that relate to the community. With respect to the former, life writing certainly offers an opportunity for writers to reflect on their lives and confer meaning upon them, either to make peace with themselves or to reconstitute their lives through writing – to "live" better and more beautifully. On the one hand, recording one's life in writing enables one to be released, to be set free of something; on the other, it allows one to attribute importance to one's life, to draw oneself on a larger scale. Thus – and this motivation must not be underrated – one immortalizes oneself. Indeed, a writer hopes that despite the finitude of life, paper will not burn and that what he or she has written will not be destroyed.

With respect to their functions for communities, memoirs and life stories help preserve history – not in the way history books do (through battles, victories, defeats, political events, and the development of economies and cultures), but rather by recording how people actually lived history. This is akin to what historiographers refer to as "the history of mentalities": what comes into focus is not so much the victories and defeats of great men, but the ways in which men, women, and children actually lived their lives – what they thought about, experienced, and ate, and what clothes they wore. In reality, history is but the sum of the stories of people's lives. There are as many different stories, as many perceptions of the times, as there are people. Of course, it is clear that it is impossible, and beyond human capacity, to write all these stories down, but there are two things that can come to our aid. First, the statistical average: if it were possible to record the biographies of a statistically significant number of people, then one could identify certain tendencies of a more general kind with great probability. Second, the best life stories resemble works of art: through a single, unique exemplar one can arrive at the general, on condition that the representation of the singular has accurately captured the essential. Thus, both the extensive and intensive approaches are important – the concerted effort to record as many stories as possible, and the artful representation of what is characteristic or essential.

Life writing in an "age of memoir" is deeply rooted in our responsibilities to remember, and those in turn are bound up with the reciprocal process of shaping an identity. Yet the value of remembering is intimately intertwined with reflections on the value of forgetting. Jeffrey

Blustein explains this very well in his recent book *The Moral Demands of Memory*:

> Remembrance is not only a good when properly constrained, but also in various circumstances morally imperative for us. Yet this is problematic because memory ... is notoriously fragile and manipulable. To fulfil the requirements of a morality of memory, therefore, individuals and groups have to engage in an ongoing struggle against the natural and social processes of forgetfulness. (4)

One of the problematics of moral memory arises from these simultaneous imperatives and their attendant paradox. There is a need to be freed from pain, but there is also a responsibility to keep what is remembered in social consciousness, to transmit it to others while coming to terms with it and conferring meaning on it through private reflection. The political context plays a significant shaping role in these processes. For example, in the case of the Second World War, Germans have been quick to take on the role of perpetrator, thereby displacing and diverting guilt from the Soviets. The public discussion of the Holocaust has been so extensive and pervasive that the Jews have become almost the only widely recognized victims of the war. Thus, the extent and the specificity of the suffering and victimhood of other people have been overshadowed. This situation, in which one group of perpetrators has taken on all the guilt, while Russians tend to see themselves as liberators and ground their identity in a heroic victory in the Second World War, continues in the post-communist era as a split between East and Central Europe, on the one hand, and Western Europe, on the other. For Western Europeans, the roles of victims and perpetrators are clearly assigned, and history is more or less worked through. For East Europeans, this is not the case.

The late president of Estonia, Lennart Meri, often expressed his sorrow that even with the availability of Stéphane Courtois and colleagues' *The Black Book of Communism*, a long-awaited publication, "the investigator of the communist crimes will be hopelessly at a disadvantage when compared to the investigator of the Nazi war crimes and crimes against humanity" (118). The investigation of the crimes of communism has never been granted similar moral and financial support to the investigation of Nazi crimes after the destruction of the Third Reich; even today, the investigators of communist crimes "only have a negligible part of the sources at their disposal" (118). Two big steps forward have been taken in 2006, when the Council of Europe Parliamentary Assembly adopted Resolution 1481 ("Need for International Condemnation of Crimes of Totalitarian Communist Regimes"), and in March 2009, when the conclusions of the public hearing in the European parliament organized by the Czech presidency of the European Union, "European Conscience and Crimes of Totalitarian Communism: 20 Years After," were adopted. However, a lot more needs to be done in order to achieve a treatment of the crimes of the communist regimes that is proportional to those of the Nazi regime. For that reason, for the nations of East and Central Europe, it is crucially important to bring forth what is remembered about past events, to work through it in history books, life writing, and public discussion, and to give it meaning.

This latter perspective finds expression in the Estonian contributions to this volume. For Estonians, there is the gnawing feeling that the past has not yet received sufficient attention and that the living have the duty to recollect what happened. In a situation where Russia continues not to accept responsibility for the criminality of communism, and where the crimes of the communist regime continue to be denied for various reasons by various people, Estonians feel the burden of explaining to the world that communism was just as criminal and unjust an ideology as Nazism, with similar driving forces and similar repressive mechanisms. (It has been said that the Nazi SD Security Police and the Soviet People's Commissariat of National Security [NKGB] developed on the basis of each other's expertise.) Communism lasted much longer than Nazism, and it cast a black shadow over the entire world: it deprived many democratic peoples of their freedom and sought the systematic destruction of groups of people and entire peoples through terror, killing, and deportations to Siberia.

The Political Dimensions of Life Writing

For those reasons, it should be possible for the reader of this volume to trace how the remembering and life writing of Estonians contrasts with the remembering and life writing of other peoples. One way to begin such a comparison is to look at language use. The majority of authors who speak about the Holocaust use the word "trauma" to point out the enormity and the singularity of the Holocaust as a historical event that in its very singularity brought about a crisis of representation. "Trauma" as defined by Freud in the aftermath of the First World War is an experience of an event so horrendous and shocking that the individual psyche cannot fully absorb it at the time; the symptomatology of the trauma's belated expression is constitutive of it. As Dominick LaCapra has pointed out, however, a considerable (and unfortunate) slippage occurs when the term is shifted from the individual to the collective level, since this entails accepting the singularity of one historical event. LaCapra finds this to be an identity-political issue, beneath which there are complex epistemological and historiographical problems. Moreover, one may ask whether notions of "collective trauma" should be used for the victims of all large-scale attacks of totalitarian regimes or only for certain victims of history such as Africans deported and sold as slaves and the survivors of the Armenian genocide and the Nazi atrocities committed against Jews, gypsies, homosexuals, and Jehovah's Witnesses. In theory, our answer to that question should depend on whether one wants to stress the singularity of events such as the Holocaust or draw attention to the vicious side of human nature, which becomes particularly visible in historical catastrophes created by totalitarian regimes. In reality, there is a strong competition about who determines the pattern and which survivors of a genocidal event "qualify."

Unfortunately, the victims of the communist regime have not been included in this group of the victims of history, although the repressions of the Soviet regime – the killing of millions of people for ideological reasons; the destruction of entire social groups by massacres, executions, and mass deportations to Siberia that included women and small children; and forced labour in the Gulag – were no less dramatic and caused no less suffering than the repressions of the Nazi regime. As Courtois explains in his introduction to *The Black Book of Communism*, both Communist and Nazi systems deemed "a part of humanity unworthy of existence. The difference is that the Communist model is based on the class system, the Nazi model on race and territory" (15). Although the massive physical repressions in the Soviet Union more or less came to an end with the death of Stalin, the ideological terror continued for the subsequent half-century in all communist countries, in differing degrees and temporalities of severity.

One of the reasons for unequal public attention to the victims of the communist regime can be traced back again to linguistic usage. Although those theoreticians who have limited the use of the term "trauma" to refer to only some groups of victims may not see that limitation as an ethical or political issue, it is precisely that insofar as it constrains our ability to understand the suffering caused by other historical configurations and events. Thus, the long tradition of speaking about the Holocaust in terms of "trauma" continues to determine the way people think about the genocides and terror regimes of the twentieth century. As the suffering caused by the Soviet regime was different from that caused by the Nazis, the former does not fit in with the prevailing discourse and is therefore better ignored. There are several political and historical reasons why the Soviet and the Nazi terror were treated differently. First, the Soviet Union's status as an ally of the United States and Western Europe in the Second World War rendered it inappropriate to critique its realpolitik. Second, a trial comparable to the Nuremberg Trials, which clarified the responsibility for the Nazi crimes, has never been held for the crimes of communism. Third, access to archives located in Russia has been difficult for researchers, so it has simply been convenient to remain silent about communist crimes. Fourth, the collapse of the Soviet empire worried many of the large nations of Western Europe, since it disturbed the sense of stability that had been achieved there. The opportunity opened by that collapse to raise awareness of the crimes of communism brought with it the discomforting obligation to revisit a past from which Western Europe thought it had finally been set free. This imposed the burden of writing a new narrative of that past, since the nations that had been freed from the yoke of communism were recalling events that had been left out of the current narrative. Finally, and not insignificantly, to this day, one can find people in Western Europe who think that communism is a positive ideology that can save the world, and who find it difficult to see and accept its criminality.

Some of these reasons have been outlined clearly and thoroughly in a collection of essays entitled *Kaiken takana oli pelko* (Behind Everything Was Fear) edited by Imbi Paju and Sofi Oksanen and published in Finland in 2009. In this book, historians, journalists, and social activists seek answers to the question of why victims of Soviet terror could not speak publicly about their experiences, and how people have coped with a system structured on fear, discrimination, and propaganda. *Kaiken takana oli pelko* also eloquently underscores one of the distinctive characteristics of Soviet terror, namely, how Soviet power constructed amnesia on the collective level, distorting or systematically denying the real past. One of the editors of the book, Sofi Oksanen, writes in her foreword that

> those people who fell victim to Soviet repressions lack public narratives which would connect the subjective experiences of the individuals with

> the broader cultural and institutional narratives. In such cases it is impossible to recognize one's own experiences in those narratives that already exist and circulate in public. Such silence impedes the individual's attempt to construct a self, to create their own identity. The mirror that would reflect back that construction is lacking. Everyone feels uncomfortable, because they cannot make their life situation comprehensible beyond their immediate environment. (19)

Oksanen concludes that there is a pressing need to inscribe the history of Estonia and Eastern Europe as part of European history. This is necessary not only for the sake of Estonians and East Europeans, but for all of Europe, since without this, the unification of Europe is nothing but a formality.

I venture to hope that our current collection will also support the move to a real unification of Europe, permitting the overcoming of socially constructed forgetting, and the systematic destruction of memory. Our contributors show that the theoretical frameworks of "life writing" and "trauma" can be fruitfully used for describing haunting memories and traumatic experiences of both the victims of Stalinist repressions and other groups and individuals across time and space. Several of our authors demonstrate that traumatic experiences result in persistent fears that remain with human beings long after the ground for the fear has disappeared. In her contribution to *Haunted Narratives* (chapter 13), Aija Sakova points out that both the German author Christa Wolf and the Estonian writer Ene Mihkelson show how fear results from atrocious crimes: "What is horrendous in the past is not dead, but rather lives on in people, be it in the form of unconscious fear, bodily suffering, illness, rage, or aggression." In this way, life writing becomes a sort of self-therapy. Paradoxically, however, remembering is closely related to the desire to forget. A writer wants to get rid of the ghosts of the past, wants to forget and to be rid of suffering, but at the same time seeks to understand what has happened. Yet self-therapy and the reconstruction of individual identity is only one side of the coin. The other side is the imperative to remember. The victims have a duty to break through the bonds of forgetting and confront injustice since forgetting is "the breeding ground of evil."

Finally, the imperative to remember is related not only to the construction of the individual but also to that of collective identity. The slogan of Estonia's Singing Revolution – "Give us back our history!" – summarizes such intentions very well. As a matter of fact, Estonia is certainly not an exception, since the collapse of the Soviet Union caused a similar "memory boom" in all the countries which re-established their freedom. In all post-communist countries, people wanted to tell what had collectively been hidden. Often, that desire was related to the wish to restore national identity. As Tiina Kirss points out in her introduction to *She Who Remembers Survives*, the collection of Estonian life histories that began in the early 1990s "framed the stories of individual lives as deeply relevant to national history and to compensatory, reclamatory, or contestatory collective impulses to remember the past" (16).

As we learn from Stefanie Preuss's article and Eva Rein's response to it in our volume (chapters 9 and 10), there are similarities beween Scottish and Estonian renegotiations of national identity. In the Scottish case, it was plays that had a major influence on the reconstruction of national identity; in Estonia, it was songs. Annie Cottier, who analyses narratives exemplifying signals of trauma, claims that Indian narratives are encouraged by the state in the service of building a national identity (chapter 21). Drawing on the work of Walter Benjamin and Theodor W. Adorno, Philipp Schweighauser brings together two notions – "trauma" and "utopia" – to suggest that the utopian imagination is needed in times of trauma to liberate the individual and open the present up to that which may transcend it (chapter 2). How is all of this related to the construction of "imagined communities" such as nations? With respect to national consciousness and trauma, there are clear differences between representations of the Holocaust and representations of traumatic experiences in other places. In this volume, those differences are reflected most prominently in the debate between Nora Anna Escherle and Eneken Laanes (chapters 5 and 6). While Escherle treats silence as a symptom of trauma, Laanes suggests that silence might instead be intentional – a conscious, deliberate decision, rather than an involuntary, subconscious response.

What is the relationship between life stories and histories? As Tiina Kirss and Jüri Kivimäe have shown in their introduction to *Estonian Life Stories*, "life stories can offer histories unique kinds of evidence; histories can in turn offer writers of life stories requisite frameworks for past events, especially those in the distant past, and help in finding chronological sequences for the composition of a narrative" (31). Can it be that in their writing of life stories, the Estonians and other post-communist peoples have been motivated by the wish to fill in perceived gaps in histories written by academics? Is there, perhaps, less of an urgent need for this on the Swiss side, as the history of the twentieth century has been worked through for a longer period in their fora of public discussion?

Europe has often been described as a community of shared memory and shared forgetting, but as the French historian Ernest Renan has said, what one nation wishes to forget, another wishes to remember. Still there must be a concerted public effort to foreground those stories that have not been heard, to embark on an analysis of why they have not been included, and to examine the contours and processes that create silences and mutings of certain categories of life writing. This requires a significant, courageous self-reflection on both the individual and the social level, and it requires the tools of historical and sociological as well as ethical analysis.

NOTES

1 I would like to thank Tiina Kirss for valuable comments and suggestions as well as for taking care of my English, and Philipp Schweighauser for good advice and helpful assistance.

2 Rutt Hinrikus's preface to *Estonian Life Stories* (2009) provides an overview of these campaigns.

WORKS CITED

Blustein, Jeffrey. *The Moral Demands of Memory*. Cambridge: Cambridge University Press, 2008.

Courtois, Stéphane, Nicolas Werth, Jean-Louis Panné, Andrzej Paczkowski, Karel Bartošek, and Jean-Louis Margolin. *The Black Book of Communism: Crimes, Terror, Repression*, trans. Jonathan Murphy and Mark Kramer. Cambridge: Harvard University Press, 1999.

Eakin, Paul John. "Introduction: Mapping the Ethics of Life Writing." In *The Ethics of Life Writing*, ed. P.J. Eakin, 1–16. Ithaca: Cornell University Press, 2004.

"European Conscience and Crimes of Totalitarian Communism: 20 Years After." Conclusions of the Public Hearing in the European Parliament Organised by the Czech Presidency of the European Union. 18 March 2010. UOK–Upplysning om kommunismen. http://www.upplysningomkommunismen.se/?page=eu2009.

European Council Parliamentary Assembly. "Need for International Condemnation of Crimes of Totalitarian Communist Regimes." Resolution 1481. 25 Jan. 2006. http://assembly.coe.int/main.asp?Link=/documents/adoptedtext/ta06/eres1481.htm.

Gilligan, Carol. *In a Different Voice: Psychological Theory and Women's Development*. Cambridge: Harvard University Press, 1982.

Hinrikus, Rutt. *Eesti rahva elulood, I – II*. Tallinn: Tänapäev, 2000.

Hinrikus, Rutt. *Eesti rahva elulood, III*. Tallinn: Tänapäev, 2003.

Hinrikus, Rutt. "Preface: On the Collection of Estonian Life Stories." In *Estonian Life Stories*, ed. and trans. Tiina Kirss, comp. Rutt Hinrikus, vii–xii. Budapest: Central European Press, 2009.

Kirss, Tiina, Ene Kõresaar, and Marju Lauristin, eds. *She Who Remembers Survives: Interpreting Women's Post-Soviet Life Stories*. Tartu: Tartu University Press, 2004.

Kirss, Tiina, ed. and trans., and Rutt Hinrikus, comp. *Estonian Life Stories*. Budapest: Central European Press, 2009.

Kirss, Tiina, and Jüri Kivimäe. "Estonian Life Stories and Histories." In *Estonian Life Stories*, ed. and trans. T. Kirss, comp. Rutt Hinrikus, 1–31. Budapest: Central European Press, 2009.

LaCapra, Dominick. *Writing History, Writing Trauma*. Baltimore: Johns Hopkins University Press, 2001.

Lotman, Juri. "Õigus biograafiale: Teksti ja autori isiksuse tüpoloogilisest suhestatusest." *Looming* 12 (1984): 1684–92.

Meri, Lennart. "Clause G: 'Singing Prohibited' – The Book of Communist Crimes Must Not Be Closed." In *Lennart Meri: A European Mind. Selected Speeches by Lennart Meri, the Late President of Estonia*, comp. Mart Meri and Edward Lucas, 54–69. Tallinn: Lennart Meri European Foundation, 2009.

Paju, Imbi, and Sofi Oksanen, comp. *Kaiken takana oli pelko*. Helsinki: WSOY, 2009.

Taylor, Charles. *Sources of the Self: The Making of the Modern Identity*. Cambridge: Harvard University Press, 1989.

Contributors

Annie Cottier is a research and teaching assistant at the English Department of the University of Berne. Her dissertation is entitled "Rewriting Histories, Reclaiming Geographies: Cosmopolitanism in Contemporary Indian Writing in English." She is the author of "Loss, Belonging, and the Vagaries of Migration: Cosmopolitanism in M.G. Vassanji's *The Assassin's Song*" (2012) and "Settlers in the Sundarbans: The Poetry and Politics of Humans and Nature in Amitav Ghosh's *The Hungry Tide*" (2012).

Nora Anna Escherle is a research and teaching assistant to the professor of literary theory of the English Department and the Center for Cultural Studies at the University of Berne. She is currently working on her dissertation project "Bad Religion? Narratives of Religious Alterity and Violence in Contemporary Pakistani and Indian Anglophone Novels."

Maarja Hollo is a researcher at the Estonian Cultural History Archives of the Estonian Literary Museum and a doctoral student in Estonian literature at the University of Tartu. Her interests range from questions concerning Estonian literature in exile to issues of memory and representations of the autobiographical in literature.

Tiina Kirss is professor of cultural theory at the Estonian Institute of Humanities at Tallinn University. She has published numerous articles on life writing, compiled several collections of Estonian life writing, and is the co-editor of *She Who Remembers, Survives: Interpreting Estonian Women's Post-Soviet Life Stories* (2004) as well as a special issue, "Baltic Life Stories," of the *Journal of Baltic Studies* (2005).

Leena Kurvet-Käosaar is associate professor of literary theory at the University of Tartu and a senior researcher of the Archives of Cultural History of the Estonian Literary Museum. She is the author of *Embodied Subjectivity in the Diaries of Virginia Woolf, Aino Kallas and Anaïs Nin* (2006) and the editor (with Lea Rojola) of *Aino Kallas: Negotiations with Modernity* (2011) and of a special issue of *Methis* on Estonian life writing (2010).

Eneken Laanes is a senior research fellow at the Under and Tuglas Literature Centre of the Estonian Academy of Sciences. She is the author of *Lepitamatud dialoogid: Subjekt ja mälu nõukogudejärgses eesti romaanis* (Unresolved Dialogues: Subjectivity and Memory in the Post-Soviet Estonian Novel, 2009).

Stefanie Preuss works as a research support officer at the University of Konstanz. She is the author of *A Scottish National Canon? Processes of Literary Canon Formation in Scotland* (2012).

Eva Rein is an assistant lecturer in English and a doctoral candidate at the University of Tartu. She has published on Canadian and comparative literature and is currently working on her dissertation, "Trauma, Memory, and Narrative in Joy Kogawa's *Obasan* and Ene Mihkelson's *Ahasveeruse uni* (The Sleep of Ahasuerus)."

Gabriele Rippl is professor and chair of literatures in English at the University of Berne. Her list of publications includes *Lebenstexte* (1998; on 17th-century autobiographies) and *Beschreibungs-Kunst* (2005; on text–picture relationships and the art of description/ekphrasis in late 19th- and 20th-century Anglo-American literature); other book-length publications which she co-edited include *Imagescapes: Studies in Intermediality* (2010), *Arbeit am Gedächtnis* (2007), and *Bilder: Ein (neues) Leitmedium* (2006).

Aija Sakova is a fourth-year PhD student of literature and cultural studies at the University of Tartu. She is the author of two essays: "The Writer's Duty to Suffer in Order to See and Understand: The Literary Vision of Ene Mihkelson and Ingeborg Bachmann" (2010) and "Die Ausgrabung der Vergangenheit in *Stadt der Engel*" (2012).

Christa Schönfelder is an assistant in the English department of the University of Zurich. She has published articles on trauma fiction, memory, and authenticity. She also co-edited "Zeitgenossenschaft / Le Contemporain / Contemporaneity," an issue of the comparativist journal *Variations*.

Philipp Schweighauser is assistant professor and head of American and general literatures at the University of Basel. He is the author of *The Noises of American Literature, 1890–1985: Toward a History of Literary Acoustics* (2006), has published widely on literary and cultural theory and history, and is the co-editor of two essay collections: *Teaching Nineteenth-Century American Poetry* (2007) and *Terrorism, Media, and the Ethics of Fiction: Transatlantic Perspectives on Don DeLillo* (2010).

Therese Steffen is professor of gender studies in the anglophone context at the University of Basel and non-resident fellow of the W.E.B. Du-Bois Institute at Harvard University. Her list of publications includes *Crossing Color: Transcultural Space and Place in Rita Dove's Poetry, Fiction, Drama* (2001) and *Gender: Grundwissen Philosophie* (2006). She has also edited "gender–literatur–kultur," a special issue of *figurationen* (2/2011), and co-edited (with Bettina Dennerlein and Elke Frietch) *Verschleierter Orient – Entschleierter Okzident? (Un)Sichtbarkeit in Politik, Recht, Kunst und Kultur seit dem 19. Jahrhundert* (2012).

Julia Straub is a senior lecturer in literatures in English at the University of Berne. She is the author of *A Victorian Muse: The Afterlife of Dante's Beatrice in Nineteenth-Century Literature* (2009) and the editor of *Authenticity: Studies on a Critical Concept* (2012).

Margit Sutrop is professor of practical philosophy, head of the Institute of Philosophy and Semiotics, and founding director of the Centre for Ethics at the University of Tartu. She has written more than 60 articles and edited 14 volumes on aesthetics, literary theory, the history of moral philosophy, bioethics, research ethics, and the ethics of technology. She is the author of *Fiction and Imagination: The Anthropological Function of Literature* (2000).

Index

www.ingramcontent.com/pod-product-compliance
Lightning Source LLC
LaVergne TN
LVHW040152080826
844660LV00014B/940/J

* 9 7 8 1 4 4 2 6 4 6 0 1 8 *